World Ditch

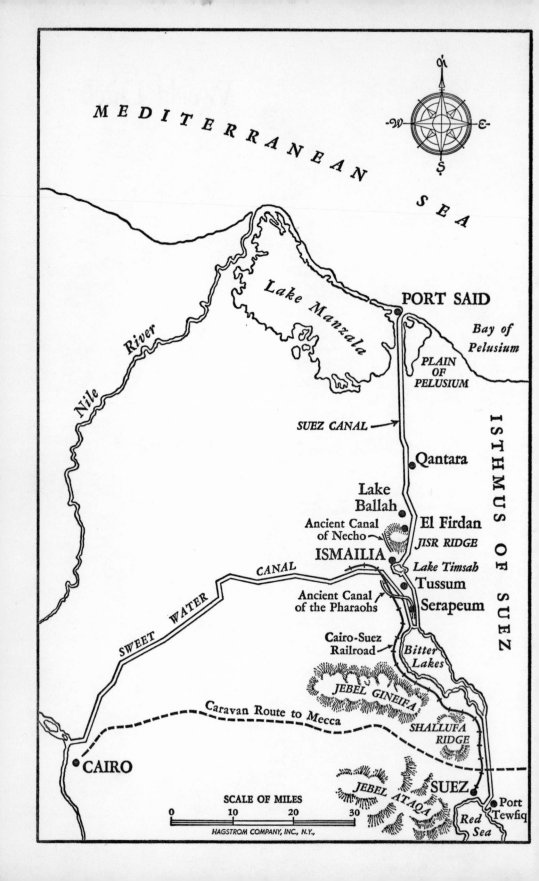

JOHN MARLOWE ᠌

WORLD DITCH

᠌ The Making of the Suez Canal

The Macmillan Company, New York

TO GILLIAN, SARA, AND JONATHAN ❧

ACKNOWLEDGMENTS

I wish to acknowledge the helpfulness of the officials of the Public Record Office, London, and of the Service des Archives, Ministère des Affaires Etrangères, Quai d'Orsay, Paris. I thank the French Embassy in London for facilitating my access to the French archives in Paris. As always, I am indebted to the resources of the London Library, and to the ever-ready helpfulness of its staff. I am grateful to the Suez Canal Company for photocopies of some of the pictures in their possession, and for some items of information. I acknowledge the assistance of Hulton's Picture Library in providing photocopies for various other illustrations. I am grateful to the numerous authors, alive and dead, who have preceded me in this field, and upon whose researches I have drawn; their names and works are listed in the Bibliography. I thank MM. Georges Edgar-Bonnet and Jean d'Elbée for permission to quote passages from their published works. I thank Mr. Nicholas Putt for assistance with the Index.

JOHN MARLOWE

DENHAM, BUCKS
March, 1964

CONTENTS

NOTE ON SOURCES

The three principal primary sources from which the narrative covering the years of the making of the Suez Canal has been compiled are:

1. Ferdinand de Lesseps, *Lettres, Journal et Documents pour Servir à l'Histoire du Canal de Suez,* published in five volumes by Didier et Cie., Paris, between 1875 and 1881 (referred to in the Notes as "Journal," followed by number of volume and page reference).

2. The French diplomatic archives at the French Ministry of Foreign Affairs, Quai d'Orsay, Paris, and in particular the two series, (*a*) "Egypte, Correspondence Politique," volumes 18 to 47 (referred to in the Notes as "CP," followed by the serial number of the volume), and "Egypte, Mémoires et Documents," volumes 13 to 15 (referred to in the Notes as "M & D," followed by the serial number of the volume).

3. The British Foreign Office archives at the Public Record Office, Chancery Lane, London, and, in particular, the "Suez Canal" series. Documents in the Foreign Office archives are referred to in the Notes by the prefix "FO," followed by the serial number of the volume.

In addition to these three primary sources covering the years of the making of the canal, I am indebted to numerous secondary sources for information and enlightenment about particular aspects. All these secondary sources are listed in the Bibliography. On some of them I have drawn heavily. For example: on Volume I of *The Great Canal at Suez,* by Percy Fitzgerald, published in two volumes by Tinsley Bros., London, in 1876, for eyewitness accounts by an engineer of the actual process of construction; on *Les Origines de l'Expédition d'Egypte* and *L'Angleterre, L'Isthme de Suez et L'Egypte,* both by F. Charles-Roux and published by Libraire Plon, Paris, in 1910 and 1922, respectively, for events in Egypt during the last three decades of the eighteenth century; on *L'Isthme et le Canal de Suez,* by J. Charles-Roux, published in two volumes by Hachette in 1901, for the French texts of various conventions, and so on, relating to the canal; on *British Routes to India,* by H. L. Hoskins, published by Longmans, Green in 1928, for much information regarding the overland route to India; on the first volume of *Ferdinand de Lesseps,* by Georges Edgar-Bonnet (incomparably the best extant biography of Lesseps), published by Libraire Plon in 1951 (Volume I dealing with Suez) and in 1959 (Volume II dealing with Panama), for much information about Lesseps; on *Règne du Khédive Ismaïl,* by Georges Douin, published in four volumes by the Société Royal de Géographie d'Egypte in 1933, and on *L'Empire Egyptien sous Ismaïl et L'Ingérence Anglo-Française,* by M. Sabry, published by Paul Guenther in 1933, for much background information about Ismail's reign.

Acknowledgment is made in the Notes for all quotations and for all information specifically and solely derived from one particular source.

NOTE ON CURRENCIES, MEASUREMENTS, AND TRANSLATIONS

Currencies and measurements have been given variously in English and French, according to the source from which the references have been taken. Usually, but not always, the currency references are in francs. The rate of exchange for the whole period of the narrative can be taken as twenty-five francs to the pound sterling (then worth about $5.00). Measurements—hectares, kilometers, cubic meters—are generally given according to the metric system, except in quotations from English sources. Where Egyptian or Turkish currency or measurements are introduced, the equivalent, according either to the English or to the metric system, is invariably given also.

Translations from the numerous French sources have been made by the author. Quotations from the original French have been avoided except, occasionally, in the Notes, but the original French has sometimes been given in parentheses alongside the translation in order to give the reader an opportunity to air his scholarship at the author's expense. Very occasionally, when quoting the text of conventions, and so on, where the official wording is important, relevent phrases in the original French text have been quoted.

PRINCIPAL CHARACTERS

Ferdinand de Lesseps. Born in 1805, he was a career diplomat in the French Foreign Service until 1849, when he retired with the rank of Minister Plenipotentiary after a disagreement with the French Government. Obtaining Concessions from the Egyptian Government for the construction of the Suez Canal in 1854 (First Concession) and 1856 (Second Concession), he formed the Compagnie Universelle du Canal Maritime de Suez in 1859 to exploit these Concessions. He successfully completed the canal, which was formally opened in 1869. Afterward he came to brief in attempting to build a canal across the Isthmus of Panama. He died in 1892.

Henry Temple, Viscount Palmerston, was Prime Minister of Great Britain (with one short interval) from 1855 to his death in 1865. He was an uncompromising opponent of the Suez Canal on the ground that it was against British Imperial interests.

Mohammed Ali Pasha. Viceroy of Egypt from 1805–1849, he has been called "The Founder of Modern Egypt." He opposed the construction of the Suez Canal throughout his reign on the ground that it would lead to a European occupation of Egypt.

Abbas Pasha, grandson of Mohammed Ali, was Viceroy of Egypt 1849–1854.

Mohammed Said Pasha. Youngest son of Mohammed Ali, and Viceroy of Egypt from 1854–1863, he awarded the two Concessions for the construction of the Suez Canal to Lesseps.

Ismail Pasha, grandson of Mohammed Ali, was Viceroy of Egypt 1863–1879, when he was deposed by the Sultan of Turkey, his Suzerain, at the instance of the British and French governments.

Napoleon III, Emperor of the French. Nephew of Napoleon I, he came into power as "Prince-President" after the 1848 Revolution in France had dethroned Louis-Philippe. He was proclaimed Emperor in 1852. He arbitrated between the Suez Canal Company and the Egyptian Government in 1864. Defeated by the Prussians at Sedan in 1870, he abdicated, and died soon afterward.

Eugénie, Empress of the French. Wife of Napoleon III, she was born of a Spanish noble family and was a distant cousin of Ferdinand de Lesseps.

Auguste, Duc de Morny, an illegitimate half-brother of Napoleon III. Président du Corps Législatif, he was a leading statesman under the French Second Empire, and became involved in intrigues against Lesseps during the construction of the canal.

Nubar Pasha, an Armenian man of affairs, served in various capacities under successive Egyptian Viceroys, occupying in turn most of the principal positions of state. He acted for Ismail Pasha in nearly all matters concerning the Suez Canal.

Prince Jérôme Napoleon, a cousin of Napoleon III, was known as "Plon-Plon." He was nominated "Protector" of the Suez Canal Company.

Benjamin Disraeli, First Earl of Beaconsfield, was Prime Minister of the British Government that purchased the Egyptian Government's shareholding in the Suez Canal Company in 1875.

Lord Stratford de Redcliffe, British ambassador at Constantinople, 1851–1857, was known as "The Great Elchi."

Sir Henry Bulwer was British ambassador at Constantinople 1858–1865.

Edouard de Thouvenel, French ambassador at Constantinople from 1855 to 1859, was French Foreign Minister from 1859 to 1862. During 1864 he presided over the Imperial Commission of Arbitration to decide matters in dispute between the Suez Canal Company and the Egyptian Government.

Count Walewski, illegitimate son of Napoleon I by a Polish countess, was French Foreign Minister from 1855 to 1859.

Edouard Drouyn de Lhuys, French Foreign Minister, 1852–1855 and 1862–1867.

Barthélemy-Prosper Enfantin was founder of the Société d'Etudes which, in 1847, made a preliminary study in Egypt of plans for the construction of the Suez Canal.

M. Ruyssenaers, Dutch consul general in Egypt, and one of Lesseps' most intimate associates in the construction of the canal, he was for some time the Company's principal agent in Egypt.

M. Linant de Bellefonds. A French engineer in the service of the Egyptian Government whose preliminary studies formed the basis of Lesseps' plans for the construction of the canal.

M. Mougel, a French engineer in the Egyptian Roads and Bridges Department, was one of Lesseps' principal collaborators in the construction of the canal.

M. le Duc d'Albufera, Vice-President of the Conseil d'Administration of the Suez Canal Company.

World Ditch

CHAPTER *one*

The Antecedents of
the Suez Canal ટ~

ₑ§ ALL accounts of the Suez Canal start with some reference to its predecessors, the first of which was constructed between the Nile and the Red Sea in Pharaonic times. From the earliest times of which there is any record, the ancient Egyptians had been adept at the art of digging canals for irrigation purposes. Some of these irrigation canals, like the Bahr Yusuf, running from Upper Egypt to the Faium, were of considerable size and were used for navigation as well as for irrigation.

According to Herodotus and Diodorus, the Pharaoh Necho of the XXVIth Dynasty, who ruled over Egypt from about 609 to 593 B.C., began to build a canal from the Pelusiac branch of the Nile to the Red Sea by way of Wadi Tumulat, a natural depression running east and west between the Nile Delta and the Isthmus of Suez.[1] Herodotus tells us that 100,000 Egyptians perished in the course of the digging of this canal which Necho left uncompleted, having "desisted from his undertaking, being admonished by an oracle that all his labour would turn to the advantage of a barbarian." According to the same account, the uncompleted canal was "wide enough to admit two triremes abreast." Strabo, Diodorus, and Pliny all tell us that this canal was continued after the Persian conquest by Darius Hystaspis (521–486 B.C.), who again discontinued it, "being told that if he cut through the isthmus, Egypt would be laid under water as the Red Sea was higher than Egypt" (Diodorus).

The canal begun by Necho and Darius, and continued as far as the Bitter Lakes, was completed to the Red Sea by Ptolemy II, named Philadelphus (285–246 B.C.). A port called Arsinoë was created at the head of the Red Sea at the terminal point of the canal (the site of Arsinoë was probably near the modern Suez), and a lock with a double gate was placed at the junction between the Red Sea and the canal to prevent the influx of salt water into the canal. Thus, for the first time, there was connection between the Nile and the Red Sea. This canal does not seem to have remained navigable for long, and had certainly fallen out of use by the beginning of the Christian Era. After the Roman conquest, it was restored to use in A.D. 98 under the Emperor Trajan, when the Nile terminal was moved to Babylon, a Roman fortress a few miles upstream from the modern Cairo, by digging the canal from the original terminal on the Pelusiac branch, which had now become silted up, to the mainstream of the Nile. Trajan's canal appears to have been used for navigation for about a century.

Nothing more was done about connecting the Nile with the Red Sea until after the Muslim conquest when Amr-ibn-al-Aas, the Arab governor of Egypt, reopened Trajan's canal in A.D. 641–642, on the orders of the Caliph Omar, for the purpose of transporting wheat from the Nile Valley to Mecca by water from Cairo to Jidda by way of Suez. This canal appears to have been used for navigation until the time of the Abbasid Caliphate when, in 776, the Caliph abu-Ja'far Abdullah al-Mansur ordered it to be blocked at the junction between the canal and the Bitter Lakes to hinder the transport of supplies between Egypt and the inhabitants of Medina, who were at that time in revolt against the Caliphate.

None of these early canals had as object the facilitation of transport between the Red Sea and the Mediterranean or, vice versa, by way of the Nile, and do not appear to have been used for this purpose. There was in fact very little movement of goods between the Red Sea and the Mediterranean until Roman times. When such movement developed, it took place either by way of the port of Myos Hormos on the west coast of the Red Sea, and from there by the Wadi Hammamat route across the desert to the Nile Valley at Qena and thence down the Nile to Alexandria;[2] or by way of Jidda on the east coast of the Red Sea and thence along the caravan route via Petra and Bosra to Damascus, and from there to the coast. The fact that the canal, whenever it was opened to navigation, invariably fell into disuse soon afterward, seems to argue that, whenever it was brought into use, it was not for the continuing purposes of trade, but for some temporary and limited purpose. We know why the canal was reopened under Omar and why it was closed under Mansur.

With regard to the earlier canals, the late Dr. G. A. Reisner[3] suggested that Necho might have started building the canal with the object of sending a seaborne expedition down the Red Sea and round to the Persian Gulf to attack his enemy Nebuchadnezzar, King of Babylon, by whom he had just been defeated in Syria. He went on to suggest that Darius continued the canal in order to facilitate sea communication between Egypt and Persia.

The desirability of this ended with the end of the Persian occupation, which may explain why the canal was allowed to silt up. According to Reisner, Ptolemy's primary object in completing the canal was to enable him to import elephants for his army from the Somali coast. He has no suggestions about the reason for the reactivation of the canal under Trajan, but surmises that it was for some military purpose, since the then considerable trade between the Mediterranean and the East was, as has been mentioned, being carried by other routes. (The prevailing north wind in the Gulf of Suez would have been a serious obstacle to the development of any considerable northbound trade via Suez until the later development of techniques for sailing into the wind; this may have been one of the reasons for the development of the Myos Hormos and Petra routes.)

It seems likely that these earlier canals were navigable only during the seasons of high Nile and that, for the rest of the year, the level of water, which depended on the level of water in the Nile, was too low for the passage of ships of any size.

Traces of these early canals were found both by Bonaparte's surveyors during the French occupation at the end of the eighteenth century and, fifty-five years later, by Lesseps' engineers when making their preliminary surveys. Although these canals were not built for the purpose of establishing marine communication between the Mediterranean and the Red Sea, the knowledge that they had been built served as an inspiration and an example, one thousand and more years later, to those who began thinking and planning in terms of a canal for this purpose.

In Roman times the principal Eastern commodities traded via the Red Sea were silk and frankincense. After the Muslim conquests, the Eastern trade with Europe languished. It revived with the Crusades and was developed by the merchant adventurers who controlled the maritime republics of Venice, Genoa, and Pisa, and by the powerful mercantile community of Marseille. The prosperity which had accrued to these communities as a result of the Eastern trade was seriously jeopardized by the Portuguese discovery and subsequent development of the Cape route to the East, which enabled the merchant adventurers of the Atlantic Powers—Portugal, followed nearly a century later by England, and then by Holland—to outflank and bypass the increasing difficulties put in the way of the overland Eastern route by the crescent power of the Ottoman Empire and to appropriate for themselves the lion's share of the Eastern trade from the Mediterranean seaports.

With the rise in wealth and living standards in western Europe—a rise which was soon to be accelerated and accentuated by the influx of gold and silver bullion from the Western Hemisphere—the Eastern trade became more extensive and more diversified. Silk and rice from China, cotton and linen from India, spices and drugs from the Spice Islands, gum and frankincense from Arabia, and, later, tea from India, China, and Ceylon and coffee from Mocha were exchanged for precious and base metals and for fine and coarse cloths. In spite of competition from the Cape route, and in spite of continual difficulties created by Bedouin marauders, by local territorial princelings, and by Ottoman pashas, a fair proportion of this increasing Eastern trade continued to be carried across one or other of the great overland routes, either via Aleppo and the Euphrates Valley, or via Cairo and the Red Sea, or via Jidda and Damascus. The Venetians, in particular, established strong connections in Constantinople, Aleppo, and Cairo, and for a long time were able to consolidate their position in the Eastern trade by occupying Cyprus.

In 1535 the French Government, actuated by the powerful Provençal merchant interest, concluded the first of the "capitulations" treaties with the Ottoman Empire which set a pattern for, and diminished many of the difficulties of, European trading in the Ottoman dominions. Under this first "capitulations" treaty, French nationals were allowed to establish themselves in certain defined quarters of the principal ports and cities of the Levant under the protection and jurisdiction of their consul, to buy, to sell, and to practice their religion freely, to be subject to their own consular jurisdiction in matters affecting their relations with one another, and so to become exempt from much of the arbitrary injustice and unpredictable depredations which afflicted the lives of most Ottoman subjects. During the next hundred years or so, the French example was followed by most of the countries of western Europe, who concluded similar "capitulations" treaties with the Sublime Porte. (England made her first "capitulations" treaty with the Ottomans in 1604.)

But, after the long decline of the Venetian Republic had set in, it was the French, by means of the friendly relations which they established at the Sublime Porte, and as a result of the commercial enterprise shewn by the Echelles (the trading stations established in the ports and cities of the Levant as a result of the 1535 "capitulations" treaty), who established an almost undisputed monopoly of the overland Eastern trade. Successive French governments, for political as well as for economic reasons, set great store by the maintenance and development of the overland route as a counterpoise to the Cape route where, in spite of the creation of a Compagnie des Indes, based on the Atlantic port of Lorient, the French were never able effectively to compete with their English and Dutch rivals who, after the virtual elimination of the Portuguese, shared most of this trade between themselves. Just as these two Atlantic Powers were geographically better placed than France to dominate the Cape route, so France, as a Mediterranean Power, was better placed than they to dominate the overland route. In this the French were assisted by the enterprise of the Marseille merchants who, in effect, controlled the operations of the Levant Echelles.

French commercial and strategic interests in the Levant have always been powerfully sustained and, it may be, exaggerated by religious and sentimental imponderables which, from the landing of the crusaders of St. Louis at Damietta in the thirteenth century to the landing of French paratroops at Port Said in the twentieth, have exercised an always potent, a sometimes ir-rational, an occasionally obsessive, and an ultimately disastrous influence on French international policies.

Although French interest in the overland route was constant from the sixteenth century onward, it does not appear that they attached any serious importance to the possibilities of a canal connecting the Red Sea and the Mediterranean until Bonaparte's expedition to Egypt at the end of the eighteenth century. Projects for such a canal were, however, put forward from time to time by various people, but they never succeeded in getting their ideas seriously considered by anyone in authority.

The first reference to the idea of opening maritime communication be-tween the Red Sea and the Mediterranean appears in 1504 when the Venetian Council of Ten, discussing the instructions to be given to a new Venetian ambassador to the Mamluk Sultan of Egypt, considered the advisability of proposing a scheme for a canal to this ruler. This was only two years before Albuquerque's expedition, via the Cape, to the Indian Ocean which marked the beginning of the diversion of the Eastern trade from the overland to the Cape route. For many years the Venetians, in alliance with the Turks, who occupied Egypt in 1514, were engaged in an unsuccessful attempt to defeat the Portuguese trading and colonizing effort in the Indian Ocean, and a joint Ottoman-Venetian fleet was maintained in the Red Sea to this end. It is interesting to speculate whether a canal would have increased the effective-ness of this attempt by facilitating the passage of warships from the Mediter-ranean to the Red Sea and Indian Ocean.

In 1586 a Turkish pasha, a certain El-Haj-Ali, proposed to reactivate the old canal between the Nile and the Red Sea with the object of enabling Turkish warships to sail from the Mediterranean to the Red Sea, via the Nile, both to deal with revolts in Arabia and to try to deal with Portuguese at-tempts to divert the Eastern trade round the Cape route. His proposal at-tracted the attention of Savary de Lancôme, the French ambassador in

Constantinople at the time, who characterized it as "seemingly impossible, or, at least, very difficult." Nothing came of the proposal.

During the course of the seventeenth century, Sully, Richelieu, and Colbert all took a practical interest in the development of the French Eastern trade by the overland route in competition with the trade by the Cape route which was being developed by the English and Dutch. (From the beginning of the seventeenth century onward, the previous Portuguese preeminence rapidly declined.) Official encouragement took the principal form of negotiation in Constantinople with a view to removing the Ottoman interdiction on Christian ships trading in the Red Sea north of Jidda. The ostensible reason for this interdiction was the proximity of the Muslim Holy Cities; the real reason was to safeguard the carriage of the Eastern trade by way of the Euphrates Valley and Damascus caravan routes. For even at this early date the Turks were concerned to prevent their Mamluk vassals in Egypt from attracting to themselves the transit profits from the Eastern trade which, it was considered, would assist them to assert their independence of their Ottoman suzerain. The French object in trying to remove the interdiction was to enable them to take advantage of the powerful position which their Cairo Echelle had built up for itself in Egypt by enabling this Echelle to profit from the greater cheapness of the short overland route via Cairo. Although for a few years the French, alone of all Christian nations, received permission from the Porte to trade in the Red Sea, this permission was soon withdrawn. French diplomatic efforts to have it renewed, or the interdiction circumvented, were continuous throughout the seventeenth and eighteenth centuries, right up to the time of Bonaparte's expedition to Egypt.

Tiring perhaps of the increasing difficulties being put in the way of the overland route by the Ottoman authorities, Colbert, in 1664, caused to be founded the Compagnie des Indes, which was given a monopoly of French trade with the East Indies and with Madagascar by the Cape route, it being stipulated that all voyages to and from the East must begin and end at the Atlantic port of Lorient. In spite of the simultaneous formation of the Compagnie de Levant, which was given a monopoly of French trade with the Levant and Red Sea (the trade in coffee from Mocha was at this time beginning to assume a considerable importance, and the French were particularly anxious to divert as much as possible of it from the Cape to the Red Sea route), the Compagnie des Indes monopoly did undoubtedly divert much of French attention from the development of the overland route until after the loss of the French Indian possessions some one hundred years later. As we shall see, the loss of these possessions greatly stimulated the by then waning

French interest in the overland route, which became primarily regarded in terms of Franco-British commercial and military rivalry.

It was inevitable that, in the course of French attempts to develop the overland route through Egypt, the idea of a canal connecting the Red Sea with the Mediterranean should frequently be revived, sometimes as part of unofficial proposals for a French occupation of Egypt. An anonymous French writer, proposing to Richelieu the French colonization of India, wrote: "A canal could be cut from Suez to Cairo, as was done under the ancient kings of Egypt and perhaps under Soliman. The Turk will hope to enrich his country; Venice will recover; the ancient commerce with Abyssinia will pick up again. By this junction of the seas the Spaniards will be weakened in the Mediterranean and all other princes strengthened."[4] In 1679 Jacques Savary, in the second edition of his work *Le Parfait Négotiant,* dealing with the possibilities of developing the Eastern trade, suggested the possibility of a canal between the Mediterranean and the Red Sea. In 1697 Benoist de Maillet, French consul in Cairo, who had spent much time in negotiating for the opening of the Red Sea to French vessels, and who had also examined a project for opening an overland route by way of Abyssinia, also suggested the possibility of a canal.

In view of the importance of Egypt to the Mediterranean Powers as a means of competing with the Atlantic Powers for a share of the Eastern trade, and in view of the obstacles placed by the Turks in the way of using Egypt and the Red Sea for transit, it is not surprising that there should have been proposals for the occupation of Egypt by one or more of the Mediterranean Powers. In 1671–1672 the German philosopher Liebnitz addressed two memorandums to Louis XIV, *Fabula Ludovisia* and *Concilium Aegyptiacum,* in which he recommended that France seize Egypt in order to secure her military preponderance over all European Powers, her supremacy in the Eastern trade, and her position as protector of the Christian Churches in the East. He described Egypt as the Holland of the East, the great commercial entrepôt of the Eastern trade. (France was at that time at war with Holland, and one of Liebnitz's principal arguments was that the occupation of Egypt would enable France to cripple Holland's Eastern trade via the Cape.)

Who indeed can expect to compete by the Cape of Good Hope when everything will arrive cheaper and more rapidly by way of Egypt? Before the discovery of the New World it was the great route for vessels; it was by this route that Venice, Genoa and . . . the free cities of Germany acquired their prosperity. The tyranny of the Turks forced the search for other routes. . . . If France, whose manufactures are already nearly the first in Europe, also acquires the spices of the Levant, what nation will dispute with her supremacy of the markets of the world? The conquest of Egypt is easier than the conquest of Holland. . . . Sovereign of the Mediterranean Powers, France will revive the Empire of the East. From Egypt she will extend the limits of her power, she will reign supreme in the Red Sea, will possess Madagascar, and will have under her control the Ethiopian Sea, the Gulf of Arabia and the island of Ormuz which dominates the Persian Gulf. . . . Once masters of Egypt, you would obtain more trade in one year than by all your recent enterprises in Madagascar. France wishes to ruin Holland, but Holland can only be conquered in Egypt where she cannot defend herself.[5]

Louis XIV and his ministers paid no attention to Liebnitz's plea. Pomponne replied to him disdainfully that "holy wars have been out of fashion in France since the time of Saint Louis." They continued France's traditional policy of alliance and attempted cooperation with the Ottoman Empire. No more attention was paid to a proposal made at about the same time by M. de Châteauneuf, French ambassador at Constantinople, for a partition of Turkey among the European Powers, or to another proposal in the same sense made by Père Jean Coppin, sometime French consul in Damietta, in a book entitled *Bouclier de l'Europe ou la Guerre Sainte,* published in 1686.

French interest in the Levant, partly practical, partly sentimental, continued into the eighteenth century. In 1740 the Abbé Mascrier, in a Preface to *Description de l'Egypte,* being the edited Memoirs of Benoist de Maillet, wrote, with some exaggeration: "The Nile is as familiar to most of our people as the Seine. Even children have heard the sound of its cataracts roaring in their ears. Everyone has seen, or has heard people talk of, mummies. Joseph's Well, Pompey's Pillar, the Pharos at Alexandria, the Pyramids, have all been so often talked of and are so well known that to try to add to people's knowledge of them is like telling a Parisian something new about St. Denis or trying to inform an inhabitant of Touraine about the whereabouts of St. Martin's tomb." A large number of French travelers—Tavernier, Morison, Lucas, Tollot, Sicard, Dubernat—visited Egypt and the Levant and published memoirs of their travels. French ambassadors at Constantinople continued their fruitless efforts to open the Red Sea to French trading vessels. But successive French governments, absorbed in unsuccessful European wars, and lacking ministers of the energy and genius of Richelieu, Mazarin, or Colbert, seem to have lost interest and paid little attention to the continual prodding they received from their ambassadors in Constantinople, their consuls in Cairo, and from the merchants of Marseille.

France was not the only Mediterranean Power to take an interest in the possibilities of the overland route via Egypt. In 1747 Dominic Jauna, an Austrian subject who had spend many years in Egypt, and who was an official of the Austrian Department of Commerce, published a book dedicated to the Empress Maria Theresa in which he proposed the conquest of Egypt and Cyprus by a coalition of Catholic European Powers in a kind of anachronistic Holy War. Although Jauna appears genuinely to have been inspired by, in his own words, "a sincere and ardent zeal to see the infidels deprived of the lands which they have usurped," and by an entirely chimerical fear of an Ottoman revival which would bring the Turkish hordes once more to the gates of Vienna, he was not insensible to the commercial advantages of his proposal, which, however, fell on deaf ears at a time when Austria was more interested in extinguishing the independence of Catholic Poland than of initiating anything in the nature of a crusade against the infidels.

England, since the establishment of the East India Company at the beginning of the seventeenth century, and until the establishment of her empire over India as a result of the Seven Years' War, had shown little official interest in the development of the Eastern trade by the overland route, although English merchants were established at Aleppo and other markets in the Levant. Although, by virtue of the 1604 and various subsequent "capitulations" treaties, English merchants in the Ottoman dominions enjoyed, on paper, much the same privileges as the French merchants, and although an English Levant Company had been formed for the development of English trade in the eastern Mediterranean,[6] the British trading position was not actively developed by diplomatic activity at Constantinople, or by consular activity in Egypt.

During the seventeenth and the first half of the eighteenth centuries England only intermittently had a consul in residence in Egypt. When one was in residence he was almost invariably harassed and impeded in his duties by the activities of his finally well-established French colleague who aimed at, and usually succeeded in achieving, a virtual French monopoly, both in foreign trade and in the privilege of protecting foreign nationals. British diplomatic activity at Constantinople, such as it was, was devoted rather to trying to prevent the grant of privileges to other foreign nations than to the obtaining of privileges for British nationals. For example, when, soon after the publication of Jauna's book referred to above, a British subject named Lander was appointed by the Austrian Government as their representative in Egypt, the British consul there, on the instructions of his ambassador in Constantinople, succeeded in securing Lander's expulsion from the country. In 1756 the British consul in Cairo was the only British national resident in that city; and, since there was no British trade and presumably no other activity for this official, the post was abolished.

In Egypt, in 1766, Ali, one of the twenty-four Mamluk beys, or governors, who ruled Egypt under the usually nominal control of the Turkish pasha, succeeded in either assassinating or exiling most of his fellow beys, packed the Turkish pasha off to Constantinople, and himself assumed control of Egypt. He remained master of the country until 1772 when he, in his turn, was driven into exile by his son-in-law and principal general, Mohammed Abu-Dahab, who took over the government of Egypt in his place. Abu-Dahab lasted until 1776, when he was killed in battle in Syria. The government of Egypt was then disputed between three Mamluk beys—Murad, Ibrahim, and Ismail. This dispute enabled the Porte to regain some semblance of authority in Egypt and a Turkish pasha was once more installed to preside, albeit somewhat impotently, over the chaos created by the three warring beys. First, Ismail expelled Murad and Ibrahim from Cairo into Upper Egypt and took over the government himself. Then, Murad and Ibrahim, in alliance, drove out Ismail and shared the government between them. In 1786 the Porte, roused from its habitual inaction by the failure of Murad and Ibrahim to pay the annual tribute due to Constantinople, sent a punitive expedition to Egypt under the command of Hasan, the captain-pasha, or admiral, of the Turkish fleet. Hasan Pasha defeated Murad and Ibrahim, who fled into Upper Egypt, and appointed their rival, Ismail, as Sheikh-al-Balad, or Governor of Cairo. Hasan Pasha himself remained in Egypt in order to restore the country effectively to Ottoman authority. But in 1787 the outbreak of war between Turkey and Russia led to his recall to Constantinople. Shortly after his departure, Murad and Ibrahim overthrew Ismail and resumed the government, or rather the misgovernment, of Egypt, which they continued until they were overthrown by Bonaparte ten years later.

Meanwhile, in 1768, Russia had begun the first of a series of victorious wars against Turkey. By the Peace of Kainardji in 1774 the Turks lost the Crimea, Bessarabia, and other provinces to Russia. In 1787 another war broke out in which Austria and Russia were in alliance against Turkey. Peace was made with Austria in 1791 and with Russia in 1793 at the price of territorial concessions by Turkey to each of these Powers.

These events made it apparent that no serious resistance was to be apprehended either from Turkey or from Egypt in the event of an attempted occupation of Egypt by a European Power. Such an occupation was, as we shall see, sedulously urged upon successive French governments by a number of people, motivated not so much by commercial reasons as by a desire both to embarrass the British in India and to secure a suitable French heritage in the apparently imminent breakup of the great Ottoman State.

But these French governments, afflicted by the inertia of a dying regime, and apprehensive of reactions from the other European Powers, took no action beyond maintaining a traditional interest in and encouragement of the overland trade. In Great Britain official interest was confined to the attempted establishment of a route through Egypt for the expedition of official dispatches to and from India. Those British individuals who attempted to develop British trade in and through Egypt were officially regarded as nuisances and interlopers with mainly discreditable motives for making mischief and creating trouble.

The most picturesque and adventurous of these British individuals was the explorer James Bruce who had previously been British consul in Algiers. In June, 1768, Bruce arrived in Cairo to find that there was no British resident in that city to offer him hospitality. After staying with some French merchants and seeing Ali Bey, who had seized the government of Egypt two years previously, Bruce went to Upper Egypt, crossed the Eastern Desert from Qena to the Red Sea by the old Roman trade route, and from there sailed over to Jidda where he found nine British merchant ships from India. The Ottoman ban on Christian ships proceeding up the Red Sea north of Jidda was still in force, and the cargo from these ships was being unloaded at Jidda for oncarriage by land through the districts controlled by the Sharif of Mecca whose exactions were a continual source of complaint from the ships' captains coming to Jidda. Bruce listened to their complaints and then departed on a long and adventurous journey through Abyssinia and the Sudan, returning to Egypt at the beginning of 1773. During his absence Ali Bey, in revolt against his Ottoman suzerain, seized the Hejaz and, in the interest of Egypt's trade, removed the Ottoman interdiction on Christian trading in the north of the Red Sea.

When Bruce returned to Cairo, fired with the possibilities of opening up trade between India and Egypt, he found that Ali Bey had disappeared and that Mohammed Abu-Dahab was ruling in his place. He arrived straight from the desert at the Coptic convent of Mar Girgis on the southern outskirts of Cairo:

> I had no shirt on and in fact had not possessed one for fourteen months. I had a waistcoat and long trousers of coarse brown wool and a blanket of the same material which I used as a cloak. I had already shaved off my long beard but I still had long moustaches. On my head was a white muslin turban wound round a red fez in the Turkish style which I wore day and night. Round my waist was a thick woollen girdle which went eight or ten times round my body. My feet were bare. Stuck in my girdle were two silver-plated English pistols and a curved Abyssinian knife with a rhinocerous-horn handle.[7]

This apparition succeeded in obtaining an audience with Abu-Dahab, who, seized by pity for a barefooted stranger whom he believed to be destitute, gave him hospitality in his palace and, with a charming tact, sent him a present of gold concealed in a basket of oranges. Bruce presented the gold to the slave who had brought him the oranges. This gesture was sufficiently unusual to excite the curiosity of Abu-Dahab, who once again sent for his mysterious guest. Bruce, by this time, had sufficiently recovered from his fatigue to discuss matters of business. Abu-Dahab treated him as an honored guest, presented him with a suit of Oriental robes and, after several meetings with him, proposed that British merchants land their goods at Suez against payment of 8 percent customs duties as compared with 14 percent which they were then paying at Jidda. He also sent a letter to his representative at Mocha, at that time in Egyptian hands, confirming this arrangement. (Mocha coffee was one of the most important items in the Eastern trade, and ships coming up the Red Sea would invariably call at Mocha for cargoes.) Bruce hastened to write letters to India to the captains with whom he had talked four years earlier, advising them of the arrangement he had made and recommending to them various reliable merchant houses in Cairo with whom they could deal. (There were no British merchant houses in Cairo at the time, and, of the four firms recommended by Bruce, three were French and one Venetian.) If they got into difficulties, Bruce recommended to them that they apply to the Venetian consul in Cairo, who appears to have been the only European consul in Egypt at the time, apart from the French consul. He also wrote to the Governor of Bengal, advising him of what he had done.

Bruce's efforts received no warm welcome from the British Government who, influenced probably by the East India Company, offered no encouragement, then or later, for the development of the Eastern trade through Egypt. (The East India Company was already trading extensively in Mocha coffee via the Cape route.) The Government of Bengal, however, was more interested, and it was probably as a result of Bruce's initiative that Warren Hastings, then Governor of Bengal, concluded, in 1775, through the intermediary of one of the British captains sailing to Suez, a treaty with Abu-Dahab that was largely a confirmation of the arrangement already made by Bruce. According to the Warren Hastings treaty, goods arriving at Suez in British ships could be imported into Egypt by paying 6½ percent duty on goods from Bengal and Madras and 8 percent duty on goods from Surat and Bombay. Moreover, British merchants were allowed to buy and export goods from Egypt without paying export duty. Detailed arrangements were also made in the treaty regarding anchorage dues, and transport of goods across the desert to Cairo, and so on.[8]

The news of this treaty caused a sharp reaction in Constantinople as a result of complaints from the Sharif of Mecca (where the Egyptian writ no longer ran), who was threatened with deprivation of his income from customs duties, and from the Constantinople merchants, who were interested in the trade via the Euphrates Valley route and were afraid of being cut out if trade were diverted to the cheaper route via Egypt. These complaints, together with the perennial Ottoman fear of Mamluk assertions of independence, led to a series of firmans between 1775 and 1779 which reiterated the traditional interdiction on Christian trading in the Red Sea and threatened with confiscation and perpetual slavery any Christian merchant attempting to defy this ban.[9] The death of Abu-Dahab in 1776, and the lack of interest shown by the British Government who, insofar as they were interested at all, were interested only in the expedition of dispatches and not in the furtherance of trade, combined to ensure the more or less effective observance of these firmans, in spite of the energetic activities of George Baldwin, who comes into our story at this point.

George Baldwin, a less picturesque but, from the point of view of our story, a more important figure than Bruce, has told the story of his Egyptian experiences in his *Political Recollections Relative to Egypt,* published in London in 1801. Baldwin had gone in 1760 to Cyprus where his brother was established as a merchant dealing with the Levant ports. In 1763 he opened a branch of the business in Acre. In 1767 he returned to England and, in 1768, went back to Cyprus as British consul. In 1773 he went to Egypt with the intention of proceeding from there to India. This plan miscarried and he remained in Egypt. In 1775 he went to Constantinople, where he made himself known to Murray, the British ambassador, and from there to London, where he got himself appointed as agent in Egypt for the East India Company. He then returned to Egypt and established himself there with offices in Cairo and Alexandria. As agent for the East India Company, Baldwin's activities were confined to trying to arrange for the rapid transport of mail through Egypt between England and India. The East India Company were not interested in trade with Egypt. They were interested only in getting swifter means of communication than the Cape route provided. But Baldwin was primarily a trader for his own account and, while determined to do his best in the matter of mail, was also determined to try to overcome the difficulties in the way of trade created by the Ottoman firmans and to develop the initiatives taken by Bruce and Warren Hastings. As he wrote somewhat flamboyantly twenty-five years later, "We composed our bowl of the Ganges, the Thames and the Nile and drank prosperity to England from the top of the Pyramids."[10]

Baldwin soon found himself at odds with Sir Robert Ainslie, Murray's successor as British ambassador at Constantinople. After Abu-Dahab's death in 1776, British merchants trading with Suez found themselves in increasing difficulties arising both from the Ottoman interdiction and from the chaos prevailing in Egypt. Appealed to by Baldwin, Ainslie took the view, first, that such trading was in contravention of the rights of the British Levant Company which had the monopoly of trade with the Ottoman Empire, and second, that, as a matter of policy, Ottoman suzerainty over Egypt must be supported against any local arrangements which might be arrived at with the Mamluk beys. Therefore, with the support of the British Government, he took the line that the Ottoman firmans forbidding trade north of the Red Sea must be respected by the British, and concentrated his efforts on trying to ensure that the Ottoman prohibition was enforced equally on the flags of all Christian nations, and on trying to secure Ottoman consent to an exception being made in favor of British vessels carrying mail to and from India. In negotiating with the Porte to these ends, Ainslie was continually embarrassed by Baldwin's attempts to evade the Ottoman firmans and by his appeals for assistance in doing so.

In order to strengthen his hand in dealing with the Egyptian authorities, Baldwin, since his arrival in Egypt, had solicited his appointment as British consul both from Ainslie and from the Levant Company, by whom British consuls in the Ottoman dominions were usually nominated. There had been no British consul in Egypt since 1756, and Baldwin was particularly incensed by the fact that, in the absence of a consul, British interests in Egypt had been provisionally placed in the hands of the chief of customs, who happened to be a Greek, and by the fact that Ainslie was accustomed to relying for his Egyptian information on an Italian correspondent. In December, 1778, Baldwin went to Constantinople to try to secure for himself an appointment from Ainslie as official British representative in Egypt. Ainslie clearly, and probably correctly, thought that Baldwin would make use of any official countenance given him to undertake, in his own interest, trading ventures that would have embarrassed Ainslie in his dealings with the Porte and that would have been in opposition to Ainslie's conception of British policy in Egypt. Baldwin, not without some justice, regarded Ainslie as a bureaucratic stick-in-the-mud who was lacking both in the vision to perceive Britain's real interests in Egypt and in the energy to pursue these interests. Ainslie turned a deaf ear to Baldwin's warnings about French designs on Egypt which, as we shall see, had a considerable basis of truth, and tried to impress on Baldwin the necessity of respecting Ottoman firmans about trade in the Red Sea and of confining himself to the facilitation of mail dispatches. He appears to have even suspected Baldwin of intriguing with the French for the encouragement of the Eastern trade via Egypt with a view to his own personal benefit. In fact, although Baldwin was certainly interested in the profit to be derived from this trade, he was a true and even a fanatical patriot; but the methods he used were those which, in every age, are calculated to make official hair stand on end.

Baldwin did not leave Constantinople entirely empty-handed. Ainslie, sweetened perhaps by an assurance from the Reis Effendi (Foreign Minister) that the prohibition on trade in the Red Sea applied not only to British but also to all Christian vessels, and by a verbal undertaking from the same official that British ships carrying mail to and from Suez would not for the time being be molested, agreed to appoint Baldwin as his unofficial *wakil* (agent) in Egypt charged with the duty of supervising the agreements Ainslie had made with the Reis Effendi. In making this appointment Ainslie, in a letter to Baldwin, gave him a solemn warning against any attempt to engage in trade in defiance of the Ottoman firmans:

As the Ministers of the Sublime Porte have frequently complained to me about the illegal trade carried on between the British establishments in India and the port of Suez in the Red Sea and have recently warned me of their determination, not only to confiscate any cargo which may in the future arrive at Suez, but also to consign the captains and crews to lifelong slavery, I recommend you most urgently to use your best efforts to suppress all traffic of this nature destined for Suez and to act in conformity with the attached copy of orders sent by the East India Company to its various Indian Presidencies, which orders have been sent to me by His Majesty's Ministers as well as by the Levant Company.

As might have been expected, Baldwin did not take very much notice of this admonition. In April, 1779, a few weeks after his return to Egypt, he was involved, with some fellow countrymen from India, in an attempt to import goods via Suez in defiance of the Ottoman firmans. He was placed under arrest and, having been set free on parole, fled the country. Returning to Constantinople with stories of having been made the victim of a plot, he met with no very welcoming reception from Ainslie. After some acrimonious exchanges between the two men, in the course of which Ainslie refused Baldwin admission to the British Embassy and Baldwin cut Ainslie dead in the street, Baldwin left for London to pursue his campaign against Ainslie with the British Government.

Meanwhile the traditional French interest in Egypt had been sharpened both by the desire to embarrass the British in India and by the increasing weakness of the Ottoman Empire as revealed by the disastrous Turkish performance in the first Russo-Turkish War. If the Ottoman Empire were to break up, it was clear that the heritage would stand to be divided between the Great Powers of Europe. In such an event France would certainly assert her claim to Egypt and Syria. The question for the French Government was whether to anticipate or to attempt to postpone the breakup. On the whole, successive French governments, up to the time of the Revolution, resisted the advice they received from their representatives on the spot to adopt a forward policy in Egypt and, whether as a result of prudence or inertia, merely continued their attempts to maintain the steadily deteriorating French commercial position in Egypt. This deterioration was due not to any encroachments by Britain or by any other foreign Power but to the deepening chaos in Egypt as a result of the misgovernment of the beys and, in some measure, to British official support of the Turkish Government in their determination to prevent Christian trading in the north of the Red Sea.

In 1769 the Duc de Choiseul, the French Foreign Minister, considered plans, which came to nothing, for occupying and colonizing Egypt in order to compensate France for her colonial losses in the Seven Years' War. In 1773 Louis de Laugier, a Marseille merchant, addressed a memorandum to the French Government in which he pointed out that the distance between Pondicherry (one of the few ports in India remaining in French hands after the Treaty of Paris in 1763) and Marseille was only one-quarter of the distance between Pondicherry and Lorient. He advocated making an agreement with the Sultan of Turkey to establish French garrisons at Alexandria, Cairo, and Suez in return for French assistance to Turkey in their war against Russia. He claimed that by this means it would be possible to send French troops to India "as easily as from Strasbourg to Marseille," and "enable us to humiliate the English in Asia and submit them, and any other Powers who trade there, to our will." In order to facilitate communications between France and India via a French-garrisoned Egypt, De Laugier, who seems to have been an optimist, advocated the construction of a canal, at Turkish expense, and with French technical assistance, between the Nile and the Red Sea.[11]

In 1775 Mure, the French consul in Egypt, advised his government that Abu-Dahab was prepared to make an agreement with France to enable French merchant vessels to come to Suez. (As we have seen, he had already made agreements with England to the same effect.) The French Government, of which Vergennes was the Foreign Minister, took no more notice of this than they had done of De Laugier's proposal. But, two years later,

Saint-Priest, the French ambassador in Constantinople, who was a strong advocate of a French occupation of Egypt, arranged, in consultation with the French Government, for a certain Baron de Tott, a Hungarian adventurer who had been in Ottoman service as a military adviser, to visit Egypt and Syria, ostensibly on a visit of inspection to the French Echelles, but in reality to make a report on the possibilities of a French occupation of Egypt. In a report subsequently made to the French Ministère de la Marine, La Laune, a French military expert accompanying De Tott, emphasized that there was no serious military obstacle to such an occupation. The baron himself, in an accompanying note, underlined its timeliness, as the British were busy trying to quell the revolt of their American colonies. He stated that such an occupation would ensure French interests in the Mediterranean against a possible Russian capture of Constantinople, and stressed that the seizure of the valuable Mocha coffee trade, which an occupation of Egypt would make possible, alone made the expedition worthwhile.[12] De Tott went on to express the view that a French occupation (which he described as "the peaceful occupation of a defenseless country") would bring the bulk of the Eastern trade once more back from the Cape route to the Mediterranean and would arm France with the means of combating any British resistance to this development. His advocated the construction of a canal between the Nile and the Red Sea after the French occupation.[13]

By the time De Tott's report was received, France was at war with Britain in alliance with their rebellious American colonies. News had already been received of Admiral Suffren's successes against British commerce in the Indian Ocean. But in spite of Saint-Priest's advice that they should either effectively sustain the Ottoman Empire or anticipate its dissolution, the French Government took no action. Either alternative might have provoked a European war and a Russian seizure of Constantinople.

But the decline in British influence as a result of the American War of Independence and the chaos in Egypt as a result of the misrule of Murad and Ibrahim kept the question of a French occupation alive in the minds of the French Government, of the Marseille merchants, of French officials in the Ottoman Empire, and of French cranks and enthusiasts of varying degrees of influence, intelligence, and imagination. French interest was also sharpened by a belief that Austria, who had shown an intermittent interest in the overland route through Egypt, and whose government was at that time in close touch with Cassis, the chief of customs in Egypt, had the same incipient ambitions toward Egypt as the French had themselves.

In 1782 a certain Baron de Waldner submitted a voluminous note to the

French Government advocating that France, Holland, and Venice should, with the agreement of the Porte, occupy Egypt, garrison it, and jointly construct a canal from Suez to Gaza with the object of capturing the Eastern trade from Britain. The note envisaged an ultimate partition of the Ottoman Empire by which France would occupy Egypt, Arabia, Yemen, and the Sultanate of Musqat; Venice, the whole of Asia Minor; Russia, Constantinople and the Dardenelles; and Austria, the rest of Turkey in Europe. This note, bordering on fantasy as it does, is principally interesting in that it advocates, for the first time, a canal running between the Red Sea and the Mediterranean direct instead of via the Nile, thus rejecting—as it happened, correctly—the traditional idea that such a direct route was impossible owing to a big difference in level between the two seas.

In 1783 Mure, the French consul in Egypt, moved by a fear lest an expected renewed outbreak of war between Turkey and Russia might tempt Austria to seize Egypt, wrote a most able and detailed report in which he advocated that France should anticipate any such Austrian initiative by occupying Egypt herself. The principal reason for his recommendation was the traditional one of bringing back the Eastern trade via the Cape to the Mediterranean route to the consequent advantage of France and the disadvantage of England. "The proximity of India, the use that could be made of the Red Sea for communication with it, the ability to transport goods from Suez to the Nile by a canal which would only need to be partly re-excavated . . . would greatly reduce the time, the expenses and the losses sustained by the Cape route and would assure the successful competition of goods taking the old route," provided, Mure went on, that the "old route" were relieved of all the obstacles placed upon it by the Turks.

Mure's military plans for an occupation were based on De Tott's recommendations made five years previously. The most interesting part of his report consists of his detailed plans for the French colonization of Egypt after the occupation. He envisaged the immigration of French peasants to cultivate the soil, the improvement of irrigation methods, and the encouragement of the import of French manufactured goods. He advocated the prohibition of the import into Egypt of woolen, silk, or cotton goods other than those of French manufacture or carried in French vessels, and the imposition of government monoplies on tobacco, salt, and other items in order to raise the necessary revenues for administration. In short, he proposed that Egypt not only be occupied for commercial and strategic reasons but that it should be converted into a French colony in accordance with the eighteenth century conception of a colony—a place of settlement for surplus population, a market for the mother country's manufactures, and a plantation for the raw materials needed for the mother country's industries.

Mure's report was the first detailed and explicit statement of the amplitude of French ambitions toward Egypt which were nourished at that time by many French officials concerned with the East, and particularly by the powerful Marseillais merchant interest. This merchant interest was gradually becoming convinced that a French occupation was the only way in which the considerable French trading position in Egypt could survive at all, let alone develop. For, by this time, internal conditions in Egypt, and the depredations of Murad and Ibrahim, had reduced French, and indeed all European, trade practically to nothing.

But the French Government would still have nothing to do with the idea of an occupation. Choiseul-Gouffier, who had replaced Saint-Priest as ambassador at Constantinople, continued trying to make arrangements for improving trading conditions and for recovering French preeminence in the Egyptian market. Eventually, in 1785, De Truguet, a French naval officer, with the assistance of Charles Magellon, a French merchant in Cairo who was, with equal enthusiasm and with more discretion, to play the same role for France as Baldwin was to try to play for England, succeeded in making a treaty with the beys very much more favorable than the Warren Hastings Treaty of 1775, which had in any case become inoperative. The Truguet Treaty provided for the free access of French vessels to Suez, for the transit of goods through Egypt against payment of 3 percent transit dues, and for the import of Eastern goods into Egypt against customs duties of 6 percent to 4 percent for the beys and 2 percent for the Turkish pasha. In a second treaty the chief of customs was designated as "protector, supervisor, and adviser" to the French merchants, and a third treaty arranged for the escort of French goods across the desert between Cairo and Suez.[14]

Excellent as these treaties were on paper, they remained almost without practical effect on the French trading position. The Porte, who in 1787 recovered their influence in Egypt for the time being as the result of Hasan Pasha's punitive expedition against Ibrahim and Murad, refused to ratify them by the lifting of the prohibition against Christian ships trading in the north of the Red Sea. Their refusal was supported by the British and other ambassadors so long as France was likely to be the sole beneficiary of a lifting of the prohibition. The French Government, for their part, found themselves in difficulties with the Compagnie des Indes, whose charter had just been renewed and who objected to the encouragement of trade which diminished the value of their monopoly via the Cape route.

One effect, however, the treaties did have. When the British Government heard of them they began to feel some concern about French designs on Egypt. Moreover, such trading as had taken place between India and England since 1773 had excited a certain amount of popular interest which was not without its effect on the attitude of the government. Baldwin, since his return to England in 1779, had been busy bringing himself and his ideas to the notice of ministers and others in high places. Consequently, when the government heard of the Truguet treaties, Dundas, President of the India Board, sent for Baldwin and asked for his advice. Baldwin replied with a note entitled "Speculations on the Situation and Resources of Egypt." In this note he warned Dundas against French ambitions in Egypt about which he knew, or suspected, more than the British Government,[15] and emphasized the importance of Egypt to England as a channel of communication with India; he reminded Dundas of how, in 1779, he had been able, from Egypt, to give to the Governor of Madras the first news of the French declaration of war against Britain and so enabled the Governor to make a surprise attack on the French port of Pondicherry.

The British Government was sufficiently impressed by Baldwin's arguments to revive the British Consulate General in Egypt and to appoint Baldwin as consul general in 1786. In a dispatch to Ainslie advising him of his old enemy's appointment, the India Board stated that "the essential object of Mr. Baldwin's mission to Cairo is to open communications with India by way of Egypt." The line taken by the India Board, which Ainslie was instructed to develop in Contantinople, was that the prohibition of British trading in the north of the Red Sea was in contravention of the various "capitulations" treaties with Turkey, as were any trading or other privileges given to France or to any other foreign nation which were not also given to England. They informed Ainslie that Baldwin had been instructed to negotiate with the beys for a treaty that would place British subjects at least on an equality with French subjects. It was emphasized that no disrespect was intended either to the Porte or to Ainslie himself but that the precedent recently created by the Truguet treaties made it clear that it was impossible effectively to safeguard British interests in Egypt except by means of a British representative in negotiation with the beys, it being understood that the result of any such negotiation, either by the British or by the French, would have to be ratified in Constantinople. The dispatch went on to state that, if the Porte refused to ratify any agreement made by Baldwin on the lines of the Truguet treaties, Ainslie was peremptorily to insist at least on the British right to carry mail through Egypt to and from India. (It is implicit in the whole tenor of the dispatch to Ainslie that the really important matter was the transit of mail and that the India Board would be quite satisfied not to press the question of trade, provided that no formal renunciation was made of the right to trade in the north of the Red Sea, and provided that France was not given any preferential trading position by a ratification of the Truguet treaties.) The India Board concluded its dispatch by stating that Baldwin had agreed to let bygones be bygones in respect of his previous relations with Ainslie, and expressing confidence that Ainslie would do the same.

In spite of this, relations between the two men were never very cordial, and little was accomplished by either of them in respect of British trade, although, partly no doubt owing to Baldwin's efforts, British mail to and from India continued to be passed more or less regularly through Egypt. But the British Government soon lost interest in Baldwin's mission, and in 1793 once more abolished the British Consulate General in Egypt. The official intimation to Baldwin of his dismissal crossed with a dispatch from Baldwin announcing the conclusion of a treaty with Murad and Ibrahim on the lines of the Truguet treaties. Baldwin, advised of his dismissal, did his best to persuade the British Government to reverse its decision and to take his treaty seriously. He also continued, presciently, to warn them about French designs on Egypt (by this time England was at war with the revolutionary Government of France). But all was in vain and, in 1796, Baldwin, discouraged, left Egypt. He was to return a few years later, as adviser to the British expedition in 1801.[16]

Baldwin was undoubtedly a somewhat tricky customer, whose trading interests, which seem to have been profitable, were often a source of embarrassment to the British authorities. But he did his country some valuable service in laying the foundations of the overland route through Egypt for mails, and in impressing upon his countrymen the importance of Egypt in the British imperial scheme of things. Little notice was taken of his advice and little appreciation was expressed of his services. (He seems to have been treated very shabbily, not only by the British Goverment but by the East India and Levant companies as well.) But he deserves to be remembered with respect. As has happened so often in British imperial history, the advice of an independent-minded and well-informed man was neglected and his activities disparaged by an "establishment" that attached more importance to protocolar behavior than to reliable information, and appreciated gentlemanly reticence more highly than pertinacious insistence.

Meanwhile the French in Egypt, since the Truguet treaties, had been faring very little better than the British. In spite of the efforts of Magellon, little French trade was done as a result of the treaties and little interest was expressed by the French Government in promoting such trade. In 1787 war broke out once more between Turkey and Russia. The Duc de Lauzun, one of the many picturesque figures in European history who, from time to time, have interested themselves in the affairs of the Levant, once more revived the question of a French occupation of Egypt. He proposed to Montmorin, Vergennes's successor as Foreign Minister, that Egypt be occupied by France as trustees for Turkey in order to prevent either Russia or Austria, who were both at war with Turkey, from seizing it themselves. Thus, in the event of the Ottoman Empire emerging more or less intact from the war, they would be under an obligation to France over Egypt and, in the expected event of the Ottoman Empire breaking up as a result of the war, France would already be in possession of Egypt. But, in spite of Montmorin's personal support of De Lauzun's proposal, no action was taken. The Ottoman Empire emerged from the war, diminished but still in existence, with her authority in Egypt reduced almost to vanishing point as a result of Murad and Ibrahim having been returned to power.

The Revolutionary Government took rather more interest than its predecessors in the maintenance of French interests in Egypt which, like all other foreign interests in that country, were steadily being annihilated under the capricious oppressiveness of Murad and Ibrahim. After Mure had left Egypt in 1788, there was no official French representative in Egypt, and the unofficial leadership of the French community had been assumed by Charles Magellon. In 1791 Magellon went to Paris to advise the new regime of the state of affairs in Egypt, and in 1793 he returned to Egypt as French consul general. Relations between the French merchants and the beys went from bad to worse. In 1795 the French Echelle was transferred from Cairo to Alexandria, and Thainville, an emissary from the French Embassy in Constantinople, was sent to Egypt to try, with Magellon, to arrive at some *modus vivendi* with the beys. The failure of Thainville's mission convinced Magellon, as Mure had previously been convinced, that the only way in which France could recover her position in Egypt was by a military occupation of the country. Magellon's report in this sense resulted in his being invited once more to Paris. He arrived in Paris in 1797, just as Talleyrand had succeeded Delacroix as Foreign Minister in the Government of the Directory. Owing to his presence in Paris, he was able to advise Talleyrand and Bonaparte over the plans which were soon to be made for the expedition to Egypt.

By the summer of 1797 France had made peace with Prussia and was engaged in peace negotiations with Austria. Great Britain remained the only active enemy. The great question was, How could the British best be attacked? The Napoleonic strategy, then as later, was to try to strangle the British by attacks on their trade. In a letter to the Directory in August, 1797, Bonaparte, fresh from his Italian victories, wrote, "The time is not far distant when, in order to destroy England, we shall have to occupy Egypt. The impending dissolution of the Ottoman Empire will soon oblige us to take steps to preserve our commerce in the Levant."[17] The previously neglected views of men like De Laugier, De Tott, Mure, De Lauzun and Magellon were at last receiving distinguished support.

At the end of September the Treaty of Campo Formio was signed, putting an end to the war with Austria and enabling Bonaparte and the Directory to concentrate on the war with England. For some months Bonaparte's efforts were directed toward the possibility of an invasion of England across the Channel. When this was abandoned, or at all events shelved, toward the end of February, the project for an occupation of Egypt was taken seriously in hand. At the beginning of February, Magellon had submitted to Talleyrand a memorandum on Egypt.[18] After describing the misgovernment of the beys and the ruin of French commerce in Egypt as a result of this misgovernment, Magellon expressed the view that it was necessary "either to renounce the French position in Egypt or establish it by force."

After stating that there would be no serious military resistance from the beys, Magellon discussed the proposed occupation in the light of the war with England. He recalled that the English had always been sensititve to the presence of the French in Egypt, and described the British diplomatic efforts to prevent the development of the French transit trade through Egypt. He said that the British had only from 15,000 to 20,000 troops in India and that the occupation of Egypt, followed by the dispatch of 15,000 French troops to India via Egypt, would, with the assistance of Tippoo Sahib, the Sultan of Mysore, then in revolt against the British and apparently in contact with French agents, would be sufficient to destroy the British position in India. Magellon ended his note by pointing out that, if Egypt was essential to France in order to get at the British in India, it was, *a fortiori*, essential to the British in order to enable them to maintain their position in India: "The British must realize that Egypt must not be allowed to fall into French hands. When they see that the moment is favorable for occupying it they will send a squadron there on the pretext of protecting it from a French attack. They could send a force of 1,500 natives together with some 5,000 to 6,000 British troops which would be more than sufficient both to occupy Egypt and to make any subsequent attempt at an occupation by us much more difficult."

A report by Talleyrand to the Directory, five days after he had received Magellon's note, was clearly influenced by Magellon's views.[19] In this report Talleyrand recommended the occupation of Egypt and expressed the view that Turkey, against whom Talleyrand set out a formidable list of French grievances, would not regard such occupation as a *casus belli*. On February 23rd Bonaparte returned from an inspection of the Channel coast and, in effect, advised the abandonment of any immediate French attempt to invade England. Instead, he recommended either an expedition into Germany or an expedition to the Levant to threaten the British position in India.[20] On April 12th the decision to invade Egypt was taken by the Directory.[21] In an order to Bonaparte, instructing him to prepare and to lead the expedition, the Directory accused the beys (incorrectly) of having allied themselves with the British and of having, as a result of this alliance, grossly oppressed French interests and maltreated French nationals in Egypt. Referring to the recent British occupation of the Cape of Good Hope, which had made French access to the Indies difficult, the order stressed the necessity of opening another route to the Indies by means of which the French could "attack the British satellites and take away from England the source of her corrupt riches." The commander in chief of the Army of the East (as the expedition was to be called) was instructed to "expel the British from all their possessions in the East, wherever they may be, and, in particular, to destroy all their trading stations on the Red Sea, to cut a canal through the Isthmus of Suez, and to take all necessary steps to ensure the free and exclusive use of the Red Sea by French vessels."[22]

The Army of the East left Toulon on March 19, 1798. The Directory's decision to occupy Egypt had been taken, as we have seen, entirely as a means toward the effective pursuit of the war against England, in the expectation that there would be no serious military resistance in Egypt, and no effective objection from Constantinople. The Directory believed, or professed to believe, that the British were taking very much more interest in Egypt than in fact they were; they may even have believed, with Magellon, that a French occupation of Egypt was necessary in order to forestall a British occupation, so obvious did it seem to the French that the British could not fail to regard Egypt as a vital link in the chain of their communications with India. In fact, the British Government did not so regard it and, in spite of Baldwin's warnings, had no serious belief in the actual extent of the French interest in Egypt. So much so that, when the French fleet accompanying the expedition left Toulon, its destination was not suspected either by the British Government or by Nelson, who was scouring the Mediterranean for it.

It was only after Bonaparte's landing in Egypt that Dundas, then Minister of War, was to write, in a note to the Foreign Secretary, that "the possession of Egypt by any independent Power would be a fatal circumstance to the interests of this country." Thereafter, this view was to govern British policy in the Eastern Mediterranean for the next 150 years, and was, in due course, to dictate the position assumed by successive British governments toward the construction, operation, and ownership of the Suez Canal.

NOTES

1. The Pelusiac branch of the Nile became silted up at about the beginning of the Christian Era. While it existed it was the most easterly of the branches (now reduced to two— the Rosetta and Damietta branches) into which the Nile was divided in the Delta just below Cairo. It flowed northeast, discharging into the Mediterranean at the ancient city of Pelusium near the modern Port Said. At the ancient city of Bubastis, near the modern Zagazig, the Pelusiac branch opened out into a large lake. It was from this lake that Necho's canal appears to have started.

2. Via the Canopic, or westernmost, branch of the Nile which, until the twelfth century of the Christian Era, when it became silted up, flowed into the sea at Alexandria. Alexandria began to lose its importance when it ceased to be directly connected, via the Nile, to Egypt's rich hinterland, and only regained it some 700 years later when Mohammed Ali once more connected it with the Nile by the Mahmudieh Canal.

3. In his Introduction to Pierre Crabites's *The Spoliation of Suez.*

4. Quoted in *Richelieu et La Monarchie Absolue,* by Vicomte d'Avenel, III, 218–219.

5. From *Œuvres de Liebnitz,* V, "Project d'Expédition d'Egypte," pp. 268 *et seq.*

6. The Levant Company, which had a monopoly of English trade with the Ottoman Empire, was not interested in the transit trade with the Indies, considering it outside the scope of their monopoly.

7. *Voyages aux Sources du Nil,* by James Bruce, French transl., IV, 718, Paris 1790.

8. For the text of this treaty, see J. Charles-Roux, *L'Isthme et le Canal de Suez,* Vol. I, Annex No. 4.

9. For text of the 1779 firman, see J. Charles-Roux, *op. cit.,* Vol. I, Annex No. 5.

10. Baldwin, *Political Recollections . . . ,* p. 6.

11. F. Charles-Roux, *Origines de l'Expédition de l'Egypte,* pp. 58–59.

12. It is noteworthy that nearly all references to the Eastern trade from the middle of the seventeenth century onward, stress the importance of the Mocha coffee trade which apparently eclipsed the previous importance attached to silks and spices.

13. This account of De Tott's mission is taken from F. Charles-Roux, *op. cit.,* pp. 61–95.

14. For texts of these treaties see J. Charles-Roux, *op. cit.,* Vol. I, Annexes 6 and 7.

15. "France, in possession of Egypt, would possess the master-key to all the trading nations of the earth. Enlightened, as the times are, in the general arts of navigation and commerce, she might make it the emporium of the world; she might make it the awe of the Western world by the facility she would command of transporting her forces thither by

surprise, in any number, at any time, and England would hold her possessions in India at the mercy of the French." Baldwin, *op. cit.*, p. 79.

16. At Malta, on his way to Egypt, he met his old rival Magellon, who had just been captured by the British on his way from Egypt. For Baldwin's account of the meeting see Baldwin, *op. cit.*, pp. 95–99.

17. F. Charles-Roux, *Origines*, p. 298. These two sentences are rather cryptic. The second sentence presumably indicates the ostensible reason, the real reason being given in the first sentence.

18. F. Charles-Roux, *L'Angleterre, L'Isthme de Suez, et L'Egypte*, p. 348.

19. F. Charles-Roux, *Origines*, p. 327.

20. F. Charles-Roux, *ibid.*, p. 333.

21. F. Charles-Roux, *L'Angleterre . . .* , p. 361.

22. F. Charles-Roux, *ibid.*, pp. 362-363.

CHAPTER *two*

The Development of

the Overland Route ❧

◀§ ALTHOUGH the immediate reason for Bona-parte's Egyptian expedition can be explained in terms of the grand strategy of the Revolutionary regime's struggle against England, the French occupation of Egypt also represented the fruition of many years of French imperial thinking, some of the manifestations of which were summarized in the preceding chapter. In this thinking, rivalry with England played only a temporary and incidental part. Even the commercial determination, which had been apparent since the discovery of the Cape route by the Portuguese in the fifteenth century, to keep open and to develop the old overland route under French auspices and in competition with the Cape route as a means of preserving France's interest in the Eastern trade vis-à-vis the Atlantic Powers was probably secondary to the impalpable, almost mystical, idea of France as the legitimate heir of the Roman Empire and as the protector and possible liberator of all Christians living under Muslim rule. As part of her Roman heritage the Mediterranean was seen by France as a potential "Mare Nostrum" and the Turkish provinces in the Levant as the fairest part of Rome's Mediterranean Empire. And, to the subjects of the Most Christian King, the Crusades had been a specifically French enterprise, and one of them—the one mostly concerned with Egypt—had been led by a French king. It is ironical that the imperial and Christian mantle of the kings of France should have been assumed with such bravura by an atheist Republic whose representatives had first supplanted and then killed a French king.

The French occupation of Egypt was intended to be a permanent one; it was intended to make of Egypt a French colony which would compensate France for the loss of her West Indian colonies and which would, in the accepted role of colonies at that time, serve as a place for French settlement, as a market for French manufactures, and as a source of raw materials for French consumption and for French industry.

27

To the immediate political reasons which caused the expedition to be decided on—fighting the British, punishing the beys for their oppression of French subjects—was added a consideration of the advantages to be derived from a permanent occupation. These advantages the French would derive, first from the exploitation of products already cultivated in Egypt—wheat, other cereals, rice, fruits of all kinds; second, from the exploitation of those more remunerative crops which would become possible as a result of the better use of the water resources of the Nile—cane sugar, linen, and indigo; third, from the exploitation of products already imported into Egypt—coffee and perfumes from Arabia, gold dust, ivory, and other articles from the interior of Africa, Eastern goods; fourth, from the supply by France of the goods which Egypt lacked—woolen cloth, wines, iron, lead, and wood. The efficient exploitation of Egypt's resources would necessitate various public works by which the wealth of the country would be increased—irrigation works for agriculture and the construction of a navigable canal from the Red Sea to the Mediterranean for commerce. Commercial relations would be established or developed with Arabia, Persia, India, and Africa. The continent of Africa would be opened up by exploration. Restored to prosperity, regenerated by wise and enlightened administration, Egypt would shed its civilizing rays upon all its Oriental neighbors.[1]

Bonaparte took with him on his expedition an impressive body of French savants—scientists, engineers, physicians, zoologists, agronomes, archaeologists, and many others—who formed themselves into an Institut d'Egypte for the purpose of documenting and making recommendations about the various aspects of Egyptian life and culture which corresponded to their several expertises. The purpose of the Institut was to assist in the economic and cultural development of a new French colony which was known to be endowed with remarkable material and cultural resources. In the event, its achievement was to lay the foundations of that French cultural penetration of Egypt which, during the first half of the nineteenth century, was to ensure that the modernization of Egypt under Mohammed Ali took place largely through the medium of the French language and with the assistance of French experts, French techniques, and French political and diplomatic backing. Among the schemes of modernization which were to come to fruition under Mohammed Ali's successors was the Suez Canal. The fact that, when this was finally achieved, it was achieved as a French enterprise, was due, first, to the long-standing French interest in the question of such a canal, and, second, to the impetus given to this interest by Bonaparte's expedition and by the activities of the Institut d'Egypte.

Bonaparte took his instruction from the Directory about cutting a canal seriously. In December, 1798, he made a personal reconnaissance in the isthmus, accompanied by members of the Institut and of the Commission des Sciences et des Arts which he had set up for the preparation of technical plans arising out of the occupation. Bonaparte and his party inspected the anchorage at Suez, explored the country between Suez and the Bitter Lakes, and claimed to have discovered traces of the old Ptolemaic canal. On his return to Cairo, Bonaparte appointed the engineer Le Père, who had been one of the party, to make a detailed preliminary survey.

Le Père and his assistants had to work under difficulties owing to lack of communications, lack of security and, above all, lack of time. As a result, probably, of these disadvantages a serious surveying error was made over the relative levels of the Red Sea and the Mediterranean, which seemed to confirm existing tradition and which was seriously to affect future thinking about the canal for the next fifty years. They found, erroneously, that the level of the Red Sea at high tide was thirty feet above that of the Mediterranean, deduced from this that a direct cut between the Mediterranean and the Red Sea was impracticable, and concluded that a new canal must follow, more or less, the route of the old Ptolemaic canal and join the Red Sea to the Mediterranean by way of the Nile.

Pressing military preoccupations, and the eventual French evacuation of Egypt within three years of their landing, prevented anything more than preliminary studies by Le Père and a preliminary report[2] which, erroneous as it was, served as an indispensable basis for all future investigations into the possibility of a canal.

British diplomacy in Constantinople saw to it that the news of the French occupation of Egypt was unfavorably received at the Porte. Part of the Turkish fleet was induced to join a Russian squadron in operations against the French in the Adriatic. The Pasha of Acre, Jazzar, with British and Turkish encouragement and assistance, sent an army to invade Egypt. This army reached al Arish, and the menace which it presented was the principal reason for Bonaparte's Syrian campaign at the beginning of 1799.

There followed the siege and successful defense of Acre, the French Army's retreat into Egypt, Bonaparte's return to France, the assassination of Kléber, Bonaparte's successor, the landing of an Anglo-Turkish expeditionary force, and the evacuation of the French from Egypt in 1801.

In 1802 the Peace of Amiens was signed between France on the one side and England and her European allies on the other. A Russian refusal to agree to Turkish representation at Amiens, although Turkey had been engaged in the war against France, gave French diplomacy at Constantinople the opportunity for a rapprochement with the Turks, who joined up with the French to secure the evacuation of Egypt by the British in 1803. The French had by no means lost their interest in Egypt. In 1802, while the British were still in Egypt, Bonaparte had sent a Colonel Sebastiani to

Egypt to report on the possibility of a French reoccupation. In 1806, when Britain and France were again at war, Sebastiani was sent as French ambassador to Constantinople. By this time the Mamluk beys, whom the British had left in control, had been ousted by Mohammed Ali, an Albanian officer who had come to Egypt with the Turkish force in 1801 and who, after the departure of the British, had rapidly taken advantage of the chaotic conditions in Egypt to raise himself to power by overthrowing the Mamluk beys and expelling the Turkish pasha. In 1805 he induced the Porte to appoint him as pasha in place of the one he had expelled. In 1807 the British Government, fearful of the possibility of a French reoccupation of Egypt, sent a force to reoccupy Egypt themselves. This force was ignominiously defeated by Mohammed Ali and forced to reembark.

In the same year the whole posture of European affairs was changed by the conclusion of the Treaty of Tilsit between Napoleon and the Czar of Russia. This treaty which, among other things, seemed to presage the partition of the Ottoman Empire between France and Russia, caused Turkey to put an end to the rapprochement with France achieved at Amiens and consolidated by Sebastiani at Constantinople, and to return to her alliance with England. By way of compensation France cultivated closer relationships with Mohammed Ali, whose increasing power and prestige were not only rendering him virtually independent of his suzerain but were beginning to create the possibility of his building an empire of his own which would absorb most of the Arab lands included within the Ottoman Empire.

Thus was created the pattern of Anglo-French policy over Egypt which was to shape events in that country for the next fifty or sixty years. Both France and Britain were concerned to prevent the dissolution of the Ottoman Empire, since such dissolution would have meant a Russian occupation of Constantinople. This would threaten France as a Mediterranean Power and increase the threat to British communications with India already presented, in the eyes of the British Government, by the beginnings of Russian overland expansion in central and southeast Asia. But France, although abandoning the idea of any direct colonization of Egypt, was prepared, by encouraging and to some extent sponsoring Mohammed Ali's ambitions, to see a loosening, and even a severance, of Turkish ties, not only with Egypt but with Syria as well, in favor of an independent or quasi-independent Arab State, ruled over by Mohammed Ali and his successors, and protected both against Turkey and against other European Powers by an alliance with France. In the exercise of this policy France counted on the possibility of the emergence of a modernized, reasonably stable, and francophile Arab State which, in the event of the dissolution of the Ottoman Empire, would be able, in alliance with France, to maintain itself in the face of Britain, Russia, and Austria. The existence of such a state would, it was reasoned, promote the supremacy of French influence in the eastern Mediterranean.

These French ambitions were no longer seriously directed against the British position in India. They were part and parcel of the French desire to consolidate their position as a Mediterranean Power and to open up the continent of Africa under French auspices. This desire was expressed, inter alia, in the French seizure of Algeria in 1830, in their designs on Tunis, and in their sedulously cultivated relations with Abyssinia. The British, although, since Bonaparte's Egypt expedition, hypersensitive about their communications with India, regarded their own occupation of Egypt as incompatible with the realities of European power politics. Instead they came to regard the effective maintenance of Ottoman suzerainty over Egypt as being the best guarantee for the continued security of these communications. Successive British governments were haunted by the possibility that some potentially hostile Power would be in a position to transport troops to India via Egypt more quickly than the British were able to reinforce India via the Cape. A virtually independent and French-protected Egypt would realize this possibility. And so British policy over Egypt and Syria, pursued more or less consistently for the first seventy years of the nineteenth century, was designed to secure the continued effective exercise of Ottoman suzerainty over these regions, to secure and to maintain a predominant British influence in Constantinople by protecting the Ottoman Empire against French and Russian encroachments and, in particular, to oppose what they regarded as French-inspired and French-supported attempts by Mohammed Ali and his successors to loosen or to sever the ties which bound them to their suzerain.

The British objections to a canal through the Suez Isthmus, as they were subsequently manifested, must be seen in relation to this general policy. These objections were not confined to the idea of a French-owned and a French-operated canal. From the British point of view, any canal, by reason of the importance it would confer on the ruler of Egypt, and by reason of the fact that it would create a physical barrier against the march of a Turkish army into Egypt, would encourage and sustain Egyptian independence of Constantinople and so defeat the basic aim of British policy toward Egypt. The fact that this British policy was, for an exceptionally long period of years, under the control or subject to the influence of one strong and single-minded individual—Lord Palmerston—gave it an unusual consistency, amounting sometimes to obstinacy. Also, British material power, and particularly British maritime power, over this period ensured that this policy was as consistently effectuated as it was consistently pursued. For, whether or not the policy was a wise one, and irrespective of whether or not it was adapted sufficiently to changing circumstances, it was a policy which, taking into account the balance of forces arrayed in support and in opposition to it, could be effectuated with the means at Britain's disposal without running any serious risk of a European war. And, as a matter of historical fact, the end result of that policy was the achievement and maintenance of British hegemony in the Mediterranean for a period of about seventy years—a circumstance which enabled Britain to survive and—if only in a Pyrrhic sense—to emerge victorious from two world wars.

The factor which made the Suez Canal project technically possible was the development of steam navigation.[3] In the days of sail the strong northerly wind prevailing in the Gulf of Suez and the difficulty of maneuvering large sailing vessels in narrow waters were strong arguments against a canal. For it was on the transit of large cargo vessels that the economics of a canal would depend. Passengers and mail could more economically continue to be sent in smaller vessels and conveyed overland between Alexandria and Suez. The use of this overland route for passengers and mail was in fact intensively developed, mainly under British auspices, until the completion of the canal. British official interest in the short route continued to be confined to the expedition of passengers and mail, and continued to ignore the possibilities of a canal for cargo even after the development of the steamship had rendered such expedition practical and potentially profitable. This myopia was almost certainly deliberate and due to political considerations. At all events, there grew up a noticeable divergence between the views of British statesmen and those of British businessmen about the desirability of a canal, and one of the first serious proposals for cutting a canal was made by a British businessman—one of the directors of Peninsular & Oriental—in 1841.

The first people to appreciate the relevance of steam navigation to the development of the overland route were the British mercantile communities in the big Indian cities who, for business and for personal reasons, were anxious to shorten and cheapen communications between England and India for both mail and passengers. In 1823 the Marquis Wellesley, the Governor-General of India, who had done much to encourage the rapid transit of dispatches between England and India during the Napoleonic Wars, began interesting himself in the use of steam for maintaining and expanding the service. In the same year the British community in Calcutta formed a "Steam Committee" to promote the idea of regular steamer services between England and India. Soon afterward "Steam Committees" were formed in Bombay and Madras as well. The Calcutta Committee offered a substantial money prize to any individual or company who should, before the end of 1826, succeed in establishing a regular service of steamers between England and Bengal, either by the Cape or by the overland route. As a result of this offer the steamer *Enterprise* was constructed and made the voyage from England to India by the Cape route.

The attempt to set up a regular service was, however, a failure, but the experiment served to show that the short Mediterranean and Red Sea route was, at that time, a more suitable one for steam vessels. Future efforts to promote such a steam service were therefore concentrated on this route. In the spring of 1830 the steamship *Hugh Lindsay* made the first successful steamship voyage from Bombay to Suez, taking about a month on the trip. Thereafter, in spite of only lukewarm support from the British Government, progress was fairly rapid. By 1840, in spite of many vicissitudes and a certain amount of official obstruction, there was a fairly regular mail and passenger service plying between England and India, by rail across Europe to the Mediterranean, by steamer to and from Alexandria, overland across Egypt between Alexandria to Suez, and by steamer between Suez and India. Apart from the steamships, the establishment of a regular service necessitated (*a*) the establishment of a coaling station between Suez and Bombay, (*b*) the preparation of accurate charts of the Red Sea, and (*c*) the proper organization of the overland route across Egypt. The annexation of Aden by the Government of India in 1838 provided the coaling station. Surveys of the Red Sea were undertaken by the Indian Navy. The organization of the overland route through Egypt, which has more direct relevance to our story, was undertaken by a number of adventurous private individuals, of whom the pioneer was Thomas Waghorn.

Waghorn was a British naval officer who had served in the Indian Navy, from which he had obtained his release in order to compete for the prize offered by the Calcutta Steam Committee. Having become convinced, as a result of the voyage of the *Enterprise,* that the Cape route was impracticable, he turned his attention to the short route via the Mediterranean and Red Sea. After trying, and failing, through lack of adequate financial backing, to organize a regular steam service, Waghorn settled in Egypt in 1835 as the agent of the East India Company, when the organization of steam services was proceeding under other auspices, and devoted himself to the organization of the overland route across Egypt. The first necessity was to lay down adequate supplies of coal at Suez. Waghorn imported coal from England to Alexandria, carried it by barge up the Nile to Cairo —communication between Alexandria and the Nile had been effected by the construction of the Mahmudieh Canal in 1819—and from Cairo to Suez by camel caravan.[4] Waghorn also arranged for the carriage of passengers and mail between Cairo and Alexandria by boat and between Cairo and Suez, where he built a hotel, by horse carriage. He charged £13 per passenger for the complete trip. It was not long before he had competitors.

Two Englishmen named Hill and Raven built hotels in Cairo and Suez and a series of five rest houses along the eighty-five-mile road between Cairo and Suez. This competition was not always advantageous for passengers, since Hill and Raven refused to allow Waghorn's passengers to use the rest houses, and Waghorn often succeeded in hiring all the available draft animals that were to be had, thus bringing his rivals' caravans to a standstill. In 1841 the three men amalgamated to form the concern of Hill & Company. Waghorn contributed his transport organization between Alexandria and Cairo and the other two their hotels and rest houses. In the same year the new company brought out a steamship, the *Jack o' Lantern,* for the Nile journey between Cairo and Atfeh, at the junction of the Nile and Mahmudieh Canal; the short journey along the Canal between Atfeh and Alexandria was made by horse-drawn barges. Hill & Company's service on the Cairo-Alexandria route was soon contested by the Peninsula & Oriental Steam Navigation Company, which had been formed in 1836 to operate a steamship service between Brindisi and Alexandria and which soon supplemented this with a steamer service between Cairo and Alexandria.

Meanwhile Mohammed Ali had been taking an increasing and constructive interest in the overland route. In 1839 he installed a semaphore signaling system between Cairo and Suez which enabled outward-bound passengers to stay in the relative comfort of Cairo until they received news that a ship was waiting for them at Suez. In the same year, and again in 1845, he concluded Postal Conventions with the British Government under which the Egyptian Government assumed responsibility for the carriage of British-Indian mail across Egypt.[5] In 1843 he caused the Egyptian Transit Company to be formed under Egyptian Government auspices and gave it the monopoly for the transport of goods, passengers, and mail by the overland route. This compelled Hill & Company to sell out to the Transit Company (whose managing director was an Englishman named Thorburn). Three years later, in 1846, Mohammed Ali terminated this concession and formed the Egyptian Transit Administration which, thereafter, managed the overland route under the direct administration of the Egyptian Government. By this time the amount of traffic carried by the overland route was rapidly increasing. In 1839 only 275 passengers had used it; in 1845 2,100 passengers were carried, and in 1847, 3,000. In that year, 2,500 camels, 440 horses, and 46 carriages were in use on the Cairo-Suez route and four steamers on the Cairo-Alexandria route. These numbers continued steadily to increase until the opening of the Suez Canal in 1869. The amenities and speed of the journey were progressively improved; a railway between Alexandria and Cairo was completed in 1855, and between Cairo and Suez in 1858.[6]

In the 1830's, the British Government and the East India Company, nervous about the security of the Mediterranean and Red Sea route owing to the growing French influence over Mohammed Ali and owing to Mohammed Ali's own increasing ambitions, made an investigation into the possibilities of establishing an alternative method of communication with India via the Euphrates Valley. The route across the desert from the Mediterranean to Baghdad and thence down the Euphrates or Tigris to the Persian Gulf was considered to have certain advantages over the Red Sea route. It was, until 1830 and after 1840, outside the area of French influence and possible interference. It was outside the area of the monsoons which, in the days of sail and the early days of steam, made navigation in the Arabian Sea dangerous for about one-third of the year. It was regarded as being more healthy than the Red Sea route and, in the early days of steam, river navigation was safer and more reliable than sea navigation. Also, the development of a regular river service on the Tigris and/or Euphrates would create the possibility of opening up Mesopotamia for trade as well as for transport, thus making the transport services pay for themselves, a consideration which appealed powerfully to the East India Company. Before the decision was taken to concentrate on the Suez route, it was therefore determined to investigate the possibilities of the Mesopotamia route for steam navigation.

In 1830 James W. Taylor who had previously, in competition with Waghorn, been investigating the possibilities of developing the Red Sea route, turned his attention to the Euphrates Valley and, under the auspices of the East India Company, left India with dispatches on a reconnaissance trip to England via Mesopotamia. He and his party proceeded from Busra to Baghdad by the Tigris and then started out on a survey of the Middle Euphrates to determine its suitability for steam navigation. The expedition ended in disaster. On leaving Mosul on their way to England, Taylor and his party were set on by bandits. Taylor and one of his companions were killed; the other three escaped with their lives after being robbed of all their belongings.

This unfortunate event did not exhaust the British Government's interest in the Euphrates Valley route. A little time before the departure of Taylor's ill-fated expedition, Captain (later General) F. R. Chesney of the Royal Artillery received a commission from Sir Robert Gordon, British ambassador at Constantinople, and from the East India Company, to make a comparative survey of various overland routes through Ottoman territory to India in order to determine which was the most suitable for regular use. He first investigated the overland route through Egypt. In the course of his investigation he took levels in the Isthmus of Suez and examined the traces of the ancient canals, and came to the (correct) conclusion, in contradiction to the findings of Le Père thirty years earlier that there was no appreciable difference in the levels of the Red Sea and the Mediterranean. But, possibly owing to lack of enthusiasm on the part of his sponsors, he soon directed his attention to the Euphrates route and conceived the idea of cutting short the long land route across the desert to Baghdad and of utilizing the Euphrates from its highest navigable point, near Aleppo. After a preliminary and exciting reconnaissance, in which he floated down the Euphrates from near Aleppo to Busra in a raft, calling in at Baghdad on the way, he returned to England full of enthusiasm for the route in spite of the various and formidable difficulties which he had encountered, including marshes, adverse currents, and hostile Arab tribes.

As a result of his enthusiasm, which chimed with the British Government's almost traditional distaste for the Suez route, an ambitious expedition was organized, on the recommendation of a Select Committee and at the expense of the British Government. This expedition, which left England in 1835, involved the recruitment of fifty officers and men, the transport of the components of two steamers overland from Antioch on the Mediterranean to the village of Bir on the Euphrates, northeast of Aleppo, for the assembly of these steamers at Bir, and for their navigation down the Euphrates to the Persian Gulf. All sorts of difficulties were encountered. The overland transport of the steamer components was a formidable task, and the technical difficulties were increased by political obstacles created by Ibrahim Pasha, the son of Mohammed Ali and Governor of Syria, which Mohammed Ali had seized from the Turks in 1830. Eventually the two ships—*Tigris* and *Euphrates*—were assembled and set off on their journey. The most difficult part of the expedition appeared to have been accomplished. But, after a few days' steaming, the convoy was struck by a severe sandstorm. One of the vessels—*Tigris*—overturned and sank. Several members of the expedition were drowned. The other vessel, after numerous difficulties and delays, eventually reached Busra, having taken about three months on the journey from Bir. Many of the difficulties encountered on the Lower Euphrates appear to have been put in the way of the expedition by M. Fontanier, the French consul in Busra, who excited the hostility of riverine Arab tribes against the expedition. The return journey was even less successful and the expedition was abandoned at Baghdad in January, 1837. It was only from the date of this abandonment that the British Government showed any serious interest in the development of the overland route across Egypt which, following the conclusion of the first Postal Convention with Mohammed Ali in 1839, began to be used on an official and regular basis.

But the Euphrates route continued to exercise its fascination. What the British Government really wanted was a transport system through Mesopotamia which would provide an excuse for a permanent British presence there and so enable them to keep an eye on Russian expansion toward India and the Persian Gulf, and which would forestall any attempt by some other Power to establish itself in Mesopotamia. In 1854–1855, R. M. Stevenson, the managing director of the East Indian Railway Company, furnished with credentials from Lord Palmerston and from the Government of India, made a survey of the route with a view to the construction of a railway. Although he reported favorably to Palmerston, nothing further was done at that time. But two years later, in 1856, W. P. (later Sir William) Andrew, chairman of the Scinde, Punjab and Delhi Railway, succeeded in forming an Association for the Promotion of the Euphrates Valley which worked out a proposal for the construction of a railway to connect the Mediterranean with the Persian Gulf via Selucia, Aleppo, Hit, and Baghdad. It was proposed, for a start, to construct a railway from Selucia to the Euphrates and to complete the journey from there to the Persian Gulf by steamer. The association succeeded in interesting the British Government on account of the supposed political advantages of the scheme, which would create a British presence along the whole length of a possible Russian line of advance toward India via Persia or the Persian Gulf.

It also happened that the British Government was interested in a scheme for an overland electric telegraph line between Europe and India running along the Euphrates Valley, such a scheme having been presented to them in June, 1856, by the European and Indian Junction Telegraph Company, whose directors included several men who were also interested in the railway. The project was taken seriously by the British Goverenment, and the British ambassador in Constantinople was instructed to obtain a firman from the Ottoman Government. He succeeded in doing this, and a concession was duly obtained. The project eventually fell through because the British Government was unwilling to underwrite the financial guarantees given by the Turkish Government to the company.[7] That was the end of the Euphrates Valley railway project until the Germans took it up some twenty years later. The telegraph scheme was developed and, during the course of the 1860's, regular telegraphic communication with India was secured by this route.[8]

During all this time, while the overland route through Egypt was being developed and the Euphrates route explored, interest continued to be taken and information collected about the possibilities of a canal through the Isthmus of Suez. Le Père's report had been published in Paris in 1810 and, after the end of the Napoleonic Wars, was available to anyone sufficiently interested. One of those so interested was R. H. Galloway, a British engineer in Mohammed Ali's service who, later, was to make plans for the construction of a railway between Alexandria and Cairo. In 1825 Galloway proposed to Mohammed Ali the construction of a canal, which he estimated would cost £1,200,000, and tried without success to interest British capitalists. At the same time the idea of a canal was mooted by several British writers in various journals interested in Anglo-Indian affairs.[9] All these proposals were based on Le Père's erroneous findings about the difference in levels between the Red Sea and the Mediterranean, and most of them assumed the necessity of building locks. As we have seen, however, Chesney, in his little-regarded survey made in 1830, had, before spending the rest of his life in the unsuccessful development of the Euphrates Valley route, established that this difference in level was negligible.

The idea of transisthmian canals was in the air. Plans were already being drawn up for cutting a canal through the Isthmus of Panama, an incomparably more difficult performance than a canal through the Isthmus of Suez. It was a time, too, when every kind of grandiose scheme was being discussed all over Europe by speculators, engineers, economists, political idealists, and plain cranks. The continent of Europe had recently emerged from a long series of wars. The Industrial Revolution was proceeding apace. Developments in steam power, rapid advances in technical knowledge, and a consequent spate of new inventions and new applications of old inventions led to a great and continuous expansion in the practical scope of engineering and to an even greater expansion in men's ideas of what that practical scope might be. There was much money available for investment and much enterprise available for speculation. Also, in a Europe sickened with war, and determined to avoid war for the future, there was a great fund of idealism which saw in this industrial development, and in all this surge of inventiveness, the means of promoting perpetual peace by the breaking down of physical barriers and by a vast increase in the production and exchange of commodities.

Prominent among the idealists were the Saint-Simonians. Claude Henri de Rouvroy, Comte de Saint-Simon, who died in 1825, has been called the founder of French socialism. Originally a soldier by profession, Saint-Simon was an amateur of philosophy, mathematics, biology, sociology, and almost every other science or pseudo-science which had any bearing on the improvement of the material state of man. He seems to have possessed considerable charm; he certainly had ample means; he gathered round him a group of devoted disciples and propounded a large number of more or less visionary schemes for the improvement of mankind. Among the more modest and less visionary of these schemes were the ideas of cutting canals through the Isthmus of Panama and the Isthmus of Suez. He made a detailed proposal for a Panama canal to the Spanish Viceroy of Mexico. He seems to have taken less interest in the Suez Isthmus, and took no practical steps about it. But the Suez idea was earnestly taken up by Prosper Enfantin, one of Saint-Simon's disciples who, between 1825 and 1832, developed the idea in articles in various Saint-Simonian publications. "To make the Mediterranean the nuptial bed for a marriage between the East and West and to consummate the marriage by the piercing of a canal through the Isthmus of Suez"—such was the type of high-flown language by which Enfantin and his friends, in their publications, recommended the idea of a Suez Canal to their readers.

In the Saint-Simonian mythology, as adapted by Enfantin, the West represented the male principle, typified by Enfantin himself, and the East the female principle. In the course of a short term of imprisonment imposed on him in 1830, after the July Revolution, in consequence of his advanced ideas, Enfantin had leisure to develop his theories. He came to the conclusion that he had been divinely appointed to bring about the junction between the Red Sea and the Mediterranean as a kind of symbolic act expressing the spiritual and material union between East and West. In 1833, attended by a small group of followers, Enfantin arrived in Egypt. Among these followers was Fournel, an engineer who was an enthusiast for the canal and who had studied wholeheartedly everything he could get hold of on the subject. On his way to Egypt Fournel had visited Constantinople, where his ideas had been coldly received and where a member of the French colony had presciently warned him that "the English have never wanted, do not want, and never will want the Suez Canal because they fear that this will still further increase the influence of Mohammed Ali in Arabia and in Persia. . . . Also they dislike the idea of the French and Austrians having access to the Indian Ocean where they have next to no genuine commercial interests."[10]

On their arrival at Alexandria the Saint-Simonians were entertained at the French Consulate. Mimaut, the French consul general, seems to have displayed the same sort of reserve toward these eccentric visitors as, for example, a British consul today might be expected to display toward an unofficial delegation of British Buchmanites or nuclear disarmers. But the vice-consul, a young man named Ferdinand de Lesseps, was more sympathetic. He was to claim later that he had himself successfully interceded with Mohammed Ali to prevent the Saint-Simonians, who were suspect as much for their eccentric dress and behavior as for their eccentric ideas, from being thrown out of the country. Young De Lesseps enjoyed a privileged position at the Court of Mohammed Ali since his father, Mathieu de Lesseps, had been French representative in Egypt during the early days of Mohammed Ali's rule, and had helped to get Mohammed Ali that French diplomatic support which was to have such an important influence on the fortunes of his reign.

After some days in Alexandria Enfantin went to Cairo where he met two compatriots who held important positions in Mohammed Ali's service. One, Colonel Sève, alias Soliman Pasha, had been a French artillery officer, had turned Muslim, and had risen to become a senior officer in the Egyptian Army. The other, Adolphe Linant de Bellefonds, was an engineer and Mohammed Ali's principal irrigation adviser. These two men entertained Enfantin lavishly and made arrangements for him to visit the isthmus. Meanwhile, Fournel and Lambert, another engineer in the party, were doing most of the real work. Fournel succeeded in obtaining an audience with Mohammed Ali, who discussed with him various engineering schemes which he had in mind, including a railway and a Nile barrage, as well as the Suez Canal. At this time the Viceroy[11] was already in consultation with Galloway about a railway from Alexandria. (Subsequently, in 1835, the scheme was abandoned, owing to British opposition, although much of the material had been ordered and was on site.) He was also in consultation with Linant about a project for a barrage at the apex of the Nile Delta to provide water storage for the irrigation of the cotton crop in the Delta at the season of low Nile without recourse to the expensive method of lifting water by steam pumps.

It seems probable that Mohammed Ali had already informed himself of the British Government's attitude toward a canal, that he had no intention of taking Fournel's proposal seriously, and that he merely discussed the possibility with him as a matter of courtesy. He even went through the formality of putting the three alternative proposals—railway, barrage, canal —before his Divan for consideration before deciding that the barrage had first priority. Enfantin, informed of this decision by Fournel, decided, *faute de mieux,* that the barrage, as humanitarian work, should have the benefit of Saint-Simonian support. The services of Lambert and some other engineers were offered to, and accepted by, Linant who was to be in charge of the construction. (The fact that the barrage was mainly constructed by Frenchmen made the British Government very suspicious of it, and Palmerston affected to believe that its real purpose was to enable the Delta to be flooded in the event of Egypt being invaded.) But the canal retained its priority in Enfantin's eyes and, when he at length left Egypt in 1836, his mind was still full of it.

Linant was already interested in the possibility of a canal. Originally a French naval officer, he had come to Egypt in 1818 and had soon afterward entered the Viceroy's service. In the course of his work on irrigation he acquired a good knowledge of the topography and geology of the isthmus. As an eminent French national living in Egypt, he was well known at the French Consulate and it is probable that Linant was the person who first interested De Lesseps, during his term of service at the consulate, in the idea of a canal.

In 1840, on Mohammed Ali's instructions, Linant published a report on his canal studies. This report, which assumed the correctness of Le Père's findings about the relative levels of the Red Sea and the Mediterranean, took the view that this assumed difference in levels did not invalidate a canal running direct from sea to sea, since this difference would provide for a scouring current running from south to north, and since strong canal banks could prevent flooding. He therefore suggested the direct route as a possible alternative to the classical route via the Nile.

Among those who read the report with interest, and who discussed it with Linant, was Arthur Anderson, a director of P. & O. who visited Egypt at the end of 1840 in connection with the development of the overland route. In February, 1841, after his return to England, Anderson addressed a letter to Lord Palmerston, then Foreign Secretary, describing his conversations with Linant and advocating the idea of a canal running direct from Suez to Pelusium. He suggested that a grant of land might be made by the Sultan to a concessionary company and that this concession might be guaranteed by the Powers and made subject to stipulations regarding neutrality, tolls, and so on. Astonishingly, he estimated the cost of such a canal at only a quarter of a million pounds.[12] Anderson followed this up in March with a more detailed proposal. He dropped the idea of a concessionary company owning the canal, and acknowledged that any such canal must be made in the name of and owned by the Sultan.[13] He suggested that tolls might be fixed at a rate of twenty shillings per registered ton and the proceeds divided fifty-fifty between the Sultan and the concessionaire.[14] He proposed that the concessionary company should be formed by British subjects, with British capital backed by a British Government guarantee.[15] These letters met with only a formal acknowledgment from Lord Palmerston, who may have indicated privately to Anderson that the British Government was not interested.

Anderson's reference to the necessity of the canal being made and owned in the name of the Sultan of Turkey refers to the contemporary series of international events which put an end to Mohammed Ali's imperial ambitions and, to some extent, restored the reality of Ottoman control over Egypt. These events must now be briefly described.

Almost from the beginning of his reign Mohammed Ali, treading his way with caution around the maze of international complications in which the Ottoman Empire was involved, had aimed at creating a position in which he or his successors would, in the event of the dissolution of the Ottoman Empire, be in secure possession of a large part of the Ottoman dominions in Asia and Africa and so be able, in the event of such dissolution, to become the principal heirs of the Ottoman Empire. To this end, during the first twenty years of his rule, with his own armies and at Egypt's expense, although acting in the name, and to some extent at the request, of his suzerain, he had conquered the Wahhabis in Arabia, occupied most of the Arabian Peninsula, and colonized the Sudan. He had assisted his suzerain during the Greek War of Independence, and the Egyptian fleet had been destroyed at Navarino as a result. Failing to obtain from the Sultan the additional pashaliks which had been promised him in return for this assistance, he had, in 1830, taken possession of Syria. His son Ibrahim, who led his armies into Syria, had, by a subsequent advance on Constantinople, precipitated a Russian occupation of that city. This provoked an intervention by the Powers leading to an arrangement by which Mohammed Ali withdrew his troops from Asia Minor in return for being confirmed for life in his possession of the pashaliks of Egypt, Crete, Syria, Damascus, and Tripoli. At the same time the Russians withdrew from Constantinople. Once more the Ottoman Empire had been reprieved.

Mohammed Ali, however, by the successful assertion of his power, had rendered himself virtually independent of, and considerably more important than, his nominal suzerain. This development had been encouraged and was welcomed by the French Government who, although they shared the British desire to keep the Russians out of Constantinople, were thinking in terms of establishing a French protectorate on the banks of the Nile. The British Government, who feared the prospect of a partition of the Ottoman Empire between France and Russia from which she would be excluded, was opposed equally to Mohammed Ali's encroachment on that empire from the south and to Russia's encroachment from the north; and Britain's Egyptian diplomacy during the 1830's was concerned to try to limit the extent of independence asserted by Mohammed Ali. The Viceroy, for his part, was aware of, and by no means acquiescent in, French ambitions for a protectorate relationship; in spite of British hostility toward his ambitions, he was at pains to try to keep an even balance in his relationships with France and Britain.

In 1838 the Turks, as a result of difficulties created by Mohammed Ali over the payment of tribute to Constantinople in respect of the pashaliks held by him, sent an army into Syria. This army was decisively defeated in northern Syria by Ibrahim. Almost simultaneously, the Turkish fleet, which had been sent to Syria to cooperate with the Turkish land forces, steered for Alexandria instead and deserted to Mohammed Ali. Once more the Ottoman Empire appeared to be on its deathbed. And once more she was dragged from the brink of the grave. There followed a complicated series of international power politics during which Britain, in conjunction with Russia and Austria, and in defiance of France, intervened forcibly against Mohammed Ali in Syria and, eventually, secured a settlement of the affair under which Mohammed Ali was compelled to abandon all his pashaliks except that of Egypt, of which he was granted the hereditary title, subject to various restrictions and definitions which were incorporated into a Hatti Sharif issued by the Sultan in February, 1841, and subsequently modified in July, 1841.

By the terms of this Hatti Sharif: "The Sultan will choose among the children of Mohammed Ali the ones who will succeed him and the successor will have to come to Constantinople to receive investiture. The prerogative of heredity conferred on the Governor of Egypt gives him no rights superior to those of other pashas. The treaties, the laws of the empire, and notably the Hatti Sharif of Gulhane[16] are applicable to Egypt in the same way as to any other Province." The Hatti Sharif also provided that the Egyptian monetary system should be the same as in Turkey, that a quarter of Egypt's revenues should be paid annually to Constantinople as tribute, that no warships were to be built by Egypt without the Sultan's consent, and that the Egyptian Army should be limited to 20,000 men, who should wear Turkish uniforms and 2,000 of whom should always be stationed in Constantinople. It was finally provided that all promotions in the Egyptian Army above the rank of lieutenant should be confirmed by the Sultan. The July amendment to this Hatti Sharif conferred the inheritance to the pashalik of Egypt on the oldest surviving member of Mohammed Ali's family at the date of the incumbent's death, allowed the Viceroy to make military appointments up to the rank of colonel, and fixed the tribute at the equivalent of £400,000 per annum.[17]

The terms of this Hatti Sharif are given in some detail, as they are relevant to the great question which arose later, in connection with Lesseps' canal concession, as to the extent of the Viceroy's autonomy vis-à-vis Constantinople. The intention of the Hatti Sharif which, in the circumstances of its promulgation, represented the intention of the British Government, was to emphasize that, apart from the question of heredity, Egypt's position vis-à-vis the Sultan was precisely the same as that of any other Ottoman province. Whether and to what extent the intention expressed in the Hatti Sharif was to become effective depended on the extent to which the European Powers were determined to make it effective. For, just as Mohammed Ali's submission to his suzerain had been brought about by the Great Powers, so his continued submission could be maintained only as a result of pressure from the Great Powers. It was predictable that Britain—the Power which had been foremost in imposing the terms of the Hatti Sharif on Mohammed Ali —would also be foremost in trying to ensure that Mohammed Ali and his successors complied with its terms. It was also predictable that France—who had, unsuccessfully, supported Mohammed Ali in his defiance of his suzerain and whose only influence on the Hatti Sharif had been slightly to modify its terms—would, in the future, connive at attempts made by Mohammed Ali and his successors to evade the full rigor of the restraints imposed upon them. It is within this framework that the complicated international negotiations which accompanied the construction of the Suez Canal will in due course be reviewed.

Meanwhile, the principal effects on Mohammed Ali of the humiliations to which he had been subjected were, first, a determination to consolidate his position and that of his successors in those parts of his previous dominions which were still left to him; second, a distrust of those French ambitions which he considered, not without reason, as having contributed to his downfall; and, third, a deference toward Britain, whose implacable and successful opposition to his expansionist ambitions had been sapiently combined with a reasonably friendly attitude toward his administration in Egypt. His attitude toward the canal project was summed up in a remark he was reported as having made to the French consul general in July, 1847. "I shall require that the construction of the canal shall be exclusively in my hands and, once the canal is in operation, I shall insist that the control of navigation and the collection of dues shall be controlled exclusively by me or by my successors."[18] But, so long as the British Government objected to the idea of a canal, he was not going to take the risk of defying them.

One of those who had studied and been impressed by Linant's report was Laurin, the Austrian consul general in Egypt who, at the end of 1843, obtained a copy of the report from Linant and sent it to Metternich. The Austrian port of Trieste had always had the same interest in the Eastern trade as the French port of Marseille, and Austria's interest in the overland route had, traditionally, been second only to that of France. Metternich was interested in the idea of a canal, expressed the view that it was practicable and capable of being financed from Egypt's own resources, and instructed Laurin to take the question up with Mohammed Ali. The Viceroy was suspicious. If there was going to be a canal, he wanted to be able to control it himself; he wanted to be assured that it would not lead him into any difficulties with any of the Great Powers; and he wanted to make certain that it would not be used as an occasion for Ottoman interference in the internal affairs of Egypt. In the light of all these objections, Laurin's negotiations came to nothing.[19]

At the beginning of 1845 a group of Leipzig businessmen who had been studying the canal project sent a representative to Mohammed Ali to try to persuade him of the advantages a canal would bring both to Egypt and to the Great Powers. Mohammed Ali's reply was succinct and to the point: "First go and get the agreement of the Powers and then come and see me."[20]

Ever since his return to France from Egypt in 1836, Prosper Enfantin had been busy on the canal project which had become the passion of his life. He kept up a correspondence with Linant and got in touch with several French and other European engineers and businessmen outside the Saint-Simonian circle with a view to interesting them in the canal project. Among these new associates was Arles-Dufour, a businessman from Lyon who was valuable to Enfantin both for the money and for the common sense he was able to provide. Enfantin's idea was to form an international Société d'Etudes comprising three national groups—French, English, and German—of ten persons each, with each group nominating an engineer who would collaborate with the other two in drawing up plans. Eventually, with the assistance of Arles-Dufour, he succeeded in getting together a group of seventeen—five Frenchmen, two Englishmen, and ten Germans—who met in Paris in November, 1846. As a result of this meeting[21] a Société d'Etudes was formally inaugurated and the three engineers chosen—Stephenson from Britain (he was a son of the Robert Stephenson who had invented the steam locomotive), Talabot from France, and Negrelli from the German group.[22] Enfantin, full of optimism, told Linant all about it and assured him that his place in the scheme would be equal to that of the three engineers who had been nominated. But he made the mistake of not advising Mohammed Ali officially of what was afoot. (He seems at all times completely to have ignored the political implications of his project.) When the Viceroy did hear about it (probably from Linant), he was very angry and suspicious, and it required all Linant's powers of persuasion to induce him to allow members of the Société to come to Egypt to make their investigations.

The British Government's reaction to the formation of the Société was predictable. In a dispatch to Murray, the British consul general in Egypt, in February, 1847, Palmerston instructed him to "lose no opportunity of impressing on the Pasha and his Ministers the costliness if not the impracticability of such a project, and you should point out that those who press upon the Pasha such a scheme do so solely for the purpose of diverting him from the railway."[23] Since 1837, when the British Government had transferred their attention from the idea of an overland route via the Euphrates Valley to the actuality of the overland route through Egypt, and since they had, in 1839 and 1845, concluded Postal Conventions with Mohammed Ali for the carriage of Anglo-Indian mails across Egypt, they had changed their minds about the desirability of a railway, and were now beginning to press upon the Viceroy the idea of a railway between Alexandria and Cairo.

In the spring of 1847 three teams of engineers from the Société d'Etudes arrived in Egypt, headed by Talabot, Stephenson, and Negrelli, respectively. Stephenson's team was to investigate the Gulf of Suez, Negrelli's the Bay of Pelusium, and Talabot's the interior of the isthmus. Stephenson, possibly owing to the counterattractions of the railway, which he himself was eventually to build, soon lost his enthusiasm for the canal and was to spend most of the rest of his life attacking it. Negrelli, who was later to be associated with Lesseps, made a survey of the northern approaches. But the bulk of the work was done, and the most voluminous report compiled, by Paulin Talabot and his team. They began inauspiciously by quarreling with Linant who, thereafter, severed all his previous connections with Enfantin. This was a heavy blow, since Linant, by reason both of his official position with Mohammed Ali and his profound knowledge of the terrain, was an almost indispensable factor in the prosecution of the scheme. In spite of the quarrel, however, he appears to have given some assistance to Talabot and his men over their technical studies. The most important outcome of these studies was to establish the erroneousness of Le Père's findings about the difference in levels between the Red Sea and the Mediterranean. Talabot established— and it was not thereafter seriously disputed—that there was practically no difference in level between the two seas. In spite of this, however, his report, published in 1848, for a variety of technical reasons, recommended the classical route via the Nile and not the direct route.

In May, 1847, when the Société d'Etudes were already engaged in their investigations, Murray wrote to Palmerston advising him of the fact and warning him that the canal was probably a practicable proposition.[24] Palmerston, in his reply, shews the first traces of that irate obstinacy which he was, for the rest of his life, to display in all matters concerning the canal. He told Murray to "remain entirely passive on the subject and to say that you have no instructions from your Government either to support or to oppose it, but that in the opinion of Her Majesty's Government the commercial advantages to be derived from the canal would be attained at much less cost by a railway." He went on to state that Austrian interests in the canal were commercial in that they were designed to benefit the port of Trieste but that French interests were political in that "it would place them as a military and naval Power in the Mediterranean much nearer to India than the English would be." He ended his dispatch with the words, "On the whole, therefore, Her Majesty's Government do not wish to oppose the canal absolutely but they would much prefer the railway."[25] He sent a copy of this dispatch to Lord Cowley, then British ambassador in Constantinople, who replied that he had discussed the matter with Rashid, the Grand Vizier, who told him that he had been advised that Mohammed Ali was "turning a deaf ear to propositions by foreigners for building a canal but is thinking of undertaking it himself." Cowley reported that the Grand Vizier had expressed the view that it would be some years before the Viceroy would be able to do this from his own resources and that in any case the consent of the Porte would be necessary.[26] In a subsequent interview Rashid told Cowley that, so long as he remained Grand Vizier, permission would not be given.[27]

In spite of Palmerston's suspicion of the French, it is fairly certain that, up to this time, no official or unofficial approaches about the canal had been made to the French Government by the Société d'Etudes. At the beginning of 1847 the French consul general, reporting the arrival of the Société d'Etudes representatives in Egypt, expressed the view that he did not think the idea of a canal practicable owing to the hostility both of the British

Government and of Mohammed Ali. He also stated that the Austrian Government were actively interested in the Société d'Etudes.[28] He would clearly not have written in this way if he had had any official, or unofficial, instructions to support the Société.

It was Enfantin's idea that, when the technical reports had been completed, the Société should approach the British, French, and Austrian governments with a detailed proposal for a canal, bypassing Constantinople and Cairo altogether. That might have been a fruitful approach had there been any reason to suppose that all these three Powers were in favor of the scheme. At all events it was never put to the test. The February, 1848, Revolution in France put an end, for the time being, to any possibility of French diplomatic assistance. And at the end of 1848 the accession of Abbas, the son of Ibrahim,[29] who did not share his grandfather's or his father's zeal for modernization, and who was reputed to be entirely subservient to the British, also put an end, for the time being, to the possibility of any favorable developments at the Egyptian end. Vain attempts were made by Enfantin and his associates to arouse interest in Constantinople, in Vienna, and even in Petersburg. Some of Enfantin's associates deserted him; some lost heart. Stephenson, the Englishman, was already attacking the idea of the canal in public and expatiating on the superior advantages of a railway. Dufour-Feronce, the Leipzig banker who had approached Mohammed Ali in 1845, was doubtful whether Talabot's canal would be big enough effectively to compete with the Cape route. Others, like the Baron de Bruck, Austrian Internuncio at Constantinople, who was an enthusiastic advocate of the scheme (he was later to be a close associate of Lesseps and a founder-member of the Suez Canal Company), advised Enfantin that the time was not yet ripe. Enfantin himself became discouraged, but neither he nor Arles-Dufour, his principal associate, lost interest. The Société d'Etudes remained in being and, as we shall see, was for some time in contact with Ferdinand de Lesseps.

As a result of Linant's work, and work by others which Linant had facilitated, it was apparent, by 1850, that, in the light of engineering techniques as they were then known, the canal was a technical possibility. It was also, *prima facie*, an economic proposition. Although such estimates as had been made—ranging from £1,200,000 to £200,000—were all very much less than the real cost would have been under the most favorable conditions, the steady growth in the Eastern trade, the development of steam navigation, and the great saving in mileage—and consequently in fuel and time—between Europe and all the principal Eastern ports which a canal would make possible, would have ensured a reasonable rate of return on any necessary capital investment. The real difficulties were neither technical nor economic, but political—although these political difficulties created economic difficulties by making capital difficult to obtain.

The principal political difficulty was the consistently hostile attitude of successive British governments. Successive British prime ministers and foreign ministers seem to have had an instinctive conviction, shared by Mohammed Ali, that the cutting of a canal would, sooner or later, compel the British themselves to occupy Egypt, with all the unpredictable international consequences of such an adventure. The record of Anglo-Egyptian relations during the nineteenth and twentieth centuries makes it clear that (*a*) British reluctance to occupy Egypt was only equaled by their reluctance to evacuate Egypt once they had occupied it and that (*b*) the existence of the Suez Canal was the principal factor overcoming their reluctance to occupy Egypt and the principal factor in their later reluctance to evacuate it.

Although France and Austria were, on the whole, in favor of the canal, and although Russia was not inclined to oppose it, neither Austria nor Russia was prepared to join France in a united front against England with the object either of coercing or of reassuring Constantinople in favor of the canal. Protagonists of the canal often spoke of making the Isthmus of Suez a second Bosphorus. The simile was an apt one. For the prospect of an alien presence either on the Bosphorus or in the isthmus was regarded in London as an assault on the integrity of the Ottoman Empire against which Britain, in her self-appointed role as that empire's guardian, was certain to react strongly. The Saint-Simonians, with their sexual imagery, regarded the isthmus as a hymen to be pierced by a lawful bridegroom. The British regarded it as a virginity to be protected from the arts of a wily and unprincipled seducer. The Ottoman Empire, whose virginity was in question, was able neither effectively to defend its virtue nor freely to enjoy the sensation of losing it.

The French had the same suspicions of a British-sponsored railway as the British had of a French-sponsored canal. Mohammed Ali, appreciating the international rivalries involved, would have nothing to do either with a canal or with a railway. Although the British Government had not been interested in a railway when the idea was first raised by Galloway in the early 1830's, they began to change their minds after the failure of the Euphrates reconnaissance in 1837. They were still primarily interested in the expedition of passengers and mail by the overland route but hardly at all in diverting cargo from the Cape route. From this point of view a railway, while greatly inferior to a canal as a means of transporting cargo, owing to the necessity for transhipment, loading and unloading wagons, and so on, was just as good as, if not better than, a canal as a means of expediting passengers and mail. Also, British engineering was preeminent in, and British finance deeply interested in, the matter of railway construction, and at that time British financiers and British engineers, and British iron and steel masters, were busy looking round the world, seeking outlets for their capital, their skills, and their products. Politically, a railway was open to the same objections from the French side as a canal was from the British side, and it not surprising that the French regarded it as a British Trojan horse in the same way as the British regarded the canal as a French Trojan horse.

In spite of British suspicions that there was some official French sponsorship for the various canal proposals put up to Mohammed Ali during the last years of his reign, the French Government, in fact, pursued the question of a canal much less energetically than the British Government pursued the question of a railway. In 1847 Barrot, the French consul general, reported having told the Viceroy that, if he wanted to open up Egypt as a route for merchandise between Europe and India, a canal would be preferable to a railway since a canal would be open to all nations, while a railway would become a British monopoly[30] After the accession of Abbas in Egypt and the February Revolution in France, Le Moyne, the new French consul general, claimed to have persuaded Abbas to give preference to a canal over a railway provided that the Porte and the Powers agreed.[31] But the French Government shewed no interest,[32] and did nothing to encourage their representatives in Constantinople or Cairo either to promote the idea of a canal or to oppose that of a railway. The first indication of an active interest by the French Government in the idea of a canal appears in a confidential dispatch from the French Foreign Minister to the consul general in Cairo in June, 1853: "Although the moment has not yet arrived to go into detail on so important a question you should not neglect any opportunity which may present itself to promote the idea with discretion." In the same dispatch[33] the Minister asked for details about costs on the overland route, terms of the railway concession which had just been awarded to a British firm, results of Linant's surveys in the Isthmus, and so on.[34]

In the summer of 1848 Mohammed Ali, by this time a very old man, went out of his mind, and his eldest son Ibrahim became *de facto* Viceroy. Ibrahim died a few months later, and his eldest son, Abbas, Mohammed Ali's oldest living descendant and so, by the terms of the 1841 Hatti Sharif, his heir, became *de facto* Viceroy, officially succeeding to the title on Mohammed Ali's death in the summer of 1849.

Abbas appears soon to have fallen deeply under British influence, partly, it appears, as a result of the personality of the British consul general, Murray, who, knowing both Arabic and Turkish, was able to converse directly with

Abbas (who knew no English or French) without the assistance of an interpreter.[35] Murray was soon able to persuade Abbas over the question of the railway, although the French consul general obtained from Abbas the assurance that the administration of the railway would not pass out of the hands of the Egyptian Government and that the transit of mail and merchandise would not be made the monopoly of any foreign Power.[36] In July, 1851, a contract was signed by the Egyptian Government with Stephenson (the British engineer who had been engaged on a survey for a canal made by the Société d'Etudes in 1847) for the construction of a railway between Cairo and Alexandria. Stephenson's company was to be responsible for the construction and for the supply of most of the materials and rolling stock, but, in accordance with Abbas's promise to the French, the railway was to be owned and operated by the Egyptian Government.

In spite of this concession to his wishes, Le Moyne viewed the whole question of the railway with the gloomiest suspicion, regarding it as a symbol of growing British ascendancy in Egypt. He prophesied, correctly, that the Alexandria-Cairo concession would be followed by the grant of a concession to the British for the construction of a Cairo-Suez railway, and expressed the opinion that it was the first step toward the establishment of a British protectorate over Egypt.[37] He had already suggested that an Ottoman firman would be necessary for the construction of the railway,[38] and it appears that the French ambassador in Constantinople attempted to prevent the issue of this firman.[39] The British Government at first took the view that a firman was unnecessary for a "domestic improvement" such as a railway, although "a canal which has an important bearing on the condition of Egypt as part of the Turkish Empire is a different thing."[40] Eventually, however, on the advice of Stratford de Redcliffe, Abbas did apply for a firman, which, as a result of Stratford de Redcliffe's influence in Constantinople, was granted without difficulty in November.[41]

Despairing of being able to counteract British influence over Abbas, Le Moyne appears to have started cultivating Mohammed Said, a younger son of Mohammed Ali and the Heir Apparent.[42] This policy, which was continued by Le Moyne's successor, Raymond Sabatier, appears to have disturbed the French Government, and Sabatier was instructed to try to maintain good relations with his British colleague and to observe discretion in his relationships with Mohammed Said.[43] The replacement of Murray by Bruce as British consul general in December, 1853, appears to have assisted Sabatier to observe these instructions,[44] at all events until Bruce, nearly a year later, showed what Sabatier regarded as the cloven hoof over the question of the canal.

Abbas died, ostensibly of apoplexy (there appear to be some reasonable grounds for suspicion that he was murdered), in July, 1854. He was succeeded by his uncle, Mohammed Said, the oldest living descendant of Mohammed Ali, according to the terms of the 1841 Hatti Sharif. By the time of his death the railway between Cairo and Alexandria had almost been completed and, as Le Moyne had foreseen, a concession for the construction of a railway between Cairo and Suez had been granted to Stephenson's company.

Since 1841 every Egyptian Viceroy had been concerned to regain as much as possible of that independence of Constantinople which had been so circumscribed by the 1841 Hatti Sharif. This could be done only through the support of the Powers. Any Power which appeared able and willing to give that support was assured of the complaisance of the Egyptian Viceroy. During Abbas's reign the aftermath of the 1848 revolutions in France and Austria had momentarily decreased the international influence of these Powers— and consequently their influence at Constantinople—vis-à-vis that of Great Britain, who, moreover, was represented at Constantinople by the redoubtable Stratford de Redcliffe. This ensured British ability to protect the Viceroy against his suzerain if it suited British policy to do so. British willingness to do so was ensured, for the time being, by Britain's desire to obtain (and Abbas's willingness to grant) a railway concession, and by the British desire to block (and by Abbas's willingness to block) any question of a canal concession. Thus, during Abbas's brief reign, one had the curious spectacle of the British Government, which had taken the lead in imposing the 1841 Hatti Sharif on Mohammed Ali, encouraging Abbas to assert his independence of the Porte, while France, "who would have gone to war with all and sundry for the interest of Mohammed Ali, intrigues to tighten the bonds of vassalage."[45]

NOTES

1. F. Charles-Roux, *Bonaparte, Gouverneur d'Egypte*, p. 3.
2. In *Description d'Egypte publié par les ordres de Napoléon le Grand en dix volumes a Paris, 1809–1822*, I *Etat Moderne*, 57–78.
3. The early steamships, which were propelled by paddlewheels (the screw propeller came into use only about 1850), were not well suited for navigating Atlantic rollers and were not successfully used on the Cape route. They were more suitable for river or narrow sea navigation.
4. Coal conveyed in this way was sold f.o.b. Suez at £3 per ton.
5. The 1845 Convention was negotiated on behalf of the British Post Office by the novelist Anthony Trollope, who was a senior Post Office official.
6. In the early days, before the organization of a regular service, a journey by the overland route through Egypt was a formidable undertaking. In 1834 a writer in the *Asiatic Journal* estimated that a traveler by it should take with him, among other things, 450 Spanish

dollars, an interpreter-servant, supplies of tea, coffee, salt, sugar, pepper, mustard, a dozen bottles each of sherry, brandy, and drinking water, two kegs of water for cooking, a good supply of candles, powder and shot, camp furniture, cooking utensils, a tent, and a milch goat with a cradle so that it could be carried on a camel. Later, as a result of the enterprise of Waghorn and his competitors, things were good deal easier, judging by a handbook for travelers published in 1841, although both the hotels at Suez are described as being uncomfortable and the water as brackish. The early steamships on the Suez-Bombay run appear to have been hideously uncomfortable. Here is a description by a young lady writing in the *Asiatic Journal* in 1839: "The cabins were small and miserable. Cockroaches abounded. Washing had to be done in a public room. Sleeping accommodation consisted of a mattress placed on some trunks or boxes, while many slept on tables or benches. The rooms were hot and smelly and the servants lazy and indolent. Food was served in the common saloon which also served for the purpose of toilet room and lounge for both sexes. . . . Piles of coal soot invaded everything." Passenger accommodation on sailing ships going round the Cape had the name of being extremely comfortable and it was some time before steamships were regarded as being a gentleman-like method of progression, either by passengers or by ships' companies. However, speed conquered comfort, and comfort gradually caught up with speed. After 1869 the prospect of direct transit between England and India by way of the Suez Canal was by no means welcomed by regular travelers, who had come to regard the overland journey across Egypt, with a stay in Shepheard's and a visit to the Pyramids and the Cairo bazaars, as a pleasant interlude breaking the monotony of a long voyage.

7. It appears that the real reason for this unwillingness was not financial, but due to objections expressed to Palmerston by Napoleon III during a visit paid by the Emperor to England in August, 1857. Palmerston, who was unwilling to abandon his opposition to the Suez Canal project which was, at that time, being pressed upon the British by the French Government, preferred, for the sake of amicable relations with France, to abandon the Euphrates Valley railway rather than abate his opposition to the Suez Canal. See Hoskins, *British Routes to India*, pp. 341–342.

8. In this case the main British objection to the alternative submarine cable route via the Red Sea appears to have been technical and not political.

9. Hoskins, *op. cit.*, pp. 292–293.

10. Most of this account of the Saint-Simonians is taken from H. R. d'Allemagne's *Prosper Enfantin* (Paris, 1930).

11. Viceroy was the title usually employed by Europeans when referring to the ruler of Egypt until 1866 when Ismail obtained the title of Khedive from Constantinople. He was also sometimes referred to as "the Pasha."

12. Galloway, fifteen years before, had estimated £1,200,000 for a canal via the Nile. These wide divergencies may have encouraged Palmerston in his belief that the whole idea was noncommercial.

13. As will be seen below, Anderson's proposal came at a singularly inopportune moment.

14. This compares with a rate of 10 francs, or about 8 shillings per ton authorized and subsequently charged under Lesseps' concession. But all of this went to the concessionaire, who merely paid 15 percent of the net profits to the Egyptian Government by way of royalty.

15. For the correspondence between Anderson and Palmerston, see FO 97/411.

16. The Hatti Sharif of Gulhane was a kind of Turkish Magna Carta imposed on Turkey by the Powers and promulgated in November, 1837. It provided for (i) security of life and property for all Ottoman subjects, (ii) regular fixing and collection of taxes, (iii) a regular system of conscription limited to five years. Needless to say, this Hatti Sharif had about as much effect on Ottoman governmental practices as Magna Carta had on English ones.

17. For details of the 1841 Hatti Sharif and amendment, see M. Sabry, *L'Empire Egyptien sous Mohamed Ali*, pp. 532 *et seq*.

18. Barrot–Guizot 10.7.47. CP 19.

19. C. W. Hallberg, *The Suez Canal*, pp. 85–88.

20. G. Edgar-Bonnet, *Ferdinand de Lesseps*, I, 179–180.

21. For the *procés verbale* of the meeting, see J. Charles-Roux, *L'Isthme* . . . , Annex No. 9.
22. For the Statutes of the Société d'Etudes, see J. Charles-Roux, *op. cit.*, Annex No. 10.
23. FO 97/411.
24. Murray-Palmerston 3.5.47. FO 97/411.
25. Palmerston-Murray 25.5.47. FO 97/411.
26. Cowley–Palmerston 3.7.47. FO 97/411.
27. Cowley–Palmerston 31.7.47. FO 97/411.
28. Barrot–Guizot 6.2.47. CP 18.
29. Mohammed Ali went out of his mind in the middle of 1848, and his son Ibrahim became *de facto* Viceroy. Ibrahim died a few months later, and his son Abbas succeeded him as *de facto* Viceroy. Abbas became Viceroy *de jure* on Mohammed Ali's death in the summer of 1849.
30. Barrot–Guizot 18.5.47 CP 19.
31. Le Moyne–Ministry of For. Affairs 1.2.50 and 25.4.50 CP 19.
32. The Minister, in a penciled note on Le Moyne's second dispatch (see Note 31), minuted he could not remember the contents of the first one.
33. Drouyn de Lhuys–Sabatier 1.6.53. CP 25.
34. Sabatier had just reported having arranged, with the agreement of the Egyptian Government, for Linant to visit the isthmus and to clear up the question of the relative levels of the Red Sea and Mediterranean. See Sabatier–Drouyn de Lhuys 19.5.53. CP 25.
35. Le Moyne-Drouyn de Lhuys 30.11.50. CP 22.
36. *Ibid.*, 13.3.51. CP 23.
37. *Ibid.*, 18.4.51. CP 23.
38. *Ibid.*, 17.4.51. CP 23.
39. *Ibid.*, 7.10.51. CP 23.
40. Palmerston–Stratford de Redcliffe 24.7.51. FO 97/411.
41. "We have just received news that the Porte is satisfied with the explanations which the Viceroy has given on the subject of the railway and has decided to give its authorization." —Le Moyne–Drouyn de Lhuys 9.11.51. CP 23.
42. Le Moyne–Drouyn de Lhuys 2.9.52. CP 24.
43. Drouyn de Lhuys–Sabatier 19.3.53. CP 24.
44. Sabatier–Drouyn de Lhuys 31.12.53. CP 25.
45. Austrian ambassador in London, quoted by Hallberg, *op. cit.*, pp. 111-112.

CHAPTER *three*

Ferdinand de Lesseps ॐ

ॐ FERDINAND DE LESSEPS was born at Versailles on November 19, 1805. He was the son of Mathieu de Lesseps of the French consular service who had just completed a four-year tour of service in Egypt during which time he had been of service to Mohammed Ali in the complicated transactions which had preceded and followed his seizure of power after the British occupation.

The Lesseps family, which originated from Bayonne, had a diplomatic tradition. Ferdinand's grandfather Martin and his great-uncle Dominique had both been in the Diplomatic Service. His uncle Barthélemy had a notable career, first under the Monarchy, then under the Empire, and finally under the Restoration, when he was appointed ambassador to Lisbon. He remained there until his death, and young Ferdinand was to start his own diplomatic career in Libson under his uncle's aegis. In his early days Barthélemy had made a remarkable journey on official business from Kamchatka back to France across Siberia. Ferdinand's father, Mathieu, was a somewhat mysterious figure who spent most of his official career in the Arab world. When the French evacuated Egypt in 1801, Mathieu had been left behind as unofficial French representative. He remained throughout the British occupation and seems to have been the first foreign official to have recognized the potentialities of Mohammed Ali and to have initiated with Mohammed Ali those close relationships with France which were later to have such important consequences.

The Lesseps family did not return to Egypt after Ferdinand's birth. Mathieu was posted to Italy, where Ferdinand spent his early years. In 1824, at the age of nineteen, Ferdinand secured a post in the Diplomatic Service through the influence of his uncle Barthélemy, and he was posted to Lisbon. In 1827 he went to Tunis as vice-consul to his father, who, after a period in Aleppo, had been posted to Tunis as consul general. Ferdinand remained in Tunis until his father's death in 1832, when he was posted to Alexandria as vice-consul. He remained in Egypt until 1837, becoming successively consul and consul general. There is a story that, on his first arrival in Alexandria, Ferdinand was detained for some days in quarantine and that Mimaud, the consul general, sent him some literature to pass away the time. This literature, so the story goes, consisted of the ten-volume *Description d'Egypte,* containing reports drawn up on various aspects of Egypt by Bonaparte's experts during the French occupation of Egypt thirty years previously, and including, in the first volume, Le Père's preliminary survey for a canal through the isthmus. The story goes that it was as a result of reading this survey that Ferdinand first became interested in the idea of building a canal. Whether or not that story be true, the young consul, during his service in Egypt, had plenty of opportunity for informing himself on the question. Enfantin and his fantastic entourage, who arrived in Egypt in 1833, were just the sort of tiresome visitors who fall to the lot of a vice-consul to entertain. And Linant de Bellefonds, Mohammed Ali's irrigation adviser, who was already interested in the possibility of a canal, and who was busy compiling information on the subject, was a frequent visitor to the French Consulate.

The memory of Mathieu de Lesseps was still green at the court of Mohammed Ali, and young Ferdinand appears to have been received there with friendship and intimacy. In this way he became acquainted with Mohammed Said, the youngest son of Mohammed Ali, then a boy of about thirteen. Mohammed Said, who was brought up *à la française*, appears to have been attracted by a sort of hero worship to the handsome young consul in whose house he sometimes sought refuge from the strict regime his father endeavored to impose upon him. Even in these early days, Mohammed Said was already running to fat. It appears that his father had prescribed a diet for him which he evaded by coming to Lesseps for supplementary rations. Twenty years later, when he came to the throne, Mohammed Said was to remember this early friendship with gratitude.[1]

Although the idea of a canal almost certainly took root in Lesseps' mind during his five years of service in Egypt, he did not, like Enfantin, become obsessed with it. Nor did he allow it to affect the progress of what was already a promising official career. In 1837, at the age of thirty-two, having acted as consul general in Egypt for two years, he was transferred, first to Rotterdam, then to Malagá, then to Barcelona. He was very much at home in Spain. He knew the language and, coming as he did from a family established on the borders of Spain, had a number of Spanish relatives. One of these relatives, Eugénie de Montijo,[2] was afterward to become Empress of the French and a powerful friend at court during her cousin's quest for French diplomatic support over the canal. Stationed at Barcelona, Lesseps was caught up in the troubles of the civil war, and appears to have distinguished himself as the French representative. He was still consul general in Barcelona when the February Revolution broke out in France in 1848. Lesseps, during his diplomatic career, always seems to have kept himself clear of internal French politics, and there is no clue to his views about the downfall of Louis Philippe. He continued to prosper under the new government, and Lamartine appointed him French Minister to Madrid. Then, in 1849, he received what proved to be his last assignment in the French public service.

During the wave of revolutionary fervor which swept western Europe in 1848, the citizens of Rome had revolted against their temporal sovereign, Pope Pius IX, chased him from the city, and set up a republic. The French republican Government, in order to forestall an Austrian expedition to restore the Pope, sent an expedition to Civita Vecchia, the port of Rome. The precise object of this expedition was never made clear either to Oudinot, the general commanding it, or to Lesseps, who was later sent to advise Oudinot in an ill-defined capacity with the rank of minister plenipotentiary. In fact, apart from desiring to avoid an accession of Austrian influence in Italy, the French Government was not clear what it wanted the expedition to achieve. Lesseps was instructed to try to negotiate a settlement, to be guaranteed by a temporary French occupation, which would lead to the restoration of a reformed papal government. The Pope refused to promise any reforms as a precondition of restoration; the elected Assembly of a Roman Republic refused to have the Pope back without a guarantee of reform, and refused to admit French forces into the city. Oudinot was anxious only for military glory. In this he was supported by Louis Napoleon, who had just been elected to office as "Prince-President," and by the clerical faction in his government, who saw the expedition simply as a means of restoring the Pope by force of French arms.

Lesseps, who throughout his diplomatic career seems to have done his best to carry out his instructions without any political *arrière-pensées,* tried to restrain Oudinot pending further negotiations. However, Oudinot attacked the citizen army, occupied Rome, and proclaimed the restoration of the Pope in his temporal dominions. Lesseps was recalled to Paris and publicly reprimanded before the Assembly for having exceeded his instructions. Lesseps, disgusted, resigned from the public service and spent the next five years in retirement at his country estate, La Chenaie, in the Berry. Without going into the details of the Rome affair, it can be stated that no discredit attaches to Lesseps for this unfortunate end to a successful diplomatic career. He was victimized by an irresolute government which had got itself into a muddle and was looking for a scapegoat. The primary responsibility appears to rest with the Prince President who, in this affair, displayed that combination of cowardice and impetuosity which was finally to lead him to Sedan.

At the time of his retirement in 1849, Lesseps was forty-four years of age. Until the Rome affair his career had been successful, indeed distinguished. In his various diplomatic posts he had shown sound judgment without timidity, independence of mind without insubordination, physical and moral courage, great energy, considerable patience, and high administrative ability. But, on the face of it, there seemed no reason to believe that this prematurely retired public servant had a career in front of him which was to make him the greatest entrepreneur of the age. Apart from being a successful diplomat, what manner of man was he?

One of his biographers[3] has called him a "Conquistador of genius." All his biographers are unanimous in regarding him as a *charmeur*. Palmerston described him as a "swindler." Colquohoun, British consul general in Egypt from 1859 to 1863, wrote of "the untiring energy both of body and mind which distinguished M. de Lesseps." It is clear that he was a man of immense vitality, great persuasiveness, and supreme self-confidence. Like many men of achievement he was extremely vain and a fairly considerable humbug. He was an admirable paterfamilias[4] and, on the whole, a good employer, since both these roles ministered to his vanity. He had a persuasive and pervasive bonhomie which enabled him to use, with charm and with effect, all the resources of flattery for the encouragement of supporters and of deception for the confounding of critics. But beneath this bonhomie was a cynicism which enabled him precisely to weigh the means and motives of those with whom he had dealings, and accurately to judge the implications and bearings of the situations in which he found himself. He had the willpower of a Conquistador controlled by the patience of a diplomat, the cynicism of a company promoter disguised by the affability of a courtier, the optimism of a gambler sustained by a belief in his own infallibility. In short, he had all the qualities of a successful buccaneer magnified to the point of genius and, perhaps, given an almost irresistible force as a result of their having been, as it were, dammed up, first by the exigencies of diplomatic life, and then by the frustrations of compulsory retirement.

Both in his qualities and in his defects Lesseps bears an extraordinary resemblance to Cecil Rhodes—that great English nineteenth century buccaneer. Both had the same mixture of idealism and egotism, of geniality and ruthlessness. Both were financially unscrupulous without being personally acquisitive. Both, with some lapses, learned how to curb a natural impetuosity with an acquired patience. They shared a gift for disguising duplicity with high-flown sentiments and, on occasion, with displays of not entirely synthetic indignation. They were both masters in the handling of men, using the resources of flattery, bribery, and blackmail as occasion served. Charm was their principal stock-in-trade, used for the seduction of opponents, for the quieting of critics, for the encouragement of friends, and for the obtaining of money. Both were men of liberal views and charitable instincts. Both regarding themselves as having many attributes of the Deity and both striving, as a matter of business, to become all things to all men, they naturally regarded the Almighty as possessing many of those attributes with which they themselves were so generously endowed. In the end, both were to overreach themselves as the result of overconfidence derived from an acquired belief in their own infallibility. And both are remembered, if not with honor, at least with respect and admiration, by a posterity which, deprived of the persuasiveness of their advocacy and informed of the defects in their characters, can yet salute the magnitude of their achievements.

At first sight, Lesseps was ill equipped technically for the great role he was to assume. He had no engineering training. He knew nothing of finance and had no close connection with the great European banking houses. He had no commercial experience and no great experience in the recruitment and handling of large bodies of men. As a result of the circumstances of his retirement he had, with one important exception, no friendly personal contacts in the high places of the Second Empire. The one exception was his cousin, the Empress Eugénie, whose benevolent and carefully cultivated interest in the canal was to be of the greatest assistance to Lesseps. But, apart from his own innate qualities, Lesseps possessed one tremendous asset with which to start on the achievement of what he was now to regard as his life's work. This asset was the devotion of the little fat boy whose hunger he had surreptitiously relieved in the days when he had been a young vice-consul at Alexandria. For, by this time, Mohammed Ali and his eldest son, Ibrahim, were both dead; Abbas, Ibrahim's eldest son, was on the throne of Egypt; and Mohammed Said, the little fat boy, by the rule of heredity laid down in the 1841 Hatti Sharif, was the Heir Apparent.

During his retirement at La Chenaie, Lesseps kept closely in touch with events in Egypt through his friend Ruyssenaers, the Dutch consul general who was later to be his principal agent in Egypt. In 1852 he sent Ruyssenaers a memorandum he had prepared on the subject of the canal (probably the same memorandum he subsequently read to Mohammed Said), telling him that "since 1849 I have been studying under all its aspects a question which has occupied my attention since we first got to know each other in Egypt twenty years ago. I admit that the whole thing is still in the clouds and I am quite aware that, as I am the only one who thinks it possible, it may indeed seem to be impossible."[5] He asked Ruyssenaers to bring the contents of the memorandum to Abbas's attention. Ruyssenaers replied that Abbas was not interested and that the time was not yet ripe to pursue the matter. Lesseps also approached the Turkish Government in Constantinople, and was told that he should address himself to Abbas.

As early as 1851 Lesseps had got into touch with Enfantin and Arles-Dufour and Talabot, who supplied him with information about the work of the Société d'Etudes and who began to recognize in Lesseps a possible means of bringing their idea to fruition. They appear to have considered, in complete good faith, that Lesseps would put his negotiating ability at the disposal of the Société d'Etudes and that Lesseps had identified himself with the ideas of the Société d'Etudes. In fact Lesseps, who had made some study both of the technical and of the political aspects of the canal, was in disagreement with the Société on two fundamental points. From the technical point of view he appears to have become convinced that the Talabot scheme for a canal via the Nile would be impracticable owing to the increasing size of the oceangoing steamships a canal would have to accommodate, and to have satisfied himself (on instinctive rather than on technical grounds) that a direct cut across the isthmus was practicable. From the political point of view—which he was better qualified to judge—he seems to have realized that Enfantin's approach, by means of diplomatic representations to the Powers and financial backing from the great European banking houses, was foredoomed to failure by reason of the known British opposition, and that the essential first step was to create as much as possible of a *fait accompli* in Egypt.

Lesseps' opportunity came in September, 1854, when Abbas died and was succeeded by his uncle Mohammed Said, then a man of about thirty-two. Lesseps received the news when on his estate in the Berry. He lost no time in writing to his old protégé to congratulate him and to propose himself for a visit to Egypt to convey his congratulations in person. He received a warm invitation in reply. He then wrote to Ruyssenaers, advising him of his imminent arrival and warning him to say nothing to anybody about his plans for the canal. On November 7th, less than two months after Mohammed Said's accession, Lesseps landed at Alexandria on his life's great adventure.

The Egypt to which Lesseps returned in 1854 was a very different place from the Egypt he had known in the 1830's, and vastly different from the Egypt which merchant adventurers like Magellon and Baldwin had known at the end of the eighteenth century. Up to the time of Bonaparte's invasion, western Europe had made little or no impact on the lives of any class of Egypt's inhabitants. The number of western-European foreigners living in or visiting Egypt was small. These who lived there were either apostates who had adopted the Muslim religion and adapted themselves entirely to local ways, or traders living in foreign enclaves under the precarious protection of their consuls and having little other than business contacts with the local inhabitants. Their way of life was regulated by the various "capitulations" treaties which gave them a status, provided them with rights, and imposed upon them responsibilities, broadly analogous to those enjoyed by the various religious and racial minorities in the Ottoman dominions. That is to say, on the one hand they were allowed to practice their religion, live according to their own laws and customs, and were exempted from conscription; on the other hand they were not allowed to own land or to acquire any civil rights other than those traditionally granted to their own particular community. In practice, the extent of their privileges, and the extent of their immunity from persecution and extortion depended, not on the terms of the various treaties from which these privileges were derived, but on the caprice or interest of whoever happened to be the effective ruler or rulers of Egypt at the time. For several hundred years the diplomatic influence of their respective governments had been ineffective or non-existent; the influence of the Porte, who had concluded the treaties and who was responsible for their observance, was for the most part similarly ineffective, and western-European residents had to depend for keeping out of trouble on the agility of their wits, on the firmness of their resolution, and on the length of their purses.

By the 1830's, after a quarter of a century of Mohammed Ali's rule, all this had been changed. The windows of Egypt had been thrown open onto the Mediterranean. There was continual contact between Egypt and western Europe. The number of western-European residents had greatly increased, and the contacts between them and the inhabitants of Egypt had increased likewise. They had emerged from the ghetto-like existence which had been imposed on them up to the end of the eighteenth century. Upper-class Egypt had begun to assume its cosmopolitan air. Upper-class Egyptians—who were for the most part not Egyptians at all but Turks, Albanians, Circassians, Greeks, or Armenians—had become more Europeanized, and western Europeans more Egyptianized. In his anxiety to attract foreign merchants and foreign technicians to Egypt, Mohamed Ali was at pains to protect western-European foreigners from the extortionate caprices of his officials. More importantly, now that the Napoleonic Wars and the hastening decline of the Ottoman Empire had drawn Egypt into the orbit of European diplomacy, the protection afforded to their nationals in Egypt by European governments became increasingly effective. Mohammed Ali needed to obtain or to retain the goodwill of the various Great Powers in his endemic struggle for independence of his Ottoman suzerain, and he soon found that the extent of this goodwill was in large part dependent on the favors accorded to the nationals of the Great Powers resident, or having interests, in Egypt.

This was a situation clearly open to abuse, and it was in fact abused, by the consuls of the various Great Powers. The extent of this abuse did not begin to become apparent until after 1841 when, as a result of events which have already been described, Mohammed Ali lost much of the power he had previously possessed to limit the growing exigencies of the foreign consuls and the European communities generally. For the next thirty-five years, until national bankruptcy put an end to the party, Egypt became the happy hunting ground for a horde of get-rich-quick foreign adventurers who, sometimes with the connivance of their governments, usually with the active assistance of their consuls, exploited Egypt's vulnerability vis-à-vis the Great Powers to obtain for themselves privileges, immunities, and indemnities far beyond anything authorized by the "capitulations" or required by legitimate enterprise.

Advancing under the cover of diplomatic immunity, capitulatory privileges encroached upon and curtailed Egyptian jurisdiction and Egyptian administration until a point was reached at which the inhabitants of Egypt were almost as much at the mercy of the foreign communities as the foreign communities had previously been at the mercy of the Mamluk beys. As a result of this stealthy and insidious encroachment, foreign residents in Egypt became virtually exempt from the payment of Egyptian taxation, from the operation of Egyptian civil and criminal laws, and from the obligation to honor any contract made with Egyptian nationals for longer than it suited them to do so. Under the aegis of these inflated capitulatory privileges, and under the threat of forcible diplomatic intervention, goods were extensively smuggled, bogus companies promoted, brothels and drinking dens established and maintained, and crimes and misdemeanors of all kinds committed by European foreigners more or less openly and with almost certain impunity. Foreigners of every class, from the aristocratic French company promoter to the humble Greek procurer, indulged in this licensed illegality and benefited from this uncovenanted immunity.

After the death of Mohammed Ali, these illegalities were encouraged by the increasing weakness of the Egyptian Government, by increasing diplomatic interference in Egypt on the part of the Great Powers, and by the continuing modernization of Egypt which created an ever-increasing demand for European contractors and suppliers and provided a golden opportunity for European sharks and share pushers. A favorite method of large-scale extortion was for some apparently distinguished foreigner to arrive in Egypt with letters of introduction to his consul and to various other distinguished people, to spend money and charm lavishly, to invent or to exaggerate an intimacy with, or sometimes to represent himself as the agent of, some European potentate, to ingratiate himself into the favor of influential members of the court circle and, finally, with the aid of, and possibly in partnership with, some member of the court circle, to form a company and to be awarded a concession which usually involved some degree of interference with Egyptian sovereignty or with the rights of various Egyptian nationals.

When the inevitable opposition arose to the implementation of the concession, the concessionaire, whose object was, not to implement the concession but to obtain an indemnity in return for its cancellation, brought pressure to bear through his consul in order to extract the maximum indemnity. This procedure was repeated on several occasions and was almost invariably successful. Many of the older-established foreign residents and some of the career consuls (at that time the consuls of most European countries were merchants who acted as their country's representative and often used their consular position to forward their trading interests) strongly objected to, and did what they could to discourage, this sort of activity on the part of their fellow nationals which tended to bring their whole community into disrepute. But these adventurers often enjoyed powerful backing in the home country, and their consul was under heavy pressure from his government to identify the satisfaction of illegitimate claims with the maintenance of his country's prestige.

On the face of it, Lesseps, when he arrived in Egypt and obtained a concession for the canal, seemed to be just such an adventurer. He was a man with distinguished manners and good address, an ex-diplomat giving the impression that he had access to the highest circles in France and other European countries, who used his personal intimacy with the Viceroy to extract from him a vaguely worded concession for a vast and somewhat chimerical scheme which he appeared to have neither the technical nor the financial organization to execute. It was widely assumed, not only by the British but also by many of the French colony in Egypt, that Lesseps was just another indemnity racketeer, who had no serious intention of building the canal but who was relying on being able to extract a large indemnity from the Egyptian Government against the eventual cancellation of the concession he had persuaded the Viceroy to award him.

In fact, as we shall see, there was a point in the history of the canal when it appeared that the whole scheme would be wound up in this way. But the difference between Lesseps and the indemnity racketeers was that Lesseps, from the beginning, was primarily interested, not in obtaining an indemnity, but in building the canal. He was to be extremely successful and extremely unscrupulous in extracting uncovenanted financial assistance from the Egyptian Government, and extremely astute in exploiting such diplomatic backing as he was able to arrange from the French Government; but his object, at all times, was not self-enrichment but the completion of the canal.

Mohammed Said, the new Viceroy, was about thirty-two years of age when he succeeded to the throne. He was a reasonably intelligent, well-intentioned, good-natured but somewhat neurotic prince whose obesity of body was matched by a flabbiness of character and an infirmity of will which prevented him from pursuing any consistent policy, which made him an easy game for charlatans and speculators, and which excited alternate contempt and suspicion from the Sublime Porte and from the European Powers. Normally placid and easygoing, he was subject to frequent fits of moroseness and ungovernable rage. He had a childish love for playing at soldiers, and was never happier than when maneuvering and drilling his army in pointless and expensive exercises. He had a real sympathy with and compassion for the Egyptian peasantry, and took some practical steps to ameliorate their lot by improvements in land tenure and by remissions in taxation. He was anxious to pursue his father's policy of modernization, but lacked his father's discrimination and firmness in selection and implementation.

Said had received a good European education, spoke French fluently, and was accustomed to European methods and European habits of thought. His fleshly appetites were as uncontrolled as his rages, his despairs, and his impulses of generosity. He was entirely unfitted to withstand the subtle and complicated pressures to which rulers of Egypt were at that time continually exposed. He lost his nerve in every crisis. He retreated before every threat. He misjudged every situation and tried to lie or to bribe his way out of every difficulty. He made himself ridiculous by his lack of reticence; he made himself distrusted by his anxiety to be agreeable. Lesseps exploited his weaknesses without mercy and without scruple, but in return appears to have given him the understanding friendship of a man of the world and to have become the confidant of the bewildered Viceroy's innermost hopes and fears.

On his arrival in Egypt, Lesseps received a warm welcome from Mohammed Said, who installed him as an honored guest in one of the royal palaces in Alexandria. Within a few days Mohammed Said invited Lesseps to accompany him on one of his favorite army maneuvers which he was holding in the Western Desert between Alexandria and Cairo. This gave Lesseps an opportunity to get the Viceroy to himself, at a time of relaxation, away from the cares of state and the tiresome nagging of the foreign consuls. Mohammed Said must have known something of the various proposals for a canal, of his father's distrust of the idea, of the British objections, and of the suspicions harbored in Constantinople. It was to be supposed that he would approach the subject with caution. But Mohammed Said was a man with generous impulses who liked to oblige his friends, and a man who wished to make his reign memorable and his name immortal by means of some public work as impressive as the Great Pyramid and a great deal more useful. Like many weak-minded despots, he was a man of large ideas who ignored difficulties while they were still distant and ran away from them as soon as they started to catch up with him. Lesseps prepared the ground by discussing his scheme with one or two courtiers whom be believed to be sympathetic. After a few days' traveling in the desert the propitious moment arrived. Let Lesseps describe it in his own words:

At sunrise the camp began to stir. I dressed myself in warm clothes and went out to look at the new day. The sun's rays were already lighting up the eastern horizon; in the west it was still dark and cloudy. Suddenly I saw a vivid-colored rainbow stretching across the sky from east to west. I must admit that I felt my heart beat violently, for, in my imagination, this token of a covenant which we read about in the Bible seemed to presage that the moment had come for the consummation of the union between East and West and that this day was fixed for the success of my project. The Viceroy's arrival brought me back to earth again. He came up to me and we wished each other good day by shaking hands in the European fashion. . . . When taking leave of the Viceroy I wanted to show him that his horse (which he had lent to me) was a fine jumper; so I cleared the compound wall at one jump and galloped up the hill to my tent. This piece of imprudence was perhaps one of the reasons which afterward caused the Viceroy's entourage to give the necessary approval to my scheme. The Generals with whom I shared breakfast congratulated me and remarked that my boldness had greatly increased their opinion of me.

At five o'clock in the evening I mounted my horse and rode back to the Viceroy's tent, once more jumping the parapet of the compound. The Viceroy was in a good humor; he held my hand in his for a few moments and led me to a seat on the divan next to him. We were by ourselves; through the opening of the tent we could see the setting of the sun whose rising had moved me so much that morning. As soon as I had decided to raise the decisive question I felt quite calm and strong. I had all the details of the scheme clearly in my mind and I felt so confident of my ability to carry it through that I felt able to communicate my confidence to the Viceroy. I explained my scheme to him without going into details and was allowed to read to him from beginning to end the memorandum which I had prepared. Mohammed Said listened with interest. I asked him if he had any questions to put to me. He raised several intelligent points, and I dealt with them in a way which appeared to satisfy him. At last he said to me, "I am satisfied; I accept your scheme; during the rest of the trip we will discuss ways and means of bringing it about; you can rely on me to see the thing through" (c'est une affaire entendue; vous pouvez compter sur moi).[6]

At the time he wrote this account Lesseps was just under fifty years old. The combination of simplicity and sophistication, which is characteristic of many of Lesseps' letters and journal entries, is not an unattractive one.

In the memorandum which he gave—or read—to Mohammed Said,[7] Lesseps, after briefly tracing the previous history of the canal and referring to the studies already made by Le Père, Talabot, and Linant, and to studies made by Gallice Bey and Mougel Bey, two French engineers in the Egyptian Government service, concluded that the project was both technically practicable and commercially viable. In support of the latter conclusion, Lesseps gave a table of comparative distances between Bombay and various European and American ports by the Cape route and via a Suez Canal. After stressing the glory and prosperity which would accrue to Egypt and to Mohammed Said himself as the result of a canal,[8] Lesseps estimated that, on the basis of canal dues charged at ten francs per ton, such a canal would benefit world commerce to the extent of 150 million francs per annum and at the same time provide an annual income of 30 million francs for the Canal Company. (He prudently made no estimate of the capital cost of the canal.) He concluded with a dissertation on the political aspects of the canal in which he recognized the existence of British objections and ascribed them to "a deplorable prejudice, founded on that political antagonism which has unhappily lasted so long between these two countries." But he expressed his confidence that the existing friendly relations between them (they were at that time allied with Turkey and with each other against Russia in the Crimean War) would enable the British to realize that any enterprise so commercially advantageous to them could not be politically dangerous.

Lesseps' proposal, unaccompanied by any detailed plan, any estimate of cost, any financial guarantee, or any governmental backing or recommendation, was a slender basis for the amplitude of the Concession which Mohammed Said awarded to Lesseps fifteen days later, after their arrival in Cairo from the desert trip. By the terms of this Concession,[9] which was dated November 20, 1854, Mohammed Said gave to "our friend M. Ferdinand de Lesseps . . . who has made known to us the possibility of forming a Company composed of capitalists of all nations . . . the exclusive right to form and direct a 'compagnie universelle' for the construction and operation of a canal through the isthmus of Suez."

The terms of the Concession provided that Lesseps should form and direct a company to be known as "la Compagnie Universelle du Canal Maritime de Suez" for the construction and operation of a canal running across the isthmus, that the president of the company should be nominated by the Egyptian Government, that the term of the Concession should be for ninety-nine years from the date of the opening of the canal to navigation, that the Egyptian Government should receive 15 percent of the net profits, that 10 percent of the net profits should be reserved for founder members who were to consist of individuals, approved by the Viceroy, whose works, studies, *soins*, or financial contributions in the early stages had contributed to the success of the enterprise, that the remaining 75 percent of net profits should be divided between the ordinary shareholders, that the transit dues should be agreed between the company and the Egyptian Government and should be nondiscriminatory between nation and nation, and that the Egyptian Government should make available such lands as might be required from the State Domains, including any land that might be required between the isthmus and the Nile.[10]

Lesseps' official copy of the Concession was not formally handed to him until the following March, and then only with an important codicil added to it which stated that "the concession awarded to the Compagnie Universelle du Canal de Suez, of which I now send you a copy, must be ratified by the Sultan. Work on the construction of the Canal must not be started until after the authority of the Sublime Porte has been received."[11]

On the evening of the signature of the Concession, Lesseps wrote a number of letters in which he made it clear that the Concession had, in effect, been drafted by himself.[12] One of his correspondents was Arles-Dufour, Enfantin's colleague in the Société d'Etudes. In this letter Lesseps referred to "*notre grande affaire*," and still seems to have been thinking in terms of cooperation with the Société. He told Arles-Dufour to make such approaches as he thought fit, without committing himself to anything, and advised him to seek an audience with the Emperor and to get into touch with the British Government. But he warned him that he would have nothing to do with the Talabot plan for cutting a canal via the Nile, since the Viceroy was opposed to it. This was the beginning of what was soon to be a complete estrangement between Lesseps and the Société. Enfantin and his friends considered that Lesseps, in obtaining the Concession, had been acting on behalf of the Société d'Etudes. Lesseps made it clear that the Concession had been awarded to him personally and that the Société had no standing in the matter. Enfantin replied that Lesseps should make over the Concession to the Société d'Etudes and, when Lesseps refused to do so, did his best to discredit him with the Emperor.

Vain attempts at conciliation were made. It was admitted that Lesseps had no formal engagement to the Société d'Etudes, but it was held, by Negrelli and others, that he had some moral obligation toward them. In the event, the Emperor refused Enfantin's request that he should intervene in the dispute, and Negrelli deserted to Lesseps by agreeing to take part in the International Commission which Lesseps set up in 1855 to make a technical study of the project. Enfantin gave up the struggle, and the Société lapsed into harmless inactivity. Before he died, Enfantin had the generosity to recognize that the canal was in better hands than his: "In my hands the affair would have failed; I no longer have the force and resilience necessary to stand up to so many enemies, to fight in Cairo, in London, in Constantinople; it would have been quite enough for me to conquer the sands, I would have been defeated by the ill-will of adversaries. In order to succeed one must, like Lesseps, have *'le diable au corps.'* "[13]

NOTES

1. At this time Lesseps could not possibly have anticipated that the greedy little fat boy would one day become ruler of Egypt. In the 1830's, although Mohammed Ali had not yet received the hereditary title to Egypt, it seemed probable that he would become independent of Constantinople and establish his own dynasty in Egypt. If he had done so, the succession would normally have descended through his eldest son, Ibrahim, and Mohammed Said, the youngest of many sons, would have had little chance of the succession. Lesseps could not have foreseen the terms of the 1841 Hatti Sharif which, by conferring the succession on the oldest living descendant of Mohammed Ali, was eventually, after the death of all Mohammed Ali's older sons, and of Abbas, Ibrahim's eldest son, to bring Mohammed Said to the throne. There is therefore no reason to suppose that Ferdinand's friendship with Mohammed Said, who could not have been a very attractive boy, had any ulterior motive.
2. The relationship was a distant one. Ferdinand's father, Mathieu, had married a Spaniard, Catherine-Marie, Basilie de Grivegnée, who had a grand-niece, Eugénie, the daughter of Cyprian Guzmán Palafox Portecarrero, Comte de Tela, who became Comte de Montijo on the death of his elder brother without issue. On her father's death Eugénie became Comtesse de Montijo and subsequently, by her marriage to Napoleon III in 1852, Empress of the French.
3. Jean d'Elbée.
4. He was happily married to his first wife, who died in 1853. For many years after that, his mother-in-law, Madame Delamalle, was one of his closest friends and confidantes. He

was married again, to a young girl, in 1869. He had several children by both his marriages. His eldest son, Charles, succeeded him as president of the Suez Canal Company, and ultimately took all the blame of the Panama scandal from off his (by then aged) father's shoulders onto his own and went to prison as a result.

5. Edgar-Bonnet, *Ferdinand de Lesseps,* I, 190.

6. Journal, I, 16. Letter to Mme. Delamalle dated Nov. 15, 1854.

7. For text see J. Charles-Roux, *L'Isthme* . . . , Vol. I, Annex No. 12.

8. "Le nom du Prince qui aura ouvert le grand canal maritime de Suez sera béni de siècle en siècle jusqu'à la postérité la plus reculée." Lesseps apparently believed in Disraeli's maxim that, when flattering royalty, one should lay it on with a trowel.

9. For text see J. Charles-Roux, *op. cit.,* Vol. I, Annex No. 13.

10. Clause 7: "Dans le cas où la Compagnie jugerait nécessaire de rattacher par une voie navigable le Nil au passage direct de l'isthme et dans celui où le canal maritime suivrait un trace indirect desservi par l'eau de Nil, le gouvernement égyptien abandonmerait à la Compagnie les terrains du domaine publique aujourd'hui incultes qui seraient arrosé et cultivés à ses frais ou par ses soins." This Clause presupposes that Lesseps was not yet committed to the direct route, although Clause 8 seems to assume a direct cut across the isthmus with a "canal d'alimentation dérivé du Nil." But it soon became apparent that Lesseps and Mohammed Said had agreed that the direct route was the only acceptable one, but that it was also necessary to link the isthmus with the Nile by a "canal d'alimentation" to provide fresh water both for the construction and for the subsequent operation of the Maritime Canal.

11. There is a distinction between ratification by the Sultan and the authority of the Sublime Porte. The ratification would be made by a firman, an imperial decree signed by the Sultan. The Sublime Porte was the expression normally used to denote the Turkish Government as distinct from the Sultan himself, and "the authority of the Sublime Porte" could be held to mean an informal permission to proceed given by the Grand Vizier or the Reis Effendi (Foreign Minister). Lesseps was later to claim that he had received this informal permission.

12. Edgar-Bonnet, *op. cit.,* I, 199–200.

13. J. Charles-Roux, *op. cit.,* I, 241.

CHAPTER *four*

The Canal Concessions ⮿

꿈 NEWS of the Concession was published to the world at a meeting of the Consular Corps, at which Lesseps was present, called by Mohammed Said in Cairo on December 1st. Sabatier, the French consul general, reporting this meeting to his government, wrote, "I immediately called upon His Highness and urged him to stand firm in face of the opposition which he could expect from my colleagues." Adding that he did not think that the British Government would persist in its previous "petty opposition," he expressed the view that "this great question is on the point of being solved." He went on to report that the Viceroy had indicated to him that he proposed immediately to ask the Porte's approval for the Canal, and requested the good offices of the French ambassador in Constantinople. "I gave him the assurance not only that our Chargé d'Affaires would exercise his good offices but that His Highness could count on the fullest support of the French Government both in Paris and Constantinople."[1]

The French Government, in their reply to Sabatier, took a very much more reserved attitude and, while expressing their support for the canal, warned him that it must be regarded as a private enterprise and that it should not be sponsored officially by the French Consulate General. The dispatch added that the British Government had been assured that Lesseps had no official backing from the French Government and again warned Sabatier to act, in the matter of the canal, with *"une certaine réserve."*[2] At the same time the French Government, instructing Benedetti, the French chargé d'affaires in Constantinople, wrote that "France and Britain have *'en quelque sorte'* agreed to let this question develop (*se vider*) without any official intervention from either Government. We must try and keep it on this basis. You must not therefore intervene in any way with the Ottoman Government in favour of Said Pasha's request. If Sir Stratford [*sic*] does not imitate your reserve and tries to persuade the Porte to oppose the project, you will arrange with the Porte to keep the matter in suspense and report the matter to me and seek new instructions."[3]

Bruce, the British consul general, reporting the meeting to the Foreign Office, wrote:

In the absence of any instructions . . . I abstained from bringing forward any objection against it, confining myself with [*sic*] urging on His Highness the expediency of not committing himself prematurely to any such scheme, on the ground that it was too large an undertaking for the resources of Egypt and that the true test of the practicability and profitability of such a speculation was only to be found in the money market. . . . I have reason to believe that this scheme has been brought forward by Mr. Lesseps without any communication with the French Government. . . . His Highness has got so far with a view to encouraging it as to approve of a canal being carried from the Nile as a feeder. The land reclaimed by means of it is to be held as property by the Company and for the first ten years to be free of all payment of land tax. . . . A direct link between Suez and the Mediterranean would give Egypt the go-by, would have a constant tendency to escape from the jurisdiction of the Egyptian Government and would in no way enrich it except in so far as it might create a demand for supplies. . . . Mr. Lesseps assured me that the French Government is not in any way to supply funds for its execution . . . [he] is anxious to present it simply as a commercial proposition but it appears to me difficult to disjoin it from political considerations. . . . It is clear that before eight million pounds could be found[4] the neutrality of the passage must be guaranteed by some arrangement in the nature of a Treaty between the Great Powers.

After referring to the possibility of European settlement in the Red Sea as a result of a canal, Bruce wondered how long Turkish authority could be maintained in Egypt were any Power to obtain a footing in its rear. He went on: "It seems to me that the political considerations affecting the question will be more properly dealt with by the Porte whose consent to the enterprise is necessary, than by the local government of Egypt . . . the impression among English engineers . . . is that the scheme is very difficult of execution and . . . will require not only a very large sum to make it, but such an annual outlay as to render it impracticable as a speculation."[5]

The British Government, having made inquiries about the attitude of the French Government, received the following reply from Lord Cowley, the British ambassador in Paris: "The French Government denies most particularly having any interest whatever in the plan put forward by M. Lesseps . . . but M. Drouyn de Lhuys says at the same time that he believes that were the work carried out it would prove of great benefit to Egypt and also to all mercantile interests and that consequently the French Government, without interfering at all, would yet see it executed with satisfaction."[6]

In January the Foreign Office informed Bruce that "Her Majesty's Government continue to hold the same opinion as they have firmly held not only as to the inexpediency for the interests of Egypt herself of any attempt to carry into execution a plan involving such a large expenditure, but also as to the impracticable nature of the plan itself. But Her Majesty's Government do not think it necessary to do more than represent to the Pasha . . . that the scheme may involve him in an extent of expenditure which the finances of Egypt are inadequate to meet and that if the capital for the undertaking is to be procured from other quarters he may find that it is only to be obtained on conditions which would very much cripple his freedom of action in administering the government of Egypt." The dispatch went on to make it clear that the French provenance of the scheme had nothing to do with the British Government's objections to it, and ended by instructing Bruce to "keep aloof from it and frankly to state to the Pasha your reasons for so doing."[7]

From the time of Mohammed Ali's defeat at the hands of the Great Powers in 1841 to the time of the British occupation of Egypt in 1882, the position of the consuls general representing the Great Powers in Egypt was one of great influence and importance. Although, since Egypt was a part of the Ottoman Empire, they were subordinate to, and depended from, their respective ambassadors in Constantinople, the quasi-autonomous status of Egypt, the importance attached to Egypt by all the Great Powers and, above all, the expanding—although largely usurped—power conferred upon the consuls by the "capitulations," gave to these officials a considerable influence in the policy of their countries, in the councils of the Egyptian Government, and in their local national communities, whose members accepted their judgment as arbitrators and invoked their influence as protectors. Their influence with their own nationals was probably less than in the ghetto days before the beginning of the nineteenth century, and was mainly dependent on their own personal qualities. The need for protection was less, and the sense of a small, closely knit community living together in a more or less disciplined hierarchy had disappeared during the spacious days of Mohammed Ali.

Many foreign residents, and many foreign interests, had powerful connections in their home countries by means of which pressure was often brought to bear on consuls to use their influence—sometimes in unjustifiable and illegitimate ways. Some of them too—like Lesseps—had their own independent connections with the Egyptian Government which enabled them to dispense with the protection, and sometimes to outflank the opposition, of their consul. For all these reasons, a consul was more important as the representative of his government than as the leader of his community. As the representative of his government the consul general of any of the Great Powers had frequent access to the Viceroy and, since the accession of Said, who spoke fluent French, was able to converse with him without the medium of an interpreter. Any important new Egyptian law or act of policy was announced to the Consular Corps, at a meeting especially convened for the purpose, either by the Viceroy himself or by his Foreign Minister.

In Constantinople the ambassadors of the Powers occupied an even more important position vis-à-vis the Ottoman Government. In 1838, when Sultan Mahmud II died a few days after the defeat of the Turkish forces by Ibrahim Pasha at Nezib, a Conference of Ambassadors had, for a few weeks, virtually ruled the Ottoman Empire. Thereafter, with a weak Sultan,[8] and in the capital of a defenseless empire whose continued existence was secured only by the balance of rivalries between the Great Powers, the influence of the British, French, and Russian ambassadors, and the Austrian Internuncio, was limited only by the extent of the endemic personal and political rivalries between these four potentates. On the rare occasions when they acted in unison, the Sublime Porte could only hear and obey.[9]

In 1855, just after the grant of the first canal Concession, Great Britain and France were allied with Turkey in the Crimean War against Russia. The British ambassador was Lord Stratford de Redcliffe (formerly Sir Stratford Canning), the Great Elchi, who had achieved an almost legendary (although certainly exaggerated) ascendancy over the Ottoman Government. The Grand Vizier, Rashid Pasha, was regarded by the French as Stratford's creature, and it was regarded by them as a great triumph when, for a few months in 1856, Rashid was replaced as Grand Vizier by Kiamil Pasha. It was similarly regarded by them as a triumph for De Redcliffe when Rashid Pasha returned to office later in the same year.

The policy of alliance with England, inaugurated by Napoleon III and implemented in the Crimean War, imposed on the British and French governments, in their Eastern policy, the necessity of presenting a more or less united front vis-à-vis the Ottoman Empire and, in consequence, the necessity for great circumspection in the pursuit of traditional Anglo-French rivalries in Egypt and elsewhere in the Ottoman Empire. In deference to the requirements of the alliance, which was no more popular in France than the regime which had inaugurated it, French representatives in Turkey and in Egypt, restrained by Paris in the interests of higher policy, were compelled impotently to watch a progressive increase in British influence in Constantinople and in Cairo. These representatives, and educated French public opinion generally, considered that *"perfide Albion"* was using a temporary and unnatural alliance to advance her own at the expense of

French interests in the Ottoman Empire, to undermine traditional French interests in the eastern Mediterranean and, in particular, to obtain a stranglehold on Egypt. There were bitter French memories of British policy toward Mohammed Ali in 1840–1841 which they regarded as having been primarily directed against French influence in Egypt and at Constantinople, and toward the establishment of British influence in these places. The British representatives, and British public opinion, whose suspicion of French designs on Egypt was at least as lively as French suspicion of British designs, neither abated their suspicions nor relaxed their vigilance as a result of the alliance, in which they clearly regarded France as the junior partner.

In the eyes of the Sublime Porte, Egypt was easily the richest, the most highly developed and, at the same time, the most tenuously held province in the empire. Just as it was the aim of every Egyptian Viceroy to loosen the bonds of Ottoman suzerainty, strengthened as they had been by the events of 1840–1841, so it was the aim of every Ottoman Government to maintain and, if possible, still further to strengthen these bonds. The predominant British influence at Constantinople was partly due to the Ottoman belief that Britain was in favor of the maintenance of effective Ottoman suzerainty over Egypt, and that the French were in favor of its relaxation. This belief had of course been implanted as a result of the events of 1840–1841, and was assiduously cultivated by the British ambassador. But while this belief clearly contributed to the influence of the British ambassador at the Sublime Porte, it also caused the Sublime Porte to pay considerable attention to French wishes lest the French, despairing of their position at Constantinople, be tempted to repeat with Mohammed Said the same separatist policy they had previously pursued with Mohammed Ali. For the Sublime Porte, unable to impose any policy in Egypt in opposition to any one of the Great Powers, and fearful of the possibility of an Anglo-French bargain at their expense, could retain its tenuous hold on Egypt only by encouraging rivalry over Egypt between Britain and France and at the same time remain on good terms with both Powers by trying to comply sufficiently with the usually contradictory wishes of each.

It is within this general framework that British, French, and Ottoman reactions to the news of the first canal Concession must be viewed.

The British Government was headed by Lord Palmerston, who had recently replaced Lord Aberdeen as Prime Minister and who, fifteen years earlier, had been the British Foreign Secretary and the moving spirit behind the defeat of Mohammed Ali's imperial ambitions. Lord Clarendon was the Foreign Secretary in Palmerston's first administration, which remained in office until the beginning of 1858, but Palmerston as Prime Minister appears to have exercised a very close supervision over foreign affairs. His views on the Eastern Question had been formed during his years as Foreign Minister, and were to remain unchanged until his death in 1865. He was convinced of the necessity, from the point of view of British interests, of maintaining Ottoman suzerainty over Egypt as defined in the 1841 Hatti Sharif; he was deeply suspicious of French designs on Egypt, and he was irrevocably opposed to the cutting of a canal through the Isthmus of Suez. His reasons for this opposition were that the scheme was a French plot designed (*a*) to colonize Egypt; (*b*) to enable the Egyptian Viceroy, with French assistance, to render himself independent of Ottoman suzerainty; and (*c*) to enable the French to threaten the British in India by their ability to send troops to India via the canal while barring the use of the same route to the British. In his public speeches it would have been injudicious to express these suspicions, and he therefore concentrated his public attacks on the practicability of the canal, on the dishonesty of its promoters, and on the gullibility of those who invested money in it. In private his views were stated with more frankness:

. . . [The canal] would be injurious to England because, in any quarrel between England and France, France, being so much nearer to the Canal, would
have much the start of us in sending ships and troops to the Indian seas.[10]
It is quite clear that this scheme is founded on ulterior intentions hostile to
British views and interests and the secret intention no doubt is to lay a foundation for a future severance of Egypt from Turkey and for placing it under French
protection. A deep and wide canal interposed between Egypt and Syria studded
with fortifications would be a military defensive line which, with the desert in
front of it, would render the task of a Turkish army very difficult . . . and if
land is to be conceded to the French Company a French colony on French
territory would be interposed between Turkey and Egypt and any attempt by
Turkish troops to cross that line would be held to be an invasion of France.
From the moment the enterprise was completed Egypt would be completely
cut off from Turkey and would be placed under the protection of France. . . .[11]

The official British attitude was, at first, rather less robust. Cowley, in reply to a complaint from Drouyn de Lhuys that Bruce had been openly opposing the scheme in Egypt, acknowledged that the British Government disapproved of the scheme, but stated that this disapproval was in no sense inspired by hostility toward France and that British opposition to it would not be pushed "beyond the bounds of courtesy."[12] In Constantinople, Stratford de Redcliffe, who was of course aware of the British Government's views and who had received copies of Clarendon's dispatches to Bruce and Cowley, told Clarendon that he had arranged with the Grand Vizier that the Viceroy would be encouraged to complete the railway but discouraged from pursuing the canal scheme.[13] A month later, Stratford de Redcliffe, advising the Foreign Office about Lesseps' arrival in Constantinople, wrote that "the Grand Vizier and Aali Pasha [Reis Effendi, or Foreign Minister] have been presently advised of my sentiments on the subject but I feel the importance of not giving any occasion for any ostensible difference of opinion between the two Embassies."[14]

When Stratford hinted to the Foreign Office that he needed some more positive support in order to sustain his opposition to the scheme, which was being actively canvassed by Lesseps in Constantinople, he was told that "in the opinion of Her Majesty's Government it would not be expedient to make any official protest against the scheme."[15] It was only after Stratford had intimated in the most urgent terms that there was a serious danger lest Lesseps seduce the Sultan into granting his firman for the construction of the canal that the British Government, galvanized by Palmerston, began to throw the whole weight of their influence into the balance against the scheme.

In spite of Palmerston's suspicions the French Government appears to have had no sinister intentions in respect of the canal. Although Ferdinand was at all times in touch with his brother Théodore, who was employed at the French Foreign Office and who frequently acted as intermediary between Ferdinand and the French Government, there is no evidence that Ferdinand had had any consultations with the French Government about his plans, and it is certain that, in obtaining the Concession, he was in no sense acting as an agent of the French Government. Lesseps was certainly at pains, both in Cairo and in Constantinople, to give the impression that the Emperor was personally interested in the canal, and almost succeeded in making both Mohammed Said and the Sublime Porte believe that any reluctance to facilitate the progress of the canal would be regarded by the Emperor as a personal affront to himself. But he found some difficulty in reconciling his assertions with the instructions received and with the attitudes adopted by the French representatives. These instructions were dominated by the importance attached by Napoleon III personally to the British alliance and by his desire to avoid doing anything which might possibly jeopardize it.

The French Government was well aware of the British Government's views about the canal in general, and Cowley had soon made them aware of the unfavorable British reaction to the news of Lesseps' Concession. The instructions given to Benedetti and Sabatier were designed to provide that, while such official backing was to be given to the scheme as might properly be given to any respectable scheme put forward by private French citizens, the French Government was not to be identified with the scheme

Ismail Pasha, Viceroy of Egypt 1863–1879

Ferdinand de Lesseps

Napoleon III, Emperor of the French

Eugénie, Empress of the French

Auguste, Duc de Morny

Edward Henry Stanley, First Earl of Derby

Benjamin Disraeli, First Earl of Beaconsfield

Dry Excavation, Sweet Water Canal

Construction: Steam Dredge

Triumphal Arch for Opening Ceremonies at Port Said

Ceremonial Opening: Procession of Ships Through the Canal

A Panoramic View of the Canal

and no pressure was to be employed or intimidation attempted in order to advance the scheme. The line to be taken was that it was a matter to be settled directly between the Viceroy and his suzerain without the intervention of the Powers. On the whole these instructions, which did not exclude some support for Lesseps, seem to have been faithfully observed. Stratford reported that "the language of the French Embassy . . . tends . . . to promote its success while disclaiming all interest or official participation in its progress."[16]

At the beginning of February, 1855, Lesseps, detaching himself from a voluminous correspondence in which he was quarreling with Arles-Dufour and his friends and recommending his project to a wide circle of acquaintances in England, Austria, the United States of America, and elsewhere, sailed from Alexandria for Constantinople. In his discussions with the Viceroy over the previous two months, he had taken the view that the canal, as a scheme of public works within Egypt, could, under the terms of the 1841 Hatti Sharif, be constructed without the necessity of a firman from his suzerain in the same way as the various irrigation canals, which were continually being dug in Egypt, were constructed. Seeing, however, that such a canal would have international ramifications, he agreed with Mohammed Said[17] that, as a matter of courtesy, the Porte's informal approval in principle should be sought.

It was therefore arranged that Lesseps should proceed to Constantinople as the Viceroy's emissary in order to obtain this approval. Lesseps was almost certainly aware that the Sultan's firman would sooner or later be necessary; he realized that the grant of this firman would be strenuously opposed by Britain, but reckoned that this opposition could eventually be overcome both by propaganda in England and by the creation of a *fait accompli* in Egypt. The object of his visit to Constantinople therefore was to obtain from the Porte, in writing, some general expression of approval which could be used to quiet Mohammed Said's misgivings, to raise money from his prospective shareholders and, generally, to invest the Concession with some appearance of legality.

Lesseps' visit to Constantinople was a great personal success. In spite of the very lukewarm support which he got from Benedetti, and in spite of the open hostility of Stratford de Redcliffe, he almost succeeded in convincing the Ottoman ministers that he enjoyed the patronage of the Emperor and that the opposition to the scheme came, not from the British Government, but from Stratford de Redcliffe personally.[18] He even tried to persuade Stratford himself to abate his opposition. In this he failed. It was a case of an irresistible force meeting an immovable obstacle. Lesseps was as convinced of the practicability and usefulness of the canal as Stratford was convinced of its impracticability as a commercial proposition and its harmfulness to British interests as a political proposition. But the ambassador retained a powerful impression of Lesseps' forcefulness and ability, and became extremely alarmed at the possible effect of his negotiations in Constantinople. On February 26th, a few days before Lesseps' return to Egypt, he wrote to the Foreign Office:

I have reason to believe that there is a strong tendency in the Grand Vizier's mind to confirm the grant . . . not that he approves the Viceroy's conduct . . . but he shrinks from a decision which may indispose His Highness towards the Porte and give umbrage to the French Emperor whose agent . . . intimates that His Majesty would not be pleased with the rejection of Mr. Lesseps' demand. I have endeavoured to dissuade the Porte from a precipitate compliance without committing Her Majesty's Government by a formal opposition to the proposed scheme. It is evident that the Porte is by no means inclined to incur the responsibility of a refusal or even of a suspension such as I have recommended confidentially. It is expected of me that I shall either declare my objections . . . or that I shall leave the Porte to confirm the Viceroy's grant without further postponement. The Council is to deliberate on the subject the day after to-morrow and I know not as yet by what means, if any, I shall be able to meet Your Lordship's wishes as to the Canal without incurring a serious hazard.[19]

In the event the Council (Divan) took the Grand Vizier's advice to delay a decision and to set up a commission to study the whole matter. Lesseps, before returning to Egypt at the beginning of March, obtained a letter from the Grand Vizier to the Viceroy which he was afterward to cite as containing that approval in principle which was all that was necessary to enable work on the canal to be started. In this letter Rashid wrote, ". . . in the matter of the Canal, which is a very useful enterprise . . . the question is at present being studied by the Council of Ministers . . . in a short time I will advise Your Highness of the detailed results of their studies."[20]

At the beginning of April, Stratford received from London the ammunition for which he had asked:

Her Majesty's Government considers that the Canal would be useless even if it were possible to execute it and the concession desired by M. de Lesseps is highly objectionable for political reasons; they recommend the Porte not to grant it on the grounds that it is not the moment for bringing so large a project into the money market and that it will require more attention and energy than the Porte has yet been able to give before a decision can be taken. In the meantime Her Majesty's Government will communicate these views to the French Government without whose sanction and assistance it is improbable that M. de Lesseps can proceed.[21]

Two months later this forthright expression of opinion was reinforced with another dispatch in which Stratford was instructed "to state confidentially to the Porte that it is very doubtful whether the Canal could be constructed and it is quite certain that it would be impossible to obtain eight or ten million sterling for such an undertaking. . . . Mr. Lesseps must therefore have political objects in view. These objects would eventually be detrimental to the interests of the Sultan and it is on that account and not for any jealousy of France that Her Majesty's Government would see with extreme regret a territorial concession, with its accompanying rights and privileges, made to any foreign Company." The dispatch went on to state that the canal would place a physical barrier between Syria and Egypt and "thus tend to render easy at some future time the severance of Egypt from the demesne of the Sultan. This consideration has probably not occurred to the Porte and the Viceroy who have no doubt been dazzled by the expectation of great profits from an enterprise which Her Majesty's Government are convinced will fail in its intended object although it might fully answer the purpose of those parties who wish to obtain a footing in Egypt independent both of the Porte and of the Viceroy."[22]

Lesseps, on his return to Egypt, found that Rashid had written a private letter to Mohammed Said, in contradiction to the views expressed in the letter he had given to Lesseps (in which he had described the canal as "a useful enterprise") and warning him against the canal project. "I observe with pain," he wrote, "that Your Highness is throwing himself into the arms of France whose government has no more stability than its agents. France can do nothing either for you or against you, while England can do you a great deal of harm. The representatives of England are always sustained and supported by their government. One cannot be too careful in dealing with them." He added that the Sultan was very angry; "the only way to appease him is to have nothing more to do with the canal." Said's brother-in-law, Kiamil Pasha, wrote to him in the same sense.[23]

A few weeks later Rashid Pasha resigned from his office as Grand Vizier as the result of a complaint made against him by the French Government in a matter unconnected with the canal.[24] This was generally regarded as a triumph for French influence at Constantinople and as a blow to the influence of the British ambassador. Lesseps, encouraged by this, decided that the time was ripe for him to prosecute his scheme in Paris and London. Through his brother Théodore he had already been in touch with the Empress, who was not without influence on the mind of the Emperor, and who had already expressed her intention of giving her patronage to the scheme.[25] With his departure from Egypt, the center of the controversy shifted from Constantinople and Cairo to Paris and London.

On his arrival in Paris toward the end of May, Lesseps found that Count Walewski, the French ambassador in London, was about to replace Drouyn de Lhuys as Foreign Minister, that Persigny, an intimate friend and faithful follower of the Emperor, was to succeed Walewski in London, and that Thouvenel, a career diplomat and an old acquaintance of Lesseps', was to go to Constantinople (where Benedetti had for some months been acting as chargé d'affaires) as ambassador. Walewski was the natural son of Napoleon I by a Polish countess and thus, on the wrong side of the blanket, a cousin of the Emperor. By reason of this relationship, and by reason of his own distinguished personal qualities, Walewski was an outstanding figure in the somewhat raffish society of the Second Empire. Owing to his hatred of Russia, derived from his Polish mother, he was an advocate of the Emperor's policy of alliance with England. Because of this he was unlikely to go to extremes in support of Lesseps' canal project, but, in spite of this, Lesseps, whose past dealings with Drouyn de Lhuys had not given him any reason for friendly intimacy—he had been Foreign Minister at the time of the Rome affair in 1849—welcomed the change at the Foreign Ministry.

Walewski's successor in London, Gilbert Fialin, Comte de Persigny, was another considerable, although somewhat comic, figure in the Second Empire. Originally a noncommissioned officer in the French Army, he had shared the Emperor's exile and, together with the exquisite Morny, had helped Napoleon to engineer the coup of December 2, 1851, which brought the Second Empire into being. He is said to have retained the manners and speech of a noncommissioned officer and, according to a mot of Morny's, "overstrained his intelligence by thinking too much" (*il méditait trop pour son intelligence*). He served the Emperor "with the fidelity of a police dog" but was never afraid to talk to him with the frankness of an old comrade. He was eventually rewarded by being, in Merimée's phrase, "embalmed" in a dukedom. Thouvenel was an able diplomat who, in Constantinople and later in Paris, was to have much to do with the fortunes of the canal project.

Walewski, soon after his appointment, replying to a complaint by Cowley about Benedetti's advocacy of the canal in Constantinople,[26] in which Cowley urged him not to disturb the harmony between the two countries by supporting Lesseps, suggested that both governments should instruct their representatives in Constantinople to "interfere no further in the matter and leave it for the decision of the Sultan and the Viceroy."

Cowley replied that the French and British governments were not on an equal footing in the matter, since Britain, unlike France, had a vital interest in transit traffic through Egypt and could not adopt an attitude of neutrality toward the project. He added, in his dispatch to Clarendon, that his experience of French agents was such[27] that, even if such an agreement were made, it would not be kept.[28]

The British Government's reaction to Walewski's proposal had been accurately foreseen by Cowley. In a long dispatch which was clearly inspired by the Prime Minister, Cowley was informed:

Her Majesty's Government consider that a proposal to leave the question to be decided by the Sultan and the Pasha would practically be to throw back the question to be fought for locally by the cabals and intrigues of the agents and partisans of the two countries in Turkey and Egypt and would tend to revive and aggravate all the jealousies and rivalries which both Governments are now labouring to extinguish. . . . The objections of Her Majesty's Government . . . are threefold. First the Canal is physically impossible except at a cost which would put out of all question its being profitable as a commercial speculation and which therefore proves that, if undertaken, it can only be undertaken for political objects. Secondly, it would interfere with and greatly delay, if not entirely prevent, the completion of railway communication between Cairo and Suez. Thirdly, it is founded on an antagonistic policy on the part of France in regard to Egypt which they hoped and believed had come to an end. . . . Previously it was natural that partisans of French policy should consider it an object of great importance to detach Egypt from Turkey in order thereby to cut off the easiest channel of communication between England and India . . . extensive fortifications planned at the War Office in Paris were erected by French engineers along the Mediterranean coast . . . it was with this view that the great Barrage was constructed on the Nile . . . it was in this view and in this spirit that the scheme was put forward, the effect of which would be to interpose between Syria and Egypt the physical barrier of a wide and deep Canal defended by military works and the physical barrier of a strip of land . . . granted away to and occupied by a company of foreigners . . . but the policy of France at the present moment is to cultivate friendly relations . . . the Canal scheme has survived the policy out of which it arose and it ought to give way to the altered and better policy. . . .[29]

Walewski, in a dispatch to Persigny protesting against the violence of this language, wrote that "if the French Government believed that the Canal project, with which it has no connection, was inspired by a spirit of hostility [toward Britain] it would oppose it without hesitation; but it is not so inspired . . . and nothing seems more calculated to revive and to nourish the old spirit of hostility and mistrust than an unjustified opposition to an enterprise of general utility."[30]

Meanwhile Persigny, in London, had become impressed with the depth and intensity of the British Government's objections to the scheme. A few weeks after his appointment he came to Paris and, in a private interview with the Emperor, appears to have impressed him with the necessity of not risking the British alliance by giving any encouragement to Lesseps. Cowley, in a dispatch dated June 30th, reported that Persigny had told him that "he had a long conversation with the Emperor on the subject of the Canal, that he had submitted to His Majesty the reasons which induced Her Majesty's Government to oppose the scheme and that the Emperor had said that whatever might be his own predilections in its favour he would not press them in opposition to the wishes of Her Majesty's Government. He was quite ready therefore to desist from further interference but desired that this should be done in a way which should not give at Constantinople the idea that the English influence had prevailed over the French. If, however, the Porte was to pronounce an adverse decision this could not be avoided and he wished rather that the question be allowed to drop and be considered '*non avenue.*' "[31] It later appeared that Walewski had no knowledge of Persigny's interview with the Emperor, and Cowley warned Clarendon that the Emperor's words to Persigny should not be regarded as indicative of French policy.[32]

At the beginning of June, Lesseps went to London. He had been in touch with Walewski before his visit, trying to get some official French countenance for his scheme to exhibit in London, but all he succeeded in getting, after a personal appeal to the Emperor, was a letter of introduction to Lord Clarendon.[33] While in London he was received both by Palmerston and by Clarendon who, courteously but firmly, expressed their opposition to his project. He made some contacts with journalists, businessmen, and engineers. He also saw Persigny, and seems to have got some inkling from him of the views about the canal which he was shortly to communicate to the Emperor.

At all events, on his return to Paris, he wrote to the Empress indicating that Persigny was not being helpful, and expressing fear that Persigny's influence on the Emperor might compromise the whole future of *"la grande Entreprise."* He asked the Empress to intervene with a view to trying to ensure that, since Persigny was not prepared to help, he should not be allowed to hinder.[34] In a more formal letter to the Emperor he reported: "The support of *The Times* has now been obtained; I have reason to believe that Prince Albert is well disposed. If during the Queen's forthcoming visit to France Your Majesty would deign to indicate to Lord Clarendon the interest which He takes in the success of this work, which already enjoys the support of public opinion in Great Britain, He will have done much to forward the success of my negotiations."[35]

Some time after this, Lesseps appears to have been granted an audience with the Emperor, who warned him that he could not expect any immediate support from the French Government, since such support might involve war with England. According to Lesseps, the Emperor went on to promise him that, if he were able to get the scheme onto a firm footing by himself, he would eventually get the support of the French Government.[36]

It was by now clear to Lesseps that, owing to British opposition, there was little likelihood of an Ottoman firman being granted except as a result of strong French diplomatic pressure. It was also clear to him that, as a result of this same British opposition, there was no immediate chance of this pressure being applied. This can hardly have come as a surprise to Lesseps. From the beginning he had taken the view that the application for the firman was merely a matter of courtesy and that, on the analogy of the railway, there was no need to await the firman before starting work. This view was based, not on any legal opinion (there is no evidence that he ever consulted one on the matter), but on an appreciation of the fact that he had to create a *fait accompli* in Egypt. In order to create this *fait accompli* he needed, first, to create sufficient public confidence in the canal as a technical and commercial proposition to enable him to float a company and raise the necessary capital, and, second, to maintain Mohammed Said's confidence by offsetting, as far as possible, the pressures against the canal being exercised on him, not only from London and Constantinople but also, to some extent, from members of his own family and entourage.

Both from the technical and commercial points of view Lesseps was on firm ground. The canal was almost certainly practicable technically and, once made, was almost certain to be advantageous commercially. It was a question of obtaining, setting out, and publicizing the relevant facts. So, during his visit to Europe in the summer of 1855, Lesseps set about forming a body of distinguished engineers of as many nationalities as possible to carry out a technical survey which could be used to demonstrate that the project was technically and commercially valid. This body, which described itself rather pompously as the International Scientific Commission, consisted of four Englishmen, four Frenchmen, an Austrian, a Prussian, a Dutchman, a Russian, an Italian, and a Spaniard. The Austrian representative was Negrelli who, it will be remembered, had previously been a member of the Société d'Etudes and a leader of one of the Société's investigation teams which had gone to Egypt in 1847.[37]

The first meeting of the commission was held in Paris on October 30th. Present at the meeting were Linant and Mougel, the French Director of Roads and Bridges in Egypt. These two French engineers had been sent

over to France by Mohammed Said at Lesseps' request and were thereafter to act in the capacity of liaison officers between the Egyptian Government and Lesseps. On November 6th the members of the commission,
together with Lesseps, Linant, and Mougel, sailed from Marseille for
Alexandria. In Egypt the commission was warmly received and hospitably
entertained by Mohammed Said, who appears to have paid all the expenses
incurred by the commission. After a holiday trip by Nile to Upper Egypt,
the members of the commission arrived at Suez on December 15th, started
their survey of the isthmus on December 21st and completed it on December
31st. On January 2nd, after this somewhat summary investigation, the
commission made a preliminary Report to the Viceroy[38] in which they
stated that "the route via the Nile from Suez to Alexandria is impracticable
both from the economic and the technical points of view," that the direct
route "only presented the ordinary difficulties attendant on the creation of
a port at either end," that the port at the Pelusium, or Mediterranean, end
should be located about twenty-eight kilometers west of the location previously recommended by Linant, and that the whole cost of construction
would not exceed 200 million francs.

The only original investigation undertaken for the commission seems to
have been done by a French engineer called Larousse, who was not a member of the commission at all and who was subsequently employed by the
Canal Company in the construction of Port Said. Larousse made a number
of soundings at the Pelusium end which led him to state that the entrance
to a port at this end would not, as had sometimes been alleged, become silted
up by Nile mud discharged at the time of flood from the Damietta branch
of the Nile. His findings led the commission to recommend the only variation they made in Linant's plan. Otherwise they seem to have adopted
Linant's conclusions—including his very optimistic cost estimate—without
any independent investigation.

The commission published its full report at the end of 1856.[39] They recommended the construction of a canal, 147 kilometers in length (as compared
with the 400 kilometers by the indirect route recommended by Talabot),
running direct from the Red Sea to the Mediterranean. The recommended
route, which, except at the northern end, was the same as Linant's, was
from Suez to the Bitter Lakes by a channel twenty kilometers long, through
the Bitter Lakes, which would be filled by gravity with seawater from the
Red Sea, from the Bitter Lakes to Lake Timsah by cutting a passage
through the Serapeum shelf, through Lake Timsah to Lake Ballah by cutting
through the Jisr shelf, through Lake Ballah to Qantara, and from Qantara
through Lake Manzala to the Mediterranean. Lake Timsah and Lake Bal-

lah, both of which were dry, would be filled by gravity with seawater from the Mediterranean. The commission recommended that the canal should have a minimum depth of 8 meters along its whole length, and a breadth of 80 meters at the surface and 44 meters at the bottom, with some stretches having a width of 100 meters at the surface and 64 meters at the botom to allow for sand erosion.

The contents of the preliminary report were immediately given the widest publicity with a view to refuting the British Government's contention that the project was technically impracticable. On January 5th, a few days after the publication of the preliminary report, the Second Concession granted by the Viceroy to Lesseps was published[40] together with the Statutes of the Company to be formed.[41]

The new Concession, which was a much more detailed document than the First Concession, in addition to repeating the principal provisions of the First Concession, provided, *inter alia:* (*a*) that the canal should be a direct cut between the Red Sea and the Mediterranean; (*b*) that there should be a navigable freshwater canal connecting the Nile with Lake Timsah and running parallel to the whole length of the Maritime Canal; (*c*) that Lesseps should be president of the Company for the first ten years after completion of the canal; (*d*) that the annexed Statutes of the Company were approved; (*e*) that at least four-fifths of the workers employed on the construction of the canal should be Egyptian; (*f*) that the Egyptian Government should give the Company, free of tax, the use of all public lands necessary for the construction of the canal and its dependencies, and that it should also give the Company, free of tax for the first ten years, the use of all public land brought into cultivation as a result of the Company's operations; (*g*) that *"sous la réserve de la ratification de SMI le Sultan"* the canal and its ports should be open to merchant ships of all nationalities without discrimination.

A Note at the end of the document, signed on the same day as the Concession itself, read: "The Concession given to the Compagnie Universelle du Canal de Suez must be ratified by His Imperial Majesty the Sultan. I give you this true copy in order that you may proceed to the formation of the Company. As to the work of cutting through the Isthmus, it may be started only after I have received the authority of the Sublime Porte." (As in the codicil to the First Concession, a careful distinction was drawn between the ratification of the Concession by the Sultan, and the "authorization of the Sublime Porte" which would enable the work of construction to proceed.)

There are some interesting differences between the First and Second Concessions:

a) In the Second Concession the Company was committed to the direct route along the approximate line set out by the International Commission, while in the First Concession the choice of route had been left open.

b) In the Second Concession it was provided that the Company would themselves fix the Canal dues up to a maximum of 10 francs per ton, while in the First Concession it had been provided that dues should be fixed in agreement between the Egyptian Government and the Company.

c) The First Concession had been for a period of ninety-nine years without provision for renewal. The Second Concession was also for ninety-nine years but with a provision for renewal subject to an increased "take" by the Egyptian Government.

d) The Second Concession provided that Lesseps should be president for ten years from the time that the canal was opened, while the First Concession provided that the president should be nominated by the Egyptian Government. (The alteration was presumably made to safeguard Lesseps against the possibility of a "take-over bid.")

e) The First Concession made provision for fortifications to be erected by the Egyptian Government at their own charge. The Second Concession made no mention of fortifications.

f) The First Concession provided that the list of founder-members who, by their work, their studies, their *soins,* or their capital, had contributed to the interests of the Company before its formation, should be approved by the Viceroy. The Second Concession provided that this list, consisting of those who, by their work, their studies, or their capital, had contributed to the interests of the Company before its formation, should be drawn up (*arrêté*) by the Viceroy. (This was presumably to prevent Lesseps from being pestered by people for founder shares. The omission in the Second Concession of the *soins* qualification is a nice touch.)

The Statutes provided that the capital of the Company was to be fixed at 200 million francs (corresponding to the cost estimate of the International Scientific Commission who had taken it from Linant) divided into 400,000 shares of 500 francs each; that each 25 shares entitled the holder to one vote at a general meeting, but that no one shareholder could have more than 10 votes irrespective of the number of shares held (another safeguard against the possibility of a "take-over bid"); and that the Company's *"siège social"* would be in Alexandria and its legal domicile in Paris.

The effect of this was that while disputes between shareholders, and between shareholders and the Company, were subject to French jurisdiction, disputes between the Company and a third party would have been subject to Egyptian jurisdiction had it not been for the existence of the "capitulations" treaties in Egypt. Under these treaties, at that time and until the establishment of the Mixed Courts in 1875, the only recognized methods of jurisdiction in respect of a dispute originating in Egypt between a foreign company or individual and another (whether Egyptian or foreign) were either (*a*) arbitration or (*b*) a hearing before the defendant's court, which, in the case of a foreign national, meant his consular court. Another point of uncertainty under the Statutes was the Company's position in the event of a dispute between the Company and the Egyptian Government. Since, in the event, the Egyptian Government was to become a shareholder, was such a dispute to be regarded as a dispute between shareholders, and so subject to French jurisdiction, even though the dispute had nothing to do with the shareholding, or was it to be regarded as a dispute between the Company and a third party? When the great dispute about compensation arose in 1863 between the Egyptian Government and the Company, both sides agreed to arbitration.

Simultaneously with his arrangements for the International Commission and for the drafting of the Statutes and the Second Concession, Lesseps launched and was for many years to sustain an extremely well-managed and almost worldwide propaganda campaign in support of the canal project with the object of offsetting the British Government's opposition by stressing not only the technical practicability and commercial advantages of the project but also its value from the wider aspects of human progress and international friendship. Lesseps sounded the keynote of this propaganda in a letter which he wrote to Richard Cobden, the great English free-trader, a few days after the signature of the First Concession, when he stated that his object, as a friend of peace and of the Anglo-French alliance was *"Aperire terram gentibus."*

Like all good propagandists, Lesseps knew how to be all things to all men. To the English business community he expatiated on the advantages which the existence of the canal would bring to the British Eastern trade; to the Austrians he stressed the wealth which the canal would bring to the declining port of Trieste; to the French bourgeoisie he harped on the theme of *gloire,* and traded on their robust anti-British sentiments; to the starry-eyed of all nations he talked of breaking barriers and facilitating communications; to believers in progress he announced the inevitability of progress; to the Pope he held out hopes of assisting missionary endeavor; to the Muslims of Turkey he boasted of how the canal would cheapen the cost of the Pilgrimage to Mecca; he warned Mohammed Said and the Sultan that if they did not do it of their own free will somebody else would sooner or later do it by force. A regular journal was issued and distributed in several languages. What we should now call "handouts" were sent to newspapers and magazines all over the world. It was perhaps the first example of a really worldwide propaganda campaign undertaken for a commercial purpose. It was still possible to oppose the canal; it was no longer possible to ignore it.

All this cost money. It appears that many of the preliminary expenses of the canal, including the cost of the International Commission, were paid by Mohammed Said. At the beginning of 1858, Green, the acting British consul general, wrote that he had evidence that the Viceroy was paying £20,000 a year to the foreign press for pro-canal propaganda.[42] Later Green reported that the Viceroy had told him that he was paying Lesseps 30,000 francs a month to cover the expenses of *L'Isthme de Suez,* the propaganda journal being published by Lesseps.[43] In addition there was the money contributed by some of the founder-members. Describing the role of the founder-members at the beginning of 1855, Lesseps wrote, "You know that I have chosen a certain number of friends who, in contributing Fcs. 5,000 each for the sole object of ensuring the success of the enterprise, will provide a sum of money to cover the initial expenses."[44] In April, 1855, Lesseps, in a letter to Mohammed Said, wrote: "Your Highness has already approved a first list of sixty founder-members. Having agreed that I shall add to this list the names of those in Europe and America who have helped to launch the Company, Your Highness has indicated that the total number of founder-members should, if possible, not exceed 100."[45] In a letter dated June 18, 1885, Lesseps wrote a circular letter to founder-members calling on them for their subscriptions of 5,000 francs per share.[46]

The total number of founder-shareholders, when the list was finally approved by the Viceroy at the end of 1860 and confirmed by the Conseil d'Administration early in 1861,[47] amounted to 170. They consisted of Lesseps himself, Ruyssenaers, Linant, and Mougel, plus eighty-nine others who had contributed funds and seventy-seven who had helped in other ways. One thousand shares were issued. The largest single founder-shareholders— Lesseps himself, Ruyssenaers, Linant, and Mougel—had twenty shares each.[48] Although these shares became very profitable for their holders after the canal had become established as a commercial success, there is no evidence, and no serious possibility, that the allocation of founder shares had any important effect on the political fortunes of the canal. At the time of allocation the value of these shares was too problematical for them to have been used as bribes on the sort of scale which would have been necessary for the purpose. The great, and seemingly unnecessary, secrecy which was always shown by the Company, and by the French Courts,[49] over the names of those to whom the founder shares were allocated has excited suspicions which are almost certainly unjustified. Historians are always apt to suspect the existence of a Bluebeard's Chamber behind a locked door.

There was one more necessary Concession which had to be obtained from the Viceroy before the canal could be regarded as a practicable proposition. As we have seen, the First and Second Concessions provided that all the necessary works of construction should be undertaken by the Company, and the Second Concession provided that four-fifths of the workers employed should be Egyptians. But there was nothing in either Concession specifying how this Egyptian labor was to be obtained. Before the construction of the Sweet Water Canal from the Nile, the isthmus was practically uninhabited except for the fishermen on Lake Manzala and for a few wandering Bedu tribesmen. There was little fresh water and, consequently, no cultivation. There was no possibility of recruiting sufficient labor locally. And there was little possibility of tempting any large number of voluntary Egyptian workers from the Nile Valley. The nature of Egypt's agriculture imposed on most of Egypt's peasants the necessity of particularly intensive work, for, apart from the sowing, tending, and harvesting of crops, irrigation canals and drains had continually to be dug, dredged, and maintained, flood banks built, manned, and kept in repair, and so on. This was particularly so in the Delta where the perennial irrigation introduced in the time of Mohammed Ali meant that two, and sometimes three, crops a year were harvested from one plot of intensively irrigated land. The Egyptian peasant was, moreover, by tradition and temperament, greatly averse to prolonged absences from his village, where he needed continually to safeguard his rights and those of his family in the endemic local feuds about land, water, and other matters which were, and are, a characteristic feature of Egyptian village life.

Labor for public works, and soldiers for the army, traditionally consisted of a *corvée,* or drafts of forced labor, pressed into service by the village headmen under the orders of the Government. When it was a question of raising a *corvée* for local works—such as flood protection, the digging or dredging of irrigation canals, and so on—which were obviously necessary in the interests of the peasants themselves, there was little resentment, particularly as the work was usually done at slack seasons of the year and did not take the peasants far from their villages. But when a *corvée* was raised for some distant public work which had no direct interest for the Upper Egypt peasantry on whom the burden of such *corvées* usually fell—such as the Mahmudieh Canal linking the Nile with Alexandria constructed in 1819, or the Cairo-Alexandria and Cairo-Suez railways—agriculture suffered and methods of coercion had to be employed both to transport the men to the place of work and to make them work when they got there. The usual method of coercion was the *courbash,* a rawhide whip wielded by the overseers on the backs of the wretched laborers. It is no great exaggeration to say that the modernization of Egypt was, to a large extent, achieved by means of those twin methods of coercion—the *corvée* and the *courbash.*

In the local circumstances it was certain that the only way of recruiting labor on the scale required would be by means of a *corvée.* Such a *corvée* would have to be raised by the Egyptian Government. In spite of the hardship and resentment involved, there was nothing unusual about this. Only a year or two before, large *corvées* of workers from Upper Egypt had been employed on the construction of the Alexandria-Cairo Railway. In 1819 Mohammed Ali had used large *corvées* to dig the Mahmudieh Canal. But both these works had been undertaken directly by the Egyptian Government and not by a foreign concessionary company. In the case of the Suez Canal the supply of labor would have to be ensured by an agreement between the Company and the Egyptian Government. Such an agreement, if incorporated into either of the Concessions, or into any published document, would have provided the opponents of the scheme with a valuable weapon of attack, particularly from the country which had, not long since, abolished slavery in its own West Indian plantations and where there was a strong and active public opinion campaigning against the slave trade in various parts of the world.

The agreement arrived at was dated July 20, 1856, and issued by the Viceroy in the form of a decree[50] based on a draft submitted to him by Lesseps.[51] This decree provided (*a*) that "the workers employed by the Company will be supplied by the Egyptian Government, in accordance with its requirements and in accordance with the requests of its chief engineers; (*b*) that workers should be paid at a rate of from two and a half to three piastres a day plus rations to the value of one piastre a day (a piastre was worth about five cents); (*c*) that the number of workers employed should be fixed after taking into account the seasonal requirements of agriculture: (*d*) that the Company should be responsible for the housing and hospitalization of workers and for their traveling expenses from (but not back to) their homes to their places of work; (*e*) that the tools for the workers—such as picks, baskets, and blasting powder—should be provided by the Egyptian Government to the Company at cost price."

On the face of it, and in spite of the saving clause about agriculture, the decree appeared to commit the government to supply on demand all the labor which the Company, in its own estimation, might require. The consular corps do not, at the time, appear to have been informed of this agreement, either officially or unofficially. Nor does it appear to have been published in any other way.

NOTES

1. Sabatier–Drouyn de Lhuys 2.12.54. CP 25.
2. Drouyn de Lhuys–Sabatier 2.1.55. M. & D., Vol. 13.
3. Drouyn de Lhuys–Benedetti. M. & D., Vol. 13. The copy of the dispatch is not dated but appears to have been sent off at about the same time as the dispatch to Sabatier as per Note 2. Although it was some weeks before HMG gave their ambassador at Constantinople unequivocal instructions to oppose the canal, it does not appear that HMG at any time made any formal "nonintervention agreement" with the French Government. The expression *"en quelque sorte"* must refer to some verbal conversation with Cowley, the British ambassador in Paris.
4. This figure was presumably mentioned by Lesseps to Bruce. It does not appear in the text of the Concession.
5. Bruce–Clarendon 3.12.54. FO 78/1156.
6. Cowley–Clarendon 26.12.54. FO 78/1156.
7. Clarendon–Bruce 9.1.55. FO 78/1156.
8. Sultan Abdul-Mejid who died in July, 1861, and was succeeded by Sultan Abdul-Aziz.
9. The Sublime Porte was the name given by Europeans to the Ottoman Government as distinct from the Seraglio, which denoted the Sultan's Household (cf. Whitehall and Buckingham Palace). It consisted principally of the Grand Vizier (or Prime Minister), the Reis Effendi (Foreign Minister), the Seraskier (Minister of War), and the Defterdar (Treasurer). These ministers and others made up the Divan (Cabinet) which, on important occasions, was sometimes joined by the Shaikh-ul-Islam (principal religious dignitary). After the death of Sultan Mahmud II, the center of power moved away from the Seraglio to the Sublime Porte, and was to remain there for the next forty years until the accession of Sultan Abdul Hamid.
10. Minute in Palmerston's handwriting on Stratford–Clarendon 22.2.55. FO 78/1156.
11. Minute in Palmerston's handwriting on Stratford–Clarendon 26.2.55. FO 78/1156.
12. Cowley–Clarendon 19.1.55. FO 78/1156. Bruce, in his reply to Drouyn de Lhuys's accusation, stated, rather disingenuously, that, in his conversations with the Viceroy, he had "steadfastly refrained from alluding to the position of Egypt with a navigable canal through it and a French province in the hands of a French Company hemmed in between Algiers on the one side and the Maronite population of Syria on the other" (Bruce–Clarendon 20.2.55. FO 78/1156).
13. Stratford–Clarendon 11.1.55. FO 78/1156.
14. Stratford–Clarendon 12.2.55. FO 78/1156.
15. Clarendon–Stratford 9.3.55. FO 78/1156.
16. Stratford–Clarendon 12.2.55. FO 78/1156. Later, however, Stratford was to complain that "M. Benedetti is actively engaged in promoting the views of M. de Lesseps." See Stratford–Clarendon 13.4.55. FO 78/1156.
17. Or, as Lesseps himself put it, he recommended to Mohammed Said. Journal, I, 107.
18. As late as April, 1855, the French Government was uncertain whether the opposition to the canal manifested in Constantinople represented the official policy of HMG or the prejudices of Stratford de Redcliffe. See Drouyn de Lhuys–Sabatier 24.4.55. CP 26.
19. Stratford–Clarendon 26.2.55. FO 78/1156.

20. Journal, I, 140.
21. Clarendon–Stratford 29.3.55. FO 78/1156.
22. Clarendon–Stratford 6.6.55. FO 78/1156. See also Note 29 below.
23. For text of these letters, see CP 26.
24. Lesseps, on hearing the news, wrote to his brother Théodore on 6.5.55: "Whatever the official reason given for his fall, it was really due to the discovery of his intrigue against France in the matter of the canal. Thus, to start our enterprise (*pour commencer la navigation*) a statesman is thrown into the sea; maybe others will follow him" (Journal, I, 193). In fact, Rashid was to climb back on board before the end of the year and become Grand Vizier again.
25. Edgar-Bonnet, *Ferdinand de Lesseps,* I, 259.
26. Stratford–Clarendon 13.4.55. FO 78/1156.
27. Cowley had previously been ambassador in Constantinople.
28. Cowley–Clarendon 4.6.55. FO 78/1156.
29. Clarendon–Cowley 18.6.55. FO 78/1156. This was presumably the dispatch referred to at the end of Clarendon–Stratford of 6.6.55 when it was stated that HMG's views were being communicated to the French Government.
30. Walewski–Persigny 21.6.55. M. & D., Vol. 13.
31. Cowley–Clarendon 30.6.55. FO 78/1156.
32. Cowley–Clarendon 4.7.55. FO 78/1156.
33. Note from the Court of Versailles to Walewski 17.6.55. M. & D., Vol. 13.
34. Lesseps to Empress Eugénie 15.7.55. M. & D., Vol. 13.
35. Journal, I, 250.
36. Journal, I, 334. In Lesseps' account of this audience, given in a letter to Negrelli dated 19.11.55, the Emperor told him: "Vous averz bien fait de ne pas initier les gouvernements á votre entreprise. Vous ferez bien de ne pas sortir de cette voie. Si je vous soutiendrai maintenant ce serait la guerre avec l'Angleterre. Mais quand les intérêts des capitaux européens seront engagés tout le monde vous soutiendra et moi le premier."
37. A letter from Lesseps to Rendel, one of the English members (who, incidentally, was unable to accompany the commission to Egypt owing to illness), makes it clear (Journal, I, 246) that the members of the commission would be inscribed as founder-members of the Canal Company. The terms of both Concessions provided that 10 percent of the net profits of the Company should be allotted to the founder-members. It was certainly a curious way of securing the impartiality with which the commission was supposed to be vested.
38. J. Charles-Roux, *L'Isthme* . . . , Vol. I, Annex No. 14.
39. *Ibid.,* I, 247 *et seq.*
40. *Ibid.,* Vol. I, Annex No. 15.
41. *Ibid.,* Vol. I. Annex No. 16.
42. Green–Hammond (U/S FO) 18.1.58. FO 78/1421.
43. Green–Clarendon 8.2.58. FO 78/1421.
44. Journal, I 158.
45. *Ibid.,* I, 189.
46. *Ibid.,* I, 207.
47. *Ibid.,* III, 417.
48. Edgar-Bonnet, *op. cit.,* I, 321.
49. In 1889, in the course of a lawsuit in a Paris Court about the ownership of some of the founder shares, the Court ordered the Company to produce a complete list of founder-share-holders. This was done, but the Court refused to allow the list to be published on the ground that it was *"le secret des familles."* See Crabites, *The Spoliation of Suez,* p. 89.
50. For text see J. Charles-Roux, *op cit.,* Vol. I, Annex No. 17.
51. Journal, I, 407.

CHAPTER *five*

The Formation of

the Company ॐ

⚜ LESSEPS had obtained all the required Concessions and agreements from Mohammed Said. The next step was to proceed with the formation of the Company and with the raising of the capital in order to be able to start work. But the ground was not yet ready. In spite of his public attitude that an Ottoman firman was not necessary and that all that was necessary in order to start work was the Sublime Porte's approval in principle which, he maintained, had already been received, Lesseps realized that it would be very desirable, if not quite essential, to obtain the Sultan's firman before appealing for capital.

In face of the official British hostility which, after second interviews with Palmerston and Clarendon in the summer of 1856, he recognized as permanent and inevitable, the direct methods he had employed in Constantinople during the winter of 1854–1855 were foredoomed to failure. He therefore devised a new strategy. He tried to secure the support of all the Great Powers except England, and particularly that of Austria, and to leave England in a minority of one in opposition to the canal. He tried to secure as much open support as possible in England in opposition to government policy, particularly among the merchant classes. He tried to squeeze as much active support and intervention as possible from the French Government in order at least to ensure that the Emperor would not be harassed into any overt declaration or act hostile to the canal. He tried to convince the Ottoman Government on the one hand that British opposition was primarily due to the influence of Stratford de Redcliffe and might not survive that ambassador's term of office, and on the other hand, that French support, although cloaked by the exigencies of the Franco-British alliance, was in fact much greater than the official attitude of the French ambassador might indicate, since the Emperor himself was interested in the project and wished to see it come to fruition as soon as possible. To this was added the hint that, if the firman was not forthcoming from Constantinople, the Viceroy might be encouraged by France to defy the Sultan and proceed with the canal without waiting for the firman.

In the playing of this complicated confidence trick, Lesseps relied on, or exploited, several persons and circumstances. In his dealings with Austria he seems to have relied principally on the services of the Baron de Bruck, Minister of Finance, who was a founder-member of the Company[1] and who was once referred to by Lesseps as *"notre illustre chef de file en Autriche."*[2] In England he relied on Sir Daniel Lange, who was his principal agent there, and on the powerful Eastern trading and shipping interests, which were in favor of the canal for commercial reasons and impatient with each successive government's political objections.[3] But Lesseps' principal weapon, apart from his own charm, plausibility, and pertinacity, appears to have been the Empress Eugénie. Although it is improbable that the Empress was able, or even willing, to exercise any very decisive influence on the Emperor with regard to the canal, the use which Lesseps made of his relationship to her (like all successful confidence men he was a great name dropper) in Constantinople, in Cairo, and even in Paris, helped him to give the impression that he enjoyed more official French support than in fact he did. In Constantinople and in Cairo particularly, it would have seemed highly unnatural if a relative of the Empress had not been able to rely on imperial backing for his commercial transactions.

In France too, Lesseps succeeded in obtaining another, scarcely less powerful, and much more active, patron in Prince Jérôme Napoleon, son of Napoleon I's brother, the King of Westphalia, and first cousin of Napoleon III. On the formation of the Company in November, 1858, Prince Napoleon was to accept the title of its "protector," and thereafter was always prepared to champion its interests, certainly in public and probably in private, with his usual vigor and indiscretion. Prince Napoleon was a florid, jolly man who, while remaining on good terms with his imperial cousin, liked to use his position to play the democrat and the demagogue, the good honest patriot with no nonsense about him. In spite of being something of a mountebank, he was a man of influence in the Second Empire, and his known support of the canal project was an important factor in helping to create the impression that Lesseps enjoyed secret but powerful support in high places.

When Lesseps arrived in Paris in March, 1856, delegates from all over Europe were assembling for the Peace Conference at the end of the Crimean War. Aali Pasha, the Turkish Reis Effendi, soon to be Grand Vizier, was there, telling the British that the Sublime Porte was against the canal, but was being bullied by France; and the French that they favored the canal but were frightened of England. He probably expressed Ottoman policy with accuracy when he told Cowley that

he was quite aware of the object of the Pasha of Egypt. Said Pasha's . . . real aim was to establish his own independence. At the same time [Aali] said that it would be very unwise on the part of the Porte peremptorily to refuse its sanction. . . . He thought that the object of the Porte might be attained by evading the question or rather by attaching such conditions to its sanction as would induce Said Pasha himself to abandon the scheme . . . he thought for example that a demand might be made that the Canal should not be undertaken without the consent of the European Powers and that it should be placed in some way under their guarantee, that the Porte should have some control over the working of the Canal and that the fortifications to be erected on it should be garrisoned by Turkish troops.[4]

Lesseps saw in the Conference a possible opportunity for France to isolate England by obtaining a declaration in favor of the canal from the other Powers and from Turkey, and was even hopeful of having some reference to the neutrality of the canal inserted in the Peace Treaty. He thought it possible that he might get the Emperor, in the flush of victory, to abandon his solicitude for British prejudices, and to take some initiative. After all he had, to all appearance, restored France to a position in Europe which she had not enjoyed for over forty years. In a letter to the Emperor dated March 29th Lesseps wrote:

"The Porte, anxious to confirm to the Viceroy the permission which it has already expressed in principle, is waiting for the French Government to safeguard them from the menaces of the British ambassador by making known their approval officially. As things stand at present it is for Your Majesty to choose the appropriate moment for overcoming the resistance of the British Government." He went on to quote Thouvenel, the French ambassador at Constantinople, as having written that British opposition at Constantinople could be overcome only if the French ambassador were officially instructed to make a formal request for the firman to be granted.[5]

While in Paris, Lesseps discussed the canal project with Count de Buol, the Austrian Foreign Minister. De Buol was sympathetic but made it clear that nothing was to be expected from his government as long as the British Government remained hostile. It was the same old story. He received greater encouragement from Metternich, the veteran Austrian statesman, then in retirement. Metternich suggested a formula separating the construction of the canal which, thought Metternich, could legally be done without Ottoman consent, from the operation of the canal, which would necessitate a Convention of Neutrality guaranteed by all the European Powers. Lesseps at first was enthusiastic but later realized that this plan too would founder on the fact of British opposition. (Lesseps always attached great importance to obtaining official Austrian support for the canal.) Austria was the only great European Power, with the exception of France and Great Britain, which had a direct interest in the canal, and its official support for it would have had a great effect on French and even, possibly, on British policy in the matter.

Any hope of this support was finally extinguished by Napoleon III's "war of liberation" against Austria on behalf of Piedmont in 1859. But, even before that, the Austrian Government had, privately, made its position clear. In a dispatch from Vienna in September, 1857, the British ambassador wrote that the Austrian Government "had decided not to press the question of the Suez Canal ... not desiring to take any measures which might put them in opposition to Her Majesty's Government upon any question of importance."[6] Clarendon, minuting a dispatch from the British consul general in Egypt, written at about the same time, wrote: "The Austrian Minister has read to me a dispatch stating that the Austrian Government was highly favourable to the Suez Canal yet, knowing that Her Majesty's Government was opposed to the scheme, had instructed the Internuncio not to give support to Lesseps when he arrived at Constantinople as the Canal ought not to be proceeded with until the Powers of Europe interested had come to an agreement on the subject."[7]

During the spring and summer of 1856, Lesseps paid several visits to London and had another interview with Palmerston. (He saw Clarendon in Paris.) According to Lesseps the English statesman "used the most contradictory, the most incoherent and the most violent language about the canal that it is possible to imagine."[8] Apart from this, however, he seems to have derived some encouragement from the generally friendly feeling displayed toward France in the aftermath of a victorious war in which the two countries had been allies, and from the contacts which he made with British businessmen and technicians. He was entertained at a banquet by MacLean, one of the British representatives on the Scientific Commission, and was received in audience by Queen Victoria and Prince Albert.

But, in spite of all this activity, nothing was really being accomplished. There was no reference to the canal in the Peace Treaty. Thouvenel received no clear instructions from his government. And, worst of all, Mohammed Said was weakening in face of British pressure, the warnings of his entourage, an ominous silence from Constantinople, and the equivocations of the French consul general.

On August 12th Lesseps, in a letter to the Emperor, wrote that Mohammed

Said, in an attempt to induce the Porte to expedite the issue of the firman, had offered to share with them the 15 percent of the net profits of the Canal Company reserved to the Egyptian Government under the terms of the two Concessions, adding that, although the Viceroy understood that French official intervention was difficult owing to the complexities of the international situation, he was finding himself increasingly in need of French support as a result of the British pressure to which he was being subjected.[9]

On August 28th Lesseps wrote to Thouvenel that "it is evident that, if you are convinced that the Porte will only give its firman to the Viceroy after having obtained the consent of England, the expedient in question [that is, the Metternich formula] falls to the ground (*péche par la base*) unless you receive instructions to support the Viceroy's request. It is on that point that my efforts have been concentrated during my stay in Paris."[10]

On October 12th Lesseps addressed another letter to the Emperor complaining that Stratford de Redcliffe was not acting in accordance with the understanding (which Lesseps, evidently and erroneously, believed to exist) that the British and French ambassadors should observe neutrality vis-à-vis the Porte in respect of the canal, and stating (correctly) that the British ambassador was at that moment negotiating with the Porte for a concession for a railway down the Euphrates Valley to the Persian Gulf.[11] He went on to suggest that the French Government should use this British activity as an occasion to instruct Thouvenel to exert a similar activity in favor of the canal project.[12]

All was in vain. On November 22nd Lesseps arrived back in Cairo to find his patron depressed, nervous, and discouraged. Weary of the strains and stresses to which he was subjected in Alexandria and Cairo, he was just about to undertake a long-cherished project and make an extensive tour of his dominions in the Sudan. He invited Lesseps to accompany him. Lesseps, always glad of occasions when he could get Mohammed Said to himself, and exert once more the remarkable influence which he had over him, gladly agreed. Their tour lasted for nearly three months.

Just before their departure, Sabatier wrote a dispatch describing an audience he had had with the Viceroy in which "without abandoning the reserve I have been instructed to maintain on the subject, I took the opportunity of using the verbal instruction which Your Excellency recently gave me in Paris to inform the Viceroy of the sympathies of the Emperor and the French Government for the canal project."[13] As we shall see, Sabatier's remarks to the Viceroy soon came to the ears of Bruce and, in due course, produced a protest from Cowley to the French Government. Walewski, apparently irritated by Sabatier's indiscretion, wrote an angry dispatch in which he warned Sabatier that "the Government of the Emperor has no reason to modify the position which it has taken up in this matter and I recommend you to act exclusively in accordance with the written instructions which have been addressed to you. You must have misunderstood me if you thought you were authorized to communicate my personal views to the Viceroy. I have been informed that M. de Lesseps is making use of the Emperor's name to the Viceroy to try and speed up the accomplishment of his project. I can hardly believe that this information is correct since the Viceroy surely understands that you are the only person in Egypt entitled to communicate to the Egyptian Government the views of His Majesty and of his Government."[14]

What had happened was that Cowley had been complaining to Walewski about Sabatier who, Bruce alleged, had, together with Lesseps, been trying to persuade the Viceroy that the Emperor was personally interested in the canal.[15] Clarendon instructed Cowley to ask the Emperor to "prevent them from putting forward His Majesty as an advocate of a scheme in which no French interest is concerned and which His Majesty's Government considers objectionable, thus creating an antagonism between British and French influence in Egypt . . . it is very unexpected that M. Sabatier should be urging on the Pasha to fresh and new expenses which are wholly unnecessary and which tend still further to increase his embarrassments."[16] In his reply Cowley stated that he had had an audience with the Emperor in which he had conveyed the contents of Clarendon's dispatch:

His Majesty replied that he had no knowledge whatever of the proceedings of MM. Sabatier and Lesseps. He did not even know where the latter was; he promised however that they should be written to on the subject. I should however deceive Your Lordship if I held out expectations that the Emperor will seriously interfere to put a stop to this gentleman's proceedings. The question of the Suez Canal is evidently one on which His Majesty does not like to converse and although he agreed politely on the conclusions which I submitted to him the promises which His Majesty made were not given with that warmth which would justify my putting any faith in their serious execution.[17]

A few days later Cowley reported that he had spoken to Walewski and asked him to tell the Viceroy that there was no foundation in the statement made to him that the Emperor took any interest in M. de Lesseps' success. Walewski told Cowley that he had no control over Lesseps but that he had "warned Lesseps that he was not to expect any countenance or assistance from the French Government . . . so long as the scheme was opposed by Her Majesty's Government. The French Government felt that Her Majesty's Government were masters of the ground at Constantinople and that they did not wish to come into discussion or collision with Her Majesty's Government on such matters." Cowley added that Walewski "was not very enthusiastic in his opposition to the Canal project."[18]

On January 12th Stratford de Redcliffe reported to Clarendon that Rashid Pasha (who had returned to office as Grand Vizier in October, 1856) had told him that "nothing had of late been said on the subject either by the French Embassy or by the Pasha of Egypt and that he was led to believe that the matter had dropped."[19]

During March, Bruce reported that Sabatier was adopting a "correct attitude" about the canal and that the Viceroy seemed to be cooling off.[20] This was just after the Viceroy's return from the Sudan.

On April 3rd Stratford de Redcliffe wrote to Bruce that "I have put the Grand Vizier confidentially in possession of all such points of information derived from your correspondence as may help to confirm his unfavourable opinion of the projected Canal. He is personally averse . . . but what we have to apprehend is the effect of strong pressure from France, especially from the Emperor himself. . . . Though not supported openly by the French Government Lesseps will probably make it appear that the rejection of his plan would be extremely unpalatable at the Tuileries."[21]

Three days later Stratford de Redcliffe was more optimistic. "It is to be expected that Lesseps will leave no stone unturned to gain his point. With Rashid Pasha at the head of the Administration I cannot entertain any serious apprehension of his succeeding as far as obtaining the Sultan's consent, but I doubt whether a decided refusal will be given."[22]

On May 7th Cowley reported that Walewski had told him that he had instructed Sabatier to tell the Viceroy to drop the idea of the canal for the time being for fear of embarrassing France's relations with Britain.[23]

On June 2nd the Foreign Office told Stratford de Redcliffe that "with reference to the report published by Lesseps in relation to the employment of forced labour in constructing his projected Canal[24] I have to state to Your Excellency that the injuries resulting to agriculture from attempting the plan should alone prevent the Porte from permitting it to be carried into effect."[25]

Two months later Cowley warned the Foreign Office that "the irritation here against Her Majesty's Government on account of the opposition shewn by them to the whole scheme is very great."[26] (Palmerston, minuting this dispatch, wrote, "Might it not be well to ask M. Walewski whether they think that such an agitation as M. Lesseps proposes to get up throughout

France against England on the subject of the Suez Canal is likely to strengthen the alliance between the two countries?" To which Clarendon, referring to Lesseps' recent propaganda campaign in England, replied, "We never interfered with him when he agitated in England.")

During the early summer of 1857 Lesseps, starting with a meeting at Liverpool on April 29th and finishing with a meeting in London on June 24th, had been addressing a series of meetings arranged by Chambers of Commerce in many of the principal cities, and particularly the ports, of Great Britain. These meetings had attracted a good deal of interest and a certain amount of support, both in the press and elsewhere. There were several questions about the canal in the House of Commons to which Palmerston (Clarendon, the Foreign Secretary, was in the House of Lords, and Palmerston, the Prime Minister, was accustomed to answering questions on foreign policy in the Commons) replied with his usual violence. On July 7th, in reply to a question, he said that "Her Majesty's Government will certainly not use its influence with the Sultan to persuade him to permit the construction of this Canal because, over the last 15 years, Her Majesty's Government has used such influence as it has at Constantinople to prevent the execution of this project. It is an enterprise which, from the commercial point of view, can be classed as one of those bubble schemes which are offered to credulous speculators. . . . I am surprised that M. de Lesseps can believe that, as a result of a tour through the provincial cities of England, he can obtain English money for a project which is at all points contrary to British interests. But no doubt it is not necessary for the enterprise to be successful to enable M. de Lesseps and the other promoters to achieve their ends."[27]

On July 17th he was even more violent: "I think I am not far wrong in describing it as one of those schemes which are sometimes put forward to deceive English capitalists into parting with their money which, in the end, leaves the capitalists poorer as a result of having made others richer."[28] On August 23rd he said: "This Company, as I have so often said, is one of the most remarkable attempts at deception which have been seen in recent times. It is a complete hoax from beginning to end."

The canal was not, however, without support in the Commons, even from a most sober and responsible quarter. On August 14th Gladstone, from the front Opposition bench, warned the government against opposing, for selfish reasons, a project which was advantageous for the general interests of Europe, and said that by treating the matter as a political one the government was risking its friendly relationships with the European Powers and particularly with France.

From England, Lesseps went on to address a series of meetings all over France where, for the most part, he was received with great enthusiasm. He also received evidences of support from Austria where the egregious Baron de Bruck embarrassed his government by a speech at Trieste in which he said that "we must not let a day pass without expressing the warmest wishes for the success of this noble idea. The opposition of one Government must not be allowed to prevent it from being accomplished."[29] A favorable message was also received from Pope Pius IX (who had apparently forgotten the reason for Lesseps' disgrace in 1849).

Opinion in England on the question of the canal was, during most of the years 1857–1858, affected by a serious mutiny which had broken out among native regiments in British India. Military reinforcements had to be sent to India from England by the long sea route via the Cape. Supporters of the canal pointed out how advantageous it would have been if it had been possible to send these reinforcements through a Suez Canal, if one had existed, since this would have taken about half the time. Opponents of the canal, on the other hand, held that the mutiny was a precise illustration of the possible danger which might arise from having a foreign Power with the canal at its disposal in possession of Egypt, since such a foreign Power would be able to use the canal for sending troops to Egypt while denying it to the British. Eventually, with the agreement of the Egyptian Government, some British military reinforcements were sent across Egypt by the overland route.

Throughout the spring and summer of 1857, Lesseps had been receiving agitated letters from Ruyssenaers, his representive in Egypt, indicating that the Viceroy was weakening in face of pressure both from the British and from his entourage, stressing the desirability of sustaining him by assurances of French official support, and imploring Lesseps to return to Egypt. Other associates advised him to remain in Paris and exercise his charm on the Tuileries. Yet others advised him to go to England in order to maintain the momentum of his propaganda drive which he had launched in the spring. Characteristically, Lesseps ignored all this advice and decided to go to Constantinople, which was the one place where he had not been advised to go. Thouvenel, immersed in negotiations with the Porte and with the British ambassador about the future of Moldavia and Wallachia, was nervous lest Lesseps' presence make these negotiations even more difficult.[30]

Nevertheless Lesseps, on October 20th, sent a letter to the Emperor through Prince Napoleon in which he told His Majesty that he was going to Constantinople to press for ratification and that he could count on the support of most European countries apart from France and Britain. "I am not asking the Emperor's government to take any initiative . . . but if, during my negotiations in Constantinople, as a Frenchman and as the concessionaire of an enterprise which is of interest to France, I find it necessary to claim the support of the French ambassador, as well as the support of the representatives of the other Powers, I hope that M. Thouvenel's protection will be forthcoming."[31] Prince Napoleon duly presented this letter to the Emperor and came back with a message that "His Majesty wishes to see this enterprise succeed and sees no objection to M. Thouvenel supporting it within the limits of the instructions he already has. He recommends prudence, and stresses that any serious difficulties with Britain must be avoided at all costs." Prince Napoleon added his own counsels of prudence and, in effect, advised Lesseps not to press the Porte too hard lest they fall down on the wrong side of the fence.[32] It was not very encouraging. However, he thanked the Prince for his advice and set off for Constantinople, arriving there during the course of December.

On Lesseps' departure for Constantinople, Walewski warned Thouvenel that he must not make any attempt to act as an intermediary between Lesseps and the Porte but that "if M. de Lesseps, who believes that he can count on the support of Austria, the United States and other Powers, asks for your support as a Frenchmen and as the concessionaire of a project in which considerable French interests are involved you are authorized to give him that support to the extent which you think fit."[33] There is no record of Thouvenel's reaction to these very equivocal instructions.

During Lesseps' stay in Constantinople a number of events occurred which, at first sight, seemed greatly to improve his prospects. In December, just about at the time of his arrival, Stratford de Redcliffe was relieved of his post as British ambassador and his long "reign" at Constantinople ended.[34] A few weeks later, in January, 1858, Rashid Pasha, the Grand Vizier, died suddenly. At about the same time an attempt by Orsini, an Italian revolutionary, to assassinate the French Emperor led to a furious outburst of French indignation against England on the ground that Orsini's plot had been prepared by Italian refugees taking advantage of England's traditional role as an asylum from Continental tyrants. Popular rage was shared to some extent by the French Government. British public opinion, in return, was roused against France. In February the Palmerston Administration, defeated in the Commons on an amendment which accused the Government of being too conciliatory toward France, resigned and was succeeded by a Conservative Administration, with Lord Derby as Prime Minister, Lord Malmesbury as Foreign Secretary, and Disraeli as Chancellor of the Exchequer and Leader in the Commons.

For a time Lesseps seems to have derived some encouragement from these events. Writing to his brother from Constantinople at the end of January, he expressed himself buoyantly, although in a style which must have alarmed those who were urging him to be cautious. "An ounce of fear is worth a ton of friendship. Imbued with this idea, I have always, in my negotiations in Constantinople, relied on the first. My weapons are either the fear of France or fear of seeing the whole question of the canal passing out of the hands of the Porte."[35]

This euphoric mood did not last. It was soon borne in on him that Britain's objection to the canal derived, not from the prejudices of individuals, such as Palmerston and Stratford de Redcliffe, but from basic conceptions of policy common to all governments of whatever political complexion. In fact, the removal of Stratford and Palmerston, by removing that element of violence and megalomania common to both, so far from weakening the British opposition, in some ways made it more formidable by making it appear more reasonable.

On New Year's Day, 1858, the Foreign Office, presumably nervous about Lesseps' activities in Constantinople, sent a dispatch to Alison (chargé d'affaires after Stratford's departure) stating: "If the Sultan were to consent to a scheme, the direct and obvious object of which would be to separate Egypt from Turkey, the Sultan must not expect that the maintenance of the integrity of the Ottoman Empire would thereafter be a principle to guide the policy of the Great Powers of Europe because the Sultan himself would have been a party to the setting aside of that principle."[36]

This was the most direct and obvious threat which the British Government had so far issued to the Porte on the subject of the canal. The Porte seems to have reacted fairly satisfactorily from the British point of view. On January 4th Alison was able to quote to the Foreign Office a report from Moore, the Embassy first secretary, which read: "The Grand Vizier being still ill, I communicated to the Minister for Foreign Affairs [Aali Pasha] Your Excellency's message and he has given me the formal assurance of the Sublime Porte that the Turkish Government will not give its consent to the construction of the Suez Canal until Her Majesty's Government sanctions that undertaking." That was all very well, but this assurance was not committed to writing by Aali Pasha, and the first secretary's report concluded: "Aali Pasha desired me to inform you that the Porte still withholds its consent to the construction of the Canal but that . . . he had been instructed by the Council [Divan] to draw up a statement setting forth the Porte's readiness to view the proposal in a favourable light on certain conditions only . . . this document would in the first instance be forwarded to Musurus [the Turkish ambassador in London] for communication to Her Majesty's Government . . . the intention of the Porte . . . is to declare itself opposed . . . and to guard its own interests for the future in the event of public opinion in England ultimately . . . modifying the views of Her Majesty's Government."[37]

When the Palmerston Government fell in February, the Ottoman Government was naturally anxious to be informed about the attitude of its successor toward the Canal since Lesseps was, equally naturally, insinuating that the change of government marked a change of British policy in respect of the canal.[38] The Foreign Office reply, communicated to Alison by cable on March 11th,[39] was quite unequivocal: "We entirely concur in the course followed by our predecessors with respect to the projected Canal and we put implicit trust in the personal assurance given by the Turkish Government that the consent of the Porte would never be given to the project until Her Majesty's Government had expressed their willingness to sanction it."[40]

The public tone of the new government, for which Disraeli was the principal spokesman on the subject of the canal, was, however, a good deal less violent than that of its predecessor. Replying to a Commons question on March 23rd, Disraeli stated that "the enterprise would be a vain one," but expressed the view that "the moment for a final verdict has not yet arrived." On June 1st there was, for the first time, a full-dress debate in the Commons on the subject on a motion by a private Member (Roebuck) calling on the government to cease its opposition to the canal. Speeches in favor of the canal were made by Lord John Russell (who was to change his mind later when he became Foreign Secretary) and by Gladstone, and against it by Disraeli, speaking for the government, and by Palmerston. Palmerston advanced all his usual arguments with all his customary violence. Disraeli, taking a subtler line, said that there was no reason to suppose that the Turkish Government needed any pressure from the British Government to induce them to oppose the scheme, and advised the House not to commit itself by any expression of approval for it. The Commons took Disraeli's advice, and the Roebuck motion was defeated by 290 votes to 62.[41]

The death of Rashid and the appointment of Aali Pasha as Grand Vizier was by no means a change for the better from Lesseps' point of view; nor was the appointment of Fuad Pasha (previously Seraskier, or War Minister) as Reis Effendi in place of Aali Pasha. These two men who were, between them, to be mainly responsible for Turkish foreign policy for the next ten years or so, were well in advance of the average level of Ottoman statesmen in probity, in intelligence, and in energy. Moreover, Aali Pasha held strong views about the desirability of effectively subordinating the Pasha of Egypt to Ottoman suzerainty, and suspected that Mohammed Said was using the canal scheme specifically, and French support generally, as a means of loosening the bonds which attached him to his suzerain.

It did not appear that the antagonism growing up between Britain and France as a result of the Orsini attempt and its aftermath would have any effect in inducing the Emperor to defy Britain over the question of the canal. Indeed, during the spring of 1858, public opinion in France seems to have been thoroughly frightened at the prospect of war with England. Barthélemy St. Hilaire, Lesseps' principal associate in Paris, warned Lesseps that, in view of the effect of the war scares on the money market, there could be no worse time for raising capital.[42]

During the weeks and months he was in Constantinople, alternately encouraged by changes and discouraged by finding that *"plus ça change plus c'est la même chose,"* Lesseps, in spite of St. Hilaire's warnings, was gradually coming to the conclusion that, unless the whole scheme was to fall to the ground through sheer inanition, he would have to proceed with the formation of the Company and with the raising of capital without waiting either for the Sultan's firman or for any more positive evidence of the Emperor's support. It was now nearly four years since he had obtained the First Concession and nearly three years since he had obtained the Second Concession and the Viceroy's approval for the Statutes of the Company. It now seemed to him that, the longer he waited, the more difficulties would accumulate, and that the only thing to do was to go boldly forward and create a *fait accompli* which, in the end, the Porte and everyone else would have to recognize and accommodate themselves to.

The prospects were not encouraging. In the absence of the Sultan's firman, and in face of British hostility, it was unlikely that Lesseps would get the support of any of the great banking houses. For the same reasons he was unlikely to be able to raise very much private capital in any European country except France. And even in France the big capitalists tended to be shy of the scheme. In the event Lesseps was to get just over half the capital from small French investors in cash and nearly all the rest from Mohammed Said in half-promises.

On his way to Paris and London in June, Lesseps had an interview in Vienna with Sir Henry Bulwer, who was on his way to Constantinople as the new British ambassador. He told him that he would only seek the assistance of the French Government "if I can establish that I am being deprived of my rights as a result of the irregular actions of another government."[43] This was the first meeting between the two men who, during subsequent years of opposition, were to develop a warm personal regard for one another.

After short visits to Paris and London, Lesseps returned to Constantinople via Egypt at the end of July. On August 10th Bulwer wrote to the Foreign Office that "M. Thouvenel and M. de Lesseps have both held to me language in conformity with what M. Walewski states, namely that the French Government took a certain interest in the project but that they would employ no diplomatic influence to further it. M. Lesseps however confides to private friends that the Emperor has a warm personal feeling on the subject, leaving it to be supposed that he [the Emperor] would be highly gratified if the scheme were carried into effect."[44]

On August 18th Lesseps, still in Constantinople, wrote to St. Hilaire that he had finally decided to come to Paris to arrange for the formation of the Company, that he had consulted Thouvenel about this and that Thouvenel had approved of it.[45] St. Hilaire, however, did not approve, and the formation of the Company marked the end of his close association with Lesseps. Other associates, too, disapproved, and Lesseps' decision to proceed against the advice of so many of his colleagues marked a fairly decisive break with the past.[46]

There are many stories, most if not all originating from Lesseps himself, about how he was offered, and how he refused, the assistance of various European bankers. There is one story of how the House of Rothschild offered to raise the capital for a commission of 5 percent; there is another story of how he turned down a similar offer from the French House of Fould. The impression given is that these banking houses took the initiative; the probability is that Lesseps approached them and was rejected. "One can't come to an understanding with these people. They are not reasonable; the bankers want to lay down the law to me but I won't have it. I will manage this business myself and I will make my appeal to the public direct."[47] So, on his arrival in Paris at the end of August, 1858, he opened a small office in the Place Vendôme and proceeded to form his Company with the assistance of three men who, three years before, had drafted the Statutes for him.[48]

In his Prospectus[49] Lesseps estimated the cost of the project at 160 million francs[50] and the annual gross income at 30 million francs. The capital of the Company would be 200 million francs in 400,000 shares of 500 francs, each bearing interest at 5 percent. Subscriptions would open on November

5, 1858, and close on November 30th. A first payment of 50 francs would fall due on each share on January 30, 1859, and second and third payments of 50 francs each in July, 1859, and January, 1860, respectively. There would be no further call until 1861 (when in the event there was a call of 150 francs per share). The Prospectus went on to state that the Concessions provided for the grant of 133,000 hectares of land to the Company, of which 70,000 hectares consisted of a strip two kilometers wide on either side of the Maritime Canal and 63,000 hectares of cultivable land bordering the Fresh Water Canal from the Nile.[51] The exploitation of this cultivable land was presented as a substantial source of income for the Company in addition to that which would be derived from canal dues.

In recognition of the universal nature of the Company, an attempt was made to spread the shareholding as widely as possible. The appeal to French nationals was limited to 220,000 shares, and it was hoped to raise the rest of the money elsewhere. Mohammed Said had, according to Lesseps, agreed to take 64,000 shares.[52] Of the shares actually subscribed, 207,111 (out of the 220,000 available) were taken up in France, and 15,247 in other countries. Thus the total number of shares taken up amounted to 286,358 out of a total of 400,000. Most of this deficiency was due to the fact that, out of 85,506 shares reserved for subscription in Great Britain, Austria, Russia, and the United States, none were taken up at all. Apart from the Viceroy's contribution, there were no subscriptions from the Ottoman Empire, and the French subscription fell short of the allocation by some 13,000 shares. There were 21,035 French subscribers, an average of about nine shares per subscriber. Of these, only 188 subscribed for more than 100 shares each. The majority of the French shareholders were therefore relatively small investors.[53] But, as the average shareholding amounted to nine shares at a nominal value of 4,500 francs (about £180), they hardly deserved the gibes of the London *Globe* which, in its issue of November 30, 1858, described them as "grocers' assistants who are accustomed to reading the advertisements of the goods they sell. . . . The whole business is a manifest piece of robbery committed on simple people who have allowed themselves to be fooled."

The *Globe*, and other critics who wished to discredit the Company, would have done better, instead, to concentrate on its subsequent proceedings. After the closing of the subscription list, the directors of the Company were nominated. Prince Jérôme Napoleon was named as "Protector." Three honorary presidents were nominated of whom two were eminent Frenchmen and the third Marshal Narvaez, the Spanish statesman whom Lesseps had known in Spain during his career as a diplomat. Lesseps himself was named president in accordance with the terms of the Second Concession. There were three vice-presidents: a Frenchman, the Duc d'Albufera who was, for the next few years, to manage the Paris end of the Company during Lesseps' frequent and prolonged absences abroad; Paul Forbes, an American banker; and Revoltella, an Austrian banker. The thirty-two members of the Conseil d'Administration included Ruyssenaers, who became the Company's Administrateur Délégué in Egypt, and Sir Daniel Lange, who was the Company's representative in England. Most of the others were Frenchmen. There was also nominated a Technical Advisory Council (Conseil Supérieure des Travaux) consisting of eight people, including Conrad, the Dutch engineer who had been president of the International Scientific Commission, and Renaud, one of the French members of the commission, and a Legal Advisory Council (Conseil Judiciaire) consisting of nine people, all French.

There was some criticism of the members nominated to the Conseil d'Administration on the ground that it contained too many of Lesseps' relatives and personal friends. But, as Lesseps wrote with some justice, "one must choose one's collaborators from those who want the business to succeed, not from those want it to fail; in order to fight our opponents we cannot take our collaborators from those whom they would choose for us."[54] The general direction of the work of construction was entrusted to Mougel. Up to that time Linant and Mougel who, at the time of the grant of the Second Concession, had been placed by the Viceroy at Lesseps' disposal, had been jointly responsible for technical supervision. But Lesseps found Linant too independent-minded and, after the formation of the Company, he was paid off with ten founder shares and a bonus.[55]

The Conseil d'Administration had its first meeting on December 20, 1858, and on December 26th applications was made to the French Minister of Commerce for the registration of the Company. This application involved making a declaration to the effect that the Company's authorized capital had been fully subscribed. As we have seen, this was not the case. A most serious irregularity had therefore been committed. According to one of Lesseps' biographers, who quoted a French journalist named Lara, Lesseps succeeded in persuading the Conseil d'Administration to consent to this illegality on receiving his assurance that the matter would be rectified within fifteen days. In spite of this, four members of the Conseil d'Administration resigned after the meeting.[56] The same biographer, quoting the same source, tells a picturesque story, which is contraverted by all the available evidence, about how Lesseps dealt with the situation:

Eighty millions were lacking from that capital which the evening papers had announced as having been fully subscribed, and it was inevitable that it would not be long before someone discovered that a false declaration had been made. It was a misdemeanor for which he would have to answer, not only to public opinion, but to the Law. It was midnight. M. de Lesseps made up his mind. He presented himself at the Tuileries and, insisting on an audience with His Majesty, put the whole situation before him. "If Your Majesty," he said, "does not come to my rescue, I am lost. That is not important, but France, who will obtain glory and wealth from my enterprise, will receive a setback which must at all costs be avoided. If the Emperor will give me a word for the Viceroy, I shall be able to go to Egypt and return within fifteen days with the eighty-four millions which are short." In reply, the Emperor, convinced by this powerful plea, wrote a few words on a piece of paper and gave it to Lesseps with the words, "Go; it must be done; I want to see the canal remain in French hands." Next morning, before sunrise, Lesseps was on his way to Egypt and, a few days later, he obtained Mohammed Said's guarantee to subscribe an additional 85 millions.[57]

The only element of truth in this story is the fact that Lesseps had already decided that the Viceroy would have to be cajoled into taking up the shortfall in the subscription.

In a letter to the Viceroy dated December 31, 1858, Lesseps advised him of the formation of the Company and formally requested permission to start work on the construction of the canal, arguing that the Grand Vizier's letter of March 1, 1855,[58] constituted sufficient approval without waiting for the Sultan's firman, and quoting the case of the Cairo-Alexandria railway on which work had been started before the firman was issued.[59] There was no mention of the shareholding in this letter. But, on the very next day, Lesseps wrote to Regny, who was acting for Ruyssenaers as the Company's Administrateur Délégué in Egypt, telling him that the 85,506 shares reserved for Great Britain, Austria, the United States, and Russia had not been taken up. "The latest news from England indicates that none will be taken there. . . . I can no longer count on any subscriptions from the United States. It will be the same probably in Russia because of the financal situation in that country." (The outbreak of war between France and Austria a few weeks later put an end to any chance of Austrian subscriptions which, as De Bruck and Revoltella had already warned him, were not very likely anyway.)[60] Lesseps went on to write that he had decided "*d'après la déclaration du Viceroi*" to take up the unsubscribed shares for his account.[61]

Lesseps, pressed by his Conseil d'Administration, made endless efforts, during the rest of Mohammed Said's reign, to get him to acknowledge the shares which he was trying to unload onto him, and then to raise a loan to enable him to pay for the shares. But, as we shall see, Mohammed

Said appears, for once, not to have given way. When Ismail, who succeeded Mohammed Said on the latter's death at the beginning of 1863, signed a convention with the Company, in circumstances which we shall examine later, by which he accepted, on behalf of the Egyptian Government, the whole of the shareholding with which the Company had credited the Viceroy, amounting to 177,642 shares, and agreed to the terms on which they were to be paid for, Lesseps, according to his biographer, enjoyed his first good night's sleep for eight years.[62]

As was usual with large Company flotations at that time, the original capital issue represented a gross underestimate of the final cost of the work. Since shareholders were reluctant to meet successive calls on shares without seeing some solid evidence of work done with the money previously called on, it followed that large construction companies were frequently driven to dubious expedients in order to raise the necessary money to keep the work going. In the case of the Canal Company the position was exacerbated in that the shares were not fully subscribed in the first place and in that the Egyptian Government, on whom the unsubscribed shares were finally unloaded, was able to pay for the shares only by long-term bills which, in view of the poor creditworthiness they enjoyed on the world's money markets, could not be cheaply or easily discounted.

The position was further exacerbated by the political difficulties and uncertainties surrounding the project, and by the dubious financial reputation earned by Lesseps and his associates as a result of the circumstances attending the formation of the Company, which made bankers shy, shareholders suspicious, and lawyers unfavorable. We shall see in the course of this narrative how the various acute financial crises that arose were successively overcome, usually at the eleventh hour, and always at the ultimate expense of the Egyptian people who had to pay, not only most of the capital cost of the canal but also the enormous sums in interest payable on the long-term bills and other postdated payments which were the only currencies available to pay the various sums which the Canal Company succeeded in extracting from the Egyptian Treasury.

NOTES

1. Crabites, *The Spoliation of Suez,* p. 91.
2. Journal, III, 94.
3. "It's anti-British but it makes sense." Their sentiments were probably the same, although less succinctly expressed, as those of another British Eastern merchant who, almost exactly

one hundred years later, was to use these words in recommending the sale of sterling to his clients.

4. Cowley–Clarendon 3.4.56. FO 78/1340.
5. Journal, I, 360.
6. Seymour–Clarendon 8.9.57. FO 78/1340.
7. Minute on Bruce–Clarendon 25.9.57. FO 78/1340.
8. Journal, I, 377.
9. Lesseps to Emperor 12.8.56. M & D, Vol. 13. This was of course an oblique way of informing the Emperor that lack of French official support for the canal was jeopardizing the French position in Egypt.
10. Journal, I, 428.
11. See Chapter Two, Note 7.
12. Journal, I, 431.
13. Sabatier–Walewski 11.12.56. CP 27.
14. Walewski–Sabatier 15.1.57. CP 27.
15. Bruce–Clarendon 26.11.56. FO 78/1340.
16. Clarendon–Cowley 24.12.56. FO 78/1340. Mohammed Said had already started borrowing from the European money market, which gave European financiers a vested interest in Egypt's solvency.
17. Cowley–Clarendon 26.12.56. FO 78/1340.
18. Cowley–Clarendon 4.1.57. FO 78/1340.
19. Stratford–Clarendon 12.1.57. FO 78/1340.
20. Bruce–Clarendon 6.3.57 and 23.3.57. FO 78/1340.
21. Stratford–Bruce 3.4.57. FO 78/1340.
22. Stratford–Clarendon 6.4.57. FO 78/1340.
23. Cowley–Clarendon 7.5.57. FO 78/1340. There is no record in the French archives of any such instruction to Sabatier.
24. This presumably refers to some publication made by Lesseps who was at that time engaged on a propaganda tour of Britain. It seems to be the first reference in diplomatic correspondence to the forced-labor question which was later to assume such importance.
25. Clarendon–Stratford 2.6.57. FO 78/1340.
26. Cowley–Clarendon 4.8.57. FO 78/1340.
27. This is an obvious reference to the belief, expressed several times by Bruce, that what Lesseps was really aiming at was a large indemnity from the Egyptian Government against the cancellation of the Concessions.
28. After Stephenson, who was an MP, had made a speech which indicated that he was in agreement with this reflection on Lesseps' honesty, Lesseps challenged him to a duel. Stephenson apologized. See Journal, II, 112.
29. J. Charles-Roux, *L'Isthme . . .* I, 273.
30. Edgar-Bonnet, *Ferdinand de Lesseps,* I, 297–298.
31. Journal, II, 128.
32. Ferdinand to Théodore de Lesseps of 3.11.57. M & D, Vol. 13.
33. Walewski–Thouvenel 20.11.57. M & D, Vol. 13.
34. Lesseps attributed his dismissal to a request made by the Emperor when on a visit to Osborne the previous August. See Journal, II, 147. But there appears to be no truth in this.
35. Journal, II, 167.
36. Clarendon–Alison 1.1.58 FO 78/1421.
37. Alison–Clarendon 4.1.58. FO 78/1421.
38. See letter from Lesseps to Aali Pasha, Journal, II, 172.
39. The use of the electric cable for diplomatic correspondence had only just started.
40. Malmesbury–Alison 11.3.58. FO 78/1421.
41. Party discipline was laxer in those days than it is now. Nevertheless, it was no mean achievement to get as many as 62 votes in favor of a project which was disapproved of both by the Government and by the official Opposition.
42. Edgar-Bonnet, *op cit.,* I, 302.
43. Journal, II, 282.
44. Bulwer–Malmesbury 10.8.58. FO 78/1421.

45. Journal, II, 340.
46. It is not quite clear whether the break with St. Hilaire and others was due to his decision to form the Company or to the serious irregularities, described below, which attended the formation of the Company.
47. J. Charles-Roux, *op. cit.,* I, 285.
48. M. Denormandie, a lawyer and family friend; M. Mocquard, Lesseps' own lawyer; and M. de Chancel, a railway engineer. When the Comapny was formed, the first two were named as members of the Conseil Judiciaire, and De Chancel as a member of the Conseil d'Administration.
49. Journal, II, 350–412.
50. The International Scientific Commission had estimated the cost at 200 million francs.
51. According to the terms of the Second Concession (Art. 10), it was provided that "the Egyptian Government will give to the Company, free of tax, the use of all land not belonging to private individuals necessary for the construction of the canal and its dependencies, and will also give to the Company the use, free of tax for the first ten years, of all land not belonging to private individuals which would be brought into cultivation as a result of the construction of the Sweet Water Canal." The extent of the land so awarded had not been officially determined, and the figures given in the Prospectus, although this was not made clear, represented Lesseps' own estimate. In the Emperor's Arbitration Award in 1864, which certainly could not be regarded as unfavorable to the Company, the area of land to be retained by the Company was fixed at 19,964 hectares and the area of land to be returned to the Egyptian Government against compensation at 60,000 hectares, a total of just under 80,000 hectares. It is clear therefore that Lesseps, in his Prospectus, greatly exaggerated the extent of the land grant.
52. Journal, III, 370.
53. J. Charles-Roux, *op. cit.,* I, 290.
54. Edgar-Bonnet, *op. cit.,* I, 331.
55. *Ibid.,* I, 333.
56. Jean d'Elbée *Un Conquistador de Génie,* p. 131.
57. *Ibid.,* pp. 132 *et seq.*
58. Journal, I, 140.
59. *Ibid.,* II, 408.
60. Edgar-Bonnet, *op. cit.,* I, 328.
61. Journal, III, 1. This is the only reference in Lesseps' Journal, which was published principally in order to justify all his transactions in connection with the canal, to any prior agreement with Mohammed Said to take up the unsubscribed shares. If there had been any prior written agreement, it can be taken that Lesseps would have published it.
62. Edgar-Bonnet, *op. cit.,* I, 330. M. Edgar-Bonnet, defending Lesseps from the charge of illegality in connection with the formation of the Company, argues that the British, American, Austrian, and Russian shares had in fact been subscribed by Lange, Forbes, Revoltella, and Yadimerovsky, respectively, but that these gentlemen had subsequently defaulted. He quotes the "Archives de la Cie. de Suez" in support, but weakens his case by producing an alternative argument, alleging that there was an agreement between Lesseps and Mohammed Said that the latter should take up any unsubscribed shares: "Said and Lesseps realized in advance that it might be impossible to hold some of the foreign subscribers to their engagements. They therefore decided that in case any banker was not able to place with the public any of the shares to which he had subscribed and thus found himself unable to take up the shares, Lesseps would himself take up the shares but that he would have as guarantee the willingness expressed by the Viceroy himself to take up any foreign subscriptions which were not honored." He goes on to say that there is no doubt that Mohammed Said made such a promise; but, of the three pieces of evidence which he cites, one is an assertion by Lesseps himself made in June, 1859, one an assertion by Ruyssenaers in September, 1859, and one a telegram by the British consul general in June, 1860, stating that the Viceroy had committed himself to the Company for 87 million francs. The first two pieces of evidence are suspect and the last is irrelevant, since the point at issue is not whether Said subsequently agreed to take up the shares but whether he had agreed to do so prior to the formation of the Company (Edgar-Bonnet *op. cit.,* I, 327–329).

CHAPTER *six*

The Emperor's

Intervention &

&§ IN February, 1859, before leaving France for Egypt, Lesseps, on behalf of the newly formed Company, concluded a contract with a French contractor, Hardon, for starting on the construction of the canal.[1] At the beginning of March, writing from Alexandria, he addressed a letter to the Grand Vizier, officially advising him of the formation of the Company and advising him that, in order to avoid any embarrassment to the Sublime Porte, the Company would proceed with preparatory work only pending the issue of the Sultan's firman. He also drew Aali Pasha's attention to Disraeli's speech in the Commons in the Roebuck debate the previous June[2] as indicating that the British Government were not themselves opposed to the project and acknowledged it to be a matter for the Turkish Government themselves to decide.[3]

On his return to Egypt, Lesseps appears to have detected a growing coolness in his relations with Mohammed Said. He assumed that this was due to the Viceroy's weakening in face of British pressures, although it may well have been due to Lesseps' attempts to unload the unsubscribed shares onto him. Egyptian officials were hampering the work of the Company's survey parties in the isthmus, and neither the Viceroy himself nor any Egyptian official representative was present at the formal *coup de pioche* with which work on the construction of the canal was inaugurated on April 25th near what was to be the northern terminal at Port Said.

This coolness on Mohammed Said's part may also have been the reflection of a growing coolness toward the canal which was being exhibited by Sabatier and, to some extent, by the French Government. On March 7th Sabatier, reporting Lesseps' return to Egypt, reminded Walewski that work on the canal could not be started before the issue of a firman from Constantinople. "Because of powerful opposition this firman has not yet been obtained, in spite of three years of incessant effort." He went on to explain the Viceroy's position: "While anxious to be agreeable to His Majesty, Said Pasha wishes neither to wound any feelings at Constantinople nor to annoy the British Government. He is therefore resolved not to involve himself deeper with the Canal Company until the three governments have come to some agreement about it." He added that Mohammed Said had already disclaimed any responsibility for the actions of the Company and that he had not acknowledged the formation of the Company. He ended his dispatch by asking for confirmation that the official French attitude on the matter, as previously communicated to him, remained unchanged.[4] In reply to this dispatch, Walewski, after noting what Sabatier had told him about the difficulties being faced both by the Company and by the Viceroy, wrote, "There is for the moment no modification to make in the instructions previously given to you for, however powerful the sympathies of the Emperor and of his government for this project, the political considerations which dominate this question would not permit the modification of our present policy without the risk of serious complications." He concluded somewhat cryptically by telling Sabatier that, while he should not give any active support to the directors of the Company, he is sure that "you will always be prepared to give them good advice and to receive them hospitably at the Consulate General."[5]

On May 6th Walne, who had replaced Bruce as British consul general, reported Lesseps' inauguration ceremony near Port Said a fortnight before ("M. de Lesseps wanted obviously to produce a favorable impression on the shareholders") and expressed the view that "so long as Said Pasha is not pressed by the French Government he may not himself take an active part in carrying out this measure. But he is of too weak a character to be relied on to prohibit the proceedings of M. de Lesseps unless he receives from Constantinople very clear and peremptory orders or from Her Majesty's Government a very distinct declaration of its wishes and intentions."[6]

This warning from the British consul general appears to have galvanized the Foreign Office. In a return to the Palmerstonian vein a telegram was sent to Bulwer stating that "the Porte should give positive orders to stop a work which is a political and private piece of swindling."[7] Five days later Bulwer replied that "the Porte will order the Viceroy to stop work on the Canal."[8]

Meanwhile Lesseps, harassed by the Viceroy's hostility, by Sabatier's coolness, and by suspicions of underground activities by Walne whom he thought, or affected to think, responsible for various acts of sabotage against his activities in the isthmus, was writing copiously to Albufera. On May 11th he complained that the "Austrian Consul General has turned against us" (France and Austria were by this time at war), "and has done everything he can to try and stop our work."[9] On May 19th he wrote, "It is not that I suspect the loyalty of Mohammed Said but . . . where he sees himself assailed by British hostility manifesting itself at Constantinople without any counteracting support from France he provisionally adopts a policy of letting it be believed that he does not approve of my proceedings and that he is doing everything he can to stop them. In fact we have agreed between ourselves that it will be better not to meet each other for the time being and, without having had it in so many words from him, I can see quite clearly that, while he gives certain orders which he knows will be reported to the British, he makes his real intentions understood to persons in his confidence." He concluded by referring to various acts of sabotage against the Company and stated that he had complained to Sabatier about them.[10]

It is clear that members of the Conseil d'Administration in Paris were getting very worried about the situation and that Lesseps was trying to reassure them. Since the formation of the Company Lesseps, in addition to trying to keep up Mohammed Said's morale, had also to "jolly along" his Conseil d'Administration who were scared to death both by the weakening of Mohammed Said and by apprehensions of what their president was going to do next.

On June 1st, writing to his brother Théodore, Lesseps expressed his dissatisfaction with Sabatier, and asked him to talk to Walewski and express the hope that the French Government would not leave him in the lurch for very much longer ("*tout en éspérant qu'on ne me laissera pour trop longtemps nager tout seul*").[11] On June 17th Cowley reported that Walewski had told him that Lesseps had been trying to obtain Sabatier's recall.[12]

In a dispatch dated May 30th Sabatier warned Walewski that the work which Lesseps had started in the isthmus was being done without the authority of the Egyptian Government and that, although the Viceroy was conniving at it for the time being, there was likely to be a crisis at any moment.[13] On June 13th he informed Walewski that the crisis had arrived and that, as a result of the publicity given to the *coup de pioche* in April, the Egyptian Government had announced that they accepted no responsibility for the finances of the Canal Company and that work in the isthmus must be stopped until a firman had been obtained. He added that the Egyptian Government's attitude posed three questions: (i) Has the Company a legal existence? (ii) if so, can the Viceroy refuse to recognize it? and (iii) can the work in the isthmus be regarded as preparatory work or not, and if not has the Viceroy the right to stop it?

Examining these three questions, Sabatier concluded that the Company had no legal existence because the legal requirements about the full sub-scription to the shares had not been fulfilled, and that the Viceroy therefore was right in not recognizing it. He went on to criticize the Company for trying to raise capital before they were in a position to start work, and expressed the view that the work being done in the isthmus could not possibly be regarded as merely preparatory and that the Egyptian Govern-ment had every right to insist on its being discontinued. He ended his dispatch by stating that he had not yet taken any steps to order French nationals to stop working for the Canal Company in the isthmus and expressed the hope that, when the first access of bad temper had subsided, Lesseps and his associates would not persist in "the detestable course on which they appear to have embarked."[14]

Walewski, in his reply, approved of Sabatier's attitude, "which you will continue to make the rule of your conduct so long as these disagreements do not lead to an infringement of the individual interests of the French subjects working in the Canal Company. . . . It must not, however, be forgotten that a large part of the Canal Company's capital is French and that we must look after these French interests to the extent that we can do so without political interference." He ended by expressing the hope that Sabatier would be able to smooth things over with the Viceroy and that the Viceroy would permit the Company to continue with preparatory work only.[15] If anything is clear from this very equivocal dispatch it is that Walewski was already beginning to feel the weight of pressure from Canal Company interests in France.

What had happened was this. At about the end of May Mohammed Said had received a letter from the Grand Vizier objecting to the fact that work had already been started on the canal. The letter stated that "enterprises of this importance must not be proceeded with before the Sultan's firman has been obtained. Your Highness will realize that the Company cannot in the meantime be permitted to undertake anything but preparatory work." The letter ended by requesting the Viceroy not to do anything to "increase those political complications everyone is trying to straighten out."[16] On June 8th, about a week after the Viceroy had received this letter, Lesseps, making one of his few serious tactical errors, wrote a most imprudent letter to Mohammed Said, which was promptly "leaked" to the local press and which caused a wave of indignation in Egypt against the Canal Company. The letter was certainly expressed in terms which Lesseps was not ac-customed to use to his *"cher Prince."*[17] "Your Highness is no longer free to default on sacred engagements, contracted in face of the whole civilized world . . . by seeking to prevent the Company, after six months of existence, from the legitimate exercise of its rights . . . by doing so you would compromise yourself in the gravest manner. . . . Your Highness would be wholly responsible if the shareholders were to claim damages arising from the nonfulfillment of engagements."

Mohammed Said was furious and asked Sabatier to draw the contents of the letter to the attention of the French Government. Sabatier, in the dispatch which has already been quoted,[18] expressed the view that Lesseps' action would grievously affect the standing of the Canal Company shares in the market. One of the Company's shareholders wrote that it was time to wind up the Company as Lesseps had conclusively demonstrated that he was incapable of making a success of the Canal. "You were known as a man of honour but now you have fallen into the same trap that thousands of others have done."[19] Albufera fumed, "What on earth is Lesseps up to in Egypt? Big talk and no results . . . we claim that we are the masters in Egypt . . . and now we know that we are not . . . with regard to England we have always deceived ourselves. We are not in nearly such a good position as some of us imagine . . . the only thing that can save us is the support of the French Government. . . . Lesseps is very busy but he is not making the Canal . . . what he is doing is of no use unless we can obtain the support of the French Government."[20]

Meanwhile the Viceroy, on receipt of these two letters—the one from the Grand Vizier and the subsequent one from Lesseps—caused a letter to the Canal Company to be circulated to the Consular Corps, which was issued on June 9th by Sharif Pasha, the Foreign Minister,[21] and stated that "His Highness has given orders that the authorization which he has given you for carrying out preliminary studies in connection with the canal must not serve as a pretext for carrying out any work on the canal itself and that no such work must take place without the authorization of H.I.M. the Sultan . . . you will therefore immediately cease work in the isthmus . . . I call upon you to submit yourself to this order immediately."[22]

Lesseps protested against this order and circularized his protest to the Consular Corps. The only sign of support which he received was from the Spanish consul general. He received none from Sabatier.[23] On June 14th he wrote to Albufera stating that, in spite of Sharif Pasha's order, work in the isthmus continued.[24] In the meantime Sharif Pasha, in reply to Lesseps' protest, had written an even stronger letter than before which was, like his previous letter, circulated to the Consular Corps, and which ordered Lesseps in the most peremptory terms "immediately to put a stop to all activities by the Company in the isthmus."[25]

Toward the end of June (the letter is undated), Lesseps wrote to Mohammed Said pointing out that, although France had agreed with Great Britain not to interfere actively in favor of the Canal Company, this did not mean that the French Government would not intervene in order to protect the commercial rights of French subjects. He went on to repeat his old argument that, while the Sultan's firman would be necessary for the operation of the canal, it was not necessary for its construction.[26] On July 3rd he wrote to Albufera complaining about Sabatier's inaction. He wrote that he had informed Sabatier that he would ignore all instructions to stop work, and told him that, as soon as the French Government could be brought to realize that the interests of the Canal Company were being gravely compromised they would not hesitate to instruct their representative to protect those interests. That, added Lesseps, in his letter to Albufera, is the nub of the question (*"la noeud de la question"*).[27]

On July 12th an extraordinary meeting of the Conseil d'Administration was held in Alexandria. Lesseps told the meeting that the recent acts of the Egyptian Government had been brought about as the result of British and Austrian pressures in Constantinople and Cairo but that Austrian pressure had now ceased. (France had beaten Austria in Napoleon III's "war of liberation" and the Treaty of Villafranca was about to be signed.) He went on to say that Mohammed Said, who for political reasons found it prudent to offer "a pretended opposition to a commercial and industrial enterprise," had canceled the order to stop work in the isthmus, that the foreign workers were in consequence remaining there, but that, in agreement with Mohammed Said, all Egyptian workers had been withdrawn.[28]

On July 18th Albufera, after his return from the extraordinary meeting, wrote a report of the meeting to Walewski, explained the Company's situation in Egypt and requested that "His Majesty, by the exercise of his powerful authority, should uphold the rights of the Company." In a covering letter he drew attention to the fact, of which Walewski must have been uncomfortably aware, that a public setback for the Company would be regarded by the world as a setback for France.[29] Walewski, replying to Albufera on July 28th, drew attention to the fact that the operation of the Concession was dependent on its ratification by the Porte and stated that, in the circumstances, the Viceroy appeared to be within his rights both in disclaiming financial responsibility for the Company and in stopping the work in the isthmus. "It would be difficult for the Government of the Emperor to make a request to the Egyptian Viceroy which is incompatible with his obligations to the Porte. I regret therefore that I am unable to satisfy the desire which you have expressed to me."[30] This was a very cold reply indeed, and represents the nadir of relations between the Canal Company and the French Government.

On July 21st Lesseps, just before he left Egypt for France, wrote to Albufera telling him that he had met, and been reconciled with, Mohammed Said, who had promised him verbally that, if the canal project did not go through, he would make himself personally responsible for reimbursing the shareholders.[31] Walne, reporting this apparent reconciliation, expressed the view that "it may be taken as an indication of fresh wavering. I have good reason to suppose that M. Sabatier has within the last few days received instructions which give him more latitude to act openly in support of M. de Lesseps."[32] He added that work was continuing in the isthmus in spite of Sharif Pasha's orders.

There had in fact been a personal reconciliation between Lesseps and Mohammed Said, and Mohammed Said had entrusted his young son, Toussoun, to Lesseps for a holiday in Europe which he spent on Lesseps' country estate at La Chenaie. The old charmer had worked his spell again. But he was not yet out of the wood and he had some anxious weeks ahead of him.

For the next few weeks the future of the canal hung in the balance. In Egypt work in the isthmus had been forbidden but was continuing on a necessarily small scale since there was no immediate possibility of getting the Egyptian Government to provide the forced labor which would have been necessary for any large-scale excavation. In Constantinople, Aali Pasha, the Grand Vizier, supported by Fuad Pasha, the Reis Effendi, and stiffened by Bulwer, the British ambassador, was showing a much more resolute attitude against the Canal than had ever been held by Rashid Pasha, and was even talking about the possibility of Mohammed Said's deposition if he did not carry out the Grand Vizier's orders. In France the shareholders were becoming restive and the members of the Conseil d'Administration increasingly distrustful of Lesseps. The Company's shares were falling on the market, and there was the ever-present possibility of the fact leaking out that not much more than half of the shares had been subscribed.

As both Lesseps and the Conseil d'Administration realized, the only possibility of salvation lay in the prospect of French diplomatic support. Such support would not necessarily result in the immediate issue of a firman, but, by counteracting British pressure at Constantinople, it would prevent the Porte from insisting on the Viceroy stopping the work of construction, would induce Mohammed Said to supply labor in accordance with his agreement of June, 1856, and might even induce him to accept, and make arrangements for paying for, the unsubscribed shares. It would also re-assure the mainly French shareholders of the subscribed shares and help to sustain their price on the European bourses.

As Lesseps was shrewd enough to realize, the embarrassment he was causing the French Government improved their prospects of supporting him. The propaganda which Lesseps had put out in favor of the project, the formation of the Company, the existence of something like 20,000 French shareholders, the starting of the work, and the extent of British opposi-tion all ensured that the abandonment of the project would mean a con-siderable blow to French prestige. The greater the publicity and the greater the opposition, the greater would be the seriousness of the blow. And if the abandonment of the project were to be accompanied, as it probably would have been, by a disclosure of the irregularities attending the forma-tion of the Company, it would constitute a very grave blow indeed. And Napoleon III, the parvenu leader of a parvenu regime, was particularly sensitive and vulnerable to considerations of prestige.

But considerations of prestige sometimes have to bow before the facts of power. A few years before Napoleon would not have dared, did not indeed dare, to do other than defer to the wishes of the British Government in a matter affecting British interests. But, in the summer of 1859, the Second Empire was at the height of its renown. As a result of two victorious wars, one against Russia in the Crimea and one against Austria in northern Italy, it had done much to restore France's traditional place in the councils of Europe. There was no such imperious need for conciliating England; there was no need at all to fear Austria.

For all these reasons, there was a growing feeling that Lesseps, nuisance that he was, would, if it came to the point, have to be rescued from the predicament in which he had placed himself. And Lesseps, who saw the situation with his usual clarity, was quite prepared to turn the screw. Whatever he might tell the Viceroy or the shareholders, there was nothing of optimism in his communications with the French Government. In deal-ing with them it was in his interest to make them realize, and even to exaggerate, the seriousness of the position.

Meanwhile it was vitally necessary to prevent the Viceroy from taking any decisive action against the Company. On August 3rd, just after he had arrived in Paris, Lesseps wrote him a very clever letter in which he intimated that he understood the reasons which had caused him to put difficulties in the way of the Canal Company and that, in conversations with the French Government, he had explained these reasons to them and had defended the Viceroy against French accusations of hostility. He re-

ferred to Mohammed Said's alleged verbal promise to reimburse shareholders in the event of the Company having to go into liquidation.
Finally, in a reference to the delicate matter of the unsubscribed shares,
he wrote, "As agreed I have reserved those foreign subscriptions that have
not been taken up owing to the circumstances of the recent war. It is
understood that His Highness will add these shares to his own portfolio,
thus giving him an important financial interest in the Canal Company."[33]

Three days later, on August 6th, he addressed a letter to the Emperor,
with a copy to the Viceroy: "The political intervention of British agents
is now an undisputed fact. It is exercised without any counterpoise from
France." He went on to write that the first annual general meeting of the
Company would be held in November and that, in view of this *"pression
sans contrepoids,"* he would be compelled to recommend to the shareholders
the liquidation of the Company against the Viceroy's promise of reimbursement. (He was obviously determined, in view of the Viceroy's obstinacy
over the unsubscribed shares, to surround this alleged verbal promise of
compensation with as much documentation as possible.) He continued that
this *"très fâcheuse"* solution seemed to be inevitable "unless steps are taken
very soon to counter this unjustifiable political pressure from Britain. . . .
The concessionaire, a private individual . . . is therefore compelled to seek
the protection of the government of his country. . . . Most of the capital
has already been subscribed. . . . There are two possible ways of counteracting the pressure being exercised at Constantinople. . . . If the French
ambassador, in the name of the Emperor, makes a formal demand for
the firman . . . it will be issued to him within twenty-four hours. If this is
considered premature . . . the Conseil d'Administration will petition the
Emperor to inquire officially from the British Government the reasons for
their opposition."[34]

Great Britain was at that time extremely unpopular in France, and many
of those who had taken shares in the Canal Company had done so because
they believed, and were encouraged by Lesseps to believe, that the Canal
would be a means of strengthening French and weakening British influence in the world. They had been confirmed in this belief, and outraged in
their *amour propre*, by the violent attacks which had appeared in the
British press when the Company had been formed, and by the remarks on
the subject emitted by Palmerston in the House of Commons, in which
insulting references had been made about the financial standing, social
position, and general intelligence of the French shareholders. It was clear
that, if the Conseil d'Administration did make such a petition, and if this
petition were made public, the French Government would be under con-

siderable pressure from French public opinion to take up the cudgels with Britain over the matter. This was something which the French Government urgently wished to avoid. It also happened that the class from which the majority of shareholders was drawn—*la moyenne bourgeoisie*—was precisely that class from which the Second Empire regime drew its principal support, since the aristocracy despised it, the working class loathed it, and *la haute bourgeoisie* merely used it. Lesseps' letter therefore was a fairly effective piece of political blackmail.

On August 10th Lesseps wrote again to the Viceroy, reassuring him: "We are going to be supported . . . but the peace negotiations[35] make it necessary for us to have patience."[36]

On August 16th Lesseps, still worried about the unsubscribed shares, wrote to Revoltella, the Austrian banker and a vice-president of the Company, through whom the Austrian share allocation was to have been subscribed, suggesting that the end of the war with France might make it possible for the Austrian allocation to be taken up and assuring Revoltella that, if this could be done, he hoped that he would be able to persuade the Viceroy to relinquish them.[37]

The following day Lesseps went to London for a week's stay. While there he wrote to his brother Théodore (his usual means of communication with the French Foreign Office) telling him he had heard that, if it had not been for the Treaty of Villafranca, Britain and Turkey would have taken the opportunity of France's preoccupation in Italy to send a fleet to Alexandria and depose Mohammed Said.[38]

Back in Paris, Lesseps continued the process of threatening the Viceroy on the one hand and soliciting the Emperor on the other. On September 2nd he wrote to the Viceroy complaining of the trouble he had had in Paris trying to protect the Egyptian Government from the unfortunate consequences of Sharif Pasha's circular, and warning him that unless he allowed the work to continue he would have against him "not only the 25,000 shareholders who would become his determined enemies and demand from him exorbitant indemnities, but also the public opinion of the whole civilized world."[39]

On September 15th Lesseps, who was being kept posted by Ruyssenaers about developments in Egypt, complained to Walewski that "M. Sabatier is showing himself to be one of the Canal Company's most determined adversaries. I am certain that he is doing everything he can to discourage the Viceroy by trying to persuade him that the Emperor will climb down in face of British opposition" (*ne contrariera pas l'opposition de l'Angleterre*).[40]

The news from Egypt was in fact serious. It became known that the

Grand Vizier was about to send an emissary, Mukhtar Bey, to Egypt with a letter for the Viceroy insisting, in the most peremptory terms, that work on the construction of the canal be stopped without any further delay. Mukhtar Bey arrived in Egypt at the beginning of October and, at a meeting of the Consular Corps in Alexandria on October 4th,[41] Sharif Pasha, the Foreign Minister, read out the Grand Vizier's letter,[42] which demanded the cessation of all work, even preparatory work, on the canal, and asked the Consular Corps to collaborate with the Egyptian Government by arranging for the removal from the isthmus of all those of these nationals who were working for the Canal Company. "To this demand the French agent declared that he at once acceded."[43]

Sabatier, advising Walewski of the impending meeting of the Consular Corps to hear the contents of the letter brought by Mukhtar Bey, reported that, in spite of the Viceroy's wishes so clearly expressed in Sharif's letter of June 9th, work still continued in the isthmus, although all Egyptian workers had been withdrawn, because no member of the Consular Corps had wished to take the initiative of withdrawing their own nationals. He went on to criticize Lesseps for having published a letter he had written to a shareholder stating that, if the canal could not be constructed, the Viceroy would have to pay an indemnity to the shareholders. "It is very regrettable that matters have come to the present pass. For the last year the promoters of the Canal Company have been on the wrong tack. They wanted at all costs to get on, when they should have been patient and waited."[44] Three days later he told Walewski about the meeting of the Consular Corps at which the vizierial letter had been read, and stated that "not only did the whole Consular Corps accede to the demand which was addressed to us (including M. Ruyssenaers, who is both Dutch consul general and Administrateur Délégué of the Canal Company) but the right of the local Government to order the cessation of the work in the isthmus was not even contested."[45]

This renewed insistence by the Porte, and Sabatier's open acquiescence in it, brought the Canal Company to the very edge of disaster. Sabatier was as good as his word. Through the French consul at Damietta he issued strict instructions to all French nationals in the isthmus to stop work on the canal.[46] In face of the Porte's insistence, in face of the known British attitude which was behind the Porte's insistence, and in face of Sabatier's surrender, rapid action was necessary or all would be lost. Lesseps was still in Paris. He did not apparently get details about the Consular Corps meeting until about ten days after the event. But he was already busy lobbying the Emperor, through the Empress Eugénie.

On October 7th Lesseps wrote to the Empress's secretary that "The Emperor's intervention has now become for us a condition of our continued existence . . . the Empress has always been our guardian angel." He added, with a touch of bathos, that the date of November 15th, as being the festival of Ste. Eugénie, had been chosen as the day for the first general meeting of the Canal Company.[47] On October 13th, still apparently ignorant of the result of the meeting in Alexandria on October 4th, he again wrote to the Empress's secretary, telling him that Mukhtar Bey was coming to Egypt to prevent the Viceroy from proceeding with the canal. "The Empress will appreciate how necessary it is for her to continue giving that assistance with which she has been so generous in the past."[48] The following day, having just received news from Egypt of the events of October 4th, he wrote yet again to the Empress's secretary, reporting that Mukhtar Bey's visit to Egypt "is beginning to have very serious consequences and there is a danger of our having to cease all work on the canal. It is very important that a dispatch should be sent to Sabatier . . . to instruct him to maintain, or if necessary to restablish, the *status quo*."[49]

On October 17th Albufera wrote to Walewski protesting against the results of the Consular Corps meeting in Alexandria on October 4th and stating that "as a result of this meeting the Conseil d'Adminstration of the Company has invoked the support and intervention of the Emperor. I request Your Excellency to give the French consul general in Egypt precise and immediate instructions to insist on the maintenance of the *status quo*."[50] It appears that, on the same day, an audience with the Emperor was arranged for October 23rd, for Lesseps, writing to Ruyssenaers about the Consular Corps meeting (about which Ruyssenaers had presumably told him) was able to say—no doubt with some exaggeration—that "the Emperor has decided to place our interests under his powerful protection. If I had a million francs at my disposal I would spend them in buying, at par, all the Suez Canal shares I could lay my hands on."[51] On the same day he wrote to his brother Théodore, giving a detailed account of Sabatier's proceedings on and after October 4th, together with the text of the Grand Vizier's letter and the letter written by Sabatier to the French consul at Damietta.[52]

October 23rd was a red-letter day in the history of the Canal Company and a red-letter day in the life of Ferdinand de Lesseps. Lesseps described his audience with the Emperor[53] in a letter written to Ruyssenaers the following day.[54] According to this account Napoleon opened the conversation by saying:

"How is it, M. de Lesseps, that everyone seems to be against your enterprise?"

"Sire, it is because everyone believes that Your Majesty does not wish to support us."

"Don't worry about that. You can count upon my support and protection. The British opposition is unimportant. We must just trim our sails to it" (*Il faut carguer les voiles*).

The Emperor then authorized Lesseps to tell the shareholders that, "negotiations being about to start, the general meeting must be adjourned, otherwise it will be necessary to liquidate the Company and refund their subscriptions." Napoleon then went on to inquire whether there was anything that could usefully be done immediately.

"Sire, the posting away of the French consul general in Egypt."
"If that is all, there will be no difficulty. Tell M. Walewski."

On October 28th, on the basis of this audience, Lesseps advised shareholders that the first general meeting, fixed for November 15th, had been postponed pending the result of the Emperor's intervention.[55] The fact that Lesseps had received the Emperor's authority to reassure the shareholders in that way was certainly something gained. A general meeting held at that time would have produced some embarrassing questions which would have taxed even Lesseps to answer satisfactorily. Apart from that, the Emperor's assurances, even according to Lesseps' account, were somewhat nebulous. But, for once, Napoleon III was nearly as good as his word.

Even before the audience and, no doubt, as a result of Lesseps' letters to the Empress, things had begun to move. On October 9th Cowley sent a dispatch to the Foreign Office stating that Walewski had told him that the Suez Canal Company had requested the Emperor's intervention in a memorandum alleging that the only obstacle to the issue of a firman was the attitude of the British Government. Walewski had asked him whether the British Government would be prepared either to agree to the canal project or to stop opposing it. Cowley had indicated to him that the British Government would probably continue to oppose it, and Walewski had replied that in that case there would be no use going on with it and that the Company must resign itself to liquidation.[56] In reply to this dispatch, Russell stated that "Her Majesty's Government regret that they cannot yield in this matter to the Government of France . . . as their objections to this scheme remain unshaken . . . the opposition hitherto given to the scheme by Her Majesty's Government will not be relaxed."[57]

That seemed to be that. But, on October 20th, Cowley reported that Walewski had told him that "if Her Majesty's Government would not adopt the proposal of the French Government that both should abstain from using their influence for or against the scheme, there would be a struggle between the two influences because it would be quite impossible for the French Government to abandon the interests of the Company which had claimed their protection." Walewski went on to tell Cowley that he had asked the Egyptian Government to ensure that the Canal Company workshops, and so on, which had already been erected should not be removed and that "he had given positive instructions to M. Sabatier that he must insist on this demand being complied with by the Egyptian Government."[58]

On October 26th, three days after Lesseps' audience with the Emperor, Walewski addressed to the unfortunate Sabatier a fulminating dispatch[59] in which he severely criticized the attitude adopted by Sabatier at the Consular Corps meeting and instructed him to ensure that the Egyptian Government did not allow the dismantling of the installations erected by the Canal Company pending a final decision from the Sultan. This dispatch, the tone of which was clearly intended to provoke Sabatier's resignation, had the desired effect. Sabatier, who had certainly been made the scapegoat in the affair, replied with a long and somewhat incoherent defense and ended with a request to be relieved of his post at the first opportunity.[60]

On November 22nd Bulwer reported that Lesseps had arrived in Constantinople; he described conversations with Thouvenel and Fuad Pasha which indicated a change in the French Government's attitude toward the canal, and added: "It will be difficult to get the Porte to resist the French Government in any decided and positive manner unless we give then a clear and positive assurance that we will stand by them whatever the consequences." Bulwer went on to advise the British Government either "to take the matter up in such a decided manner as to carry the Ottoman Government with them or, by some timely arrangment with France, to avoid the appearance of a conflict in which Great Britain will seem to have succeeded."[61]

On December 5th Cowley quoted Walewski as saying that "M. de Thouvenel has been desired to give the Company all the protection in his power but to be careful in so doing to show as little antagonism as possible towards England . . . the Ambassador had no specific instructions and much had been left to his discretion."[62]

On December 21st Russell, in reply to Bulwer's dispatch of November 22nd, cabled to Bulwer in the following terms: "Great Britain cannot undertake to make on behalf of her secondary interest a resistance to the scheme which Turkey on behalf of her primary interest should decline to make."[63] Behind the smoke screen of this turbid verbiage unmistakable signs of a retreat can be discerned. By referring to the canal as "a secondary interest" the British Government appear to have recognized that the scheme could no longer effectively be opposed, although it still might be modified and obstructed.

On December 28th Bulwer, in a long dispatch, set out what was to become the British Government's future line of policy over the canal. After describing various discussions with Turkish Ministers, Bulwer wrote: "I got accepted as the basis of all future proceedings, first that the Turkish Government should not give their consent to the Canal without the project being stripped of its features of colonisation and forced labour. . . . Secondly that such consent should be withheld until the advantages and expenses of the said Canal had been fairly and fully gone into. Thirdly that if fortresses should be made they should be kept in the hands of the Sultan, and fifthly that the guarantee of England, which implies its assent, should be held as a *sine qua non* to the whole undertaking."[64] Bulwer enclosed with his dispatch a copy of a note from the Porte to the British and French governments asking them, as allies of Turkey, for their views on the canal. This note stated that the Porte's consent to the project was undoubtedly necessary, that the Porte had already given the Viceroy orders to stop preliminary work until this consent had been obtained, and that such consent would depend on a consideration of three matters: (i) the effect of a canal on relations between Egypt and Turkey; (ii) its effect on relations between Turkey and foreign Powers; and (iii) the obtaining of a guarantee of neutrality from the Powers.

On January 21st the Foreign Office, replying to this dispatch, stated that the British Government objected to the canal under all three heads set out in the Turkish note.[65] On February 21st Bulwer sent to the Foreign Office a copy of a dispatch sent by the Porte to Musurus Bey, the Turkish ambassador in London, telling him, in effect, that the Sultan would not issue his firman until agreement had been reached between the British and French governments.[66] The British Government, having attempted to pass the ball to Turkey in their cable to Bulwer of December 21st, now saw it firmly hit back into their own court.

Meanwhile, in Egypt, the immediate crisis was past. But it was not all plain sailing. Sabatier was duly relieved as consul general by Béclard,[67] who had certainly received clearer instructions to support the Canal Company than Sabatier had ever been given. Sabatier's resignation certainly had its effect on the foreign colony in Egypt, which, including the French colony, was, on the whole, against the canal, and it must have had some effect on the Viceroy as being evidence of Lesseps' oft-repeated assurances that the French Government was, *au fond,* in favor of the canal and determined to see it accomplished. But he continued to be obstinate, both about taking up the unsubscribed shares and about supplying the necessary labor, although work on the canal went forward steadily, if slowly, during the whole of 1860.

NOTES

1. Journal, III, 20.
2. See Chapter Five, p. 104.
3. Journal, III, 34. This is a good example of Lesseps' propaganda methods. Disraeli had not said that HMG was not opposed. He had merely said, or implied, that British pressure was not the decisive factor in holding the Turkish Government back from approving the scheme.
4. Sabatier–Walewski 7.3.59. M & D, Vol. 13.
5. Walewski–Sabatier 30.3.59. CP 28.
6. Walne–Malmesbury 6.5.59. FO 78/1489.
7. Malmesbury–Bulwer 17.5.59. FO 78/1489. That this view was shared by Walne is shown by a dispatch (Walne–Malmesbury 24.5.59. FO 78/1489) in which he wrote that "The patrons of the Canal in Egypt are very limited in number and pretty well confined to M. de Lesseps and his associates, most of whom are supposed to have in view, not so much the digging of a canal across the Isthmus, as the opening of a trench to the Egyptian Treasury."
8. Bulwer–Malmesbury 23.5.59. FO 78/1489.
9. Journal, III, 95.
10. *Ibid.,* III, 100.
11. *Ibid.,* III, 117.
12. Cowley–Malmesbury 17.6.59. FO 78/1489.
13. Sabatier–Walewski 30.5.59. M & D, Vol. 13.
14. Sabatier–Walewski 13.6.59. M & D, Vol. 13.
15. Walewski–Sabatier 7.7.59. CP 28.
16. Journal, III, 156.
17. For text see Journal, III, 131.
18. See Note 14 above.
19. Edgar-Bonnet, *Ferdinand de Lesseps,* I, 346–347.
20. Edgar-Bonnet, *op. cit.,* I, 347.
21. Sharif Pasha, who for some twenty years was to play an important part in Egyptian affairs and who was later to become one of the "constitutionalist" leaders in opposition to the exercise of supreme power by the Khedive, was a Turk from Constantinople who had been sent to France for his education by Mohammed Ali. He entered the Egyptian service in 1844 and married the daughter of Soliman Pasha, ex-Colonel Sève. He became Mohammed Said's Minister for Foreign Affairs in 1857. Later, he served Ismail in various ministerial capacities and was usually a member of the Regency Council during Ismail's frequent absences abroad. He was, at various times, Prime Minister under Tewfiq both before and after the British occupation. He was a relatively honest Turkish gentleman whom Ismail was accustomed to using for the more creditable of his transactions with the Porte and with foreign Powers.
22. Journal, III, 133. Also Walne–Malmesbury 10.6.59. FO 78/1489.
23. Journal, III, 134.
24. *Ibid.,* III, 143.
25. Walne–Russell 18.6.59. FO 78/1489. The Derby Government had been replaced in the early part of June by an Administration headed once more by Palmerston in which Lord John Russell was Foreign Secretary.
26. Journal, III, 160. This is in contradiction to his letter to the Grand Vizier at the beginning of March when he wrote that the Company would confine itself to preliminary work pending the issue of the firman.

27. Journal, III, 170.
28. For report of meeting see Journal, III, 181. There appears to have been no truth in Lesseps' assertion that the order to cease work on the canal had been canceled.
29. Albufera–Walewski 18.7.59. M & D, Vol. 13.
30. Walewski–Albufera 28.7.59. M & D, Vol. 13. See also Cowley–Russell 4.8.59. FO 78/1489.
31. Journal, III, 189.
32. Walne–Russell 21.7.59. FO 78/1489. He is presumably referring to Walewski's dispatch of July 7th. See Note 15 above.
33. Journal, III, 196.
34. *Ibid.,* III, 198.
35. The negotiations at the end of the war between France and Austria, which were concluded by the Treaty of Villafranca, had only just been completed.
36. Journal, III, 201.
37. *Ibid.,* III, 202. Eventually the Austrian allocation was not taken up in Austria.
38. Journal, III, 204. There is no evidence in the British archives that there was any truth in this rumor, although the possibility of Mohammed Said's deposition does appear to have been discussed in Constantinople.
39. Journal, III, 211.
40. *Ibid.,* III, 215.
41. The alternations between Cairo and Alexandria as the center of political events in Egypt are explained by the fact that Cairo was the winter and Alexandria the summer capital. Court, Ministers and Consular Corps normally resided in Alexandria from about May to October and in Cairo during the rest of the year.
42. For text of this letter see Journal, III, 231.
43. Colquhoun–Bulwer 6.10.59. FO 78/1489. Colquhoun had just replaced Walne as British consul general.
44. Sabatier–Walewski 4.10.59. CP 28.
45. *Ibid.,* 7.10.59. CP 28.
46. Journal III, 232.
47. *Ibid.,* p. 219.
48. *Ibid.,* p. 221.
49. *Ibid.,* p. 222.
50. Albufera–Walewski 17.10.59. CP 28.
51. Journal, III, 224.
52. *Ibid.,* p. 226.
53. In fact, the audience was not with Lesseps alone but with a delegation from the Conseil d'Administration.
54. Journal, III, 235 *et seq.*
55. *Ibid.,* p. 239.
56. Cowley–Russell 9.10.59. FO 78/1489.
57. Russell–Cowley 11.10.59. FO 78/1489.
58. Cowley–Russell 20.10.59. FO 78/1489. In fact a telegram had been sent to Sabatier on October 19th instructing him to advise the Viceroy to maintain the *status quo* over the canal pending receipt of a dispatch which would be sent by the following mail. See Walewski–Sabatier 19.10.59. CP 28.
59. Walewski–Sabatier 26.10.59. CP 28.
60. Sabatier–Walewski 10.11.59. CP 28. It was probably coincidental that Walewski was replaced as Foreign Minister by Thouvenel, the ambassador in Constantinople, before the end of the year.
61. Bulwer–Russell 22.11.59. FO 78/1489.
62. Cowley–Russell 5.12.59. FO 78/1489.
63. Russell–Bulwer 21.12.59. FO 78/1489.
64. Bulwer–Russell 28.12.59. FO 78/1489.
65. Russell–Bulwer 21.1.60. FO 78/1556.
66. Bulwer–Russell 21.2.60. FO 78/1556.
67. Sabatier remained in Egypt in a private capacity and was afterward employed by various French banking interests in negotiations for loans to the Egyptian Government.

CHAPTER *seven*

The Corvée ?~

~§ On January 3rd, Lesseps, who had just arrived in Egypt from Constantinople, wrote to Zulfikar Pasha, the court chamberlain, asking him to inform the Viceroy that the Porte, after sixteen meetings of the Divan, had agreed that they would not for their part raise any objections to the canal project.[1] This was Lesseps' method of interpreting, for the Viceroy's benefit, the Porte's decision to make the issue of the firman dependent on the prior agreement of Britain and France. He also presented the Viceroy with his *"compte courant"* showing, on the basis of the 177,642 shares which Lesseps was trying to unload onto him, that he owed the Company a matter of 15,248,042 francs for the first call of 100 francs per share after crediting him with various reimbursable sums which he had advanced to pay for preliminary work.[2] Lesseps then returned to Paris where he learned, with great satisfaction, that Thouvenel was about to replace Walewski as Minister for Foreign Affairs.[3] He also learned that the Marquis de Lavallette was to replace Thouvenel at Constantinople.[4]

The first general meeting of the Company was held in Paris on May 15th and, in the comparatively calm waters which had succeeded the storms of the preceding summer and autumn, passed uneventfully. The Conseil d'Administration however, still very concerned about the unsubscribed shares and were pressing Lesseps strongly about them. There was also the less important question of the founder-shareholders, the list of which had not yet been approved by the Viceroy. After the general meeting, the news of which produced some sneers from the London *Times* about digging holes in the ground which would soon be filled up with sand, Lesseps returned to Egypt to try to settle these two financial matters, as well as the matter of the labor contract, with the Viceroy. The matter of the founder shares was settled without difficulty.[5] The originally intended number of 100 founder-shareholders[6] had grown to 170,[7] which seems to indicate that a certain amount of palm grease had been distributed in Egypt and in Paris, since the list had originally been instituted in 1855. The final list, as approved by the Viceroy, was confirmed by the Conseil d'Administration in January, 1861.[8]

The other two matters were more difficult. In the matter of the share-holding the Viceroy had, in March, 1860, sent Paolini Bey,[9] one of his foreign advisers, to Paris, to obtain a legal opinion about the regularity or otherwise of the Company's constitution and the legal position of his commitments toward the Company in respect of the ordinary shares.[10] An opinion was obtained from Odilon Barrot, an eminent lawyer and politician and a considerable figure in France at the time, and two other lawyers, to the effect that the Company had not been regularly constituted.[11]

On his return to Egypt in June, Lesseps returned to the matter of the *"compte courant"* which he had presented to the Viceroy in January.[12] He also appears to have broached the question of arrangements for eventually paying the sums which would become due on future calls. Colquhoun, the British consul general, reported that the Viceroy had been presented with his current account, as drawn up by the Conseil d'Administration,[13] "by which he stands committed to the Company for the enormous sum of 87 million francs."[14] Colquhoun went on to describe a conversation he had had with the Viceroy on the subject. "Last week the Viceroy said in his usual gay manner that the Canal Company had endeavoured to fasten onto his shoulders the whole of the Shares remaining unclaimed and which had been assigned to various nations, *'de sorte que* [quoting Mohammed Said] *je me trouve, je ne sais pas quel tour de passe-passe, inscrit pour près de cent millions de francs.'* " When Colquhoun asked him whether he had accepted this, he laughed, and replied, *"Pas si bête."* Colquhoun then stated that he had later asked Sharif Pasha, the Foreign Minister, about this and that Sharif had replied that the Viceroy was in no way committed as he had put no signature or seal on the various papers submitted to him.[15] The very next day, however, Colquhoun cabled London to say that the Viceroy had committed himself to the Company for 87 million francs and that Colquhoun had told him that, by doing so, he had legalized the Company.[16]

In fact Mohammed Said had not agreed to take up the shares at that time, and there appears to be some doubt whether he ever did agree to do so. Soon after his return to Egypt, Lesseps, in correspondence about the *"compte courant"* with Koenig Bey, one of the Viceroy's secretaries with whom these financial negotiations were carried on, had offered to reduce the debt of 15,248,042 francs as per the *"compte courant"* by 4 million francs in return for a concession to the Canal Company for fishing and navigation rights of Lake Manzala.[17] A fortnight later Béclard reported that the Lake Manzala proposal had been dropped owing to British opposition,[18] and that negotiations had been opened for the settlement of the 15 million-odd francs said to be owing in five annual payments. On July 23rd, Béclard told Paris that, after negotiations between the Company and Ragheb Pasha, the Finance Minister, the Egyptian Government had agreed that payment of the 15 million-odd francs said to be owing on the first call should be made by installments between January, 1863, and August, 1866. He added that this agreement would be drawn up into a formal convention, and commented that "this is a very important success for the Company which now, for the first time, finds itself regularly constituted from the financial point of view."[19]

Béclard had started cheering too soon. In his next dispatch on the subject,[20] he reported that the Finance Minister had raised difficulties about signing any agreement and the Lesseps, *"de guerre lasse,"* had returned to France, leaving the conduct of the negotiations to two of the Company's administrators, MM. De Chancel and Girardin. He went on to state that these two had finally come to an agreement which he regarded as "the most important event which has happened for several years in the history of the Company." According to this agreement, which was dated August 6, 1860, and of which Béclard appended a copy to his dispatch, the Egyptian Government agreed to pay the 15,248,042 francs owing on the first call by installments falling due between January, 1863, and December, 1866, with 10 percent interest payable on unpaid balances since the date of the call. The agreement also provided for the payments of the uncalled balance of 400 francs per share by installments between January, 1867, and January, 1875.

There are four curious points about this "agreement." The first is that the two copies of the agreement extant in the French archives[21] have no reference to any signatory on behalf of the Egyptian Government, although they contain the names of the two Canal Company negotiators, De Chancel and Girardin. The second is that no reference is made to this agreement in Lesseps' published Journal. The third is that no contemporary publicity was given to the terms of the agreement or even to the fact that it had been made. The fourth is that Lesseps' biographer, M. Georges Edgar-Bonnet, who had access to the records of the Canal Company, and to Lesseps' private papers, states categorically that the agreement was not completed.[22] There does in fact seem to be a considerable doubt (to say the least of it) whether a valid agreement over the shareholding was ever made with the Egyptian Government during Mohammed Said's lifetime, and the balance of evidence seems to be against the validity of the "agreement" of August 6, 1860.

Even on the assumption that the agreement was a valid and genuine one, it was by no means satisfactory from the Canal Company's point of view, apart from the fact that it could be held to have legitimated the Company in the eyes of the French law. Pressed by his Conseil d'Administration, Lesseps, for the remaining two and a half years of Mohammed Said's lifetime, assiduously but unsuccessfully tried to persuade Mohammed Said to make an issue of thirty-year government bonds which would enable him to pay cash to the Company for the whole of his shareholding.[23] But Mohammed Said always refused to agree, and died a few days before the first installment under the August, 1860, "agreement" fell due.

The question of labor supply was the third point about which Lesseps had to negotiate on his return to Egypt after the first general meeting. It was a very tricky point. The June, 1856, agreement with the Viceroy for the supply of labor had never been published. The Porte's ban on construction was still theoretically in force. Forced labor had, theoretically, been abolished in the rest of the Ottoman Empire and might be held to be forbidden in Egypt by the terms of the 1841 Hatti Sharif. It was true that the *corvée* had, from time immemorial, been the normal and, perhaps, the only practicable method of getting any large public works done in Egypt at all. Nevertheless, when so many people were looking for the opportunity to criticize and to condemn, a proposal for a *corvée* on this scale, to be sent far away into the desert to work on a private, and foreign, enterprise which was of no direct interest to the Egyptian peasant, was certain to be criticized and condemned. But there was a written agreement, there was the certainty of a demand for indemnities if this written agreement were not honored, and there was the near certainty, in the light of recent events, that this demand would be supported by the French Government. Lesseps had a much better case than he had over the shareholding where there was no written agreement. And, in spite of everything—this, incidentally, applied to the shareholding as well—Mohammed Said's prestige was almost as much committed to the Canal project as was that of Lesseps himself. And, in spite of everything, Mohammed Said still wanted to see the Canal completed as a memorial to himself during the course of his lifetime. And he may have realized that his would not be a very long life.

During the course of 1860, Lesseps tried to make do with freely recruited labor from the Bedouin of the Eastern Desert and with imported foreign labor. But this was insufficient in quantity, unsuitable in quality, and expensive in cost. The time was approaching when he would have once more to start applying pressure to the Viceroy. In March, 1861, he told Ruyssenaers that the Company must insist on the Viceroy observing his agreement regarding the supply of labor.[24] At the same time he was telling Albufera that the supply of free labor was going well and that this was a very important question for the Company, "since the theme of the *corvée* would become the pivot of attacks launched against the Canal by its adversaries."[25] He explained that the motive of his letter to Ruyssenaers was to convince Mohammed Said that he would have to insist on the fulfillment of the labor contract if difficulties were put in his way about the recruitment of free labor.

Meanwhile the Viceroy was having his own difficulties with Constantinople. Toward the end of 1860 the Grand Vizier sent him a copy of the note which had been sent to London and Paris[26] setting out the considerations which had to be taken into account by the Porte before the firman could be issued. The Grand Vizier's letter was a polite one, but it showed evidence of the British pressure which was again being exercized in Constantinople. The Viceroy, in reply, stated that it was quite understood that work could not be started on the canal until the firman had been received but that, in the meantime, "M. de Lesseps has engaged a few hundred workers—some Egyptians and some foreigners—to do preparatory work." He went on to warn the Grand Vizier of Lesseps' threat that any attempt to stop this work would result in a demand for indemnity from the Company's 25,000 shareholders.

The Viceroy sent copies of the Grand Vizier's letter and his reply to Benedetti, the French chargé d'affaires in Constantinople, who had previously been a consul in Egypt, with a covering letter indicating that more French support was required at Constantinople in order to counteract British pressure.[27] Benedetti, after consulting Paris, replied, "I am authorized to inform you that the reply which has been sent by the French Government to the Turkish Government's communication is in conformity with the wishes of all those interested in the canal. The Ottoman Government has in effect agreed to the preparatory works which have as their object to demonstrate the practicability of constructing a navigable canal to link the two seas. . . . I do not think that there is any fear of the Porte changing their mind about this." He concluded by assuring the Viceroy that if there was any trouble he would be supported by the French Government.[28]

The Viceroy apparently felt sufficiently encouraged by Benedetti's reassurances to give way to Lesseps' demands and to start supplying contingents of forced labor for the isthmus. A first contingent of about 2,500 men appears to have arrived in the isthmus about the beginning of March. But Beauval, the new French consul general, was not happy about the labor question, or about the Company's attitude in general. In the middle of March he reported to Thouvenel that Lesseps had asked him to intervene with the Viceroy in order to get the *corvée* raised from 2,500 to 12,000 men at least. He went on to make some criticisms of the Company's exigencies, which he said were mainly for the purpose of satisfying the shareholders, but said that he would continue to give the Company *"un appui suffisant mais jamais compromettant."*[29]

A few days later Beauval returned to the labor question, stating that he had had an audience with the Viceroy, who had expressed his willingness to supply the necessary labor but had insisted that the 1856 labor agreement must be kept secret and that there must be no reference to it in the press or at shareholders' meetings.[30]

Thouvenel, replying to these dispatches, agreed that the Viceroy was in a difficult position in that the labor could not be recruited without his order and that such an order might well get him into difficulties with his suzerain. "Without going into political considerations . . . it does not appear that the Company has any right to insist on the execution of a contract which is dependent for its validity on a condition which has not yet been fulfilled." He then approved the general line taken by Beauval, and added, "It is essential that the measures taken to supply labor to the Company do not lead to any abuses." He pointed out that there had already been considerable international criticism of the Viceroy's use of forced labor. "Our situation is very delicate over the isthmus, and we must see that nothing is done which might provoke the intervention of the Porte."[31]

In spite of the somewhat cautious French attitude revealed by this dispatch, the Viceroy appears to have started supplying the Company with a large part of the labor they were demanding. Colquhoun, reporting to the Foreign Office on May 18th, wrote: "M. de Lesseps would appear to have extorted from the Viceroy a promise of efficient assistance in men for work in the Isthmus of Suez. I learn that verbal orders were issued to the effect that 10,000 men, fellahs, should be sent down to the line."[32] On August 5th Lesseps, then in Paris, wrote to the Empress, asking her to get Thouvenel to instruct Beauval to press the Viceroy about the supply of labor.[33] The effect of this intervention is seen in a dispatch by Beauval in November when he told Thouvenel that he had urged the Viceroy to increase the labor supply from 12,000 to 15,000.[34]

A few days later Beauval wrote complaining about the Company's tactlessness, and pointing out that it was his business as French consul general to support the idea of a canal but not necessarily to support all the demands of the Canal Company. In a reference to the Company's efforts to persuade the Viceroy to raise a thirty-year loan to enable him to pay cash for the canal shares, he expressed his regret that Ruyssenaers (who had just resigned as the Company's Administrateur Délégué in Egypt) "should put his bank at the disposal of the Viceroy with a view to assisting him in the ruination of Egypt."[35] He complained that the Company were not satisfied with the 15,000 laborers with which the Viceroy had promised to supply them and wanted to be supplied with an army. After criticizing the Company once more for being stampeded into indiscretions by the demands of their shareholders, he restated in succinct terms the line of policy he was pursuing: "I will not deviate from the instructions which have been given me in this matter—a discreet but steady support for the Canal itself; an absolute indifference toward the personal convenience of the directors of the Canal Company."[36]

At the beginning of December, Lesseps, from Cairo, wrote one of his more euphoric letters to Albufera describing a meeting with the Viceroy at which his continual demands for more labor had at last been satisfied: *"Nos meilleurs jours étaient revenus."*[37] In the middle of December, Colquhoun reported that the Viceroy had agreed to increase the supply of labor from 10,000 to 40,000.[38] In January, Lesseps complained to Koenig Bey of the insufficiency of the labor being supplied, and pointed out that the rapid progress of the work, which depended on an ample labor supply, was an essential condition for the placing of the thirty-year bonds, to which Lesseps was still trying to get the Viceroy's agreement.[39] On the one hand Lesseps was being pressed by the Conseil d'Administration to speed up the work; on the other hand he was being warned by Beauval of the probable effect on international opinion of ever-increasing numbers of forced laborers.[40] In March, 1862, Lesseps again complained to the Viceroy about the shortage and low productivity of the labor, saying that he expected an excavation rate of thirty cubic meters per month per man.[41]

As might have been expected, the employment of forced labor did not pass unnoticed in London and in Constantinople. In a debate in the House of Lords on May 6, 1861, the government spokesman (Lord Wodehouse) stated that the Ottoman Government objected both to the use of forced labor and to the cession of lands to the Company.[42] On May 29th Bulwer reported that he had taken up the question of forced labor with Aali Pasha the Grand Vizier.[43] In the House of Commons in June, Lord John Russell, the Foreign Secretary, attacked the Company for the use of forced labor. Beauval, with reference to this attack, sent Thouvenel details of the actual conditions under which the labor was employed.[44] In May, 1862, Lesseps sent to Lord Layard, the British Under-Secretary for Foreign Affairs, a long, witty, and trenchant letter replying to further criticisms about forced labor made in the British Parliament and referring, *inter alia,* to factory conditions in England, and the condition of peasants in India, in a not unsuccessful attempt to expose the hypocrisy of the British attitude toward the use of forced labor in the isthmus.[45]

In spite of all the criticisms, and in spite of all the doubts expressed by Thouvenel and Beauval, the supply of forced labor for the isthmus continued to increase. In October, 1862, between 22,000 and 25,000 laborers were at work.[46]

As a result of the labor which had been supplied in steadily increasing quantities during 1861 and 1862, the Sweet Water Canal from Ras al Wadi (where it joined the Zagazig Canal) to Lake Timsah was completed on February 21, 1862,[47] and Lesseps hoped, but did not get, the service channel (*rigole de service*) from Port Said to Lake Timsah completed by May. It was actually finished in November. The digging of the Sweet Water Canal from Ras al Wadi to Timsah, which took from April, 1861, to February, 1862, involved excavating 1,103,200 cubic meters of soil and the simultaneous employment of between 3,000 and 7,000 laborers, virtually all of them *corvée* workers. The digging of the *rigole de service* between Port Said and Lake Timsah involved the excavation of about 4,000,000 cubic meters of soil and the simultaneous employment of between 15,000 and 25,000 laborers.[48] That, together with the partial construction of a port at the northern terminal, was the extent of the work which had been done on the canal by the end of 1862. On Lesseps' calculation of 30 cubic meters per man per month (as one would have expected from Lesseps, it was an exaggerated estimate, since he was apt to expect from other people what he would probably have been capable of himself), it represented about one million man-days spread over about two years.

In the midst of all the trouble about forced labor, busy preparations were going on for a visit by the Viceroy to Paris in the summer of 1862. The object of this visit, from the French point of view, was the consolidation of those close relationships with Mohammed Said which the French had been building up since the beginning of his reign. Mohammed Said's object was to obtain as much support as possible in his perpetual tug of war with Constantinople for the retention and extension of that measure of independence afforded by the 1841 Hatti Sharif. The Canal Company hoped to use the visit to demonstrate the extent to which they enjoyed the support of the Emperor, of the French Government, and of French public opinion.

Beauval, in a dispatch dealing with arrangements for the impending visit, gives an interesting character study of Mohammed Said:

He never dares to face up to any question or to any difficulty. Under pretense of arriving at a satisfactory compromise, he involves himself in endless complications and burdens himself with inextricable embarrassments. As a result he has to make enormous sacrifices of money. At the same time as he is making pathetic little efforts at economy, he throws away millions in order to try and obtain a tranquillity which becomes more and more remote as he spends more and more money in trying to achieve it, since his weakness encourages the demands which people make on him. There is hardly anyone in Egypt who has not the more or less open ambition of making a fortune either by provoking an act of generosity, or by a threat, or by starting a lawsuit, or by exploiting some verbal promise made by the Viceroy who, if he is not firmly sustained against this sort of greed on the one hand, and against British pressures on the other, will soon lose courage altogether.[49]

It was this weakness of Mohammed Said's which had been played upon by Lesseps in the original granting of the Concessions, in the attempted offloading of the unsubscribed shares, and in the demands for labor.

It does not appear that the Canal Company was altogether successful in impressing Mohammed Said with the strength of the support they enjoyed in France. Describing an audience he had had with the Viceroy after his return, Beauval wrote: "The Prince did not get from the Tuileries that impression of enthusiastic support for the Company which is claimed and announced with so much éclat by ill-advised friends of the Company. In view of this, and knowing the ease with which he is discouraged, I made it my business, in the matter of the isthmus, to persuade him to maintain the *status quo,* that is to say, to continue supplying from 22,000 to 23,000 laborers." As evidence of the Viceroy's wavering, Beauval mentioned that Mohammed Said was particularly worried by Colquhoun's opinion that the canal might be used as a barrier against a possible invasion from Turkey. He was clearly alarmed at the effect on the Porte of such an insinuation.[50]

During that summer the Conseil d'Administration in Paris was occupied with other and even more important matters than making a good impression on Mohammed Said. It was quite clear that, for political and technical reasons, the use of forced labor could be only a temporary measure to be used to create sufficient of a *fait accompli* as eventually to compel the Porte to disgorge the long-awaited firman. It was clear, from the British attitude, that the firman would be issued only on condition that forced labor was abandoned. Moreover, from the technical point of view, it was clear that, once excavation on the Maritime Canal had got down to the waterline, the use of hand labor would become almost impracticable and the use of excavating machinery would become necessary. Negotiations were already in train with various contractors for the supply of this machinery and for its operation. The difficulty, as always, was finance. Mohammed Said was still resisting Lesseps' attempts to persuade him to raise a loan in order to enable him to pay the Company in cash for the whole of the shareholding attributed to him. One hundred francs a share had already been called in, producing some 22 million francs from shareholders other than the Egyptian Government. The Egyptian Government had paid, apart from interest, and in the form of advances before the formation of the Company, only about 2.5 million francs on the first call of 100 francs and, by the terms of the 1860 agreement (the validity of which was uncertain) were due to pay only the balance in installments between 1863 and 1866. The shareholders were already restive (in July, 1862, the ordinary shares were being quoted at 470 francs against a par value of 500 francs),[51] and an additional call of 200 francs per share, which was actually made toward the end of 1862, was the most that could immediately be extracted from them. By the end of 1862 some 50 million francs had been spent.[52] All that had been received in cash was about 67 million francs from shareholders other than the Egyptian Government on the calls amounting to 300 francs per share (on the assumption that they had all paid up), about 2.5 million francs in advances from the Viceroy,[53] about 500,000 francs from the Viceroy "on which he does not claim reimbursement,"[54] and about another 500,000 francs from the founder-shareholders,[55] making a total of some 70 million francs against the 120 million francs which Lesseps claimed to have received.[56] In view of the doubtful validity of the August, 1860, agreement, it is doubtful whether the Company had been able to discount any paper which the Egyptian Government may—or may not—have given them to cover the installments due under this alleged agreement. Large additional cash resources would soon be needed to finance the purchase of machinery. One can appreciate the anxiety of the Conseil d'Adminstration for an arrangement with the Viceroy which would enable the whole of the shareholding attributed to the Egyptian Government to be paid in cash and so produce an immediate sum of some 85 million francs. Failing this, or a similar, sum from elsewhere, it did in fact seem that the Company was faced with bankruptcy. It is possible that, during the course of the winter of 1862–1863, the minds of some of the more astute members of the Conseil d'Administration were already thinking in terms of indemnities in compensation for the relinquishment of those "rights"—forced labor and use of lands— which were already under such heavy fire from London and Constantinople.

Before proceeding in the next chapter to an account of the initial work of
of construction, there is one other important transaction to record. On
March 19, 1861, the Canal Company purchased from the Egyptian Government 10,000 hectares of cultivable land along the Zagazig Canal—referred
to hereafter as the "Wadi lands"—for 2 million francs.[57] The ostensible
object of this purchase was, by obtaining control of the water outflow from
the Zagazig Canal (which was connected with the Damietta branch of
the Nile) to ensure the level of water in the Sweet Water Canal for purposes of navigation, irrigation, and drinking water pending the completion
of the Sweet Water Canal to the mainstream of the Nile at Cairo. The
principal real object was almost certainly to develop this land by irrigation
and to augment the Company's income by leasing the land so irrigated. In
fact, an extremely efficient and successful scheme of land development and
land settlement was put in hand, and a number of Bedouin from the Eastern
Desert took up leases of the land and settled down to farming. Eventually the
scheme became incompatible with the revision of the Concessions which came
about as a result of the Emperor's Arbitration Award in 1864, and the
Wadi lands were sold back to the Egyptian Government for 10 million
francs. They thus made a useful contribution to the capital cost of the canal.

NOTES

1. Journal, III, 274.
2. *Ibid.*, pp. 274, 370.
3. *Ibid.*, p. 282.
4. *Ibid.*, p. 316.
5. *Ibid.*, p. 417.
6. Journal, I, 189.
7. Edgar–Bonnet, *Ferdinand de Lesseps*, I, 321.
8. J. Charles-Roux, *L'Isthme* . . . , I, 285.
9. Otherwise known as Drahent Bey.
10. Colquhoun–Russell 24.3.60. FO 78/1556; Béclard-Thouvenel 20.3.60. CP 29.
11. Colquhoun–Russell 2.4.60. FO 78/1556; J. Charles-Roux, *op. cit.*, I, 294. Charles-Roux adds,
    without quoting his source, that the Viceroy subsequently told Lesseps, "I accept the opinion
    of your lawyers and reject that of mine."
12. Béclard–Thouvenel 11.6.60. CP 29.
13. He had actually presented him with it in January. See Journal, III, 274.
14. This of course was for the total value of the 177,000-odd shares.
15. Colquhoun–Russell 2.6.60. FO 78/1556.
16. Colquhoun–Russell 3.6.60. FO 78/1556.
17. Béclard–Thouvenel 11.6.60. CP 29.
18. Béclard–Thouvenel 23.6.60. CP 29. There is no reference to this opposition in the British
    archives.
19. Béclard–Thouvenel 23.7.60. CP 29.
20. Béclard–Thouvenel 9.9.60. CP 29.
21. One in CP 29 and one in M & D, Vol. 13.

22. Edgar–Bonnet, *op. cit.*, I, 330. His actual words are: *"En 1860, sous ses ordres, une convention sera preparée comportant explicitement la reconnaissance par le vice-roi des sommes dont il est dèbiteur, á la fois pour les actions qu'il a souscrites et pour celles abandonnées par les divers defaillants. Le fait sera connu des Anglais et confirmé par leur consul. Devant leur campagne d'intimidation, Mohamed en ajourera la signature officielle, et ce ne sera qu'en avril 1863 que son successeur signera l'accord définitif."*
23. Journal, IV, 110, 133, 187, 268, 272.
24. *Ibid.*, p. 26.
25. *Ibid.*, p. 28.
26. See p. 127.
27. See copy of letter from Mohammed Said to Benedetti dated 1.1.61 in CP 29 to which are attached copies of the Grand Vizier's letter and Mohammed Said's reply.
28. Benedetti–Mohammed Said 12.2.61. CP 29.
29. Beauval–Thouvenel 14.3.61. CP 29.
30. Beauval–Thouvenel 19.3.61. CP 29.
31. Thouvenel–Beauval 12.4.61. CP 29.
32. Colquhoun–Russell 18.5.61. FO 78/1715.
33. Journal, IV, 87.
34. Beauval–Thouvenel 9.11.61. CP 30.
35. It appears that Ruyssenaers, who had a finger in a number of dubious Egyptian pies, had undertaken to float a thirty-year loan for the Egyptian Government for 90 million francs in order to enable them to pay cash to the Canal Company for the whole of the shares which Lesseps was trying to unload onto them.
36. Beauval–Thouvenel 12.11.61. CP 30.
37. Journal, IV, 87.
38. Colquhoun–Russell 18.12.61. FO 78/1715.
39. Journal, IV, 145.
40. *Ibid.*, p. 164.
41. *Ibid.*, p. 176.
42. *Ibid.*, p. 64. After the debate Lesseps challenged Lord Carnarvon to a duel for saying that the Canal Company was bankrupt (*ibid.*, pp. 73–74). There is no record of Lord Carnarvon either having apologized or accepted the challenge.
43. Bulwer–Russell 29.5.61. FO 78/1715.
44. Beauval–Thouvenel 7.7.61. CP 29.
45. Journal, IV, 225.
46. Beauval–Thouvenel 14.10.62. CP 30.
47. Journal, IV, 160. The second Concession provided for the eventual extension of the Sweet Water Canal to the Nile at Cairo, as the water supplied via the Zagazig Canal was insufficient for the ultimate needs of the Company.
48. G. Douin, *Règne du Khédive Ismaïl*, I, 128.
49. Beauval–Thouvenel 19.4.62. CP 30.
50. *Ibid.*, 6.10.62. CP 30.
51. Journal, IV, 238.
52. *Ibid.*, p. 259.
53. Journal, III, 370.
54. *Ibid.*, p. 227.
55. Edgar–Bonnet, *op. cit.*, I, 321.
56. Journal, IV, 259.
57. *Ibid.*, p. 31.

CHAPTER *eight*

Construction—

First Phase &

&§ SINCE the development of regular mercantile sea traffic between Europe and the East, and particularly after the introduction of steam navigation, the one-hundred-mile strip of desert which separated the Mediterranean from the Red Sea had, like the narrow Isthmus of Panama separating the Atlantic from the Pacific, tantalized sailors and merchants, worried politicians, and presented a challenge to engineers and entrepreneurs. In an age of steam, in an age of trade expansion, in an age of capital accumulation and consequent speculation, it was almost inevitable that a canal should be attempted. Had it not been for the political obstacles, it would have been attempted sooner. For, at first sight, the physical difficulties did not seem very formidable in an age which had had much experience of canal construction and when mechanical dredgers and excavators were being invented, developed, and progressively improved. The commercial prospects for such a canal were far less chimerical than those for many of the vast schemes for which public subscriptions were almost daily being solicited and obtained. These commercial prospects were, perhaps, more readily apparent to the merchants of Marseille, Trieste, and other Mediterranean ports which were at a disadvantage in their Eastern trading by comparison with the merchants of the Atlantic ports of London, Liverpool, and Hamburg, the fortunate heirs of that Mediterranean supremacy which had been lost with the development of ocean navigation and the discovery of America and the Indies. But even those who would not have initiated a route which was of more advantage to their competitors than to themselves could certainly not afford to abstain from using a route initiated by these competitors.

Today, when the Canal Zone presents an appearance of lushness, orderliness, and busyness, it is difficult to imagine that, in 1855, it was just a part of that almost uninhabited, waterless, and windblown desert which stretches eastward from the Nile Valley across Sinai to Syria. Some eighty miles eastward from the Nile Valley, the flat and low-lying desert narrows to a belt, some one hundred miles wide, between the Mediterranean and Red Sea, before broadening out again into the rocky and mountainous Sinai Peninsula. This narrow belt was known as the Isthmus of Suez. The isthmus was formed by an arm of the Red Sea, known as the Gulf of Suez, extending northwest along the west coast of the Sinai Peninsula toward the Mediterranean and ending, about one hundred miles from the Medi-terranean, in the little roadstead of Suez at the head of the gulf. At the northern end of the isthmus the low, featureless coastline of the Medi-terranean, consisting of low sand dunes and salty, shallow lagoons, stretched from the Damietta mouth of the Nile to Gaza, three hundred miles and more to the northeast, without a port, without a navigable inlet, without even a roadstead, a barren, inhospitable and, by reason of its shoals and currents, treacherous coast. In the one hundred-mile stretch of land between the Red Sea and the Mediterranean the land was flat, rising to a maximum of only fifty-nine feet above sea-level, and presented some natural features which, it seemed, would facilitate piercing the isthmus with a canal.

Suez, at the time the canal was begun, in spite of being a terminal and starting point for quite a considerable volume of passenger and mail traffic between Europe and the East via Egypt, was little more than a village, with an open roadstead for ships, a couple of hotels for transit passengers, very limited supplies of fresh water from a few wells and, consequently, no surrounding cultivation. The Cairo-Suez railway was not yet begun (it was to be completed in 1859), but there was a well-beaten track across the eighty-five-mile stretch of desert between Suez and Cairo, used by camel caravans, wheeled vehicles, and pack and riding animals of all kinds. North of Suez was a low ridge of land, known as the Shallufa Ridge, separating the head of the Gulf from a depression known as the Bitter Lakes, the southern end of which was about thirteen miles north of Suez. At that time the Bitter Lakes consisted of a series of dry, salt-encrusted depressions, stretching for a distance of some twenty-seven miles from south to north and slightly below the level of the Red Sea. They had, almost certainly, at one time formed part of the Gulf of Suez and had become separated from it by the gradual piling up of windblown sand to form the Shallufa Ridge. North of the Bitter Lakes was a ridge, twenty-nine feet above sea level, known as the Serapeum, stretching some ten miles from south to north and separating the Bitter Lakes from another, and smaller, natural depres-sion known as Lake Timsah, about four miles long from north to south, lying halfway between the Mediterranean and Red Sea, and at the bottom of the shallow Wadi Tumulat running between the isthmus and the Nile Valley. Between Lake Timsah and El Firdan, some nine miles to the north, lay a ridge, called Jisr, rising to a height of thirty-six feet above sea level, the highest ground along the direct route between Suez and the Mediterranean. Between Firdan and Qantara, a station on the caravan route between Egypt and Syria, lay a marshy depression known as Lake Ballah, covering about five miles from south to north. Between Qantara and the Mediterranean, a distance of some thirty-two miles, lay the large, shallow lagoon of Lake Manzala, stretching away to the northwest corner of the Delta near the Damietta mouth and separated from the Mediterranean by a narrow sandbar.

The construction of a Maritime Canal through the isthmus involved essentially: (*a*) cutting through the Shallufa Ridge between Suez and the Bitter Lakes and filling the Bitter Lakes with water from the Red Sea; (*b*) digging a navigable canal through Lake Manzala and the Jisr Ridge to Lake Timsah and filling Lake Timsah with water from the Mediterranean; and, finally, (*c*) joining Lake Timsah and the Bitter Lakes by cutting through the Serapeum Ridge. There were two essential, and preliminary, adjuncts to the construction of the Maritime Canal itself. These were: (*a*) the creation of an artificial harbor and port at the Mediterranean terminal of the Maritime Canal to provide for the import of supplies, and so on, and (*b*) the provision of a regular and copious supply of fresh water in the isthmus by bringing the waters of the Nile to the isthmus by digging a canal from the Nile Valley to the isthmus.

The building of an artificial port was the most difficult part of the scheme, the digging of a freshwater canal the easiest. After all, the latter had been done some two thousand years earlier, when the Pharaoh Necho had built his canal between the Nile and the Bitter Lakes. The line of Necho's canal, which was followed for most of its length by Lesseps' Sweet Water Canal, was along a natural depression, called the Wadi Tumulat, running east and west between the Nile Valley near Zagazig and the middle of the isthmus. The digging of such a canal, and its extension along the Maritime Canal southward to Suez and northward to Port Said (the name chosen for the northern terminal in honor of Mohammed Said), had been stipulated in the Second Concession, which had also provided that the Sweet Water Canal should lead off from the Nile at Cairo so as to provide an adequate flow of water. The artificial port was a much more difficult enterprise. Since there was no natural inlet, a breakwater would have to be built for shelter against the prevailing northwest wind. Since the sea was very shallow inshore, there would have to be dredging. Since there was no dry land except for a narrow spit of sand, an artificial island would have to be raised up out of the water. There was a question whether the silt discharge from the Damietta mouth at high Nile would not be carried along the coast by currents and defeat any attempts at dredging a navigable channel; the breakwater to be constructed would have to look after this as well as provide shelter. Much masonry would be needed which, according to the terms of the Second Concession, could be obtained from the stone quarries at Mex, west of Alexandria (there was no stone in the isthmus), and transported to Port Said by sea. Land communication would be almost impossible since the new port would virtually be an island, surrounded on three sides by Lake Manzala and on the fourth side by the sea. And the necessity for sea communication meant that some sort of port, with a jetty, would have to be built before supplies could be brought in.

The construction of the canal was started on two fronts simultaneously: (*a*) the digging of the Sweet Water Canal from the end of the Zagazig Canal at the head of Wadi Tumulat to Lake Timsah and thence southward to Suez;[1] and (*b*) the construction of the northern terminal port and the digging of a service canal (*rigole de service*) from there to Lake Timsah, across Lake Manzala, and through the Jisr Ridge, to enable seaborne supplies to be carried up to Lake Timsah for work on the southern half of the canal. (The Sweet Water Canal, when it was completed, could also be used for bringing supplies to the isthmus from the Nile Valley.)[2]

The digging of the Sweet Water Canal was quite straightforward and was done mainly with forced labor and by hand. It was completed from Ras al Wadi (at the junction of the Zagazig Canal) to Timsah in February, 1862. The extension to Suez was completed in December, 1863. The stretch from Timsah to Port Said was at first supplied with fresh water by pipeline, after the completion of the Sweet Water Canal to Timsah, but the extension of the Sweet Water Canal to Port Said was completed before the opening of the Maritime Canal in 1869. The digging of the stretch from Cairo to Ras al Wadi was undertaken by the Egyptian Government under the terms of a convention signed between the Canal Company and the Egyptian Government in March, 1863, and was completed (by means of forced labor) during 1866.

The first idea had been the crude one of a stream of fresh water from end to end [of the Maritime Canal]. . . . But a more advantageous project was soon conceived. It was found that only half of this conduit need be made, for while the northern portion of the larger canal was in progress the workmen were supplied by native sources and by distillation. The embarrassments of carrying on a vast undertaking where from 15,000 to 20,000 laborers were employed, without a supply of water, seemed unconquerable. Even Suez was without a supply of its own. . . . If then, while this northern half of the Canal proper were being made, the portion of the Fresh Water Canal from Lake Timsah down to Suez was also being constructed, the result would be that there would be a through-water communication of some description along the whole route from end to end.

On the principle that the same length of fresh water, or perhaps a little more, could be made infinitely more profitable as a permanent benefit to the country, instead of being a mere convenience to the workmen, it was determined to bring the water from the centre of the country to the east[3] where it would meet the Canal, or the portion of it that was finished, at right angles and thence make a continuation of it southwards. It started from Zagazig . . . and took its course across the country for fifty miles. Reaching Lake Timsah, it joined the northern portion of the sea Canal from which it was separated by a double lock. This was necessary as the level of the Nile is seventeen feet above that of the sea. This portion of the Fresh Water Canal was an important work in itself, being sixty feet in width by eighty in depth. Above the locks an arm branched out southward which maintained the same level. The northern portion was therefore on a different level from the southern. . . .

The course of this conduit . . . takes the shape of an arc. It starts from Cairo, ascends [*sic*] to Ras-al-Wadi and descends again to Suez, after shooting out a branch to Lake Timsah. Originally, however, advantage was taken of a branch of the Nile which . . . came from near Zagazig;[4] but as this source was attenuated and liable to run dry . . . it was later determined to draw the water from the mainstream itself from Cairo.[5]

The short length of canal joining Lake Timsah and Ras-al-Wadi was twenty miles; it was eight feet deep and about sixty wide. Its cost was £28,000. The portion from Timsah to Suez was about fifty miles in length, and that from Cairo to Ras-al-Wadi fifty-six, the cost of both being estimated [in 1862] at £280,000.[6]

The more formidable initial work was in the north—the construction of a northern terminal and the digging of a service canal through Lake Manzala and into Lake Ballah and then through the Jisr Ridge to Lake Timsah:

Nothing less promising than the aspect of the coast could be conceived, and the forebodings of mariners who thought of the difficulties and dangers of "making" it in foul weather might seem to be fully justified. Pelusium indeed offered the shelter of a bay but there was no water and the whole was a series of lagoons; in parts large ships could not approach within four or five miles . . . A rather curious configuration of the coast here occurs. The sea is separated from a huge lake, known as Lake Menzaleh, by a long strip of "slob," that seems on the map like the rim of a tea cup, a few hundred feet wide. This sort of sea-wall stretches across for about forty miles and joins the two capes of the mainland together. Somewhere in this rim an opening was to be made for the Canal; further on a port and town would have to be formed, with docks to shelter and repair vessels, warehouses to store goods, and all on a strip of slob land. A few fishermen gained a precarious livelihood here, there was no water, save only what could be transported on camels from Damietta. There was no stone.[7]

South from Port Said was Lake Manzala,

a shallow lake, which would have from four to five feet of depth, and in which for twenty-nine miles the Canal would have to be excavated. The mainland is then reached at Kantara, where for about three miles it proceeds along a small tongue of land which separates the great lake from a smaller one, called Lake Ballah. It would then have to pass through Lake Ballah, a distance of about five miles, and there reach a hilly tract extending for nearly ten miles, and consisting of a gradually ascending series of hills culminating in El Jisr, thought to be one of the serious difficulties of the work. This plateau was about ten miles in length and rose about 50 feet above the waterline.[8] This surmounted, comes Lake Timsah, where was to be the half-way port. . . . Across this hollow it was now to proceed for four miles. Though called a lake it had long been dried up. . . . As regards the character of the soil, it may generally be stated that the higher portion, from Lake Menzaleh to about the middle, was formed of a sea sand easy to work.[9]

It may be mentioned here that though, by the Concession, the Canal was required to run in a straight line from sea to sea, the question of arranging the Canal was left an open one and Mr. McLean, the well-known English engineer on the Commission, submitted a proposal which was seriously considered, debated, and finally rejected. This was to construct high banks all along the course of the Canal and raise the waterline almost to the level of these banks, confining the water between locks at both ends. The Canal being thus raised many feet above the level of the sea, no dredging would be required, while its bed would be sheltered from the sands by the high banks. But there were obvious objections to the scheme; danger of the banks bursting, or of the water infiltrating through the sand, to say nothing of the check on traffic owing to the locks at each end.[10]

Work began in April, 1859, on the construction of the artificial port. A temporary jetty three hundred feet long was constructed for the reception of material by sea, and particularly for the reception of stone from the Mex quarries. Stone was also made on the spot with a mixture of one-third hydraulic lime and two-thirds sand, machine-mixed with salt water and made into blocks 12 cubic yards in size and weighing 22 tons each. Nearly 30,000 of these blocks were used in the construction of piers, jetties, and breakwaters.[11] The work was carried out under exceptional difficulties. They were almost literally on a desert island. Drinking water, fresh food and, indeed, all supplies which could not be brought in by sea had to be brought across Lake Manzala, after having been transported to Damietta by camel from the railhead at Sammanud, forty-five miles away. (In addition it was sometimes possible to receive supplies by camel direct from Damietta, twenty miles away, along the narrow spit of land between the sea and the lake.) Nevertheless, fair progress was made. The area of land was extended; a village grew up; a port began to take shape. In the autumn of 1860 a visitor, Comte Colonna-Ceccaldi, went to stay with Lesseps at Port Said. From Cairo he went to Sammanud by rail, from there to Mansura by mule and from Mansura to Damietta by boat down the Nile. At Damietta the party embarked on Lake Manzala in six half-decked boats:

in which we were very seasick. We passed a bad night being bitten by mosquitoes and other insects. At five o'clock in the morning we could see the lighthouse at Port Said through field glasses. Half a mile from shore a rowing boat took us off as there was not sufficient depth of water for our boats. We got on shore at nine o'clock. . . . All of the little colony at Port Said came to greet us. There was not far to go. The whole of Port Said consists of a narrow lido. Fourteen months ago this place was a desert; today there are fourteen houses or shops; a lighthouse fifty feet high can be seen at night up to fifteen miles away; a pier stretching 2,000 yards into the Mediterranean has been built to receive supplies by seagoing vessels, one of which at least arrives every week; there are two plants for distilling water. There is a population of 120 Europeans, and 250 Arabs are camped in tents behind the houses.[12]

Lesseps showed his guests a little ditch connecting the Mediterranean with Lake Manzala. "It is only a little ditch, but it is the beginning of the Suez Canal."[13] All the work was done by free labor—Bedouin from the desert, Druzes from Syria, Europeans from everywhere. The big *corvées* who were to dig the Sweet Water Canal and the *rigole de service* from Port Said to Timsah with their bare hands did not become available until the end of 1860.

The next stage in the work was the carrying of the canal across Lake Menzaleh, a distance of about twenty miles,[14] from Port Said to Kantara, the first point on the mainland. This large tract was little more than five feet deep[15] while below the water was slob. Here the opponents of the scheme had decided that the scheme must break down, for the reason that when the Canal was scooped out the bottom would not hold water, the shifting mud or sand sucking it all up like sponges. . . . Further, the Canal banks resting on such a treacherous foundation would melt away through their very weight. An admitted difficulty, too, was the removal of the stuff, which was liquid mud, and when applied as material for the banks would dissolve away as fast as laid down. But for this a special kind of laborer was found on the banks of the lake . . . who were accustomed to "treat" this mud. The mode they adopted was simply to scoop up large masses, out of which they squeezed the water by pressing it against their chests; then they laid it in lumps one on the other. By this laborious process a small channel not more than twelve feet wide was formed . . . as soon as the small cutting was ready dredgers were set to work whose operations soon reached below the mud to a stiff clay. This it discharged upon the banks at each side, raised and widened them, and allowed the Canal also to be widened to its proper extent. The simple

precaution of allowing the discharge of slob and clay to dry in the sun before
another layer was added gave cohesion and solidity. There were many dishearten-
ing incidents owing to the gales and storms which arose at times and swept away
portions of the banks; but these casualties were promptly repaired and only
caused delay. When finished, these banks stood about six feet high above the
water. Then the sun cooperated and baked the whole into a firm, solid mass, so
firm that the banks were used as roads on which heavy loads were transported.[16]

Having now reached the mainland, there were about two miles of channel to
be made when they found themselves at Lake Ballah, an irregular swamp, almost
dry, through which the cutting had to be carried for about eight miles.[17] Here
the soil excavated was found to be gypsum which, when used for the banks,
cracked and decomposed. So other material had to be carried for some distance.
But when they had done with the slob and plaster they had to encounter difficulties
of a more serious kind. A huge plateau, known as El Guisr, stopped the way
and here, said the opponents, "one of the most disastrous surprises awaited them
. . . this series of hills was all sand . . . no art can maintain a cutting through
sand . . . for as soon as any portion is taken out, the rest falls in by its own
weight and fills up the rest." . . . the workmen, it was urged, would infallibly
be buried alive. None of the anticipated evils occurred. Though it was not until
1868 that the excavation of this plateau was completed, it was made passable as
early as 1862. For the wise system, on which the progress of the work was arranged,
was to have it open in some shape so as to hold water—were it only enough to float
a skiff. But, water once present, a most powerful mode of excavation could be
employed, viz: that of steam dredging, which would enlarge the Canal to any
extent desired.[18]

This, then, was the extent of physical progress by the end of 1862, seven
years after the grant of the Second Concession, four years after the formation of the Company, three and a half years after the first *coup de pioche,*
and only a few short days before the death of Mohammed Said. The Sweet
Water Canal had been completed from Ras al Wadi to Lake Timsah and
about halfway from Timsah to Suez. A terminal port, of a kind, had been
established at Port Said. A *rigole de service* had been completed between
Port Said and Lake Timsah. About 5 million cubic meters had been excavated out of a total estimated excavation required of 65 million cubic meters.
Fifty million francs had been spent out of a total capital of 200 million francs.
Physically, with the aid of the *corvées* provided by Mohammed Said, they
had got over the "hump" of Jisr. Politically, they had created enough
of a *fait accompli* to ensure that the canal would eventually be completed
and put into operation, although it was to be another three years before
the Sultan's firman was at last issued.

Sir Henry Bulwer, the British ambassador at Constantinople, when on a
visit to Egypt toward the end of 1862, wrote that "all the accounts which I

hitherto seen . . . underrate what has been done and overrate the remaining difficulties . . . now it is being pursued with an energy and an enthusiasm which is striking . . . the only question as to its completion is a question of money."[19]

With his usual rather long-winded perspicacity, Sir Henry Bulwer had made a just appreciation. The principal problem the Company now faced was a financial one. In the following chapters we shall see how they addressed themselves to it.

NOTES

1. This would provide Nile water via the Zagazig Canal. The link-up with the mainstream of the Nile at Cairo was to be left until later, as was the northern extension from Timsah to Port Said. Fresh water on the Timsah-Port Said stretch was provided, at first either by distillation or by supplies in drums from Damietta across Lake Manzala, and then, when the Sweet Water Canal had been completed to Timsah, by pipeline.
2. The original intention, forecast in the Second Concession, was that the canal's principal port and the place of entry to and egress from Egypt of goods and passengers would be constructed on Lake Timsah at the junction between the Maritime and Sweet Water canals. In the event, although Ismailia, the town constructed on Lake Timsah, was to serve as the headquarters of the Company, it never, for technical reasons, became a port, and either Port Said or Suez were used for loading and unloading, bunkering, et cetera.
3. There was in fact no alternative.
4. It was not a branch of the Nile but an artificial canal dug from the Nile.
5. The eventual extension of the Sweet Water Canal to Cairo had been stipulated in the Second Concession.
6. Fitzgerald, *The Great Canal at Suez,* I, 180–185.
7. *Ibid.,* I, 154–155.
8. Actually, about thirty feet.
9. Fitzgerald, *op. cit.,* I, 157–158.
10. *Ibid.,* pp. 159–160.
11. *Ibid.,* pp. 169–171.
12. Quoted in Edgar-Bonnet, *Ferdinand de Lesseps,* 459–460.
13. *Ibid.*
14. Actually, about thirty miles.
15. Actually, it was much less.
16. Fitzgerald, *op. cit.,* I, 172–174.
17. Actually, about five miles.
18. Fitzgerald, *op. cit.,* I, 174–176.
19. Bulwer–Russell 3.1.63. FO 78/1795.

CHAPTER *nine*

Ismail ?~

TOWARD the end of 1862 Sir Henry Bulwer, the British ambassador in Constantinople, paid a visit to Egypt with, it appears, the principal object of seeing for himself the progress which had been made on the construction of the canal. As we have seen,[1] he came to the conclusion that the Company was likely to be able to complete the canal successfully if they could raise enough money to do so. He estimated, with some prescience, that the total cost of the canal would be about £15 million, of which about £2 million had already been spent. He recognized that the original capital, even if it were subscribed in full, would not be sufficient to complete the canal, but, "I would not think it safe to count positively on such embarrassment breaking up the Company," since they could do enough work with the available capital to prove the canal to be a practicable proposition and so enable them to raise the additional capital required. He deprecated the view that the canal, as such, would be disastrous to British interests: "If I see no great advantage to us in the Canal I see no loss; neither do I think that it will in itself cripple our maritime power." But he was concerned with the risk of French colonization. "Port Said, Timsah and Suez will be French towns . . . the new lands called into cultivation will become French territory and governed by French authority. The native government will become a cipher as well as the Porte." He objected to the forced labor being employed: "On general grounds of progress and humanity there are great objections as to the mode under which the French scheme is carried out." He summed up his objections in the following words: "My objections are not to the Canal and its adjuncts but to the Canal as made by the French Company in the way it is now proceeding and according to the terms it has now obtained . . . it is not so much the Canal that we have to combat as the French Company and the power it is being possessed of."[2] In an immediately following dispatch Bulwer recommended that the British Government should be ready to assist the Porte with a loan to buy out the Canal Company and enable them to complete the canal themselves.[3]

Mohammed Said was already ill while Bulwer was in Egypt. Bulwer reports having an interview with him in which they spoke about the canal. He quotes Mohammed Said as saying:

> As to the Canal we have all been wrong, you, the Porte, me; I have yielded to the pressure which has been put on me; I have not taken all the implications into account; and the rest of you, the British Government and the Porte, never spoke to me decisively and clearly enough against the Canal while I was still free . . . the idea of foreign colonisation is just a piece of nonsense to help them sell the Shares. . . . I intended to take 30,000 Shares but they have put me down for 80,000;[4] I didn't dispute it; the damage is done; now they're talking to me about a loan, but I haven't committed myself to that so far.

Mohammed Said was clearly a sick and demoralized man (he had only a month longer to live). Sir Henry dealt gently with him. He told him that the British Government "had no sort of wish either to govern in Egypt or to have any exclusive or greatly preponderating influence in it, but . . . we could never permit any other foreign Power either forcibly to possess itself of Egypt or indirectly to acquire a greatly preponderating influence over it." With regard to the canal, he told Mohammed Said that "if it could be constructed at all it could only be constructed after many more years and much more expense than had been counted on," and tried to dissuade him from raising a loan to pay for the shares he had taken in the Company.[5]

On January 18, 1863, just over four weeks after his audience with Bulwer, Mohammed Said breathed his last. He was only just over forty years of age. According to the law of heredity set out in the Hatti Sharif of 1841, he was succeeded by Ismail, the oldest male member of the family in the direct line, a son of Ibrahim, a grandson of Mohammed Ali, and a nephew of the late Viceroy.

Lesseps was in the isthmus when he received news that his patron was dying. He hurried to Alexandria to find that Mohammed Said had already expired. According to his biographer he then spent two days *"tout entiers consacrés au culte du souvenir et de l'amitié"* before presenting his respects to the new Viceroy.[6]

Ismail was a very different manner of a man from Mohammed Said. About thirty-three years of age when he ascended the throne, he had the name of being a good man of business and an excellent manager of his large agricultural estates. He was more *rusé* than Mohammed Said; he had none of that monarch's warmhearted lack of reticence and little of his spontaneous generosity. As enthusiastic as Mohammed Said on the modernization of Egypt, he had little of Mohammed Said's consideration for the fellahin of Egypt, whom he was to use ruthlessly throughout his reign, taxing them to pay for his extravagances and conscribing them for his public works and for his army. His great ambition was to make himself independent of the Porte and, in particular, to establish the line of heredity in Egypt through his eldest son, as was the custom in Europe, and not according to the Muslim tradition as laid down in the 1841 Hatti Sharif by virtue of which he himself had ascended the throne. He soon realized that this independence which he so much desired could be obtained only with the assistance of France, since Britain appeared to be too deeply committed to her by now traditional policy of upholding the integrity of the Ottoman Empire, and by wholesale bribery at Constantinople. This need for French support and this reliance on bribery in Constantinople as a principal instrument of policy are the keys both to Ismail's apparently tortuous dealing with the Canal Company and to the Rake's Progress of financial extravagance which was eventually to lead to his deposition.

The desire for independence of Constantinople manifested by Ismail, and by his predecessors, was not merely a matter of personal ambition. The rule of heredity imposed by the 1841 Hatti Sharif was productive of endless intrigue. In Ismail's case, his uncle Halim and his brother Mustafa, both of whom were candidates for the succession in the event of Ismail's death or deposition, were continually intriguing against him both in Cairo and in Constantinople. There were other disadvantages. The chaotic question of jurisdiction over foreigners could not, owing to the connection with Turkey, be resolved without the consent both of the Porte and of the Powers which were parties to the various "capitulations" treaties. Commercial treaties with foreign Powers could not be negotiated without the consent of the Porte, which wished to use Egypt as a dumping ground for its own surplus products, for example, tobacco, and as a means of supplying Turkey with the Egyptian products which it needed, such as cotton. The necessity to seek the Porte's permission before contracting a foreign loan might have proved beneficial to Egypt. But in this matter the Porte's permission was either evaded or else obtained as a result of pressure in Constantinople by the bankers who were anxious to make the loan. Also, the need for these loans arose, in part, from the enormous bribes which had to be paid in Constantinople for the successive relaxations which Ismail managed to obtain in the terms of the 1841 Hatti Sharif. These relaxations, incorporated in two firmans issued in 1867 and 1873, did relieve Egypt from most of the disabilities attaching to the Ottoman connection but did not prevent Ismail from being deposed by the Sultan, at the request of Great Britain and France, in 1879.

Lesseps had no intimate acquaintance with Ismail before his accession. His subsequent relations with him were never on the same rather emotional level that they had achieved with Mohammed Said. They were rather those of business rivals who later became rather unscrupulous business associates, each quite prepared to cheat the other but each realizing that the other was useful to himself. Lesseps wanted the canal, and Ismail wanted sovereign independence. After an attempt, at the outset of his reign, to shake himself free of Lesseps, Ismail came to the conclusion that a complaisance toward the Canal Company would procure for him that French diplomatic support which would assist him toward sovereign independence. Lesseps knew that a demonstration of French official support for the Canal Company would induce such complaisance. Lesseps succeeded in fooling Ismail most of the time because he was a more intelligent and, from the point of view of his ambition, a more dedicated man than Ismail. But Ismail was by no means a fool. He knew what he was doing most of the time. But he was a man who thought that everything could be done with money, and a man who thought that the rulership of Egypt gave him, and would continue indefinitely to give him, access to unlimited sums of money. He was always prepared to buy what he wanted because he had no idea of the value of money. Ismail, as Viceroy, was, in this respect, a totally different person from the prudent manager of his estates which he had been before he became Viceroy. All in all he was a baffling character. He was a man of some charm and presence who never excited in foreign consuls the contempt which his predecessor had done. Like his grandfather, he was a strange mixture of barbarism and enlightenment. But he was too clever by half. He tried to use people; he was nearly always used by them. He was used by Lesseps to finance the canal to a far greater extent than Lesseps had ever been able to use Mohammed Said. He was used by innumerable ministers in Constantinople who took enormous bribes from him without ever doing very much of what he was trying to get them to do. He was used by the eccentric Sultan Abdul Aziz to stock his exotic aviaries with rare and expensive birds. He was used by France against Great Britain and by Great Britain against France and was finally deposed at the instance of both governments acting, for once, in unison.

Aali Pasha, who as Grand Vizier or as Reis Effendi, had much to do with Ismail during the first nine years of his reign, wrote of him:

Ismail Pasha is the victim of whoever knows how to exploit his vanity, his pretensions to magnificence and, above all, his fears; for he is afraid of everything; he is afraid of European opinion and has tried to bribe it; he is afraid of his harem and tries to purchase the good opinion of his wives, his slaves and his eunuchs by means of costly presents. . . . Convinced that everyone is venal, he is surrounded by a horde of people whose greed confirms him in his view. He tries to satisfy everyone with money, and that is the reason for his excessive taxation and for his ruinous loans.[7]

Another portrait is given by a European observer who knew him well:

He had a sort of dignity which you gradually recognised, a strikingly gentle-manlike dignity. . . . With all his keenness and insight into character his knowl-edge both of men and things was superficial, and rather the result of rapidly-formed impressions than of study. . . . Ismail's power of fascination was his most extraordinary gift, and I have never met a man who failed for the moment to succumb to it. Long afterwards, when I saw him daily, and was able five minutes after I left him to expose the deceptions he had been uttering, I had to admit that, so long as I was in his presence, it was almost impossible to avoid being persuaded for the moment.[8]

At the beginning of his reign Ismail appears to have kept Lesseps at arm's length. A few days after his accession, when receiving the congratulations of the Consular Corps, he announced that he proposed to abolish forced labor in Egypt, but privately assured Beauval that he did not intend this to apply to the provision of forced labor for the canal. At the same time, he saw to it that supplies of forced labor for the isthmus were progressively cut down. Beauval, immediately after his conversation with Ismail, tele-graphed: "The Pasha, after proclaiming the abolition of the *corvée,* recog-nized that this abolition was inapplicable to the isthmus and corrected the published version of his speech in that respect. Moreover he has ordered that the next detachment of workers should proceed. He is, however, nervous about the matter and has telegraphed Constantinople for instructions."[9] A few days later, in a long dispatch, Beauval, describing another audi-ence with Ismail, quoted the Viceroy as saying: "I am even more keen on the canal than Lesseps himself, but I approach it in a positive spirit. I believe that it will be of great benefit to Egypt, but at present it is not on a sufficiently secure basis. I will secure it and I will do more than my predeces-sor in this respect. I will see that it gets finished." Beauval then asked him about the labor supply. Ismail said that he could not replace the contingent then working. Beauval protested, and Ismail replied: "Listen to me. I'm going to write to Constantinople tomorrow that such-and-such a situation exists in the isthmus; tell me what to do about it." Beauval ob-jected that such a reference to Constantinople would get to the ears of the British and inevitably provoke an unfavorable reply. He went on to refer to the interests of French shareholders. Ismail replied that the Porte was bound to send some equivocal reply, promised that he would take no notice of it, but indicated that he wanted to behave correctly toward the Porte until after his investiture. "And, between ourselves, after the investiture, I shall be able to do as I like."[10]

Soon after his accession, in accordance with the terms of the 1841 Hatti Sharif, Ismail proceeded to Constantinople for his investiture. Here, besides the Sultan, he saw Kiamil Pasha, the Grand Vizier; Fuad Pasha, the Reis Effendi; Sir Henry Bulwer, the British ambassador; and the Marquis de Moustier, the French ambassador. As a result of his conversations with these dignitaries, he formed certain conclusions about the canal, and about other things. He concluded that the canal enjoyed the support of the French Government. He concluded that the British Government objected particularly to the territorial concessions and to the forced labor. He gathered that none of the Ottoman authorities had strong views for or against the canal but that they were likely to be pushed by Britain into renewed opposition to it unless France asserted herself in favor of it. In general he concluded that British policy was unchanged since the time of Mohammed Ali, that Britain was determined on Egypt's continued subordination to the Porte, and that she was urging the Porte to renew its opposition to the canal principally on that ground. It was not a bad appreciation. Having invited the Sultan to pay a state visit to Egypt the following month, and having distributed, with perhaps more than the usual lavishness, the presents appropriate to the occasion, he took his leave. Back in Egypt, he seems to have decided that, from the point of view of his predominant ambition— sovereign independence—he would have to seek the goodwill of France through complaisance toward the canal, since no support was to be expected from Great Britain, but that he would have to try to avoid British hostility by making some modifications of the Concessions in respect of forced labor and territorial grants.

Almost immediately after his return to Egypt, Ismail concluded two conventions with the Canal Company. By the first of these conventions[11] the Egyptian Government agreed to construct at its own expense that part of the Sweet Water Canal between Cairo and Ras al Wadi which had been stipulated in the Second Concession. Under the terms of this Concession the Company was to be responsible for the construction of the Sweet Water Canal along its whole length and in return was to have the use (without payment of taxes for the first ten years) of all land brought into cultivation by the canal. By the terms of the Convention the Company was relieved of the expenses of digging the Cairo–Ras al Wadi part of the canal against relinquishing all rights in the lands brought into cultivation by the construction of that part. From all points of view, given the terms of the Concession, it was quite a reasonable arrangement. There were a number of complicated land titles near Cairo which it would have been almost impossible to settle satisfactorily. A canal starting from Cairo had been stipulated in the Concession, and it would probably have been impossible to get sufficient water merely by tapping the Damietta branch via the Zagazig Canal. The arrangement went some way to meet British objections about forced labor and territorial concessions, for it was to be assumed that British objections to forced labor would not be extended to its use by the Egyptian Government direct. Eventually, the Cairo–Ras al Wadi stretch of the Sweet Water Canal was dug by the Egyptian Government, with forced labor, and completed in 1866, after having been delayed by a cholera outbreak in Egypt during the summer of 1865.

The Second Convention[12] was more important. The subject of the Egyptian Government shareholding had been the subject of considerable correspondence between Cairo and Paris ever since Ismail's accession. In a note dated January 20th, apparently written by the Duc d'Albufera and sent to Beauval,[13] which set out the terms of the alleged agreement with Mohammed Said in August, 1860, it was stated: "This arrangement for payment, which does not provide the Company with the whole price of the shares until 1875, was not satisfactory to it and they proposed a new arrangement with Said by which these payments would be consolidated into an issue of 500-franc bonds repayable in thirty years. Said Pasha accepted this, and the new arrangement was announced at a meeting of Shareholders on May 22, 1862. But this public announcement aroused so much opposition in Egypt that Said put off signing the new agreement, and in the end he died before signing it. It is therefore very important for the Company to bring these facts to the attention of the new Viceroy and to get him to acknowledge and arrange to pay for the shareholding as soon as possible." On February 9th Beauval, in a dispatch dealing with this note, wrote: "I am not entirely in agreement with M. le Duc d'Albufera in what he says about Said's verbal agreement to the thirty-year bonds. I have spoken to M. de Lesseps about this and I am sure he understands that, in order to enable me to give the Company effective assistance in this matter, I must preserve that impartiality of which Your Excellency sets me so good an example." In a postscript to this dispatch Beauval stated that Lesseps had abandoned the idea of thirty-year bonds and that Ismail had agreed to acknowledge the shareholding and pay for it by installments. He con-

cluded by remarking that relations between Ismail and the Canal Company
were better than they had seemed likely to be on Ismail's accession a month
before.[14] On February 17th, in his last dispatch on the subject of the canal
(he was replaced as consul general by Tastu on February 24th) Beauval
wrote: "I have once more to congratulate myself on His Highness' apparent
benevolence toward the canal without my having tried to press any con-
troversial matters on the Company's behalf. The Company has cash in hand
amounting to 12 million francs, of which they are spending 1,900,000 francs
a month. They must therefore obtain fresh resources in order to continue
the work. They cannot in justice make another application to their non-
Egyptian shareholders, who have already paid 300 francs per share, while
the Egyptian Government still owes 52 million francs on account of their
shareholding, particularly as there is a financial crisis in Europe from which
Egypt is profiting.[15] In view of all this His Highness has authorized me to
inform Your Excellency that he will give the Company satisfaction."[16]

The promised satisfaction was given by a convention, signed on March
19, 1863, which constituted a formal acknowledgment by the Egyptian
Government of the shares attributed to them by the Company, and an
undertaking to pay off by installments the calls for three-fifths of the nominal value of the shares which had already been put out. The convention
provided that the balance of the money owing on the first call of 100 francs
per share for the 177,642 shares should be paid immediately and that the
money owing on the remaining calls, amounting to 200 francs per share,
should be paid off in seventeen monthly installments of 1.5 million francs
each starting from July 1, 1863. The effect of the convention was to legalize
the Company and to provide it with a much-needed supply of money.
(The bills which the Egyptian Government signed to cover the installments
could be discounted fairly easily and cheaply now that the whole matter
was aboveboard).

The effect of these two conventions was to regularize the status of the
Company and to make Ismail the largest shareholder in it. What made
Ismail so forthcoming? Partly, of course, his wish to placate France. But
there is no doubt that he was also thinking in terms of transferring the
effective control of the Company from Lesseps to himself. The technical
status of the canal had just been placed beyond serious doubt as the result
of the publication of a favorable report by Sir John Hawkshaw, a noted
British engineer, who had no financial interest in the canal and whose views
carried weight. The Company was known to be short of money. There
might be difficulties about raising more money unless the support of some
powerful European bankers could be obtained. Lesseps was continually com-

plaining that the value of the shares was being artificially depressed by the activities of *"agioteurs"* on the European money markets. It was felt, certainly by some of the shareholders, possibly by some of the members of the Conseil d'Administration, that the canal was undoubtedly a viable proposition but that the political situation was still delicate, and that what was needed was the transference of control from the dictatorship of Lesseps to the administration of some more tactful, less unpredictable, and generally more respectable group of people who would have the confidence of bankers, who would not frighten statesmen quite so much and who would therefore be more likely to raise the extra capital which would soon be needed. It was a classic situation for an attempt at a "take-over bid." Lesseps had tried to guard against the possibility of this by providing, in the Second Concession, for his presidency of the Company for a period of ten years after the opening of the canal to navigation. But that might easily be remedied. It soon appeared that a new Concession might probably be necessary anyway as a result of the British-inspired insistence about revising the terms of the original Concessions in respect of forced labor and the territorial grants made to the Company. The intricate negotiations of the next few months were, in fact, dominated by this possibility of a "take-over bid," and Lesseps found himself fighting, not for the future of the canal, which was now, as a result of his own efforts, assured, but for his own continued control of the Canal Company which was now being threatened from two sides—by Bulwer, who wanted the British Government to raise money to enable the Porte to buy the Company out,[17] and by various Parisian financiers and speculators who wanted to take advantage of the difficulties of the Company to buy themselves in.

The full details of the intrigues which surrounded the Company during the next two years will now never be known. They are concealed, together with more unsavory scandals, beneath the debris of the Second Empire. But, from the murk and the mist, two principal protagonists emerge with some clarity—the Duc de Morny and Nubar Bey. Of Morny we shall hear later. Nubar demands our immediate attention. Nubar was an Armenian Christian, a nephew of Boghos Bey who had for years been Mohammed Ali's Minister of Commerce. He was born in Smyrna in 1826 and educated in France. He spoke Turkish, French, and English perfectly and Arabic indifferently. He entered Mohammed Ali's service as an interpreter. Abbas made him chief interpreter and a bey, and appears also to have used him on various important missions to Constantinople and to London.[18] He continued to flourish under Mohammed Said, for whom he acted as a go-between in various negotiations. He became regarded by the French as a creature of the British. Beauval, in a private letter to Thouvenel, described him as *"L'ennemi le plus zèle, le plus constant et le plus dangereux de la France."*[19] He certainly appears to have been on good terms with a long succession of British representatives in Egypt. He rose to his full stature after the accession of Ismail, who made him responsible for all negotiations in connection with the Suez Canal and for various other important financial transactions in Constantinople, Paris, and London. Ismail made him a pasha, and he was, at various times, Minister Without Portfolio, Minister of Public Works, Minister of Justice, Foreign Minister, and, eventually, Prime Minister. His tenure of these high offices was interspersed with various periods of disgrace and exile. When out of disgrace he was enormously powerful. Apart from the Suez Canal negotiations which we are about to describe, he was for some time the *homme de confiance* employed by Ismail to negotiate in Constantinople for the various installments of independence which he managed to bribe out of the Seraglio and the Sublime Porte. He negotiated a number of Ismail's international loans. He was the astute lawyer who managed the long-drawn-out and intricate negotiations with the Porte and with the European Powers which resulted in the creation of the Mixed Courts of Justice in Egypt in 1875. In the same year he appears as an assiduous go-between in the negotiations which led to the purchase of the Egyptian Government's canal shares by the British. He was the devious financier whom Ismail employed to cooperate with and to bamboozle the Anglo-French Commission of Control after his extravagance had driven Egypt to bankruptcy. Later still, after the British occupation, Nubar was the accomplished administrator whom Cromer caused to be made Prime Minister in an attempt to clear up the administrative muddle which the British occupiers had inherited.

Nubar was the very prototype of those Levantine *hommes de confiance* who, in Constantinople and Cairo, in Baghdad and Beirut, were the *éminences grises* of their Muslim masters, negotiating with foreign Powers, extorting and borrowing money, dispensing bribes, collecting information, whispering advice. Often feared, sometimes hated, always mistrusted, both by their masters and by those with whom they dealt on behalf of their masters, they ensured their continued survival by making themselves indispensable. Often publicly humiliated, sometimes temporarily exiled, they almost always managed to avoid the ultimate punishment of death, either by execution or by assassination. Gliding through sultans' palaces, through bankers' parlors, and through ministerial antechambers, whispering, cajoling, threatening, and cringing, giving a bribe here, accepting a bribe there, knowing by what means certain people could be conciliated, and with what secrets certain other people could be effectively threatened, they developed a marvelous sense of self-preservation, and died, most often, peaceably in their beds, long after some of their Muslim rivals had met their violent ends by means of the poisoned cup, the knife, or the strangling cord. When Nubar, full of years and honor, died in his bed, he achieved the surprising apotheosis of a memorial tablet in the Anglican Cathedral in Cairo, bearing the inscription "Justice is the Foundation of Empires."

Nubar's first important experience in international negotiations was in the matter of the canal. He negotiated with Lesseps the two conventions which have just been described. And, after the Sultan's state visit, which seems to have passed off without any reference to the canal having been made, he was sent by Ismail to Constantinople to open negotiations for a revision of the canal concessions.

The British Government's reaction to news of the two conventions was one of extreme annoyance with Ismail. On April 7th they cabled to Colquhoun instructing him to use all his influence to get the conventions canceled.[20] Meanwhile, Bulwer had been engaged with the Porte in drafting a stiff note to the Viceroy. This note, as a result of interventions from Bulwer on the one side and from Moustier on the other, took a lot of drafting, and needed to be approved at a meeting of the Divan before it could be sent off. The text was finally approved on April 6th and a copy[21] given to the British and French ambassadors. The original was sent to the Viceroy on April 6th but does not appear to have reached Egypt until some weeks later.[22] In spite of Moustier's intervention, it was still fairly stiffly worded:

Neither the Porte nor the Powers which are so keenly interested in the progress of civilization in the Orient can permit that this great work is brought about by methods which are severely and justly condemned by all civilised nations and of which one of the disastrous consequences in Egypt has been to take as many as 60,000 men at a time away from agriculture. . . . Nor can the Sublime Porte recognise that other stipulation by which a considerable part of Egyptian territory has been ceded to a foreign Company. . . . In spite of the lack of consideration which the Company has shewn up to now towards the rights of the territorial Suzerain, it will be given preference in carrying on the construction of the Canal if it is prepared to forego those conditions in the Concession which have been indicated as inadmissible. If so we will consider in good faith all the other conditions of the contract. . . . If the Company does not wish to continue with the enterprise under these new conditions the Sublime Porte will be prepared to consult with Your Highness on the means to be adopted for indemnifying the Company for the expenses which it has so far incurred and for continuing the construction of the Canal in a more acceptable and practicable way.

It ended by stating that the supply of forced labor was to be cut off immediately and all work on the canal stopped.

This note did not arrive in Egypt until after the Sultan's visit was over and just before Nubar left for Constantinople at the end of May. Tastu, the new French consul general, who became notable for his uncritical support of the Canal Company, had already been informed of the contents of the note in a telegram from Drouyn de Lhuys dated April 4th:

An energetic pressure of a nature to compromise the French interests in the isthmus appears to have been exercised on the Sultan before his departure for Egypt by the British ambassador. At the same time a communication was prepared in Constantinople which will be sent to the British and French governments. According to this communication the Porte's agreement to the continuation of work in the isthmus will be subject to certain conditions which would be to the detriment of the Canal Company and which would involve a modification of the Concession. The Turkish Government claims that these conditions are being insisted on by Ismail himself. In view of the fact that Ismail has given the Company proof of his good intentions toward them we do not believe this. We do not doubt the sincerity of his assurances, and it will no doubt be sufficient for you to remind him that we count on his firmness and that he can count on our support.[23]

Later in April, while the note was on its way to Egypt, Colquhoun received a dispatch drafted by Palmerston personally, in which he had written that "the Pasha should be made to understand that M. de Lesseps is undermining his authority as Viceroy and that soon . . . he will be the nominal while Lesseps will be the real Viceroy of Egypt."[24] On May 27th Colquhoun, reporting Nubar's imminent departure for Constantinople, added that the publication of the note to Ismail (which had apparently only just arrived in Egypt) had caused a great sensation: "The language held by the French is very violent and it has been reported to me that that of the French Agent is characterised by a total absence of moderation . . . and he declares that his Government will not fail to support the interests of French subjects."[25] On the following day Colquhoun reported that Prince Napoleon, the Protector of the Company, had arrived in Egypt and was making a tour of the isthmus.[26]

When Nubar, who had just been created a pasha,[27] arrived in Constantinople at the beginning of June, he found that Kiamil Pasha had just been replaced as Grand Vizier by Fuad Pasha, previously Reis Effendi. Nubar appears to have improved the occasion by offering to pay off a pressing debt of 30,000 mejidiehs (about £30,000) owing by the new Grand Vizier, an offer which Fuad, who had the reputation of being unusually honest as Ottoman ministers went, accepted.[28]

When Ismail was in Constantinople, the Porte, at Bulwer's instigation, had presented him with a questionnaire about the canal in which he had been asked (*a*) the position about the shareholding, (*b*) the estimated total cost of the canal, (*c*) the amount of labor employed on the canal, and the effect of this on agriculture in Egypt, and (*d*) whether the canal could be completed by the Egyptian Government out of its own resources.[29] Ismail had not answered this questionnaire at the time, but Nubar carried a letter from Ismail to the Grand Vizier in which he set out his ideas about the canal. In this letter Ismail wrote that "the canal having been agreed in principle by the Sublime Porte, the Company should be allowed to continue and complete the work of construction on condition that the Viceroy revises the Company's Concessions so as to delete the objectionable provisions mentioned in the Grand Vizier's letter of April 6 [forced labor and the land grants]. To this end the Viceroy . . . proposes to make an arrangement with the Company with regard to the lands granted and will also repurchase from the Company the Wadi lands. Furthermore, with regard to the question of forced labor, the Viceroy will endeavor to make an arrangement with the Company which will reconcile the needs of construction with the effective abolition of the *corvée*."[30]

Nubar also carried with him a letter from Ismail to Moustier, the French ambassador. In this letter the Viceroy requested Moustier's good offices in helping Nubar to come to an arrangement with the Porte over the canal, stating that the Company would be allowed to retain such land as they needed for the construction and operation of the canal and would be compensated for the rest. The letter added that the continuation of the *corvée* was impossible as the fellahin had become more prosperous as a result of the American Civil War,[31] and *"Je ne peux plus faire ce que mon grandpère a fait impunément."* Instead of a *corvée* he suggested that free labor could be organized, and indicated that he would be prepared to assist. He went on to assure Moustier that he would see that the canal was completed but that he would need French assistance to ensure the neutrality of the canal and also to ensure that the canal was not garrisoned by Turkish troops. He concluded by saying that he would also need French diplomatic support in the efforts he was making in Constantinople to secure for his eldest son the right of succession to the Egyptian throne.[32] When presenting this letter, Nubar made a verbal communication to Moustier, who passed it on to Drouyn de Lhuys, to the effect that "if the French Government wishes to intervene in this matter, as Prince Napoleon seemed to indicate during his recent visit to Egypt, and to use its influence on M. de Lesseps to induce him to hand back the land against financial compensation, which would be agreed between the Viceroy and Lesseps, Ismail, if he were sure of the French Government's agreement, would allow the work to continue without taking any notice either of the British Government or of the Porte." Nubar indicated to Moustier that he would like an urgent reply from the French Government and that, if the reply were favorable, he would be prepared to break off all negotiations in Constantinople and come to Paris to negotiate with Lesseps and the French Government.[33]

Nubar then went to see Bulwer. "What Nubar stated to me was that the Viceroy recognised the necessity of getting the lands that Said had ceded to the Company from that body and that he was able and willing to do this by purchasing them . . . but that, as to forced labour, he was afraid to abolish it since the Company would declare that this was a clear though indirect method of stopping the construction of the Canal altogether. . . . I told him that I was certain that any attempt to continue forced labour would never receive the approval of Her Majesty's Government."[34] Afterward Bulwer tentatively suggested a limitation of the supply of forced labor to a maximum of 6,000 for the following two years only.[35]

There followed a series of intricate negotiations involving Fuad Pasha, the Grand Vizier, Aali Pasha, who had replaced Fuad as Reis Effendi, Moustier, Bulwer, and Nubar. Another grand-vizierial letter was sent to Ismail[36] which contained some modifications of the terms of the letter of April 6th in that it expressed the Porte's agreement to the construction of the canal subject (*a*) to the completed canal being used only for commerce and not for the passage of warships or troop transports, (*b*) to the return of the alienated lands to the Egyptian Government, and (*c*) to the abolition of forced labor. The letter gave Ismail six months to agree with the Company over (*b*) and (*c*), during which period work was to be allowed to continue. With regard to (*a*) Ismail was asked to make a technical study of the proposed size of the canal to see whether warships could be excluded without excluding merchant vessels.

At the beginning of August, Nubar returned to Alexandria from Constantinople, and Ismail, apparently pleased with the services of his *homme de confiance,* made him a present of a fully equipped farm.[37] After spending only a few days in Alexandria, Nubar set off for Paris armed with a letter of introduction from Ismail to Drouyn de Lhuys. In this letter Ismail wrote that he was sending Nubar to Paris to "negotiate with M. de Lesseps the modifications which had to be introduced into the Concessions in accordance with the orders of the Porte." He added that the Porte had authorized him to negotiate these amendments direct with the Company and that he wanted these negotiations to take place in Paris under the benevolent auspices of the French Government.[38] Before Nubar's departure Tastu saw him, and pointed out that Lesseps was already on his way back to Egypt. In reply Nubar indicated that he was going to Paris to see the French Government to try to induce them to make Lesseps see reason. Tastu remarked that the French Government would not intervene in the matter unless the Canal Company asked them.[39]

Nubar was determined to bypass Lesseps and settle the matter in Paris. He appears to have been advised by Moustier to go to Paris,[40] a circumstance which greatly annoyed Lesseps when he got to hear of it. But he had other and more cogent reasons for making the trip. Intrigues were proceeding in Paris which had as their object the buying out of the existing Canal Company and the removal of Lesseps. A mysterious "chief engineer of the Roads and Bridges Department" had been sent to Egypt by a certain *"homme d'état"* to inspect the canal works and had returned to France with a most unfavorable report which was going to be used by the *"homme d'état"* in question "to have the existing Company liquidated and to replace it by another one which is already in process of being set up."[41]

The *"homme d'état"* was Auguste, Duc de Morny, President of the Corps Législatif, an illegitimate half-brother and intimate political associate of the Emperor. Auguste Morny, who took his surname from the French *petit-bourgeois* family by whom he had been brought up, was the illegitimate grandson of Talleyrand and the illegitimate son of Hortense Beauharnais, Queen of Holland, and daughter, by her first marriage, of the Empress Josephine, first wife of Emperor Napoleon I. It may be worth while explaining in a little more detail the circumstances of these untoward conceptions. Talleyrand, during the interval between his being a priest and becoming a statesman, had a son by a certain Mme. Flahaut, née Adelaide Filleul, wife of Comte de Flahaut de la Billarderie. This son, who was known by the surname of Flahaut, became a dashing cavalry officer during the Napoleonic wars. The Emperor Napoleon, in the course of providing thrones and wives for his relatives and associates, had given the throne of Holland to his syphilitic and degenerate brother Louis and had bestowed on him as consort his stepdaughter Hortense, daughter of his wife Josephine by her first marriage. With such an unsatisfactory husband, and possessing something of her mother's taste for gallantry, Hortense had many lovers. One of these was the dashing Captain Flahaut by whom she had a son, Auguste, who was born in decent obscurity in the year 1811 and boarded out with a family of the name of Morny. This son was well looked after, at a distance, by his various distinguished relatives. He spent some years in the army, became a man-about-town in Paris, and dabbled in the arts, politics, and high finance. After the 1848 Revolution he abandoned his old Orléanist associates and threw in his lot with his half-brother. The blood relationship was universally known but never officially acknowledged. Morny was one of Napoleon's principal aides in the December *coup d'état*. He became President of the Corps Législatif and was for a time ambassador at the court of the Czar. He was made a duke. In foreign affairs he was an advocate of an alliance with Russia and an opponent of the British alliance. But his real influence was in home affairs, where his dexterous management of the Corps Législatif helped to lend a deceptive air of stability to a hollow and corrupt regime. In this corruption Morny himself took no small share. He was deeply involved in the Mexican scandals. He was a great speculator. He had a finger in most of the larger pies. "*Morny est dans l'affaire*" was a warning for the prudent investor to run for cover. He knew everyone; he heard everything. It was to be expected that he would turn a speculative eye toward the tangled affairs of the Canal Company. It is impossible now to discover the extent to which he did become interested.[42] But it is certain that there was a move in Paris to buy out the Canal Company and to eliminate Lesseps from it; it is certain that Morny was concerned in this movement; and it is certain that Morny was in correspondence with Ismail about the canal independently either of the Canal Company or of the French Government.

Lesseps returned to Egypt on August 25th, six days after Nubar had left for Paris. Ismail, anxious to avoid meeting him, had left the day before for Upper Egypt.[43] One way and another, Lesseps was very angry indeed. He was angry about Nubar's visit to Constantinople; he was even more angry about his visit to Paris. He was angry about the two grand-vizierial letters, the second of which he regarded, not incorrectly, as having been partly inspired by Nubar. He was angry at Ismail's evasiveness. For the first time in the history of the canal, he must have felt that he was no longer at the center of things, that the whole affair was in danger of passing out of his control. On August 27th he wrote to Albufera warning the Conseil d'Administration to have nothing to do with Nubar in Paris.[44] On August 28th he wrote to his brother Théodore the letter which has already been quoted about the mysterious engineer and the "*homme d'état*."[45] On September 1st he wrote a long and detailed protest to Ismail about the contents of the two grand-vizierial letters. "If . . . they were to be taken seriously, it would mean a denial of the Company's rights and the practical impossibility of finishing the canal." After ridiculing the suggestion that the canal should be made big enough for merchant ships but not big enough for warships, he warned Ismail that, if he took any notice of the Grand Vizier's instructions, he would in effect be transferring the capital of Egypt from Cairo to Constantinople. He pointed out that the supply of forced labor had been guaranteed by a contract with Mohammed Said. Finally, with reference to the question of an Ottoman firman, he pointed out that Ismail's predecessor had recognized that, since the withholding of the firman was due solely to British objections, it had always been an understood thing between him and the Porte that no written permission would be given but that verbal permission had already been given.[46]

During the course of September, Lesseps received a report from the isthmus stating that the number of workers, which had amounted to 20,000 at Mohammed Said's death, had been steadily reduced since, and now amounted to less than 15,000. There were other complaints too, to the effect that officials were "dragging their feet" and generally being obstructive, as they had been in 1859, and that the interests of the Company were being "neglected and sacrificed."[47]

Meanwhile, Nubar was busy in Paris. He saw Morny and wrote to Ismail that, in accordance with Morny's advice, he should not negotiate with Lesseps: "Continue to act toward M. de Lesseps as you have been doing. Plenty of politeness, no negotiations. That is M. de Morny's advice. The Viceroy, in deciding to negotiate in Paris, is exercising his rights as a sovereign. M. de Lesseps must accept this; try to persuade him that in his own interests it is advisable for him to come to Paris as soon as possible. That is M. de Morny's advice."[48] He saw Drouyn de Lhuys, who told him that the French Government would take no action except at the request of the Company.[49] He obtained a legal opinion from an eminent French lawyer, Nogart St. Laurent, about the labor contract, in which St. Laurent stated that, according to the terms of the contract, the wage rates were subject to modification at the Viceroy's discretion and that the amount of labor supplied could be regulated at the Viceroy's discretion according to his estimate of the needs of Egyptian agriculture.[50]

On October 12th Nubar, on behalf of the Viceroy, formally presented the Conseil d'Administration with the Egyptian Government's proposal for a revision of the Concessions. According to this proposal[51] the labor supply was to be maintained at a maximum of 6,000[52] and the laborers' pay increased to two francs (or about nine piastres) a day. (The 1856 contract provided that adult workers were to be paid from two and one-half to three piastres a day plus rations to the equivalent of one piastre a day. The proposed rate—whether or not it included rations is not clear—was thus a very considerable increase on the old. But wage rates had gone up in Egypt since 1856 as a result of the cotton boom. Many of the complaints which had arisen over the supply of forced labor were due to the inadequacy of the wage rates, which the Company does not seem to have done anything to correct.) The alienated lands were to be restored to the Egyptian Government, which by way of compensation to the Company would bear the whole of the expenses of digging the Sweet Water Canal for its own account. The offer also stipulated that the sale of the Wadi lands to the Company must be canceled against the return of the purchase price to the Company.

When this proposal was received by the Conseil d'Administration, Lesseps was still in Egypt, in spite of a request by Drouyn de Lhuys, conveyed to him through Tastu, that he should return as soon as possible for direct negotiations with Nubar.[53] An extraordinary meeting of the Conseil d'Administration was held in Alexandria toward the end of October to consider Nubar's proposal, the rest of the members of the Conseil d'Administration having made the journey from Paris to Alexandria for this purpose. At this meeting it was decided formally to reject Nubar's proposal; this was done in a letter to Nubar dated October 29th, a copy of which was sent to Drouyn de Lhuys.[54] On the same date the Conseil d'Administration addressed a circular to shareholders denying rumors of a pending agreement between the Egyptian Government and the Company for a revision of the Concessions.[55]

On October 18th Tastu, reporting the coming meeting of the Conseil d'Administration in Alexandria, and perhaps echoing the anxieties of Lesseps himself, pointed out to Drouyn de Lhuys that Ismail clearly felt himself sustained by the French Government in his quarrel with the Canal Company, since otherwise he would have made some attempt to take advantage of the presence of the Conseil d'Administration in Egypt to negotiate with them direct. He went on to express fear that Nubar had misinterpreted the courtesy with which he had been received in Paris as an indication that the French Government were in sympathy with his point of view.[56] Beneath the polite phrasing of this dispatch can be seen Tastu's suspicion that the French Government was conniving at some intrigue which was going on in Paris behind the backs of Lesseps and the French consul general in Egypt.

There was in fact some reason for Tastu's suspicions. It appears that Nubar, on his arrival in Paris, had delivered to the Emperor a letter from Ismail in which the Viceroy had asked Napoleon for his intervention in the differences which had arisen between the Egyptian Government and the Company.[57] The Emperor, instead of passing this letter to the Foreign Minister as would have been normal, passed it to Morny, asking him to investigate the matter. (It seems that there must have been some pre-arrangement about this between Nubar and Morny.) Nubar then gave Morny a long note detailing the Egyptian Government's grievances against the Canal Company.[58] These complaints were listed under two main heads. Under the head of forced labor, Nubar expatiated on the ill-effects which the *corvée* was having on Egyptian agriculture, pointed out that the wages paid were inadequate, and complained that the laborers were ill-treated by the Company's supervisors. In an impressive passage he gave details of this alleged ill-treatment and related how he had wept when he had witnessed it. (Lesseps, when he was later given a copy of this note to read, minuted drily that Nubar had never set foot in the isthmus.)[59] Under the head of lands, Nubar, while admitting the principle of paying compensation to the Company for the return of the ceded lands to the Egyptian Government, pointed out that the lands had very little present value and that it would be many years before they could become cultivable: "The sand, like the sea, takes a long time to conquer." He ended on a gently blackmailing note: "For my part I am very anxious that I should not be compelled to go back to Constantinople and knock on Sir Henry Bulwer's door."[60]

Morny, who was too busy and too important to do any detailed work on the matter himself, asked Emile Ollivier, an Opposition leader in the Corps Législatif, whom Morny had adopted as a kind of protégé in order to moderate his criticisms of the Government, to study the whole question and make a report for the Emperor.[61] At the same time Nubar, spending the Viceroy's money with a free hand, started a vigorous campaign against the Canal Company in the Paris press. Lesseps, who was of course aware of much of what was going on in Paris, seems at last to have decided that he could no longer afford to be absent from the arena. On October 31st he left Alexandria for Marseille, having characteristically informed Tastu that he had intended to return to France at the end of October in any case in order to take his son back to college at the beginning of term.[62]

Once in Paris, Lesseps, exasperated and, it may be, alarmed by Nubar's activities, tried to reestablish direct contact with Ismail. He wrote to Ruyssenaers and asked him to try and warn Ismail against Nubar's activities and announced his intention of returning to Egypt forthwith to open negotiations with Ismail direct. Ismail replied to this by promoting Nubar to the post of Minister Without Portfolio as a sign of confidence in him, and by threatening to withdraw all labor from the isthmus immediately if Lesseps embarked at Marseille.[63] At about the same time, in Constantinople, Aali Pasha told Moustier that, since Lesseps was refusing to negotiate with the Viceroy's representative, the six-month delay period provided for in the Grand Vizier's second letter was deemed to have started.[64] Ruyssenaers advised Lesseps to try to secure the intervention of the French Government.[65] That was all very well, but the French Government's intervention would be of use only if it were certain that this intervention would not be inspired by Morny, since such inspiration as Morny might import into the matter would be disastrous to the Company, or at all events to Lesseps personally.

On November 11th Drouyn de Lhuys informed Tastu that there was likely to be an arbitration over the differences existing between the Egyptian Government and the Canal Company, and warned Tastu to make certain that the *status quo* was maintained in Egypt in all matters affecting the Company and that no action was taken which might affect the matter to be arbitrated.[66] In reply, Tastu telegraphed that the Viceroy professed to know nothing about the possibility of arbitration.[67]

At the beginning of December, Lesseps went to see Morny, apparently at Morny's request. He sent an account of the interview to Ruyssenaers.[68] Morny told him that he had offered himself as a mediator between the Egyptian Government and the Canal Company. Lesseps, according to his account, told Morny that he was the last person who, in the matter of the Canal Company, was qualified to act as a mediator. He referred Morny to the rumors which were rife in Egypt about his relationships with Nubar and, in effect, warned him to watch his step. In reply Morny showed him a letter from the Emperor, referring to a request made by Ismail that the Emperor should arbitrate between the Company and the Egyptian Government, and asking Morny to see Lesseps on his behalf and discuss the matter with him. Morny then told him that he had asked "a certain deputy" in the Corps Législatif to study the whole dispute between the Company and the Egyptian Government and make a report about it which would be submitted to the Emperor.[69]

After his interview with Morny, Lesseps went to see Drouyn de Lhuys and told him all about it.[70] Drouyn de Lhuys, as Foreign Minister, had been naturally and justifiably irritated at the Emperor's action in placing the matter in Morny's hands and, while Morny was referring inquirers about the canal to Drouyn de Lhuys, Drouyn de Lhuys was referring them to Morny.[71] On January 6th Erskine, the British chargé d'affaires in Constantinople (Bulwer, as we shall see, was in Paris) reported Aali Pasha as saying that he was still without the least clue to the Emperor's intentions, that Morny had advised Jamil Pasha (the Turkish Ambassador in Paris) to speak either to the Emperor himself or to Drouyn de Lhuys, and that Drouyn de Lhuys had told him that, the question being still in Morny's hands, he could say nothing. He further reported that Morny, being anxious to avoid the appearance of taking a part against Lesseps, had placed the matter in the hands of Emile Ollivier.[72]

By this time Ollivier had made his report,[73] which had been submitted to the Emperor. In it he expressed the opinion: (*a*) that the lands which had been ceded to the Company were unnecessary for its operations and should be given up against "*une indemnité suffisante*" to be settled by negotiation; (*b*) that the Sweet Water Canal should remain under the Company's control; (*c*) that the Porte's ratification was necessary before any more work could be done on the canal; (*d*) that the *corvée* should be abolished, that no compensation was due to the Company in consequence of its abolition, but that the stipulation in the Second Concession about four-fifths of the workers having to be Egyptian should be revoked. It was certainly not an opinion on which Lesseps would have wished the Emperor to base his arbitration.

On December 28th Lesseps told Drouyn de Lhuys that the Conseil d'Administration had decided to sue Nubar for defamation as a result of the press attacks which he had, for the past two months, been making on the Company, and that an extraordinary general meeting of the Company would be held at the beginning of March.[74] (The Company's case against Nubar was heard before the Tribunal de la Seine two months later; the Tribunal refused to hear the Company on the ground that, since the issuance of the writ, and when the matter was in consequence *sub judice,* they had taken steps to answer Nubar in public. The accusation against Nubar was based on the charge that Nubar, on the strength of legal opinion which he had obtained,[75] was making propaganda to the effect that the Company had no legal existence until the Sultan's firman had been obtained. The Company replied with propaganda for its own account and, for several months, a brisk war of words proceeded in the venal Paris press in which no expense was spared by either party.)

On January 4th the Conseil d'Administration addressed a formal petition to the Emperor asking for his intervention at Constantinople in the light of the Grand Vizier's two letters to Ismail in April and July of the previous year.[76] On the same day Lesseps wrote a letter to his old ally, the Empress, enclosing a copy of the petition to the Emperor and asking her to arrange for him to have an audience with the Emperor. He told the Empress that what he was principally concerned about was to stop Morny from interfering in the affairs of the Company.[77]

Sir Henry Bulwer, who was on a short visit to Paris, saw the Emperor on

January 8th and discussed with him the whole range of those Near Eastern affairs in which Britain and France were both interested. On the subject of the Canal, Napoleon told Bulwer:

"Lesseps is making a great fuss about it. I am to see him tomorrow. I hear you have been over the ground. Give me freely your opinion and that of your Government as to the whole of this affair." I said that as to the Canal itself I did not see any objection to it nor any objection that my Government had to it; that I myself thought it executable though at much larger cost than had been calculated; that I could not however say that it would be profitable; this however was the concern of those who made it. But while the Canal was one thing, the question which the Company wanted to connect with it was another. . . . By an agreement which the Company had made with the Viceroy, which to be binding had to be sanctioned by the Porte but had never been so sanctioned, the Company would get possession of all the lands adjacent to the Canal; that people would see, not unnaturally even if erroneously, a scheme of French ambition and not of general utility . . . that in regard to Egypt especially His Imperial Majesty knew only too well the interest we had in India to suppose that we could ever see established with indifference such a state of affairs as Lesseps proposed to constitute, and that the Porte, and even the Ruler of Egypt, must believe him, from manifest interest, opposed to it. "But supposing," said the Emperor, "the Company sell the lands you speak of, may not this be merely part of a commercial speculation?" I said that if the Company sold its lands, they would probably be sold to French or other foreigners; they would be subject (owing to the Capitulations) to the laws of their own country and not to those of Egypt, which would render the position of the native Government almost impossible. . . . I would say that without the land scheme the Canal would meet with no opposition . . . that with it . . . the most resolute opposition would be the consequence. "But if the Egyptian Government were to purchase the lands?" "Exactly, Sir. That is what the Egyptian Government have been endeavouring to do and what Lesseps is resisting . . . notwithstanding that various distinguished French lawyers had decided that Lesseps' claim was illegal he still persisted in this and seemed disposed to try and drag his Government and his country into difficulties for the sake of his own pecuniary interests." The Emperor said, "I am seeing him tomorrow. We must try and arrange the affair."[78]

Three days later, Bulwer saw Morny, and reported, "The Duke told me that he had seen the Emperor who told him 'I am happy to find that Bulwer and you are quite agreed and that we all three entertain the same opinion.' "[79] Later, on January 15th, Bulwer wrote, "It is better not to touch the matter with Drouyn de Lhuys at present; M. Ollivier's Report is against Lesseps; Morny's opinion will be against him, and the Emperor is prepared to agree with Morny."[80]

But Bulwer had underestimated either the Lesseps magic or Eugénie's influence on the Emperor. Lesseps had his audience with the Emperor on

January 9th. An entertaining, but probably apocryphal, account of the audience is given by one of Lesseps' biographers:

The Court was at Fontainebleau. The Emperor invited Ferdinand de Lesseps to luncheon. The Empress was present. She had just received a luxurious Bosphorus barge, complete with bargemaster, which "Fernando" had sent her as a present. The conversation, which was extremely cordial and in which Lesseps took the lead with his usual verve and charm, dwelt on the varied and picturesque incidents which had marked the already long process of the canal's construction. Lesseps had the tact and good taste not to expatiate on the difficulties which he had experienced, and on the tremendous efforts which he had had to make, and which he was still making, but it was easy to appreciate them beneath the deliberate lightheartedness of his conversation. Eugénie understood. Her beautiful eyes, wet with tears, were fixed upon those of Napoleon while Lesseps was talking. That look of Eugénie's was one of the few which was able to penetrate the Emperor's heavy eyelids and get through to his heart. After luncheon Napoleon III took Ferdinand de Lesseps affectionately by the arm and led him into the park. Smoking their cigars, they arrived at the lakeside where the Bosphorus barge, Lesseps' gift to the Empress, was moored. "Let us get into the barge and have a turn on the lake," suggested the Emperor.[81] "It will be a good opportunity for a chat." They sent for the bargemaster, who was deaf and dumb, a discreet Oriental bodyguard. The barge glided silently through the water, its gold fittings and its precious woods reflected in the mirror-like surface of the lake which was broken from time to time by the leaping of the carp with which the lake had been stocked by Francis I. Neither the bargemaster nor the carp ever told the secret of that conversation, but when, on their return, Lesseps took leave of his Sovereign, his face shone with ardor and confidence.[82]

Whatever may have happened at this audience, a conversation between the Emperor and Lesseps was once more to prove a turning point in the history of the Canal Company. And once more Eugénie had proved herself to be the "guardian angel" of the Canal Company. Immediately after the audience, Napoleon instructed Drouyn de Lhuys to take the matter of the canal in hand.[83]

NOTES

1. See pp. 149–150.
2. Bulwer–Russell, No. 2 of 3.1.63. FO 78/1795.
3. *Ibid.*, No. 3 of 3.1.63. FO 78/1795.
4. Presumably he said (or meant) that he had intended to subscribe 30 million francs but that they had put him down for 80 million.
5. Bulwer–Russell 15.12.62. FO 78/1715. Bulwer seems to have assumed that Mohammed had formally agreed to take up the 177,000 unsubscribed shares.
6. Edgar-Bonnet, *Ferdinand de Lesseps*, I, 363.
7. Quoted by G. Douin, *Règne du Khédive Ismaïl*, II, 362.

8. McCoan, *Egypt Under Ismail*, pp. 283-284.
9. Beauval–de Lhuys 23.1.63. CP 31. Drouyn de Lhuys had once more become Foreign Minister in place of Thouvenel.
10. Beauval–de Lhuys 5.2.63. CP 31.
11. M & D, Vol. 13.
12. *Ibid.*
13. See CP 31.
14. Beauval–de Lhuys 9.2.63. CP 31.
15. This is a reference to the steep rise in cotton prices which was taking place as a result of the American Civil War and the blockade of the southern cotton ports by the North.
16. Beauval–de Lhuys 17.1.63. CP 31.
17. See Note 3 above.
18. Le Moyne 9.7.50. CP 22 and 20.4.51. CP 23.
19. Beauval–Thouvenel 14.10.61. CP 30.
20. Russell–Colquhoun 7.4.63. FO 78/1795.
21. See M & D, Vol. 13.
22. Journal, IV, 311.
23. De Lhuys–Tastu 4.4.63. CP 31.
24. Russell–Colquhoun 27.4.63. FO 78/1795.
25. Colquhoun–Russell 27.5.63. FO 78/1795.
26. *Ibid.*, 28.5.63. FO 78/1795.
27. Tastu–de Lhuys 18.4.63. CP 31.
28. Douin, *op. cit.*, I, 59.
29. *Ibid.*, p. 32.
30. Journal, IV, 312.
31. Which had led to a great rise in the demand for Egyptian cotton.
32. Douin, *op. cit.*, I, 583.
33. Journal, IV, 312 *et seq.*, quoting dispatch from Moustier to Drouyn de Lhuys.
34. Bulwer–Russell 11.6.63. FO 78/1795.
35. *Ibid.*, 27.6.63. FO 78/1795.
36. M & D, Vol. 13.
37. Tastu–de Lhuys 4.8.63. CP 32.
38. Ismail–de Lhuys 18.8.63. CP 32.
39. Tastu–de Lhuys 19.8.63. CP 32.
40. Douin, *op. cit.*, I, 67.
41. Journal, IV, 339.
42. The British ambassador in Vienna, in a dispatch dated March, 1856, names Morny as one of the founder-shareholders in the Canal Company. (Seymour–Clarendon 4.3.56. FO 78/1340). There was also a later suggestion that Morny had been asked by the Russian Government to interest himself in the Canal Company (Cowley–Russell 2.8.64. FO 78/1849).
43. Colquhoun–Russell 26.8.63. FO 78/1795, and Tastu–de Lhuys 30.8.63. CP 32.
44. Journal, IV, 337.
45. *Ibid.*, p. 339.
46. Journal, IV, 319–336.
47. *Ibid.*, p. 344.
48. This letter is quoted in Tastu–de Lhuys 7.8.63. CP 32. The name "Morny" has been cut out of the original dispatch and left as M.
49. De Lhuys–Tastu 18.9.63. CP 32.
50. Text of St. Laurent's opinion dated 1.10.63 in CP 32.
51. Douin, *op. cit.*, I, 72–73.
52. Refer to Bulwer's suggestion to HMG in 27.6.63. See Note 35 above.
53. Cable de Lhuys–Tastu 7.10.63. CP 32.
54. Lesseps–de Lhuys 31.10.63. CP 32.
55. Journal, IV, 363.
56. Tastu–de Lhuys 19.10.63. CP 32.
57. De Lhuys–Tastu 7.12.63. CP 32.
58. For text of this note see CP 32.

59. Minute by Lesseps on text of note in CP 32.

60. Lesseps' minuted comment was *"Quelle impudence."*

61. It was from Emile Ollivier that Lesseps received a copy of Nubar's note to Morny. After minuting it, Lesseps passed it on to Drouyn de Lhuys (Lesseps–de Lhuys 28.12.63. CP 32).

62. Tastu–de Lhuys 18.10.63. CP 32.

63. *Ibid.,* 9.11.63 and 10.11.63. CP 32.

64. Douin, *op. cit.,* I, 76.

65. Ruyssenaers–Lesseps 9.11.63. CP 32.

66. De Lhuys–Tastu 11.11.63. CP 32.

67. Tastu–de Lhuys 19.11.63. CP 32.

68. Journal, IV, 364.

69. It is not clear whether Morny told him that the "certain deputy" was Emile Ollivier. In any case Lesseps soon found out, and obtained from Ollivier a copy of Nubar's note to Morny. See Note 61.

70. Douin, *op. cit.,* I, 79.

71. Drouyn de Lhuys's irritation is apparent in a dispatch to Tastu, dated December 7th, in which he writes that he is unaware of the contents of Ismail's letter to the Emperor or of the Emperor's reply but that it can be assumed that the reply, insofar as it concerned the isthmus, was favorable to the Canal Company (De Lhuys–Tastu 7.12.63. CP 32). There appear to be no extant copies of Ismail's letter or of the Emperor's reply.

72. Erskine–Russell 6.1.64. FO 78/1849.

73. For text see M & D, Vol. 14.

74. Journal, IV, 370.

75. On the basis, the Company alleged, of a falsified document.

76. M & D, Vol. 14.

77. *Ibid.*

78. Bulwer–Russell 9.1.64. FO 78/1849.

79. *Ibid.,* 12.1.64. FO 78/1849.

80. *Ibid.,* 15.1.64. FO 78/1849.

81. On a January afternoon in Paris!

82. D'Elbée, *Un Conquistador de Génie,* I, 166–167.

83. Douin, *op. cit.,* I, 81.

CHAPTER *ten*

The Imperial

Arbitration ?~

⊷§ THE principle of arbitration by the Emperor had now been accepted by both sides. Ismail had asked for it informally in the belief that it would be put into Morny's hands. The Company, apparently satisfied that the matter was back in the right channels, had asked for it formally. On November 19th Drouyn de Lhuys, on receipt of a dossier of information about the Company from Lesseps, had given instructions that a single person should be made responsible for the custody and study of all documents relative to the canal in preparation for an eventual Government intervention.[1] On January 16th Drouyn de Lhuys instructed Tastu that "the Emperor, wishing to bring the Company to a transaction, desires that the Viceroy will maintain the *status quo* in the Isthmus until April 1st."[2] Ismail, in due course, agreed to this.[3] A week later, Tastu was informed of the lines on which it was proposed that the Emperor should arbitrate the dispute. These were: (*a*) reduction of forced labor to 6,000 with no mention of compensation; (*b*) return of ceded lands to the Egyptian Government against substantial compensation ("*une large indemnité*"); (*c*) the Sweet Water Canal to remain in possession of the Company.[4] All this was closely in accordance with Emile Ollivier's recommendations and seemed to indicate that Morny was still in charge of the affair. Ismail was certainly under this impression when, on January 30th, he wrote to the Emperor officially asking for his arbitration,[5] since, on February 3rd, Tastu reported that the Viceroy had already been informed, by some third party, of the proposed terms of the Emperor's arbitration, and "did not conceal the pleasure which he derived from the success of his campaign against the Company."[6]

On January 22nd Lesseps submitted to Drouyn de Lhuys the Canal Company's counterproposal to Nubar's, which the Company had rejected at the end of October, and asked him to submit it to the Egyptian Government.

In this counterproposal the Company offered (*a*) to give up all cultivable lands except those necessary for working the canal—which were estimated at 33,000 hectares out of the total of 133,000 hectares claimed to have been ceded to the Company under the Second Concession,[7] against a compensation of 500 francs per hectare for the 100,000 hectares to be given up, plus the cancellation of the provision in the Concession which reserved to the Egyptian Government 15 percent of the Company's net profits; (*b*) to agree to limit requirements of forced labor to a maximum of 6,000 at a time against compensation of 40 million francs. It was proposed that payment of compensation for the lands and for the labor should be effected by the Egyptian Government surrendering the whole of its shareholding to the Company at par, that is, 88,821,000 francs, plus Treasury bills for the balance of 1,179,000 francs, and it was stipulated that the whole proposal was conditional on the immediate issue of a firman by the Porte.[8]

By this proposal, which, like Nubar's, was in the time-honored tradition of Oriental bargaining, the Egyptian Government would have had to give up its entire financial interest in the canal as compensation for those revisions on which the Porte was insisting as a prior condition of the issue of the firman. Even so, the Company would not only keep lands far in excess of those which even the Emperor's commission was later to adjudge necessary for the Company's operations, but would also retain as much forced labor as they would still have been in a position to use.

Drouyn de Lhuys communicated the Company's counterproposal to Tastu for submission to the Viceroy. (It was a sign of the changed atmosphere brought about by Lesseps' audience with the Emperor that these counterproposals were submitted to Ismail through French Government channels and not by the Company to Nubar, who was still in Paris.) At the same time De Lhuys instructed Moustier to ask the Porte to extend until April 1st the six-month delay laid down in the Grand Vizier's letter to Ismail in July. This was agreed to by the Porte.[9]

Tastu, when communicating the Company's counterproposal to Ismail, was disconcerted by Ismail's air of arrogant confidence. "The Viceroy, so far from being in a conciliatory mood toward the Company, has got a new plan of attack." After remarking that he reckoned he had already succeeded in getting the land back, the Viceroy explained to Tastu that it was now a question of getting control of the canal itself. He had become the largest shareholder as the result of the Convention of March 19, 1863, and was arranging to send nominees to the general meeting of shareholders, to be held in March, with instructions to launch an attack on the current administration of the Company, charging them with wanton waste of the shareholders' money. The object of this plan, wrote Tastu, was to bring about Lesseps' retirement from the presidency of the Company. "Once this powerful personality has been got rid of, he hopes that the rest of the shareholders will leave the control of the Company's affairs in the hands of the largest shareholder, that is, the Viceroy."[10]

The Viceroy was still in this euphoric mood when Tastu saw him just over a week later. On this occasion he rejected the Company's counter-proposal which Tastu had left with him on his previous visit, telling Tastu: "I cannot accept M. de Lesseps' note. The time for negotiations has passed. I sent someone to M. de Lesseps to negotiate with him. M. de Lesseps refused to have anything to do with him, and now it is too late." During the course of the conversation Ismail, obviously relying on a letter he had received from Morny, made clear his belief that the arbitration would be in the nature of a pistol held at the Company's head and that, while a moderate compensation would be awarded for the lands to be returned, there would be no question of compensation for the withdrawal of forced labor.[11]

It is apparent that the object of the Canal Company's opponents in Paris was to try to use the proposed arbitration as a means of discrediting the actual administration of the Canal Company and so to depress the shares; to obtain control of sufficient of the shares to enable them, with the addition of the Viceroy's shareholding, to control the Company; to use this control to extrude Lesseps; and, benefiting from the Viceroy's complaisance earned by the generous terms of the arbitration, to complete the construction of the canal themselves, raising such additional capital as was necessary on the Paris money market. Since the validity of the Viceroy's shareholding was an essential part of such a scheme, it is possible that it was matured between Nubar and his Paris backers very soon after Ismail's accession and that Ismail's signature of the March convention, by which he established his ownership of just under half the total shareholding, was an essential part of the scheme. At all events, there is no doubt that there was a scheme, to which Ismail, Morny, Nubar, and probably some of the Canal Company shareholders, were privy (there is a cryptic reference in a letter from Nubar to Ismail to the effect that *"les principaux actionnaires sont favorables"*),[12] to oust Lesseps from the Company and to take it over. The success of the scheme depended on the continued ability of Morny to manage the terms of the arbitration. It was at this point that Lesseps directed himself, relying on his relationship with the Empress, to whom he wrote very frankly about Morny's tactics, and using Drouyn de Lhuys's natural resentment at being bypassed over a matter of foreign policy.

What actually happened is obscure. But, some time during February, the wind at Court changed. On February 18th Drouyn de Lhuys wrote to Tastu pooh-poohing Tastu's fears about Ismail's intrigues and giving the impression that he had the whole matter firmly under control.[13] On February 27th the Emperor, replying to Ismail's request for his arbitration, accepted, but made it clear that his arbitration would not be confined to deciding the amount of indemnity to be paid to the Company for the lands, but would deal with the whole range of differences existing between the Egyptian Government and the Company.[14] The significance of this was that it was a departure from the Ollivier report according to which the only matter to be decided was the amount of compensation for the lands to be returned by the Company. The Emperor's condition was accepted by Ismail.[15] He may, or may not, have realized that he had been outwitted. At all events, his confidence in Nubar remained undiminished. On February 27th he advised Lesseps, through Nubar, that he had dismissed the Dutch engineer Conrad (a member of the Conseil d'Administration) as the Viceroy's commissary and that he would be replaced by anyone whom Nubar might choose to nominate.[16] Nubar's hat was still in the ring. So was Morny's.

On February 14th, as a counterblast to the anti–Canal Company propaganda being disseminated in Paris by Nubar, Morny, and the other enemies of the Company, Prince Napoleon, the Company's Protector, gave a great banquet in Lesseps' honor at the Palais de l'Industrie in the Champs-Elysées to which sixteen hundred guests were invited. At this banquet the Prince made a characteristically eloquent, long-winded, and bombastic speech which, we are told, succeeded in arousing the enthusiasm of the guests on a very cold winter's evening in an insufficiently heated hall.[17] More important than the effect on the guests was the effect on the world at large, for the occasion, and the speech, were widely reported. Ridiculous as he was in some of his attitudes, Prince Napoleon was an important person in the Second Empire, quite as important as Morny, whose personality and methods were so different from those of the bluff and hearty "Plon-Plon." Opposed as he was by Morny, the support of Prince Napoleon and the Empress (who, incidentally, detested one another) was a valuable reinforcement for Lesseps when it was a question of making representations to the Emperor. In the course of his speech the Prince ridiculed the idea that French support for the canal would lead to any serious trouble with England: *"Une guerre à cause du Canal de Suez? Allons donc!"* He expatiated on the advantages of the canal to Egypt, and attacked Nubar by name and Morny by implication: *Qu'est-ce que ces interventions, dont on fait tant de bruit? Je n'en sais rien et je n'en veux rien savoir. Ne vous occupez pas de cela. Tout ce qui ne se fait pas au grand jour officiel, tout ce qu'affecte l'ombre, est mauvais."*[18]

On March 1st an extraordinary general meeting of the Canal Company was held in Paris, at which Lesseps gave a long and reasonably accurate account of the recent crisis, and concluded by saying that "the Viceroy has now declared that he has requested the Emperor to solve, amicably and definitively, all the questions at issue between the Company and the Egyptian Government and that the Emperor has condescended to make himself responsible for the final decision in all these questions."[19] At this meeting Lesseps seems to have had very little trouble with the shareholders. As a result of the counterpropaganda launched against Nubar, the Canal Company shares, which had been down to 461 francs at the beginning of January, had risen to 475 francs.[20] A remarkable feature of the attacks made on the Company during 1863–1864 was the steadiness of the share prices. There was in fact a very narrow market in Canal Company shares, since they were mainly held in small blocks by individuals who had bought the shares for patriotic reasons and who were not used to "playing the markets." The 188 biggest shareholders averaged only 170 shares each. There was only one block of 1,000 shares.[21] It was therefore very difficult for Lesseps' adversaries either to buy any very large number of shares or greatly to depress their price. It was probably this fact that saved Lesseps.

On March 7th *Le Moniteur* (the contemporary French equivalent of the *Official Gazette*) published the following communication, addressed by Drouyn de Lhuys to the Emperor, dated March 3rd and approved by the Emperor:

> The Viceroy of Egypt having written to Your Majesty praying him to arbitrate on certain questions at issue between the Egyptian Government and the Suez Canal Company, Your Majesty has condescended to reply to Ismail Pasha that you will accede to his request.

The note went on to nominate four names for membership of the Arbitration Commission. The nomination for president of the Commission was Edouard-Antoine Thouvenel who, during the long diplomatic history of the canal, had been, first, French ambassador in Constantinople and, afterward, Foreign Minister. Emile Ollivier was not among the nominated members of the commission.

The Arbitration Commission got to work immediately. It held its first meeting on March 18th to settle its Terms of Reference. At this meeting the Porte was asked to extend until June 1st the six-month time limit laid down in the Grand Vizier's letter to Ismail in the previous July. (It had already been extended, at the request of the French Government, until April 1st.) The Porte agreed to this, and thereby embarked on a course of equivocation over the arbitration which was to cause much trouble and delay later. There was a little preliminary skirmishing by Nubar as to whether the Sweet Water Canal should be regarded as part and parcel of the lands whose retrocession had already been agreed in principle, or whether it should be regarded as a separate issue. Nubar eventually agreed that it should be treated separately.[22] (The point was that, if the Sweet Water Canal were treated separately from the lands, the Company would have an additional claim for compensation in the event of their giving up the Sweet Water Canal. It was compensation that the Company was after, not the Sweet Water Canal.) At last, on April 21st, the Terms of Reference were agreed on by both parties,[23] with Nubar making the provision that he could answer for the Egyptian Government but not for the Sublime Porte.[24] It was agreed that the Arbitration should consist of an answer to the following five questions: (1) Was the June, 1856, agreement for the supply of labor to be regarded as a contract between the Egyptian Government and the Canal Company? (2) If so, what indemnity was due to the Company from the Egyptian Government to compensate for its termination? (3) Should the Sweet Water Canal be regarded as an annex to the Maritime Canal and be retained by the Company or should it be regarded as separate from the Maritime Canal and be returned to the Egyptian Government? (4) How much land was it necessary for the Company to retain for the purpose of its operations? (5) What compensation was payable to the Company for the balance of land handed back to the Egyptian Government?

On returning to his hotel after having signed, on behalf of the Egyptian Government, his agreement to these Terms of Reference, Nubar was met by Jamil Pasha, the Turkish ambassador, who showed him a telegram from Aali Pasha, dated April 18th and received in Paris on April 19th, stating that the Turkish Government did not accept the Terms of Reference and that, in particular, they insisted on the Sweet Water Canal being returned to the Egyptian Government as a precondition of arbitration. Nubar told him that it was too late to go back on his agreement to the Terms of Reference, and asked him why on earth he had kept the telegram in his pocket for two whole days until after the Terms of Reference had been agreed on.[25] He does not appear to have received any satisfactory reply. What had apparently happened was this: After the Porte had heard about the arbitration as a result of having been asked to extend the time limit laid down in the Grand Vizier's letter of the previous July, they had instructed Jamil *"de ne pas s'immiscer dans cette transaction, de laisser libre le representant de Son Altesse* [Nubar] *d'agir."* When Jamil received the telegram objecting to the Terms of Reference, he went by his previous instructions and did nothing about it. Subsequently Jamil was instructed by Aali Pasha on no account to divulge to the French Government the contents of the telegram of April 18th.[26] Aali Pasha, by a characteristic tactic, had avoided embroiling the Porte with the French Government or the commission and had at the same time left the door open for a subsequent refusal to issue a firman on the basis of the Arbitral Award. In a subsequent telegram to Jamil dated May 17th, Aali Pasha made it clear that Nubar's agreement to the Terms of Reference was irrelevant (*"n'implique nullement"*) since the Porte had not given its agreement to them.[27]

Meanwhile the commission was pursuing its labors, hearing the arguments from both parties. The Company, in putting its case, asked for 57 million francs as compensation for the cancellation of the labor contract and, suddenly producing a figure of 573,712 hectares as the amount of land which would become cultivable as a result of the Company's operations (thereby taking advantage of the fact that the exact area had never been demarcated),[28] stated that 30,000 hectares of this were necessary for the Company's operations, and demanded 50 million francs in compensation, plus cancellation of the Egyptian Government's 15 percent share of net profits against returning the rest of it.[29] Nubar rested his case on the proposal made to, and rejected by, the Company in October, 1863.

During the sittings of the commission, Lesseps and his friends showed signs of considerable nervousness at evidence they were receiving about intrigues which were still on foot against the Canal Company. Having lost the game in Paris, it appeared that the Company's adversaries were now concentrating on Constantinople. Ismail, having been jockeyed into accepting the Emperor's arbitration as a result of a too optimistic estimate of the strength of Nubar's connections in Paris, had left himself a loophole in that he had deliberately not associated the Porte with his request for arbitration, reckoning that this would enable him to use the Porte to evade the results of the arbitration, should these be unfavorable to him. What was at stake was not so much the amount the Egyptian Government would have to pay, as the confidence of the Canal Company's shareholders in the actual administration of the Company. This confidence, shaken by Nubar's press campaign and, as it appears, restored in time for the March general meeting by the Company's counterpropaganda and by such evidence as Lesseps was able to produce of French official support for the actual administration of the Company, could be maintained only as the result of a swift implementation of a reasonably favorable arbitration award.

A dispatch from Tastu on May 9th suggests that considerable publicity was being given in Egypt to the Porte's refusal to recognize the Arbitration Commission.[30] An anonymous letter to Lesseps from Alexandria[31] of the same date informs him that the objections being raised in Constantinople did not come spontaneously from the Porte, but originated from Ismail, who had arranged with the banker Oppenheim (who had considerable financial dealing both with Ismail and with the Ottoman Government) to persuade the Porte to oppose the terms of the arbitration: "I have already spoken to you about the proposed formation of a Company which would take over the Canal Company after you have been successfully removed from it. This Company has now been formed; although its real object is to take over the Canal Company, it is at present concealing this. It has a capital of nine millions sterling. The principal shareholders are English. Both Oppenheim and Nubar are involved in it." The mention of Oppenheim (presumably Henry Oppenheim) lifts a corner of the veil from the mystery surrounding the attempts to take over the Canal Company. He had been responsible for floating Egypt's first international loan, for Mohammed Said, in 1862. He was subsequently responsible for floating several loans for Ismail. Although a German national, with his banking house based in Frankfurt, he was closely connected with British banking interests and was generally regarded by the French as a protagonist of British, and as an opponent of French, influence in Egypt. It was this same Oppenheim who, in 1875, was said to have "tipped off" the British Government, through the editor of the *Pall Mall Gazette,* about the availability of the Egyptian Government shareholding in the Canal Company.

Lesseps, presumably nervous about the effect on public opinion of a continuance of forced labor in the isthmus, had already written to Girardin, his representative in Egypt, telling him that the Company was prepared to waive any further demands for forced labor for work on the Canal, but pointing out that the substitution of machinery for hand labor would be an expensive matter for the Company.[32] Curiously, this letter makes no reference to an indemnity, but Drouyn de Lhuys, in a dispatch to Tastu on May 18th, referring to Lesseps' offer, makes it clear that it was made "on condition that an indemnity would be paid to the Company to recompense them for the losses involved."[33]

After having received the letter from his correspondent in Alexandria,[34] Lesseps again turned for support to the Empress, urging her to use her influence to hasten the completion of the commission's labors and the publication of their award, since the delay was injuring the Company's credit: "When the public attacks being made against the Company were defeated by our publicity, our adversaries, counting on the support of Morny and the

efficacy of his intervention, proposed that the Emperor should arbitrate. . . .
But the commission nominated by His Majesty being obviously an impartial
one, these adversaries, still supported by M. de Morny who continues to interfere almost daily, have no other resource than to try and hold up the
course of the commission's inquiry. . . . I implore the Empress to ask the
commission to complete their report without any further delay."[35]

On June 7th Lesseps wrote in the same sense to Drouyn de Lhuys, protesting against a proposal that the commission should visit Egypt before completing their report, and attributing this proposal to the machinations of his
adversaries "who hope that a delay in arriving at the award will lead to the
disorganization of the Company, which they are planning to take over."[36]
On June 16th Lesseps made a further protest to Drouyn de Lhuys about delay,
stating that "our adversaries are now representing to the commission that
the amount of indemnity which they propose is so great that the Egyptian
Treasury will be unable to pay it and will be compelled to seek a loan from
Britain." After remarking that indemnities are fixed according to the amount
of damage suffered by the injured party and not according to the means
of the party inflicting the injury, he mentioned a figure of 90 million francs
(which seems to indicate that he was being kept well informed of the de-
liberations of the commission) and expressed the view that "the Egyptian
Government possesses the necessary resources to make such a payment." He
went on to state that, unless the matter was settled by the time of the Company's general meeting in August, the Company would be compelled to insist on the validity of the labor contract and to seek by *"les voies gouvern-
mentales"* an indemnity to cover the additional costs of mechanical excavation.
With regard to the lands, he said that the Company would simply refuse to
give them up. He concluded by indicating that the Company would be prepared to accept the Egyptian Government's shareholding at par in settlement
of the indemnity awarded. This would dispense with the need for any application for a loan by the Egyptian Government.[37]

This hectoring letter indicates either that Lesseps was prepared to appeal
to public opinion if necessary over the heads of the French Government, or
that he had received some very definite assurances of support from the
Emperor.

On June 20th the commission presented its recommendations to Drouyn
de Lhuys.[38] In answer to the agreed five questions, the commission found:
(1) that the labor agreement of June, 1856, was a valid contract; (2) that the
compensation payable for the cancellation of this contract amounted to 38
million francs, being 42.5 million francs, less 4.5 million francs which had
been underpaid by the Company under the terms of the agreement; (3) that

the Sweet Water Canal was to be reserved for the exclusive use of the Company until the completion of the Maritime Canal, after which the section Ras al Wadi–Timsah–Suez was to be returned to the Egyptian Government against a payment of 10 million francs in respect of expenses incurred in digging the canal and 6 million francs as compensation for loss of navigation charges, the Company thereafter to maintain the Sweet Water Canal for the account and at the expense of the Egyptian Government against a charge of 300,000 francs per annum to be paid to the Company by the Egyptian Government; that the Egyptian Government was to be responsible for supplying the Company with adequate supplies of water via the Sweet Water Canal and that the Company was to be responsible for making its own arrangements for the supply of sweet water along the line of the Maritime Canal between Timsah and Port Said;[39] (4) that the area of land deemed necessary for the Company's operations amounted to 10,264 hectares on the Maritime Canal and 9,600 hectares along the Sweet Water Canal; (5) that the area of land to be restored by the Company to the Egyptian Government was calculated to be 60,000 hectares, for which the compensation due from the Egyptian Government to the Company was assessed at 30 million francs.

The compensation awarded, amounting to 84 million francs, was to be paid by the Egyptian Government in the following installments: (*a*) 38 million francs in respect of the cancellation of the labor contract payable in installments over six years starting from February 1, 1864; (*b*) 30 million francs in respect of lands payable over ten years starting from February 1, 1870; (*c*) 6 million francs for loss of navigation dues on the Sweet Water Canal payable over ten years starting from February 1, 1870; (*d*) 10 million francs in respect of expenses incurred by the Company in digging the Sweet Water Canal payable on the date on which the Sweet Water Canal was handed back to the Egyptian Government.

Thouvenel, in a covering note to the recommendations of the commission,[40] recommended that the actual area to be left to the Company should be determined by a commission of investigation on the spot. He expressed the opinion that the Turkish Government would not object to the terms of the award: "The understanding which five years of residence in Constantinople has given me leads me to suppose that the Sublime Porte will not create any difficulties over an indemnity which they will not themselves have to pay." He went on to say that although, as a matter of form, they might complain about these indemnities, they would, in fact, not be ill-pleased to see their vassal punished for having, in spite of their reiterated orders, granted Concessions to a foreign Company. He added that Ismail was spending each year, in various extravagances, sums far larger than those which he was being condemned to pay, over a period of ten years, as indemnity to a Company in which he held almost half the shares. He ended up by suggesting that, as a concession to Turkish *amour propre,* the "delimitation" of the lands necessary to the Company be fixed by a commission on which the Porte was represented.[41]

The Emperor's Award was published in *Le Moniteur* of August 2, 1864, after having been communicated to the Canal Company, the Viceroy, and the Sublime Porte. It was entirely in accordance with the recommendations of the commission, except that Thouvenel's advice about the appointment of a commission to "delimit" the lands to be retained by the Company had not been taken.[42]

The Canal Company had every reason to be satisfied with the terms of the Award. To some extent the British Government had played into their hands by making it politically impossible for them either to continue using forced labor or to retain the lands which had been ceded to them. By the end of 1863 when the Sweet Water Canal had been completed to Suez and the *rigole de service* completed from Port Said to Timsah, the forced labor contract had almost exhausted its usefulness, since, once excavation on the Maritime Canal had reached the waterline, hand labor on any extensive scale was no longer practicable, and the use of machinery became necessary. And the lands, although potentially valuable, needed money for their development which the Company was unlikely to have at its disposal for some time. Even if there had been no political objections, it would have been financially advantageous—it would almost have been financially necessary—for the Company to have "traded in" these privileges in return for an indemnity. The effect of the political agitation was to place upon the Viceroy the onus of objecting to these privileges and of thus making the Company's claim for an indemnity plausible. The vociferous objections raised by the Company to the loss of labor and lands postulated in the Grand Vizier's letters of April and July, 1863, were simply conventional gestures made for the purpose of establishing the foundations of a claim for indemnity. The Company concentrated on the mobilization of sufficient support from the French Government to ensure that a handsome indemnity was awarded and its payment enforced. This was a well-worn path for foreign concessionaires in Egypt. The affair departed from what had become a conventional pattern only in that the preparations for extracting an indemnity coincided with an attempt by third parties who, in concert with Ismail, tried to deprive the Company of the support of the French Government, and so make its position untenable, as a preliminary to taking over the Company themselves with the assistance of Ismail's shareholding.

In view of Ismail's demonstration that he was prepared to use the shareholding which he had accepted—and which made him easily the largest shareholder—as a means of disputing the control of the Company with Lesseps[43] (and he may well have agreed to take up the shares with that specific object in view), it seems possible that the amount of the indemnity—which approximated to the par value of Ismail's shareholding—was so designed as to encourage Ismail to surrender his shareholding to the Company as a means of paying off this indemnity; we know that this was in Lesseps' mind from his letter to Drouyn de Lhuys of June 16th.[44]

Ismail accepted the Award "as far as I am concerned as Viceroy of Egypt. But as far as the rights of the Sublime Porte are concerned I cannot commit them, and if any difficulties arise in this respect I hope that the good relations existing between France and Turkey will enable them to be overcome."[45] The Award was accepted by a general meeting of the Canal Company which was held on August 6, 1864.[46]

The Porte, with the connivance of Ismail, and encouraged by Bulwer, then settled down to a long delaying action. The first shot in this was fired when Aali Pasha, the Reis Effendi, expressed the opinion that a new convention should be drawn up between the Viceroy and the Company embodying the terms of the Arbitral Award, and indicated that the Sultan would issue his firman on the basis of this convention.[47] This sounded quite straightforward and satisfactory. But it soon became apparent that all concerned, with the exception of the French Government and the Canal Company, were determined to use the drafting of a new convention as a means of modifying the original Concessions in a number of ways other than those involved in a simple implementation of the Arbitral Award. It also became apparent that the exact delimitation of the lands awarded to the Company by the Arbitral Award was to be the subject of a determined rear guard action by the British Government.

NOTES

1. Note on letter Lesseps–de Lhuys 19.11.63. CP 32.
2. De Lhuys–Tastu 16.1.64. CP 33.
3. Ismail–Napoleon 3.2.64. CP 33.
4. De Lhuys–Tastu 28.1.64. CP 33.
5. Ismail–Napoleon 30.1.64. CP 33.
6. Tastu–de Lhuys 3.2.64. CP 33.
7. This was the figure mentioned in Lesseps' Prospectus, but it had never been authoritatively established.
8. For text of counterproposal see Journal, IV, 379 *et seq.*

9. Note from Turkish Embassy in Paris to Drouyn de Lhuys 30.1.64. CP 33.
10. Tastu–de Lhuys 9.2.64. CP 33.
11. *Ibid.*, 18.2.64. CP 33.
12. Quoted in *ibid.*, 7.9.63. CP 32.
13. De Lhuys–Tastu 18.2.64. CP 33.
14. Napoleon–Ismail 27.2.64, M & D, Vol. 14.
15. Ismail–Napoleon 14.3.64. CP 33.
16. Nubar–Lesseps 27.2.64. CP 33.
17. Edgar–Bonnet, *Ferdinand de Lesseps*, I, 397.
18. *Ibid.*, p. 399.
19. Journal, IV, 422.
20. See Landes, *Bankers and Pashas*, p. 187.
21. *Ibid.*, p. 183.
22. Tastu–de Lhuys 21.3.64. CP 33.
23. For text of Terms of Reference, see CP 33.
24. Referring to Nubar's reservation, Drouyn de Lhuys wrote to Thouvenel that he had spoken to Jamil Pasha, the Turkish ambassador in Paris, and, "I can say that he told me nothing to justify Nubar's reservation" (de Lhuys–Thouvenel 18.4.64. CP 33).
25. Douin, *Règne du Khédive Ismaïl*, I, 97.
26. Colquhoun–Russell 7.5.64. FO 78/1849.
27. Telegram from Aali Pasha to Jamil Pasha of 15.5.64, of which copy in FO 78/1849.
28. They appear to have arrived at this figure by including a lot of land on the borders of Lake Manzala.
29. Douin, *op. cit.*, I, 98-99.
30. Tastu–de Lhuys 9.5.64. CP 33.
31. Original in CP 33 dated 9.5.64. The signature has been cut out.
32. Lesseps–Girardin 26.4.64. CP 33.
33. De Lhuys–Tastu 18.5.64. CP 33. This statement of Drouyn de Lhuys, prejudging as it does one of the matters to be decided by the commission, casts a considerable doubt on the commission's impartiality, particularly as Ollivier's opinion, which was before the commission, was to the effect that no indemnity was payable for the withdrawal of forced labor.
34. See Note 31.
35. Lesseps–Eugénie 2.6.64. CP 33.
36. Lesseps–de Lhuys 7.6.64. CP 33.
37. *Ibid.*, 16.6.64. CP 33.
38. M & D, Vol. 14.
39. The Sweet Water Canal Ras al Wadi–Timsah–Suez had been completed by the Company in December, 1863. The stretch Cairo–Ras al Wadi had been handed over to the Egyptian Government for construction according to the terms of the March, 1863, Convention. The stretch Timsah–Port Said was being supplied by pipeline.
40. Thouvenel–Napoleon 20.6.64, M & D, Vol. 14.
41. The exact meaning of the term "delimitation" was to cause much trouble later, the French Government maintaining that it simply implied the allotment of the area awarded to the Company by the commission, the British and Turkish governments maintaining that a reduction in the area awarded by the commission was not excluded.
42. For text of Aribitral Award see J. Charles-Roux, *L'Isthme . . .* , Vol. I, Annex No. 19. The neglect of Thouvenel's advice (which was accepted later after pressure from the British Government) may perhaps be attributed to Lesseps' lobbying.
43. See p. 178.
44. See p. 184.
45. Tastu–de Lhuys 19.7.64, quoting written declaration given to him by the Viceroy, CP 34.
46. Lesseps–de Lhuys 10.8.64. CP 34.
47. De Lhuys–Tastu 19.8.64. CP 34.

CHAPTER *eleven*

The Firman ॐ

◆§ EIGHTEEN months of extremely wearisome negotiation preceded the promulgation of the firman by Sultan Abdul Aziz on March 19, 1866.[1]

The attitude of the French Government was expressed by Drouyn de Lhuys in an interview with Cowley. After Cowley had described the Emperor's Award (truthfully if tactlessly) as a "scheme to indemnify M. de Lesseps for losses which he had sustained in persisting in a ruinous speculation," and had expressed surprise that "M. de Thouvenel had lent himself to such a transaction," Drouyn de Lhuys replied that "the award must now be carried into execution." Cowley reported that Drouyn de Lhuys seemed to think that the execution of the Award was now a matter of national honor, and added that the Minister had stated more than once in the course of conversation that both he and the Emperor were heartily sick of the whole affair.[2]

Lesseps regarded the rights of the Company as having been *"consacrés"* by the Arbitral Award.[3]

The attitude of the British Government, after they had ascertained that the supply of forced labor for the canal had been stopped,[4] is expressed in the following two dispatches from the Foreign Office. They informed Constantinople that the forced-labor question being settled, Her Majesty's Government had only to take care: "(i) that not more land than is wanted is granted to the Canal Company; (ii) that no one but the Sultan or the Viceroy erects fortifications or maintains garrisons on the Company's land; (iii) that everything required for commerce should be granted to the Company; (iv) that everything that appertains to sovereignty should be kept by the Sultan and administered by the Viceroy."[5] And they informed Paris: "It is impossible that the Sultan can be required in this peremptory manner to give up territory which forms part of his Empire. Let the Emperor order a fair enquiry by a Mixed Commission as to the quantity of land required for the purposes of the Canal Company. When this quantity has been fairly ascertained the Sultan will doubtless be ready to grant a Firman for the Canal and Her Majesty's Government will support the Sultan in any proposals which he may make. But Her Majesty's Government cannot acquiesce in a foreign transfer from the Sultan to the Lesseps Company of a portion of the Ottoman Empire for purposes other than those of making a Canal."[6]

The Ottoman Government, with Fuad Pasha as Grand Vizier and Aali Pasha as Reis Effendi,[7] was behaving rather more actively than usual and was, with British support, trying to use the occasion as a means of reasserting Ottoman suzerainty over Ismail.

Nubar Pasha, representing the Egyptian Government, was furious at the terms of the Arbitration Award, considering, not without reason, that he had been misled by Morny.[8] Therefore, having in the first place taken the initiative in going behind the back of the Porte in appealing to the French Government against the Canal Company, he now attempted to use the Porte to nullify the results of the French Government's intervention.

The firman was eventually obtained at the end of two series of negotiations, proceeding side by side, occasionally impinging on the other, and ultimately intersecting. The one set of negotiations, in which the principal figure was Lord Cowley, led to the setting up of a Mixed Commission to demarcate and, if necessary, to revise the area of land allotted to the Company by the Arbitration Award. The other set of negotiations, in which the principal figure was the Marquis de Moustier, the French Ambassador in Constantinople, led, much more importantly, to the conclusion of two conventions between the Company and the Egyptian Government and, through these conventions, to the promulgation of the Sultan's firman.

The British Government's suspicion that far too much land had been awarded to the Company, and that the Company intended to use their surplus land for colonization, was heightened by two events which took place at the beginning of 1865. First, a Turkish commissioner, Osman Nury Pasha, who, at Bulwer's instigation, had been sent by the Porte to Egypt in the autumn of 1864 to make an independent estimate of the amount of land required by the Company for its operations, reported that the area properly required was 1,784 hectares adjacent to the Maritime Canal (as compared with the 10,264 hectares in the Arbitral Award) and 615 hectares adjacent to the Sweet Water Canal (as compared with 9,600 hectares in the Arbitral Award).[9]

The second event was the Abdul Qader incident. Lesseps had formed a friendship with Abdul Qader, the Algerian leader who, after having led the Algerian forces against the French invaders in 1830, had become reconciled to the French occupation of his country. He was at that time living in Damascus and, on the way back from a pilgrimage to Mecca, paid a visit to Lesseps in the isthmus. Lesseps, without consulting Ismail, made Abdul Qader an offer of 300 hectares of land occupied by the Company at Deir Abu Ballah, on the Sweet Water Canal. This offer, which Abdul Qader had the good sense to decline, exasperated Ismail, who made an official protest to the French Government, and confirmed the British Government in their suspicions of the Canal Company.[10]

Meanwhile Cowley in Paris and Stuart, the chargé d'affaires in Constantinople (Bulwer went to Cairo at the end of January and stayed there until the end of May), were making little progress either in getting the Ottoman Government to propose or the French Government to agree to the idea of a Mixed Commission. The Porte was afraid of questioning the Emperor's Award, and Drouyn de Lhuys refused to do so. Eventually Cowley, on April 12th, had an audience with the Emperor in which "His Majesty was pleased to give me the assurance that he would have no objection to the immediate appointment of a Mixed Commission . . . to enquire into the amount of ground necessary for the completion and working of the Canal, provided that the Sultan should engage, after the enquiry should have terminated, to issue the necessary Firman."[11] Stuart, thus able to assure the Porte of the Emperor's approval in advance, arranged for a formal letter to be written by the Sultan to the Emperor proposing that a Mixed Commission should be set up, composed of one representative each from the Turkish, Egyptian, and French Governments and one from the Canal Company, to determine the extent and location of the lands needed by the Company for their operations. In this letter the Sultan undertook to accept the findings of such a commission and to issue his firman as soon as these findings had been submitted to him.[12]

When this letter arrived in Paris on May 9th, by the hand of Aali Pasha's son-in-law, the Emperor had departed on a visit to Algeria, leaving the Empress Eugénie as Regent. Cowley, knowing the influence the Empress had previously exerted in favor of Lesseps, and knowing that Lesseps was opposed to the idea of a commission, showed some nervousness about the fate of the Sultan's proposal, "the Empress having taken on herself all the functions of the Chief of State," including the opening of all letters addressed personally to the Emperor.[13] However, all went well. The Turkish Ambassador presented the letter to the Empress,[14] and in due course a letter was sent to the Sultan accepting his proposal. It was also accepted by Ismail, after an abortive attempt by Lesseps to avoid the commission by getting Ismail to agree that, when the canal was finished, the Company would voluntarily give back to the Egyptian Government such lands as they found they did not need.[15]

The Turkish nominee on the commission was Osman Nury Pasha, who had already made a report recommending a drastic reduction in the lands to be allotted to the Company.[16] Possibly for this reason, Lesseps at first refused to accept the French Government's invitation to nominate a Canal Company representative to the commission, and addressed an appeal to the Emperor asking him to demand an immediate issue of the firman from Constantinople.[17] After some prodding from Cowley, Drouyn de Lhuys eventually told Lesseps that the commission would proceed with its task whether or not a Canal Company representative was nominated.[18] As a result of this threat, which coincided with the timely death of Osman Nury, who was replaced by Server Effendi as the Turkish nominee, Lesseps appointed Admiral Janvier as the Canal Company's representative, and the commission got to work.[19]

While the negotiations about the commission were proceeding, several changes had been taking place in British and French diplomatic representation in Cairo and Constantinople. In April, 1865, Outrey replaced Tastu as French consul general in Egypt. In June, Colquhoun was replaced as British consul general by Colonel Stanton, of the Royal Engineers, who was apparently chosen partly because his professional qualifications would enable him expertly to appraise various technical aspects of the canal question.[20] In September Sir Henry Bulwer was replaced by Lord Lyons as British ambassador in Constantinople. And in October the British Prime Minister, Lord Palmerston, the oldest, the greatest, and the most uncompromising opponent of the canal, died at the age of eighty-two. He was succeeded as Prime Minister by Lord John Russell, previously Foreign Secretary. Lord Clarendon, who had been Foreign Secretary in Palmerston's previous Administration, replaced Russell at the Foreign Office.

Soon after his appointment to Egypt, Stanton reported two disquieting facts. First, an inspection of the ground at Suez had confirmed a previous report by Colquhoun that the Messageries Impériales, a French shipping line, had secured a concession for a dock at Suez which appeared to give them a monopoly of all future docking facilities at that port. This heightened British suspicions that the French Government was engaged in a plot, with the Canal Company and the Messageries as accomplices, to create a French monopoly of the canal route via Suez. Secondly, as revealed to him by Nubar Pasha, now Minister of Public Works, the Canal Company was leasing to third parties land occupied by them in the vicinity of the canal, thus confirming the British Government's suspicion that the land awarded to them was far in excess of their requirements. Eventually, both these matters were settled as a result of the intervention of Outrey, the newly appointed French consul general, who appears also to have persuaded Lesseps to appoint a Canal Company representative to the Mixed Commission and to sell the Wadi lands back to the Egyptian Government.

In fact, all parties were drawing closer together as the result of a series of negotiations which had been taking place in Constantinople ever since the publication of the Arbitral Award. After the issue of the Arbitral Award, and its acceptance by the Egyptian Government and the Canal Company, it became necessary to draw up a convention for signature by the two parties, incorporating the terms of the Award. From these negotiations the British Government, owing to the absence of Bulwer in Egypt, and owing to their concentration on the question of a Mixed Commission, were almost entirely excluded. Apart from the British Government, there were four parties to these negotiations, each wanting something different. There was Lesseps, for the Canal Company, who simply wanted the terms of the Emperor's Award to be ratified in the form of a convention without any alterations in those terms of the two Concessions which had not been affected by the Arbitral Award. There was Moustier, the French ambassador, who, like Drouyn de Lhuys, regarded it as a matter of honor that the Emperor's Award should be adopted in its entirety and without qualification but who, subject to this stipulation, was anxious to pacify both the British and Ottoman governments. There was the Ottoman Government, represented by Fuad Pasha and Aali Pasha, who were—determined is too strong a word in this connection—certainly in favor of using the necessity for a new convention to force upon the Viceroy and the Canal Company conditions which would limit the Viceroy's independence of his suzerain in the matter of the canal. And there was the Viceroy, represented by Nubar, who wanted to incorporate into the convention some conditions which would transfer back to the Viceroy some of that autonomy which had been conferred on the Company as a result of the Concessions granted by Mohammed Said.

After the issue of the Arbitral Award, Lesseps got out a draft convention on the lines desired by the Canal Company, and submitted it to Drouyn de Lhuys, who sent it to Moustier, instructing him to try to get Ottoman approval for this draft.[21] Meanwhile Nubar, who went straight from Paris to Constantinople after the issue of the Arbitral Award, had obtained the Porte's agreement to a draft convention which made several radical alterations in the terms of the original Concessions other than those necessitated by the Arbitral Award. This draft provided, *inter alia*: (*a*) for the nomination by the Egyptian Government of the presidency of the Company instead of reserving the presidency to Lesseps for the first ten years and thereafter providing that the Company's nomination of a president was subject to the approval of the

Egyptian Government; (*b*) for the fixing of Canal dues by agreement between the Company and the Egyptian Government instead of their being fixed unilaterally by the Company; (*c*) for the supervision of construction work by the Egyptian Government; (*d*) for the possibility of reducing the area of land allocated to the Company under the Arbitral Award; (*e*) for Egyptian jurisdiction over all matters affecting the Company: (*f*) for the nomination of additional founder-shareholders by the Viceroy; (*g*) for the deduction of 15 percent from all sums awarded to the Company under the Arbitral Award on the ground that the sums awarded represented a net profit to the Company and that the Egyptian Government, under the terms of the Concessions, was entitled to 15 percent of the net profit.[22] This draft, having been accepted by the Porte, was sent by Aali Pasha to Drouyn de Lhuys, who sent it on to Lesseps, who had by that time arrived in Egypt to try to induce Ismail to agree to his own draft convention. But Nubar, coming from Constantinople, had just forestalled him and had obtained Ismail's agreement to his draft, which had already been approved by the Porte.[23] Lesseps furiously protested to the Emperor that "the Porte recognizes neither the Arbitral Award nor the rights of the Company as confirmed (*consacrés*) by this Award," and requested that Moustier be instructed to demand the promulgation of the firman forthwith.[24] Moustier was instructed accordingly but, having been told by Aali Pasha that the firman would be promulgated only as the result of a request from the Viceroy,[25] and following a protest from the British Government,[26] did not persist in his request.

At the beginning of March, Lesseps, in Constantinople, produced a third draft convention which was discussed between Moustier, Fuad, and Aali. Moustier maintained the view that the terms of the Emperor's Award were not subject to discussion. The Grand Vizier and Reis Effendi intimated to Moustier that the real difficulty lay in British opposition to the land question and that this could be solved only by direct negotiations between France and Britain.[27] There followed the direct Franco-British negotiations which have already been described and which led to the setting up of the Mixed Commission.

On March 10, 1865, the Duc de Morny died. After his death the letters which Ismail had written to him during 1863–1864 came into the hands of Aali Pasha. These letters which, according to Aali Pasha, stated that Ismail "felt it necessary for the time being to show a certain amount of deference to the Sultan but that, if the French Government would aid him to secure his independence, he would be ready to make any concessions which might be required for the advancement of French interests in Egypt,"[28] naturally increased Aali's endemic suspicion of Ismail and, to that extent, hindered the progress of negotiations. During the recriminations which followed, Bulwer, who had seen the whole of the Ismail-Morny correspondence, told the Foreign Office that he did not believe that Ismail had been intriguing with Morny, and blamed Mustafa, Ismail's half-brother, who lived in Constantinople, for spreading rumors about him. Referring to the correspondence, he expressed the view that "nothing could be more clear than Ismail Pasha's complaints or more reasonable and moderate than the Duc de Morny's counsels and opinions. The Viceroy's desire to be well with the Sultan is at this time serious . . . it suits his favourite wish and hope to get the Sultan's ultimate sanction . . . to a change in the hereditary succession. Nothing but fear or surprise will make him act against the policy he has now adopted."[29] This was probably a correct view, seeing the amount of money Ismail was to lavish in Constantinople over the next year or two in order to obtain the desired change in the succession, and it is unlikely that at this stage he would have done anything seriously to annoy the Porte over the matter of the canal. In fact, the rest of the negotiations regarding the text of the convention were carried out entirely between Moustier and the Porte, although these negotiations, and the agreed text which eventually emerged from them, were considerably affected by the matters which Nubar had managed to import into the second draft of the proposed convention.

In July, 1865, a fourth draft convention was produced which Lesseps objected to on the ground that it did not make it clear that foreign employees of the Canal Company were protected by the "capitulations." Moustier, after getting from Outrey a report about various British objections regarding land use, fortifications, and so on, which Outrey had discussed with Stanton,[30] and after having received legal advice about the question of jurisdiction, produced a fifth, and final, draft, which received the approval of Aali Pasha and which was also, after some persuasion by Outrey, approved by Lesseps. It was then shown to Lord Lyons, the new British ambassador, by Aali Pasha on what appears to be the first occasion on which the British Government had been brought into the discussion. Lyons described the document as "a draft drawn up at the Porte of the Convention to be eventually concluded between the Viceroy of Egypt and the Canal Company. This paper was communicated to me, very confidentially, by Aali Pasha. He told me that it was founded on two drafts which had been drawn up some months before, one by the Porte and the other by the Company . . . articles had been introduced into the draft . . . with a view to securing the control of the Egyptian Government over the Canal and the jurisdiction of that Government in cases in which the Company was concerned."[31]

The end was now in sight. The draft was agreed to by Nubar on Ismail's behalf and formed the basis of two conventions, one dated January 30 and the other February 22, 1866, between the Egyptian Government and the Canal Company which settled all matters outstanding between the two parties on the lines laid down in the Emperor's Arbitral Award, and also provided for clarification of certain matters regarding use of lands, fortifications, and so on. These "clarifications" went some way toward meeting the objections expressed to the terms of the original Concessions by both the British and the Ottoman Governments.

The first of these two conventions[32] provided: (i) that the Egyptian Government should have the right, at their discretion, to establish strategic and administrative posts along the line of the Maritime Canal; (ii) that private individuals should, with the consent of the Egyptian Government, be allowed to occupy land along the line of the Maritime Canal; (iii) that the Wadi lands would be resold to the Egyptian Government for the price of 10 million francs;[33] (iv) that the Sweet Water Canal be handed over to the Egyptian Government before the end of the year against payment by the Egyptian Government of 10 million francs as laid down in the Arbitral Award; (v) that the sum of 57,750,000 francs out of the Arbitral Award which would still remain payable after November, 1866, that is, 84 million francs less 10 million francs for the Sweet Water Canal and less three installments of 5 million francs due, according to the terms of the Arbitral Award, by November, 1866, would be paid in thirty-six monthly installments between January, 1867, and December, 1869.

The second of the two conventions[34] started by recapitulating the various agreements which had been come to between Lesseps and the Egyptian Government—the First Concession of November 30, 1854, the Second Concession of January 5, 1856, the labor agreement of June 20, 1856, the two conventions of March 16, 1863, and March 20, 1863, and the most recent convention of January 30, 1866.[35] It went on to quote the Grand Vizier's letter of April 6, 1863, and stated that the purpose of the convention was to meet the conditions laid down by the Porte in that letter. It cancelled the various clauses in the two Concessions and in the labor agreement relating to forced labor, lands, and the Sweet Water Canal, and set out the compensation awarded by the Emperor in consideration of these cancellations. It recapitulated arrangements already made, in the March, 1863, and March, 1866, conventions, for the payment of the Egyptian Government's shareholding, for the payment of the indemnities and for the repurchase of the Wadi lands. It recapitulated the clauses in the January 30, 1866, convention about the right of the Egyptian Government to establish strategic and administrative posts along the line of the Maritime Canal and the right of private individuals to settle along the line of the Canal with the consent of the Egyptian Government. It specified that "the Maritime Canal and its appurtenancies" were subject to the authority of the Egyptian police "which shall exercise its functions freely, as at every other point in the territory, so as to secure good order, the public peace, and the execution of the laws and regulations of the country." It laid down that goods in transit through the canal were exempt from customs duties "without distinction, exclusion, or preference in respect of person or nationality." It gave the Egyptian Government the right to appoint a special commissioner to be attached to the Canal Company "in order to ensure the faithful execution of the agreements between it and the Company." It clarified the question of jurisdiction, stating that "La Compagnie Universelle du Canal Maritime de Suez, being Egyptian, is governed by the laws and usages of the country; at the same time, as regards its constitution in the character of a Company, and the relations of its members among themselves, it is, by virtue of a special agreement, regulated by the laws which in France govern '*sociétés anonymes*'. It is agreed that all disputes under this head shall be decided in France by arbitrators with appeal to the Imperial Court at Paris as referee. Differences in Egypt between the Company and individuals, to whatever nationality they belong, shall be judged by the local tribunals according to the forms prescribed by the laws and usages of the country and the treaties.[36] Disputes arising between the Egyptian Government and the Company shall also be submitted to the local tribunals and decided according to the laws of the country." (This appeared to provide that disputes between the Egyptian Government and the Company, unlike disputes between private individuals and the Company, should be dealt with in the national courts, on the basis of the Company being of Egyptian nationality, and without reference to the "capitulations".) The last article provided that all previous agreements between the Egyptian Government and the Company which were "not inconsistent with the present agreement" should remain in force.

In this convention the Company appeared to have met all the criticisms of substance which had been raised, either by the British Government or by the Porte or by the Egyptian Government, in respect of jurisdiction, land use, and so on—that is to say, all the criticisms about the Company trying to establish itself on Egyptian soil as an *imperium in imperio*. It had also, by renouncing any special rights in respect of land which was still retained by it for its operations, rendered largely irrelevant the long wrangle about the proper extent of that land, on which the Mixed Commission, which was in Egypt at the time of the signature of the convention, was about to adjudicate. In return for these considerable concessions, the Company had succeeded:

(i) in regularizing its position vis-á-vis the Porte, which had already sig-
nified its approval of the terms of the convention and thereby committed itself
to the promulgation of the firman as soon as the convention had been signed;
and (ii) in securing an appreciable acceleration in the rate of payment of indemnities as compared with the installments stipulated in the Arbitral Award.
Both these considerations were important in the light of the Company's
financial position, which, at the beginning of 1866, was described in the following terms by a Colonel Laffan of the British Royal Engineers, who investigated the matter and whose appreciation was acknowledged by Lesseps himself to be *"très exacte et très loyale"*:

While the Agreement [that is, the two conventions which were about to be
signed] is advantageous to Egypt, it has proved the salvation of M. de Lesseps,
for he was literally [sic] aground for want of money . . . he had in hand some
Fcs.45 million in Egyptian Treasury Bonds and Shares in his own Canal bought up
to keep them afloat on the market. He could not realise these, though he had
probably been able to borrow some Fcs.30 million upon them with which he
enabled his contractors to pay for a portion of their enormous matériel. But
the contractors would want some Fcs.50 million more advanced to pay for the
remainder of their working stocks, the total outlay on which would be Fcs.80
million. And where was Lesseps to find the money? To call up the last Fcs.40
million due on the Shares would have raised a storm in France, for it would
have amounted to a confession of bankruptcy while the real work of the Canal
could scarcely be said to have begun. The Pasha's money comes just in time to
relieve him from a disagreeable dilemma [sic]. It will enable him to defer his
call on the Shareholders until after the next general Meeting in May next, and
it will enable him to work on for nearly three years more.[37]

The promulgation of the firman would facilitate the collection of the remaining calls on the original share issue and make it possible to issue a further
appeal to the public for capital. The acceleration of the indemnity payments
enabled the Company to have access to this money during the time that they
would need money most, that is, during the actual period of construction.
In short, the convention demonstrated that the canal project was not, as Palmerston had tried to make out, a French imperialist plot directed against
Britain, but an extremely hazardous financial speculation, and that the Company, provided that it got a good enough price, was quite prepared to trade
strategic advantages and colonial opportunities in return for Egyptian
money and in return for the prospect of European capital which would have
been frightened off by a continuance of political complications.

The British Government expressed their satisfaction at the signature of the
Convention and, in so doing, put an end to the long warfare they had
waged against the canal project. In a letter from Clarendon to Ismail dated

May 12th, the Foreign Secretary wrote: "Your Highness' letter of 15 April was duly delivered to me by Nubar Pasha whom I had great pleasure in receiving. Her Majesty's Government have learnt with great satisfaction of the termination of the difficulties connected with the Suez Canal Company and I have to express the earnest hope that the position in which the affair is now placed will be firmly maintained by Your Highness."[38]

A month after the signature of the convention, on March 19, 1866, the Sultan's firman was promulgated,[39] nearly eleven years and four months after the grant of the First Concession by Mohammed Said to Lesseps. It had for long been inevitable, and when it came it was something of an anticlimax. On March 25th Ismail wrote to Napoleon III indicating that he would require "the powerful support of France in a new era," meaning that he wanted French support for his various campaigns at Constantinople as a *quid pro quo* for his complaisance toward the Canal Company.

Meanwhile the Mixed Commission, on February 25th, had issued its report, awarding to the Company much the same area of land as had been awarded to them in the Arbitral Award—10,214 hectares as compared with 10,264 hectares in the Arbitral Award.[40]

On August 1st, at the Annual general meeting of the Canal Company, Lesseps told his shareholders, without éclat, of the promulgation of the firman.[41]

On December 19, 1865, the British Government had produced a paper[42] for internal circulation in which they estimated the results of the opposition which they had offered to various aspects of the canal project. These results were tabulated under various headings:

(i) Abolition of forced labour. "Its cessation was entirely owing to the exertions of Her Majesty's Government."

(ii) Restriction of the amount of land to be conceded to the Canal Company. "Mr. Lesseps did not seek merely to construct a Canal, but he also endeavoured, under different pretences, to obtain possession of a large tract of country amounting to . . . about 80,000 hectares. . . . The opposition of Her Majesty's Government —for the Porte were passive—was doubtless the only reason why, by the Emperor's award, the amount of land to be conceded to the Company was fixed at 10,264 hectares."

(iii) Defeat of the colonisation scheme. "The chief object for which Mr. Lesseps sought to obtain possession of so large an extent of land was for the purpose of introducing a foreign colony into Egypt. The reduction of the amount of land to be conceded, and the definitive understanding come to with the French Government that only so much land is to be conceded as is actually wanted for the construction of the Canal, effectively puts a stop to this and to any other similar scheme which Mr. Lesseps may have in view."

(iv) Damage to British interests at Suez. "The steps taken by Her Majesty's

Government to check the hostile proceedings of the Canal and Messageries Companies have been attended with complete success."

(v) Fortifications and (vi) the maintenance of Egyptian jurisdiction "are on a footing favourable to a satisfactory settlement of these matters."

Lastly, "Her Majesty's Government have established that the Sultan's sovereignty is to be as fully recognised in Egypt as in any other part of the Ottoman dominions."

Given the reality of the British fears about the purposes of the Canal—that it was a French imperialist plot designed to lead to a French colonization of Egypt, to the separation of Egypt from Turkey, and to a French threat to India—the various modifications which had been secured in the terms of the original Concessions did represent some sort of paper safeguard. But if there really had been a French imperialist plot with these aims in view, such paper safeguards would have been useless. Since the canal was a financial speculation and not an imperialist plot, the only effect of these modifications was to load the Egyptian Treasury with a burden of indemnity and, correspondingly, to relieve part of the Company's financial embarrassments. If, between the First Concession in November, 1855, and the Second Concession in January, 1856, the British Government had advanced their detailed objections about forced labor, lands, jurisdiction, fortifications, and so on, there is little doubt that most of these objections would have been met in the terms of the Second Concession. Instead, the British Government assumed that the strength of their opposition would prevent the Canal from materializing at all. When it did materialize, the Egyptian Treasury had to bear the cost of the face-saving revisions on which the British Government were able to insist and about which they were able to issue the somewhat muted apologia which has been quoted.

The French Government, on the assumption that they were not interested in an imperialist plot against Great Britain, had considerably more reason for satisfaction. In a matter in which their prestige had, willy-nilly, become involved, they had, without seriously antagonizing Britain, and without any open bullying of Turkey, and without any expenditure either of force or of money, succeeded in accomplishing that which, ten years before, could not have been attempted without risking war with Great Britain.

The Ottoman Government had even greater reason for satisfaction. In spite of British gibes at Ottoman passivity, they had really achieved all their relevant objectives in the matter of the canal. They had established the necessity for obtaining the Sultan's firman and, by so doing, had reaffirmed the reality of the Sultan's suzerainty over Egypt. They had, with remarkable dexterity, managed simultaneously to satisfy the most urgently expressed requirements of both Great Britain and France, and had thus kept the good-will of both, without any serious derogation from any vital Ottoman interest. Time after time, the Ottoman Ministers had, by judicious procrastination, avoided either a precipitate surrender or a direct resistance to threats, and by so doing had preserved intact those few tatters of independence still left to the Ottoman Empire. Time after time, with a virtuosity which compels a reluctant admiration, they had turned crisis into anticlimax. Time after time, when seemingly faced with the necessity of an embarrassing decision, they had made their escape behind a cloud of equivocation. And when eventually the firman was produced, it appeared to be the inevitable and spontaneous result of some long process of gestation, safely brought to birth in the privacy of the Sultan's Seraglio.

Ismail was the real loser. He had been condemned to pay an 84-million-franc indemnity as the result of British suspicions of French imperialist intrigues. He had been forced to make an ostentatious parade of his subservience to Constantinople. He had greatly increased the chances of having his country invaded either by Britain or France or both. And he had delivered himself into the clutches of a peculiarly rapacious concessionaire who was, moreover, supported by the French Government and with whom he could no longer break without consequences even more dismal than those attendant on continued collaboration. All in all, Ismail's ghost must have viewed the events of July–November, 1956, with a good deal of satisfaction.

NOTES

1. Sultan Abdul Aziz, who had succeeded to the throne after the death of his predecessor, Sultan Abdul Mejid, in 1861, seems to have played as little a personal part as Abdul Mejid in the affairs of the canal. He was described by Bulwer as being "possessed of the best intentions but his knowledge was necessarily limited as it was difficult for him to know more than it was convenient to tell him." (Bulwer–Russell 9.11.64. FO 78/1850.) His principal power lay in his ability, which he used freely, to make and unmake Grand Viziers. This gave him some influence in domestic policy, but in foreign affairs all Grand Viziers were equally subject to pressures from the Powers and their influence, and consequently that of the Sultan, was limited and virtually nonexistent. Sultan Abdul Aziz had a passion for exotic birds, of which he made a large collection, largely at the expense of Ismail, who made lavish presents of these birds to the Sultan in his various endeavors to obtain modifications of the 1841 Hatti Sharif. The Sultan's aviary, like the Suez Canal, was based almost entirely on the unrequited toil and sweat of the Egyptian fellahin.
2. Cowley–Russell 25.3.65. FO 78/1895.
3. Journal, V, 88.
4. Stevens–Bulwer 18.6.64. FO 78/1895. Stevens was a secretary at the Constantinople Embassy who had been sent by Bulwer to Egypt to report on the canal.
5. Russell–Stuart 20.1.65. FO 78/1895.
6. Russell–Cowley 26.2.65. FO 78/1895.
7. Of these two remarkable men, one or the other occupied the post of Reis Effendi for the

whole period of the canal transaction from 1854 until 1869. (Fuad died in 1869.) In addition, one was Grand Vizier while the other was Reis Effendi, from August, 1861, until Fuad's death in February, 1869. This combination gave an unusual air of continuity, as well as firmness, to Ottoman foreign policy during this period. Given the powerful and diverse pressures operating upon them, and given the lack of material forces at their disposal, they did by no means so badly as the dispatches of foreign ambassadors might lead one to believe. In the matter of the canal they secured most of what Turkish interests required without coming down decisively either on the side of Britain or of France, and without throwing Ismail into the hands of either. The exasperation at their tactics so often expressed by both British and French ambassadors is really a tribute to their virtuosity.

8. Douin, *Règne du Khédive Ismaïl*, I, 137. There is a story that Nubar, visiting Morny after the Arbitral Award had been announced, was told by Morny that the Emperor had charged him to present Nubar with the insignia of a Commandant de la Légion d'Honneur. As Nubar was tall and Morny short, Nubar had to bend low to enable Morny to place the collar round his neck. "Eighty-four millions francs round my neck," mused Nubar, "is quite a heavy enough weight to make me stoop."
9. Bulwer–Russell 10.1.65. FO 78/1895.
10. For an account of this matter see correspondence between Tastu and Drouyn de Lhuys in CP 34. See also Bulwer–Russell 8.1.65. FO 78/1895.
11. Cowley–Russell 13.4.65. FO 78/1896.
12. Stuart–Russell 25.4.65. FO 78/1895.
13. Cowley–Russell 9.5.65. FO 78/1896.
14. *Ibid.*, 26.5.65. FO 78/1896.
15. Douin, *op. cit.*, I, 170–171.
16. See p. 190.
17. Journal, V, 206.
18. Cowley–Russell 20.7.65. FO 78/1896.
19. After Bulwer had expressed a fear lest the two Frenchmen on the commission, presumably acting in unison, would be able to impose their wishes on the Turkish and Egyptian members, Cowley made a halfhearted attempt to get the French Government to agree to the nomination of a British Government representative on the commission. This attempt was unsuccessful, since Drouyn de Lhuys pointed out that the Sultan's letter to the Emperor had not proposed the inclusion of a British Government representative. Cowley did not press the matter, but got Drouyn de Lhuys to agree that, in the event of the four members of the commission not being able to agree among themselves, there would be no question of the Emperor being called upon to arbitrate between them. Eventually, as the result of strong pressure from Outrey, the four members of the commission did agree to make only a nominal variation in the extent of the land allotted to the Company in the Arbitral Award.
20. Cowley–Russell 25.4.65. FO 78/1895.
21. Douin, *op. cit.*, I, 136.
22. *Ibid.*, pp. 139–140.
23. *Ibid.*, p. 141.
24. Journal, V, 88. Letter dated 4.2.65.
25. Stuart–Russell 21.2.65. FO 78/1895.
26. Russell–Cowley 25.2.65. FO 78/1895.
27. Douin, *op. cit.* I, 156-158.
28. Stuart–Russell 8.4.65. FO 78/1896.
29. Bulwer–Russell 5.6.65. FO 78/1896.
30. This seems to have been the first occasion on which detailed questions arising out of the canal project were amicably and constructively discussed between the British and French consuls general in Egypt, a circumstance which reflects credit on the good sense of Stanton and Outrey and less credit on the good sense of their various predecessors.
31. Lyons–Clarendon 19.12.65. FO 78/1897.
32. For text see J. Charles–Roux, *L'Isthme* . . . , Vol. I, Annex No. 21.
33. They had been bought from the Egyptian Government five years previously for 2 million francs.
34. For text see J. Charles-Roux, *op. cit.*, Vol. I, Annex No. 22.

35. Significantly, the alleged financial agreement with Mohammed Said of August, 1860, is not included in this recapitulation.
36. Capitulations Treaties.
37. Report to Foreign Office by Colonel Laffan, R.E., 31.1.66. FO 78/2014.
38. Clarendon–Ismail 12.5.66. FO 78/2014.
39. For text see J. Charles-Roux, *op. cit.,* Vol. I, Annex No. 20.
40. Douin, *op. cit.,* I, 193.
41. Journal, V, 247.
42. Text in FO 78/1896.

CHAPTER *twelve*

Construction—

Second Phase ॰ॐ

॰ॐ IN spite of all the political alarms and excursions, work on the canal proceeded uninterruptedly throughout 1863, mostly by means of *corvée* labor. At the beginning of the year about 20,000 laborers were being employed, but this had fallen to under 13,000 a year later[1] when the six-month time limit fixed by the Grand Vizier for the cessation of all forced labor was drawing to an end. The Timsah-Suez stretch of the Sweet Water Canal was completed in December, 1863,[2] and for the first time the waters of the Nile were brought to the Port of Suez, a circumstance which was, of course, of immense advantage to the inhabitants, and particularly to the landowners, of the town. A start was also made on the excavation of the Serapeum Ridge between Timsah and the Bitter Lakes. During the year a total of 3,347,000 cubic meters was estimated to have been excavated, making a total of about 8,500,000 cubic meters, nearly all of which had been done by hand labor.[3] Here are extracts from an eyewitness account of the state of the canal, at the beginning of 1864, contributed by the British consulate chaplain in Alexandria,[4] who had just made a tour of the isthmus, traveling mainly in a barge pulled by dromedaries:

None of the work of the Maritime Canal has been commenced at or near Suez. Ismailia (the intended port on Lake Timsah) has only been commenced 18 months ago but is now a considerable town; we estimated it to contain 1,800 people. . . . A large body of corvée labourers are at work a little to the south of Lake Timsah . . . the fresh water from Ismailia to Port Said flows in large iron tubes along the side of the Canal. . . . Only half of the distance (to Kantara) is yet finished . . . a small side canal (salt) leads from Ismailia to the Canal Maritime; the latter enters Timsah at its north-east corner. About an hour from Ismailia we reached El Guisr, an enormous cutting in the sand some four miles long and very deep; the canal in the cutting was but a mere thread of water and very shallow. . . . Beyond Kantara all through Lake Menzala the Canal is of full breadth but nowhere at present is there a depth of more than 2 metres and in most places much less. Near Kantara there were some 7,000 corvée labourers at work and, according to our estimates, there were altogether 13,000 employed. When they had reached water level it was intended to execute the rest by dredging machines which could not be employed till the earth had been removed by manual labour to water level. . . . Their appearance (that of the corvée labourers) was very pitiable. All told us that they did not come of their own free will; they came by force, "*b'il nabut*" (driven by sticks). . . . Port Said may contain some 4,000 people . . . we returned by the Canal Maritime to Ismailia and then passed along the Sweet Water Canal to Zagazig . . . at nightfall we reached Tel el Kebir, the estate purchased by the Company for £60,000. It is said to be 22,000 feddans.[5]

At the end of 1862 the contract with Hardon, who had up to that time been the sole contractor for the canal works, had been amicably terminated and the work of construction contracted out to three separate contractors— Ayton, an Englishman, who was responsible for the 61-kilometer stretch from Port Said to Jisr; Couvreux, who was responsible for the 15-kilometer stretch through the Jisr Ridge; and Borel, Lavalley et Cie., who were responsible for the whole 64 kilometers from Timsah to Suez. (Ayton subsequently went bankrupt, and his contract was taken over by Borel, Lavalley et Cie. The construction was thus virtually a piece of all-French engineering).

Very little work was done during 1864. Forced labor was stopped, and the new machinery had not yet arrived. But, near the beginning of 1865, work was resumed at high pressure and continued uninterruptedly until completion.

Mechanical devices . . . of great originality and power, that supplied the want of human labour, were soon at work. . . . No one who has seen an ordinary dredge at its slow work in an English river could have an idea of the bold fashion in which the principle was now applied. . . . The dredges vary in size according to the work for which they are required and the ulterior disposal of the dredgings. The lesser ones are of 15 h.p.; there is also an intermediate size; and then follow the largest machines of 75 h.p., 110 feet in length, with 27 feet beam, and having their drums 48 feet above the water-line. . . . If the dredgings are required, as at Port Said, for reclaiming land, or for making concrete blocks, when raised from the water they are made to fall into large boxes having a capacity of four cubic yards. Seven of these fit into a barge which is moored under the spout of the dredge. When all are filled, the barge is floated under a steam crane by which the boxes are lifted out and placed on tracks running on tramways. On arriving at their destination, one end of these boxes opens on hinges and the contents are thus readily deposited. . . . The greater part of the Port Said dredgings are however conveyed in large sea-going barges some four or five miles out to sea and there dropped into deep water. . . . These barges are in use in the ports and in some of the lakes; but a large proportion of the dredgings is discharged from the machines either into an apparatus which has been named the "long couloir" or into the "elevateur."[6]

The *long couloir* was a chute used for depositing dredged material on the banks when the dredger was working at or not far below the level of the land on each side of the canal. The chute, which was anything up to one hundred feet long, was carried on a barge with an iron framework superstructure which was moored at right angles to the dredger between the dredger and the bank. The upper end of the chute, which was attached to the dredger, and which was at a height of up to about forty feet above water level, was fed by an endless chain of buckets containing the dredged material which was then washed down the inclined chute with the help of a stream of water pumped up from the barge and deposited on the bank. The *élévateur* was used when the dredgers were working well below the level of the side banks. It consisted of an inclined plane up to about 200 feet long, carrying two lines of tramrail, one up, one down, worked on a steel cable. The dredged material was dropped into hinged boxes on barges which, when loaded, were floated under the *élévateur*. The filled boxes were hoisted onto the tramway, carried up to the top, discharged their contents onto the canal bank, and were sent down again into a waiting barge. Lesseps told a general meeting of the Company that "our dredging machines, of which the ducts are one-and-a-half times as long as the column in the Place Vendôme, carried off from two to three thousand cubic metres a day; and as we had sixty of them, we succeeded in extracting monthly as much as two million cubic metres."[7]

The dredgers were brought progressively along the line from Port Said by the *rigole de service* to deepen the Maritime Canal to the required depth after excavation to water level had been done by manual labor. It proved impossible, however, to obtain the manual labor required for excavating the Serapeum Ridge, south of Lake Timsah, down to water level. Mechanical dredgers were therefore adapted to dry excavation. Having been brought from Port Said into Lake Timsah by the *rigole de service,* the dredgers were taken seventeen feet above sea level into the Sweet Water Canal through the locks at Ismailia between the Maritime and Sweet Water canals. Cross-cuttings were then made from the Sweet Water Canal to near the line of the Maritime Canal opposite the points where the ridge had to be excavated. Dams were maintained between the cross-cuttings and the Maritime Canal until the Maritime Canal had been excavated to sea level; then the cross-cuttings were damned off from the Sweet Water Canal and the dams were opened between the cross-cuttings and the Maritime Canal, thus enabling the dredgers to float into the Maritime Canal and revert to their normal task of underwater excavation.[8]

After the withdrawal of forced labor, freely recruited hand labor was to some extent employed, particularly for excavation through the Shallufa Ridge between Suez and the Bitter Lakes:

The curious spectacle was now witnessed of a rush of able-bodied European workmen arriving from all parts of Italy, Belgium, France, England, to give their services. But most of the workmen are again "les indigenes," but coming now as volunteers and attracted by the good and certain wages which they earn. The greater part of the excavation is accomplished by piece work from which excellent results are obtained . . . the price is such as enables the labourer to earn from 1s. 6d. to 2s. 6d. a day, but usually he manages to make more than the minimum sum.[9]

The Company was fortunate in that nearly all the material to be excavated was sand. The only place where any rock was found was in the Shallufa Ridge, where 52,000 cubic meters of rock had to be removed by blasting.[10]

Apart from the work of excavation, it was also necessary to create out of nothing the northern terminal at Port Said, to construct the headquarters and intended loading and discharging port of Ismailia on Lake Timsah, and to develop the docks and roadstead of Suez at the southern terminal. As we have seen, the work had to start with the creation of Port Said where all the material for construction was received and where the excavation of the Maritime Canal began by the digging of a *rigole de service* southward to Lake Timsah to enable dredgers and other construction machinery to be brought forward along the line of the canal.

It proved impossible to use Ismailia, as had been intended, as the principal canal port, but it was developed into a considerable and attractive town which, in 1869, had a population of some 6,000 and contained the Egypt Headquarters of the Canal Company.

Suez had been transformed by the completion of the Cairo-Suez railway in 1859, and by the advent of Nile water at the end of 1863. Considerable work in the harbor was also done, both by the Canal Company and by the Messageries Impériales and the Peninsula and Oriental Steam Navigation Company, as well as by the Egyptian Government, in anticipation of what would be required there after the canal had been opened to navigation.

Not more than four or five years ago, Suez was an insignificant village containing 4,000 inhabitants, but exhibiting no signs of life except when the steamers of the Peninsula and Oriental Company, and subsequently those of the Messageries Impériales, were embarking or disembarking their passengers and merchandise. The absence of water, and the dearness of provisions, both of which had to be brought from Cairo and the surrounding districts, rendered it as uninviting a spot as can well be imagined. The advent of the Fresh Water Canal has brought about a marvellous change. The population has now increased to 25,000 and there is a degree of life and activity about the place clearly indicating the energy that is being displayed on all sides. The principal operations of the Company consist; firstly in constructing a mole, 850 yards in length, at the mouth of the Canal to serve as a protection against southerly gales and against the action of the tide at high water; secondly, in dredging to the requisite depth the channel leading from the Canal to the anchorage in the roads of Suez; and thirdly, the reclamation of land.[11]

Up to the end of 1864, about 15 million cubic meters had been excavated (including the Sweet Water Canal), mainly by hand labor.[12] By September, 1869, when construction had been virtually completed, a total of about 75 million cubic meters had been excavated.[13] Of this, some 60 million cubic meters had been excavated during the 4¾ years since the end of 1864, almost entirely by mechanical means. The price paid to the contractors for mechanical excavation was estimated at from 2.5 francs to 3 francs per cubic meter.[14] Taking the lower figure, this would have involved payments to contractors of about 150 million francs for mechanical excavation alone. Even at Lesseps' exaggerated expectation of one cubic meter per man per day, and ignoring the difficulties of using hand labor for excavation below sea level (which could have been partly overcome by damming), the excavation of 75 million cubic meters by hand would have taken 75 million man-days. With an average *corvée* of 20,000 men working 300 days a year, this would have taken 12½ years for excavation alone, without taking into account the necessities of port construction, and so on.

When the canal was completed in 1869, it had been excavated to a minimum depth of 26 feet across a minimum bottom width of 72 feet. The width at surface level varied from 327 feet to 196 feet. In the narrower sections the slope of the banks was 1 in 2, the banks being terraced by one or more horizontal "benches" 10 feet wide, according to the depth of the cutting. In the wider sections the bank was divided into two terraces by a horizontal "bench" 58 feet wide, the lower terrace having a slope of 1 in 2 and the upper terrace a slope of 1 in 5. The narrower sections were those through which deep cuttings had to be made and where the further widening of the canal at surface level would have involved the excavation of vast additional quantities of soil.[15] In the northern section of the canal, between Port Said and Timsah, the canal was widened by *gares,* or sidings, at intervals of five or six miles, to enable ships to pass one another or to moor in the canal.[16] Ships could also pass each other or moor in Lake Timsah or in the Bitter Lakes.

As to the question of a current through the Canal, it was anticipated that the difference of level between the seas would have produced a sort of fall. This, it seems, has been neutralised by the great lakes which act as water "buffers." The difference of level between the two seas, so far as it has had any effect in producing a current one way or the other, is inappreciable.[17]

The total cost of the canal up to the end of 1869, according to the Company's books, was 453,645,000 francs.[18] Of this sum, 200,000,000 francs was found from the original capital, all of which, including the Egyptian Government shareholding, had been fully paid up by the end of 1869. Where did the balance of 253,645,000 francs come from? It came mainly from four sources, two of which have been described in a previous chapter, and two of which will be described in this chapter:

(i) The 84 million francs indemnity.

(ii) The 10 million francs received from the resale of the Wadi lands to the Egyptian Government.

(iii) A sum of 100,000,000 francs obtained from two bond issues in 1867–1868.

(iv) A sum of 30 million francs paid by the Egyptian Government to the Company for various physical assets, customs, fishing rights, and so on, purchased by the Egyptian Government from the Company in accordance with the terms of a convention signed on April 23, 1869.

These sums account for a total of 224 million francs. The balance of nearly 30 million francs would seem to have been obtained from interest paid by the Egyptian Government to the Company, under the terms of the March, 1863, and January, 1866, conventions, on amounts owing on the Egyptian Government's ordinary shareholding and on the indemnity.

Apart from the sum of 453,645,000 francs appearing in the Company's books, there were a large number of expenses incurred by the Egyptian Government in connection with the canal, details of which were given by M. Edouard Dervieu, a French banker resident in Egypt, of whom we shall hear more later:[19]

Cost of construction of Sweet Water Canal from Cairo to Ras al Wadi	francs	21,500,000
Cost of construction of Radoub Basin at Suez		9,000,000
Cost of construction of port works at Suez		23,395,000
Construction of lighthouses at northern terminal of canal		1,250,000
TOTAL	francs	55,145,000

The money spent by the Egyptian Government on the canal, whether in the form of share capital, indemnities, or on public works connected with the canal, or on the expenses of Nubar's missions to Paris and Constantinople, or on the lavish entertainments which accompanied the formal opening of the canal in 1869, nearly all had to be raised by foreign loans. It has been estimated[20] that the total amount of indebtedness incurred by the Egyptian Government in the course of raising the money spent by them on the canal amounted to some 400 million francs. In return, the Egyptian Government received ordinary shares at a par value of some 87,000,000 francs (on which, as we shall see, they had to forego all interest and dividends until 1894, and which were, in 1875, sold to the British Government for 100,000,000 francs), plus a 15 percent interest in the net profits of the Company, which interest was, in 1880, sold to the Crédit Foncier for a sum of 22,000,000 francs.[21] The 400-million-franc indebtedness incurred because of the Suez Canal represents an appreciable proportion of the Egyptian Government's total indebtedness of some 2,225,000,000 francs at the time of Egypt's bankruptcy in 1876.

The 1867–1868 bond issues were designed to raise additional capital of 100 million francs, or a sum equal to 50 percent of the original capital. In the first issue 333,333 bonds were offered at 300 francs each, repayable at 500 francs each after fifty years, and bearing interest at 25 francs per bond per annum. In spite of these relatively favorable terms only 108,393 of the 333,333 bonds had been taken up when subscriptions closed on September 30, 1867, making a total subscription of some 33 million francs out of the 100 million francs called for. The Company then sought, and obtained, from the Conseil d'Etat, special permission[22] which enabled them, in July, 1868, to ask subscriptions for the balance of money required—some 66 million francs—on the same terms as before, but with the additional incentive of another 1 percent interest distributed in lottery prizes (on the same principle as for premium bonds). The addition of this incentive proved successful, and the issue was fully subscribed.

It is apparent from the vicissitudes attending this bond issue that, in spite of the removal of all the political difficulties, there was still only a modified enthusiasm in the money markets about the canal's commercial prospects. The success of the issue after the addition of the lottery incentive was perhaps due more to the favor manifested by the French Government, which had secured legislative assent to the lottery, than to its intrinsic attractions. (A later attempt by Lesseps to receive legislative permission for a lottery issue in connection with the Panama Canal was unsuccessful, and this setback contributed largely to the failure of the Panama project.) A failure to secure permission for the lottery issue in 1868 might well have precipitated the failure of the Company, even though the canal was nearly finished.

This continued financial stringency explains Lesseps' repeated, and not unsuccessful, attempts, between 1866 and 1869, to extract money from the Egyptian Government on every conceivable pretext.

Arrangements, incorporated in the March, 1863, convention, had been made that the remaining calls on the Egyptian Government's shareholding should be paid in monthly installments of 1,500,000 francs. When the final call of 100 francs a share was made in 1866, the Egyptian Treasury found itself unable to meet the installments. Lesseps raised a loan in Paris, in the name of the Egyptian Government, for 17 million francs at 11½ percent interest, to enable the Egyptian Government to pay off the whole of this final call. Lesseps appears to have committed Ismail to the loan without previously consulting him. And, not for the first time, he succeeded in persuading the Khedive, as we must now call Ismail,[23] to legalize his transaction *ex post facto,* although the Canal Company had to agree to pay some of the interest on the loan. This transaction, although it cost the Company some 500,000 francs in interest payments, was considered by Outrey, the French consul general, as a *"bonne opération"* for the Company, which was thus able "immediately to realise a large sum for which they had the most pressing need."[24]

This pressing need for money also dictated a proposition made by Lesseps to the Khedive in January, 1867, when he proposed that the Company should renounce to the Egyptian Government all their remaining privileges in the isthmus except for the possession of the canal itself *("tout ce qu'elle possède dans l'Isthme à l'exception du Canal proprement dit")* in return for the surrender by the Egyptian Government to the Company of the whole of its ordinary shareholding.[25] On British advice Ismail rejected this offer and refused to part with his shares which, as Colonel Stanton pointed out to him, gave him some means of control over the Company's activities.[26]

It was not long before Lesseps was again making impudent demands on the Egyptian Government, this time by the time-honored method of trying to insist on an extreme construction of a clause in a Concession as a preliminary to claiming an indemnity for waiving it. Article 13 of the Second Concession provided that the company was "exempted from all payment of customs duty or dues in respect of the import of all machinery and other material necessary for the work of construction." Until Egyptian customs posts had been established in the isthmus in accordance with the relative provisions of the January, 1866, convention, the isthmus had in practice become a Free Zone into which had been imported, via

Port Said, free of duty, not only the materials required by the Company in their work, in accordance with Article 13 of the Second Concession, but also furniture, foodstuffs, luxury articles, and other items of every kind, for consumption and for resale, by the Company itself, by its contractors and employees, and by merchants and private individuals who happened to have established themselves in the isthmus.

A great abuse had thus grown up and, with the improvement of communications between the isthmus and the rest of Egypt, there was the danger and, to some extent, the fact of large-scale smuggling, via the isthmus, into the interior of Egypt, to the detriment both of the Egyptian revenue and the prosperity of the port of Alexandria. When Egyptian customs officials established themselves at Port Said, they took immediate steps to put an end to this abuse, while continuing to respect the legitimate franchise of the Canal Company as laid down in the Concession. It was a classic opportunity for a characteristic piece of *"chantage."*

On April 18, 1868, Lesseps addressed a letter to his chief representative in the isthmus, instructing him that "in consideration of the 15 percent of the net profits of the Canal Company reserved for the Egyptian Government, everything coming into and consumed in the isthmus is free of all customs duty." On August 8th he addressed a letter to all the consuls general, calling on them to protect the rights of their nationals in the isthmus who were being forced to pay customs duty, and stating that the customs administration in Port Said had the right to collect customs duties only on goods "going to or coming from those parts of Egypt independent of the Company." "Thus M. de Lesseps . . . wished to incite the consuls to open wide the doors for the legalization of large-scale smuggling . . . his obvious intention was to provoke a conflict with the Egyptian Government in order to compel them to have recourse to another imperial arbitration."[27]

This *"tentative d'une grande hardiesse"* was not even approved by Poujade, the French consul general, who wrote to his Ministry that

this circular was immediately brought to the attention of Sharif Pasha[28] by Colonel Stanton. . . . I know that there was a very lively interview yesterday between Sharif Pasha and M. de Lesseps. . . . Sharif Pasha told him that there was no foundation for the claims made by him on behalf of the Company; that there has never been any question of giving franchise to anything other than machinery and other items necessary for the work of construction, and that anything over and above this previously admitted to franchise had been simply because of the toleration exercised by the previous Viceroy . . . that the Egyptian Government had no intention of creating a state within a state, and that to make a free zone of the isthmus would be tantamount to setting up a nest of smugglers. M. de Lesseps has, once more, proposed to Sharif Pasha that the Emperor be asked to arbitrate on this matter, but the proposal was not welcomed. I have already made investigations to try to discover in the various conventions which have been concluded between the Company and the Egyptian Government a text which might be held to support M. de Lesseps' claim, but so far I have not been successful. I asked M. de Lesseps to show me those clauses on which he bases his claim, but he went away without doing so.[29]

On August 10th Lesseps addressed a public meeting at Port Said, calling upon his audience to resist the "pretensions" of the customs. On August 25th four French merchants, obeying Lesseps' exhortations, visited the customs and forcibly removed some goods consigned to them without paying customs duties. Poujade, equally objective as, if less courageous than, his predecessor Outrey, expressed his disquiet: "If Sharif Pasha can neither excuse nor explain M. de Lesseps' telegram stating that all goods except gunpowder, arms and tobacco should be imported into the isthmus free of duty, after Sharif Pasha had clearly told Lesseps that his claims were without foundation, what on earth is he going to say when he hears that M. de Lesseps has been trying to incite foreigners to violate the laws of the country?"[30]

At this time the Khedive was in Constantinople. Lesseps, who had had previous clashes with Sharif Pasha and who disliked dealing with him, went off to Constantinople and persuaded Ismail to set up a commission to determine the rights and obligations of the Company in the matter of the customs franchise. To this commission were appointed Server Bey, representing the Turkish Government; Ali Pasha Mubarak, representing the Egyptian Government;[31] Poujade, representing the French Government; and a M. de Leclercq, representing the Canal Company. The commissioners, or rather three of them, proved unexpectedly obdurate. On March 1, 1869, three of the commissioners, with M. de Leclercq dissenting, made their award: "The Company should receive in franchise not only all those materials necessary for its works, but also food, drink, clothes, and medicines necessary for its contractors, employees and workers during the period of construction and subsequent operations. The Company shall not delegate this privilege and wholesale and retail merchants have no right of franchise."[32] This was a generous interpretation of Article 13. Nevertheless, the Canal Company representative refused to associate himself with the award, and the French consul general found it politic to write a long and revealing dispatch to his Ministry, excusing himself for having "let the side down":

I ask Your Excellency to consider that Article 13 is very obscure in translation and that the words "*matières quelconques*" are not, strictly speaking, applicable . . . to everything for which I have been able to obtain franchise. . . . The creation of a free port at Port Said would have meant either the ruin of Alexandria or the abolition of customs duties throughout Egypt. All my colleagues were opposed to the extension which the Canal Company sought to give to Article 13, and the Viceroy maintained that nobody, however powerful, had the right to dictate to him in the matter of customs duties. The Company's advocate told M. de Lesseps that the recommendations of the commission had exceeded his most optimistic expectations. However, I know that the Company is not satisfied; it had hoped to bring the Viceroy to purchase from them a "right" which it did not possess, and it has been evident, all through the sittings of the commission, that what M. de Lesseps was really after was money. I understood that from the beginning, and the vigor with which I defended the interests of the Canal Company during the sittings of the commission had no aim other than to facilitate an arrangement between M. de Lesseps and the Viceroy. I went so far in that direction that the Viceroy himself complained of my attitude, and M. de Lesseps tried to dissociate himself from me in the eyes of the Viceroy. But, in spite of everything, the President of the Company has not succeeded in getting the Viceroy to pay him the sum of 40 million francs which, I am given to understand, is necessary for the Company if they are to finish the canal by October 1st. What M. de Lesseps wanted, and what could be understood from the attitude of the Company's representative on the commission, was for me to demand that the Company's right to a free port at Port Said should have been conceded without argument and that, in face of the resistance offered by the Egyptian and Ottoman representatives, I should have retired from the commission together with M. de Leclercq. But I could not have taken that course without openly violating all considerations of justice and equity.[33]

This, surely, must be one of the most remarkable consular dispatches ever penned. But it illustrates, not unfairly, the sort of role which many consuls general in Egypt at this time were expected to play. Poujade, in another matter connected with the canal, had written shortly before that "the tone of the communications from the Company's administration, which seems to regard the Company as a State within a State, is greatly disliked and has drawn unfavorable comment from the Turkish authorities; they ought to be more careful." He was soon to pay the price which, some ten years previously, Sabatier had paid for his independence. In July, 1869, he was relieved of his post and succeeded by M. Tricou.

Lesseps, with that delayed reasonableness which so often saved him from serious trouble, accepted the award with outward good grace, and took the opportunity to repair his somewhat frayed relations with Ismail. He had the best of reasons for doing so. The Company was still in urgent need of money. In March, 1869, Ismail paid his first visit to the isthmus, where he was received with the honors due to his rank and with the *empressement* due to a man from whom one is about to try and extract a large sum of money. While he was in the isthmus the opportunity was taken to breach the dam which divided the waters of the Mediterranean from the

Bitter Lakes. As Lesseps, in courtly mood, said to the Khedive, "Moses ordered the waters of the sea to go back and they obeyed him; now Your Highness orders these same waters to return, and again they obey."[34]

On Ismail's return to Cairo, Lesseps got back to business. On April 22nd he addressed a long letter to the Viceroy[35] of which the opening theme was that, with the work on the construction of the canal nearing completion, the Company were anxious to relinquish any privileges which placed them outside the *"droit commun"* of all the other inhabitants of Egypt. "It is natural," he wrote, in sharp contradistinction to the tone he had adopted less than a year before over the matter of the customs franchise, "that the Company's agents, established on Egyptian soil, should pay the same taxes and enjoy the same rights as the other inhabitants of Egypt." To this end Lesseps proposed the renunciation by the Company and its employees of all customs privileges, of all exclusive navigation rights on the Sweet Water Canal, of special quarrying rights conferred on it in the Second Concession, of fishing rights in the Sweet Water Canal and in Lake Manzala (where it did not possess any rights anyway), and of the "right" to maintain its own postal service in the isthmus. "The Company," he wrote, "should and will confine itself to the facilitation of navigation between Suez and Port Said and vice versa and to the maintenance of the canal."

After outlining these remarkable acts of sacrifice, Lesseps proceeded: "Another point which has been brought to my attention is that of the sale of lands situated alongside the Maritime Canal. . . . It is certain that the sale of these lands would in all cases require Your Highness' prior consent. . . . In my opinion, and subject to Your Highness' agreement, these lands should be divided into plots, and offices of sale established in all the various towns of the isthmus. The sales proceeds would be divided equally between the Government and the Company. The purchasers would receive their title deeds only after they had paid the purchase price in full. It is superfluous to add that the purchasers of these lands would be in exactly the same legal position as any other inhabitants of Egypt." In this way did Lesseps propose that the Company dispose of those lands judged, by the Emperor and by the Mixed Commission, to be necessary to the Company for the construction and operation of the canal.

But Lesseps had another point to make. This, again, was preceded with an expression of extremely high-minded sentiments: "It would, Sire, be a very ill return for the many shining examples of Your Highness' royal benevolence toward the work of joining the two seas for the Company to look backward toward past disagreements, especially just after the auspicious occasion on which Your Highness condescended to pay his first visit to the isthmus. Your Highness will have realized the necessity for the Company to safeguard those rights which they believed to belong to the Company, or to its employees or agents, and that I had the duty studiously and personally to examine any claim put forward by the Company or its agents. I am now happy to be able to inform Your Highness that the Company take their stand on justice and equity and that they hereby renounce any claim against the Egyptian Government brought forward prior to the date of this letter. There is therefore at this moment no matter of dispute between the Company and the Egyptian Government. I am happy to give Your Highness this solemn assurance on behalf of the Company and on behalf of its contractors."

As might have been expected, this was the prelude to another extremely unreasonable demand:

There is one thing which I now have to request of Your Highness. He has seen on his visit to the isthmus that the phase of construction has now almost come to an end. It follows from this that large installations, made by the Company at great expense for the purposes of construction, have now outlived their usefulness to the Company. At the same time Your Highness' Government is on the point of establishing important administrations in the isthmus. It would be advantageous to the Government as well as to the Company if, instead of the Government proceeding with the erection of new installations, Your Highness would consent to take over from us, at an agreed valuation, the Company's hospitals and telegraphic installations, apart from those required by the Company for the supervision of navigation through the canal, and any other installations which might be useful for the public service. I have already informally suggested something of the kind to Your Highness which he has condescended to say that he will consider favorably.

Given Ismail's character, this was a much more intelligent approach than the previous attempts at bluster. But it is a little difficult to understand how Ismail was led, on April 23, 1863, to sign a convention with the Canal Company[36] under the terms of which the Egyptian Government agreed to pay to the Company a sum of 20 million francs in respect of various privileges voluntarily ceded by the Company in accordance with the terms of Lesseps' letter to the Khedive, and a further 10 million francs in payment for the various installations—the hospitals in the isthmus, the warehouses at Bulaq and Damietta, and the quarries at Mex—for which the Company had no further use.

In order properly to appreciate the reasons for Ismail's extreme complaisance toward the Canal Company's exactions, it is necessary to take a glance at Ismail's relations with his suzerain since the issue of the 1867 firman which had conferred on Ismail the title of Khedive and, more importantly, had conferred on him the long-sought right of primogeniture in the succession to the throne of Egypt. This, in Ismail's eyes, was merely the first installment of that complete measure of independence which he was determined at length to achieve. The next installment which he sought was the right to negotiate loans on the security of Egyptian revenues, and the right to make treaties with foreign Powers.[37] To this end he continued lavishly to distribute bribes at Constantinople and assiduously to seek the support of the French Government, in the same way as he had done over the matter of the succession in 1864–1865. And having become convinced, as a result of the failure of Nubar's negotiations with Morny, and as a result of the terms of the Arbitral Award, that the best available channel to the French Government's favour was via Lesseps and the Canal Company, he seems to have decided that the Canal Company must be bribed in the same way as he was bribing Ottoman ministers in Constantinople and for the same object. As the British consul general wrote, "I believe that the desire of the Viceroy to secure the support of the French Government in his present negotiations with the Porte will induce His Highness to cede, without much pressure, to any suggestion or solicitation that may be made to him by Lesseps or Outrey."[38] When the Khedive visited Paris for the Exposition in the summer of 1867, Lesseps acted as his cicerone, and appears to have succeeded in convincing him both of his devotion to the cause of Egyptian independence and of his ability to influence the French Government in favor of this cause. At all events, relations between the two men which, before the Khedive's visit to Paris, had been invariably cold and often hostile, became very much more friendly. But it was always a relationship, not between intimates, but between accomplices. Lesseps wanted money for the Canal Company; Ismail wanted the help which he believed that the Canal Company, in return for money, was able and willing to give in connection with his ambitions for independence. It is probably fair to say that Lesseps did his best for Ismail in this respect. But there is no evidence that the Canal Company's influence was of the slightest practical use to Ismail, since the French Government seems to have made no move at Constantinople, then or later, to mitigate the redoubtable opposition offered by Aali Pasha to any extension of the privileges granted to Ismail. It was only after Aali Pasha's retirement that Ismail was to make any further headway, and not until 1873 that he was able, at long last, and after great expenditure, to obtain the firman he desired.

The proposal made by Lesseps, in his letter to the Khedive, for the joint exploitation, by the Canal Company and by the Egyptian Government, of the lands allocated to the Canal Company by the Mixed Commission in 1866, had for some time been the subject of negotiations between the Khedive and the Company.[39] In these negotiations Ismail had made it a condition of his agreement to Lesseps' proposal that the Canal Company should obtain the French Government's support for proposals for a revision of the "capitulations" which were, at that time, being discussed between the Egyptian Government and the Powers. The proposals of the Egyptian Government, who were represented by Nubar Pasha, provided for the establishment in Egypt of mixed courts, composed of both Egyptian and foreign judges, to adjudicate disputes between Egyptians and foreigners and between foreigners of different nationalities. As we have seen, the lack of any suitable machinery for the settlement of such disputes had meant that they had usually been settled, to the great disadvantage of any Egyptian interests involved, by means of diplomatic pressure exerted on the Egyptian Government. In view particularly of the rapidly increasing importance and value of foreign interests in Egypt, and the increasing diplomatic pressures being exercised in defense of these foreign interests, it was important for the Egyptian Government to get the agreement of the Powers to some procedure by which disputes with Egyptian nationals and with the Egyptian Government involving these interests should be adjudicated in some fair and impartial way. The principal stumbling block in the way of an agreement was the attitude of the French Government, which was traditionally reluctant to do anything which might tend to limit the extensive privileges acquired by their nationals in Egypt. If, therefore, the Canal Company could be persuaded effectively to intervene with the French Government in favor of the Egyptian Government's proposals for the setting up of mixed courts, it might well have been worth while for the Egyptian Government to extend substantial privileges to the Canal Company in return. There is no doubt that Ismail's complaisance toward the Company was dictated, in part, by the hope and expectation that the Company's influence in this matter would be effective. On April 23rd, on the same day on which the convention committing the Egyptian Government to pay 30 million francs to the Canal Company was signed, a second convention was concluded,[40] providing for the joint exploitation of lands reserved to the Canal Company, on condition that it should not come into effect pending a satisfactory conclusion of the negotiations then taking place with the Powers on the question of the mixed courts.[41] (Eventually the convention came into operation in May, 1870, and the mixed courts were not set up until 1875, after numerous delays, and after numerous modifications to the original proposals, mostly inserted at the insistence of the French Government.)

The method of raising the 30 million francs, agreed to be paid by the Egyptian Government to the Company under the terms of the first of these two conventions, was not devoid of ingenuity. There was, of course, no sum of 30 million francs available in the Egyptian Treasury. Egyptian Treasury bills were no longer readily discountable in the European money markets. Recourse was had to the ordinary shareholding in the Canal Company held by the Egyptian Government, which had by this time been reduced to 176,-602 shares—the difference of 1,040 shares between this and the original holding having apparently been disposed of. Coupons from these shares, entitling the holder to 5 percent interest for the next twenty-five years, in addition to any dividend which might be declared during that period, were detached from the shares held by the Egyptian Government and offered to other ordinary shareholders against an issue of 120,000 bonds of 270 francs each—making a total sum of 32,400,000 francs, representing the capital sum of 30,000,000 francs plus interest. In return for their subscriptions the fortunate ordinary shareholders were to receive, over the next twenty-five years, sums amounting to no less than 110,376,250 francs, exclusive of any dividends which might be declared by the Company, representing 5 percent interest per annum for twenty-five years on the 176,602 shares belonging to the Egyptian Government from which the coupons had been detached. Thus every purchaser of the 270-franc bonds was entitled to receive, in respect of each bond purchased, over the next twenty-five years, a total of 919 francs in return for his original investment, plus whatever dividends the Company might declare during that period. This munificent offer was confined to the ordinary shareholders of the Company, who thus received a handsome reward for the ten anxious years they had spent since the Company had been floated. It was the worst financial bargain Ismail had ever made, which is saying a good deal. And it was an unnecessary bargain, since, in return for this sum of 30 million francs, raised on such expensive terms, the Canal Company was, in respect of 20 million francs, giving up for the second time rights which had already, either explicitly or implicitly, been given up under the terms of the convention of January, 1866, and, in respect of 10 million francs, selling installations which were of no further use to them and which the Egyptian Government could not, under the terms of the Concessions, have been compelled to buy.

As soon as the canal was completed and opened to navigation, the Khedive had served his turn. At a general meeting of shareholders held on August 24, 1871, Lesseps proposed that holders of ordinary shares from which the coupons had been detached should be deprived of their voting rights at general meetings for the period covered by the detached coupons.[42] This proposal was carried, and the Egyptian Government thereby lost the influence which, as the largest single shareholders, they might have possessed in the affairs of the Company which had so systematically pillaged them.

NOTES

1. The numbers employed during January and February, 1864, were 13,702 and 12,150 respectively (Voisin–Lesseps 14.4.64. CP 33).
2. Tastu–de Lhuys 14.12.63. CP 32.
3. Douin, *Règne du Khédive Ismaïl*, I, 128–129.
4. Report to British consul in Alexandria dated 11.3.64. FO 78/1849.
5. One feddan equals approximately one acre; about 2½ feddans, one hectare.
6. Fitzgerald, *The Great Canal at Suez*, I, 202–205.
7. This description is derived from Fitzgerald, *op. cit.*, I, 206–211.
8. Derived from *ibid.*, I, 193–194.
9. Fitzgerald, *op. cit.*, I, 200–201. The standard rate under the Labor Agreement of 1856 was about tenpence a day, including an allowance for rations.
10. Fitzgerald, *op. cit.*, I, 195–196.
11. *Ibid.*, 197–198.
12. Douin, *op. cit.*, I, 128–129.
13. *Ibid.*, II, 431.
14. Stanton–Clarendon 6.4.67. FO 78/2014.
15. Fitzgerald, *op. cit.*, I, 213–214.
16. *Ibid.*, p. 224.
17. *Ibid.*, p. 228.
18. Wilson, *The Suez Canal*, p. 44.
19. Quoted by Sabry, *L'Empire Egyptien* . . . , note, p. 312.
20. *Ibid.*, p. 312.
21. Wilson, *op. cit.*, p. 109.
22. In the form of an Imperial Decree dated 28.5.68, issued by the Conseil d'Etat to the Corps Législatif "in consideration of the exceptional character of the enterprise and the interest which France has in the Suez Canal."
23. In 1867 Ismail obtained the title of Khedive from the Sultan, together with the grant of primogeniture in the succession to the Egyptian throne.
24. Sabry, *op. cit.*, p. 296.
25. Stanton–Clarendon 1.3.67. FO 78/2014.
26. It will be remembered that Lesseps had previously considered getting Ismail to part with his shares in payment of the 84-million-franc indemnity.
27. Sabry, *op. cit.*, p. 300.
28. Foreign Minister, and in Ismail's absence in Constantinople, a member of the Regency Council.
29. Sabry, *op. cit.*, pp. 300–301.
30. *Ibid.*, pp. 301–302.
31. Both these men had served on the Mixed Commission in 1865–1866. Their complaisance to the Company on that occasion may have encouraged Lesseps to believe that they would display a similar complaisance over the franchise.
32. Sabry, *op. cit.* pp. 302–303.
33. Quoted by Douin, *op. cit.*, II, 146–147.
34. *Ibid.*, p. 148.
35. *Ibid.*, pp. 151–154.
36. For text see J. Charles–Roux, *L'Isthme* . . . , Vol. I, Annex No. 23, p. 501.
37. This was an important matter for Egypt from the point of view of commercial treaties, since, under existing arrangements, Egypt's tariff system was completely subordinated to the interests of Turkey. For example, Turkish tobacco came into Egypt duty free, and foreign tobaccos were kept out by a prohibitive duty. Thus Egypt lost the potential revenue she might have derived from a moderate import duty on all tobaccos.
38. Stanton–Clarendon 1.3.67. FO 78/2014.
39. See Report of Canal Company general meeting on 2.6.68; Journal, V, 270.
40. For text see J. Charles–Roux, *op. cit.*, Vol. I, Annex No. 23, p. 504.
41. Douin, *op. cit.*, II, 156.
42. Sabry, *op. cit.*, pp. 313–314.

CHAPTER *thirteen*

The Opening

Ceremonies ?~

~§ ACCORDING to Lesseps[1] the month of October, 1869, was fixed for the formal opening of the canal as early as April, 1867, at a time when, in terms of cubic meters excavated and to be excavated, the canal was not much more than half finished. However, by that time some, though by no means all, of the financial obstacles had been overcome, and all the excavation machinery was already on site and working smoothly. The principal contractor, Lavalley, apparently had a penalty clause in his contract condemning him to a fine of 1 million francs a month for any delay after October 1, 1869, and another clause providing for a bonus of 6 million francs for completion by October 1, 1869.[2]

In July, 1869, when invitations had already gone out and when intensive preparations were already being made for the lavish ceremonies planned to mark the opening, 6.5 million cubic meters still remained to be excavated, and difficulties were still being experienced with rock formations in the Shallufa Channel between Suez and the Bitter Lakes. It was not until August 15th that the dam erected across this channel was breached to allow the waters of the Red Sea to flow into the Bitter Lakes and there to mingle with the waters of the Mediterranean which had been admitted the previous March. The junction between the two seas had been completed. At the beginning of October a French steamer, *Louise-et-Marie,* made the first complete transit of the canal by an oceangoing vessel from Suez to Port Said. But the difficulties were not yet over. It was intended that the canal should have a depth of 26 feet in the middle of the channel, and it was necessary for it to have a minimum depth of at least 18 feet in order to ensure the safe passage of the various ships participating in the opening ceremonies. Within a month of these ceremonies a rocky ledge was discovered in the Shallufa Channel which reduced the depth to a minimum of 14 feet for a distance of about 150 yards. The ledge was too hard for removal by dredging. There was no proper equipment for underwater blasting, which up to that time had not been necessary. It was necessary to improvise. Something was improvised, and the situation was saved.

During 1869, the year of the opening, Ismail's relations with his suzerain were particularly bad. Aali Pasha, Ismail's old enemy, had become Grand Vizier on the death of Fuad Pasha in February. He was, as always, strongly opposed to Ismail's efforts to obtain an increased measure of independence, and took the view that Ismail, in his foreign loan transactions, in the size of his army, and in other matters, was already exceeding the powers which had been given to him under the 1841 Hatti Sharif and the firman of 1867. Aali Pasha was assiduous in trying to turn the weak mind of Sultan Abdul Aziz against his ambitious vassal, and was credited with the desire to procure Ismail's deposition. In theory, such deposition was in the power of the Sultan; in practice it could not have been done without the consent of the Powers.

Egypt was easily the richest and most advanced province of the Ottoman Empire, which relied heavily on Egypt's increasing financial resources at a time when other Ottoman revenues were either stagnant or diminishing. (The Egyptian tribute which, up to 1867, had amounted to the equivalent of £414,000 (about $2,070,000) a year, was increased to the equivalent of £690,000 (about $3,450,000) a year in 1867 in consideration of the additional privileges granted to the Viceroy under the firman promulgated in that year.) The loss of Egypt would, moreover, have been a great blow to Ottoman prestige, and might well have marked the final stage in the dissolution of that tottering Empire. For this reason Ismail's ambitions were a source of concern, not only to the Porte but also to the Powers for whom a breakup of the Ottoman Empire would have presented a number of vexing problems. Both the Porte and the Powers were becoming concerned at Ismail's extravagance, at the high taxation which he was imposing on the fellahin, and at his military adventures in the Horn of Africa and in the Sudan. Both the Porte and the Powers had a vested interest in Egypt's solvency and in Egypt's internal tranquillity, both of which were threatened by Ismail's waywardness. On the other hand, there was some sympathy among the Powers for Egypt's anomalous position, which she owed to her association with the Porte and which brought her manifold disadvantages.

As we have seen, Egypt was exposed to difficulties over the "capitulations" and over her inability to make advantageous commercial agreements. She got nothing from the Porte in return for these disadvantages. While it was clearly in the Ottoman interest to keep Egypt's state of subordination unimpaired, it could reasonably be expected that the Powers, from considerations both of equity and of self-interest, would use their influence to mitigate the worst effects of that subordination, if it could be done without jeopardizing the survival of the Ottoman Empire and without freeing Egypt from those bonds, conferred by the "capitulations," which it was to the advantage of the Powers to have retained.

Just before the date fixed for the ceremonial opening, Ismail's relations with the Porte reached a point of crisis. When Ismail came back from his European tour in the summer of 1869, during which he had been occupied in inviting the crowned heads of Europe to be his guests at the opening ceremonies (an initiative which still further irritated the Porte), he found awaiting him what was virtually an ultimatum from the Grand Vizier demanding: (*a*) a reduction in the size of the Egyptian Army, (*b*) the delivery to the Porte of two warships and a large amount of arms which had been ordered by Ismail and which Aali Pasha regarded as being in excess of Egypt's legitimate requirements, (*c*) the submission of Egypt's annual budget to the Porte for approval, (*d*) the cessation of all independent negotiations between Egypt and foreign Powers, (*e*) an undertaking to raise no more foreign loans without the prior consent of the Porte, and (*f*) an immediate reduction in Egyptian taxation. Ismail sent a reply rejecting most of these demands. Now, nothing but the goodwill of the Powers stood between him and deposition. His half-brother Mustafa, the Heir Apparent before the 1867 firman, had been recalled to Constantinople and made Minister of the Interior as a steppingstone to the khedivial throne. A very real shadow was therefore hanging over Ismail during the course of the glittering ceremonies, which he went through with the panache of the born gambler that he was.

After the ceremonies, during which he had taken the opportunity for long and confidential talks with the ambassadors of the Powers, a special commissioner from the Sultan arrived in Cairo with a letter demanding compliance with the Grand Vizier's demands. Eventually the matter was settled. The ambassadors recommended moderation to both parties. The warships were surrendered to the Porte. Various promises were made by Ismail. Nubar Pasha went to Constantinople with gold on an errand to which he had become well accustomed. A particularly seductive lady from Ismail's harem was transferred to the Sultan's seraglio. And so, what with the ambassadors, Nubar Pasha, and the lady, Ismail was able to retain his throne and to carry on in much the same way as before, increasing taxes, contracting foreign loans, and negotiating with whom he pleased until, in 1873, after the death of Aali Pasha, and as a result of further bribery from the proceeds of previous loans, Ismail was able to obtain a firman specifically allowing him to do most of those things which Aali Pasha's ultimatum of 1869 had ordered him to stop doing. He celebrated the occasion by contracting the most ruinous of all his loans.

Given the critical state of his relations with his suzerain, it was natural that Ismail should wish to use the occasion of the opening of the canal to make himself agreeable to the Powers and to demonstrate to them the considerable extent of the material progress which had been made in Egypt during his six-year rule. The heads of all European states and the President of the United States of America were invited either to honor the occasion with their own presence or to delegate members of their personal or official families to represent them. Men of eminence in all walks of life—statesmen, scientists, men-of-letters, artists, musicians, and businessmen—received invitations. Learned societies and chambers of commerce were asked to send representatives. As was fitting, the guest of honor was to be Eugénie, Empress of the French, to whose advocacy with her imperial husband the canal owed so much. The Empress, and many of the European sovereigns, received their invitations personally from the hand of Ismail during his tour of Europe. The Sultan of Turkey appears to have expressed considerable irritation at Ismail's action at having invited heads of states without any previous consultation or even communication with him.[3] Eugénie, visiting Constantinople on her way to Egypt for the ceremonies, graciously did her best to excuse Ismail, telling the Sultan that she had expressed to Ismail her wish to go and that Ismail had had no option but to invite her on the spot. She also quoted Ismail as having told her that it would have been an impertinence for him to have invited the Sultan to be present at a ceremony in his own house. (In fact, if the Sultan had come, he would have to have been the host. Ismail was therefore determined that he should not come.)

The replies from the heads of states were reasonably gratifying. The Emperor Francis Joseph of Austria decided to come himself. The King of Prussia sent the Crown Prince. The King of Holland sent his brother, Prince Henry. Great Britain was represented by Mr. Henry Elliot, the British ambassador at Constantinople, and Russia by General Ignatiev, the Russian ambassador at Constantinople. Most of the lesser celebrities, who included Ibsen, Théophile Gautier, and Emile Zola among the men-of-letters, accepted with alacrity their invitations to what seemed likely to prove the party of the century.

The Khedive made the most elaborate preparations to receive his distinguished guests:

Apart from crowned heads he wished to invite as many celebrities as possible. When Lesseps expressed the intention of inviting several journalists, he replied that he would invite them himself at his own expense. For months, under the impulse of his personal authority and under the efficient superintendence of Nubar Pasha, a number of high officials, assisted by an army of clerks, worked out the program of ceremonies, the order of precedence, the accommodation arrangements, and the lavish entertainments for hundreds of guests to whom the Khedive wished to display hospitality on an unprecedented scale. Several times Ismail intervened in the arrangements to extend the already overfull program or to add to the already excessive guest list. A thousand people were invited from all parts of the world and their expenses paid for the whole voyage. A hundred especially privileged persons were invited to make a tour of the antiquities of Upper Egypt before going to the isthmus for the opening ceremonies.[4]

Among the first to arrive were the one hundred distinguished guests who were to make the tour of Upper Egypt. They disembarked at Alexandria on October 15th and went up to Cairo by railway on October 17th. "Many of the travelers had got themselves up for this four-hour railway journey as if for a voyage on the Upper Nile above the Cataracts, although the temperature did not exceed that of Marseille or Algiers at the same time of year." The headgear was particularly bizarre. In spite of the fact that the temperature was only about 70 degrees Fahrenheit, most of the distinguished guests were pipe-clayed helmets fitted with veils to protect the neck and face from the sun. Others wore turbans, headcloths, or fezzes. Some contented themselves with large Panamas. One man, a chemist of European reputation, was dressed in a "stove-pipe" hat, black coat, white tie, and patent-leather shoes, pleading that he always dressed in that way, that he would feel naked dressed in any other way, and that such a feeling would add to the fatigue and spoil the pleasure of the trip.

On their arrival in Cairo the guests were conducted to their various hotels. Théophile Gautier was taken to Shepheards', "from the outside a large, bare and austere building, more like an English barracks than like an Eastern caravanserai, and inside like a great monastery with half-lit stairways and bedrooms like monastic cells." On October 18th they were received by the Khedive, and on the evening of the same day a reception was held in their honor at the Kasr-el-Nil Palace. "Those who expected a scene from the Arabian Nights were disappointed; it was a typical Parisian evening. They saw a performance of *Caprice* by Alfred de Musset, followed by a concert." During their four days in Cairo they had some time for sightseeing. "The wonderful city of the Caliphs, adorned with some of the most magnificent productions of Arab architecture, was decked out to receive the visitors. But, alas, she chose to receive us in new clothes and with a made-up face. Almost all the monuments have been painted red and white; all the original delicate traceries and arabesques have disappeared under a thick coating of colour. . . ."

Near the Ezbekieh Gardens, the center of the European part of the city, the guests could see the Hotel d'Orient where Lesseps usually stayed when in Cairo. In this hotel, "M. le Comte," as Lesseps was usually known, was *chez lui.* The comfort was only passable, but the food was excellent and the view magnificent. The Ezbekieh Gardens, once a fashionable promenade, were, in 1869, "infested by thieves during the day and by assassins during the night," but in appearance they were still full of charm. All the time he had been in Egypt, Lesseps had been accustomed to entertaining visiting Frenchmen at the Hotel d'Orient, introducing them to his contractors, to his engineers, and to well-known French residents of Cairo. There, the invited guests met Mariette Pasha, the great Egyptologist; Clot Bey, a French doctor in the Egyptian service who probably did more than anyone else to improve public health in Egypt during the nineteenth century; the amazing Soliman Pasha, and many others. Mariette, who had come to Egypt several years before . . . had created the Egyptian Department of Antiquities. He was rather a terrifying figure with his great height, his red tarboosh, his stern face, his staccato talk, and his tinted spectacles. But when he was in the mood he sparkled with wit and gaiety. Soliman, son of a small factory owner near Lyon and an army officer under the First Empire, had, after the Restoration, become the organizer of Mohammed Ali's army and an intimate friend of the great Viceroy. Now, in his old age, he was a little deaf, and a little pompous, but his vitality and gaiety made people forgive ex-Colonel Sève for having changed his religion in exchange for a great position and the title of Pasha. Cursing at the Fast of Ramadan, he seemed to be no more of a good Muslim than he had been a good Christian. Nevertheless, there were few people who did not like him and enjoy his company. These, and other strange characters, with their fascinating reminiscences of the past, could be seen among Lesseps' intimates at the Hotel d'Orient during those autumn days of 1869. But, at this moment of time, it was the present that was important, and Lesseps, the hero of the hour, dominated them all.

On October 22nd, after four days in Cairo, the party left for Upper Egypt, traveling up the Nile as far as Aswan in steamers provided by the Khedive, and returning to Cairo on November 13th in time for the ceremonies in the isthmus.

The isthmus was *en fête,* with tens of thousands of sightseers, celebrated and humble, invited and uninvited, who had gathered there from all parts of the world for the great occasion: "Muslim notables with their carpets, their tents, their wives, their servants, their camels, their horses, their sheep . . . nearly 30,000 Arabs were camped along the shores of Lake Timsah, which was a Babel where every race, every language, and every color were mixed up with one another . . . yellow, black, and copper-colored people, thousands of camels, donkeys, horsemen, and carriages . . . a Saint-Cloud fair under Egyptian skies." The careful organization had completely broken down under the weight of numbers. The most important visitors were able to sleep on shipboard. But the rest had to fend for themselves. Somehow or other they got accommodated, fed, and transported in a district which had until recently been nothing but desert.

Apart from the few most privileged guests, it was quite a problem to get to the isthmus at all. Boats from Alexandria, trains from Cairo were full to overflowing. "In our train," wrote Fromentin, who was one of the less privileged guests:

there was an immense crowd of Asiatic pilgrims—Anatolians, Circassians, Bokharans, some in silken caftans, some in sheepskin mantles, hadjis in green turbans, women, children, old men, cripples, blind men, paralyzed men. Mostly old people, bearing with them their bedding and cooking utensils. Bashi-bazouks with their lofty headgear looking like bandits, with an arsenal of weapons stuck into broad sashes wound round their waists. A few Turkish women dressed in white, with veils which revealed plucked eyebrows and almond-shaped eyes. Some Egyptian peasant women, with pretty laughing eyes, pretending to hide themselves behind their veils. We arrived at Ismailia at about midnight. A strange place at such an hour. Somehow or other, everyone found somewhere to sleep, at a friend's house, in a tent, or, if one was lucky, in one of the houseboats moored in the Sweet Water Canal.

Meanwhile, the really important guests were converging on Port Said. The Empress Eugénie and her suite, on the imperial yacht *l'Aigle,* had left Marseille at the beginning of October and, after paying an official visit to Constantinople, arrived at Alexandria on October 19th. She was to enjoy a month's holiday in Egypt before taking her place as the guest of honor at the great ceremony. Afterward she was to describe this holiday as her last happy memory. Immediately in front of her lay defeat, deposition, widowhood, and fifty years of exile at Chislehurst, embittered by the death in battle of her only child, the Prince Imperial. But no presentiment of disaster seems to have cast a shadow across those last golden days when, with her entourage of lively young nieces and handsome army officers, she was borne, like Cleopatra, in silken and jeweled luxury, to the sound of music and laughter, upon the waters of the Nile in the clear light and crisp air of an Egyptian autumn.

On her return from Upper Egypt the Empress disembarked at Sakkara and, after visting the tombs there, was driven some ten miles across the desert to the Pyramids, where the Khedive was awaiting her. A chalet had been built especially for the occasion near the foot of the Great Pyramid. Here Ismail entertained Eugénie with a dinner and afterward led her out to see the Great Pyramid, lit up from the glow of a magnificent fireworks display. At nine o'clock in the evening she returned to the Gezira Palace, near Cairo, along a ten-mile avenue which had been constructed especially for her journey.

On November 14th the Empress rejoined *l'Aigle* at Alexandria. The great party was ready to begin.

The first ceremonies were to take place at Port Said:

On November 13th the Prince and Princess of Holland had arrived in their yacht and were received by His Highness the Khedive, who had already arrived from Alexandria in his yacht *Mahroussa,* accompanied by Nubar Pasha, Sharif Pasha, and a number of high Egyptian officials. On November 14th Ferdinand de Lesseps, with those members of his family present in the isthmus, arrived at Port Said where, by this time, a whole fleet of warships and merchant vessels was lying in the harbor. On November 15th the Emperor of Austria, escorted by a frigate, entered the port to the sound of salvos of ships' batteries and the cheering of ships' crews. Early on November 16th more ships entered the port. Among them was the *Péluse,* one of the finest steamships belonging to the Messageries Impériales, bringing to Port Said the members of the Conseil d'Administration of the Canal Company. At eight o'clock the Crown Prince of Prussia, on board the frigate *Herta,* arrived and received the same honors as the Emperor of Austria. At last *l'Aigle* was sighted. It was greeted with a tremendous salute of cannon both from the ships and from the shore batteries; every ship was fully dressed, with national flags flying and crews drawn up on deck as *l'Aigle* entered the harbor, which was by this time so crowded that it seemed impossible for it to accommodate any more vessels. More than eighty ships, of which fifty were men-of-war, were anchored there. All the flags of Europe were represented. *L'Aigle* came slowly to anchor amid cheers from all the assembled crews and from the crowds on shore.

The Khedive, M. de Lesseps and his sons, followed, during the course of the morning, by the Emperor of Austria and the various foreign princes, went on board *l'Aigle* to pay their respects to the Empress. In the afternoon the religious ceremonies took place. On the beach, in front of the Eugénie Quay, three pavilions had been erected. The first, the one nearest the quay, was for the Viceroy's special guests; in front of it, between it and the sea, and facing each other, were two pavilions reserved respectively for Muslim and Christian religious dignitaries. It was a noble and generous inspiration of the Khedive's by which he wished to symbolize the brotherhood of Man without distinction of religion. It was the first time that a joint Muslim and Christian religious service had even been held.

At one o'clock Egyptian troops formed a guard of honor between the quay and the pavilions. . . . There arrived the Amir Abdul Qader, who had come from Beirut on the French warship *Forbin;* M. Ferdinand de Lesseps, the members of the Conseil d'Administration, the senior officers of the warships in the port, the ambassadors of the Powers, the consuls, the Catholic clergy. There was a huge crowd on the beach, presenting a most varied and colorful spectacle. Nearly every race was represented. . . . One could see, gathered at this ceremony, men of the East clothed in brightly colored garments, the chiefs of African tribes in their native dress, Circassians in their warlike costumes, British-Indian Army officers in their sun helmets, Hungarian magnates in their national dress.

The Khedive received his illustrious guests on the quay. The Prince of Holland was the first to disembark, accompanied by his Princess, whom the Khedive's son and heir, Mohammed Tewfiq, conducted to the pavilion; then came the Crown Prince of Prussia, the Emperor Francis Joseph of Austria and, at last, the Empress. . . . The procession moved toward the pavilion, the Empress giving her arm to the Emperor, followed by the Khedive and the princes. Guns were fired in salute, the crowds cheered, and the drums beat. The Empress took her place in the pavilion, with Ismail Pasha on her right and the Austrian Emperor on her left. Their Majesties remained standing during the two religious ceremonies which followed. . . .

After these ceremonies the sovereigns returned to their ships, and some of the less important guests went walking about the town. One of them wrote this description of it: "In its improvised character and in the habits of its population, which are entirely given up to money-grubbing and crude amusements, it is like a San Francisco in miniature. One sees storehouses, factories, and shops side by side with brothels, nightclubs and a casino at which people come to lose at night the money they have made during the day." In the evening the lights from a grand fireworks display were reflected in the waters of the harbor.

On the following day, November 17th, the great procession of ships through the canal was to begin. All manner of rumors began to spread about the town. It was said that the procession would have to be postponed because an enormous rock was blocking the passage, because sixty houses had been burned down at Ismailia. It was said that all the engineers had fled, that Lesseps had gone mad, that the principal contractor had committed suicide. All this was false. But there had been a mishap. On November 16th an Egyptian corvette, *Latif,* had been proceeding along the canal from Port Said to Timsah to make sure that the passage was clear. It ran aground near Qantara, blocking the channel. When the news was received at Port Said on the night of November 16-17, the Khedive went in person to the scene of the accident, so anxious was he that there should be no hitch next day. After a short time the *Latif* was refloated, and all was well.

At eight o'clock on the morning of November 17th the procession of ships began to enter the canal. There was an interval of about ten minutes between the departure of each ship, which meant a distance of about three-quarters of a mile between them in their passage through the canal. The Empress had expressed a wish that *l'Aigle* should lead the procession. So, at 0830 hours, the imperial yacht, which had Lesseps on board, entered the canal between the two navigation buoys marking the channel. It was followed by the frigate *Greif,* carrying the Emperor of Austria, and by two Austrian corvettes, *Elisabeth* and *Gargano.* The Crown Prince of Prussia came next in *Grille,* followed by *Dolphin,* a Prussian gunboat. Then came

Walk, with the Prince and Princess of Holland; the Russian corvette *Yachut,* with General Ignatiev; the British Admiralty yacht *Psyche,* carrying the British ambassador; the Austrian corvette *Vulcan,* and *Péluse,* carrying the members of the Conseil d'Administration. Some forty other vessels—yachts, gunboats, frigates, and corvettes—followed at regular intervals, entering the canal in a procession which lasted until evening.

Most of the population of Ismailia was lined up along the cutting of Jisr, anxiously awaiting the arrival of the procession. Batteries of artillery and regiments of Lancers were drawn up on the beach. At four o'clock three beflagged steamers arrived at the southern end of Lake Timsah from Suez. At half-past five a faint wisp of smoke and a masthead appeared over the sandy banks of al Jisr to the north. It was *l'Aigle,* flying the French imperial flag: "She came slowly into the lake, her paddle wheels hardly turning. She was saluted by salvos of artillery. The Empress was on the bridge, waving her handkerchief; beside her was M. de Lesseps."

As soon as *l'Aigle* cast anchor, the Khedive went on board, greeted the Empress, and enthusiastically congratulated M. de Lesseps. The procession of ships continued to arrive, and cast anchor until well into the night.

On shore in Ismailia lavish entertainments had been provided. Fromentin tells us about some of them:

Fireworks in front of the Viceroy's Palace. Open house everywhere. In one marquee there was a dinner party for five hundred guests, in another for two or three hundred. . . . Luxurious dinners, vintage wines, exquisite fish, partridges, wild duck. Seven or eight thousand people sitting down to dinner in the middle of the desert. It was like something out of the Arabian Nights. An extraordinary mixture of sumptuosity and barrenness. After dinner an amazing variety of entertainment. Dancers, jugglers and singers. . . . Outside, it was like a huge fair. Everywhere a deafening music of fifes and drums. One found oneself separated from one's companions and swallowed up in the vast crowd. At last I got back to my houseboat, which was comfortable enough for a king. Linen sheets and no vermin. All through the night I could hear the noise of the fair—the sound of music, the banging of fireworks, and the shouting of happy revelers.

The next day—November 18th—was spent in Ismailia. It had become a town of tents. Between Lake Timsah and the Sweet Water Canal were the multicolored tents of the tribesmen from the neighboring desert. Beside these were no less than twelve hundred tents arranged in regular lines to accommodate the Khedive's less important guests. The Sweet Water Canal was covered with houseboats on which Egyptian notables had brought themselves and their families down from Cairo for the celebrations. Just outside the town was the Khedive's Palace, a two-story building which had been erected in less than six months. Facing south, it commanded a view over Lake Timsah and the far-away hills of the Red Sea coast. In the gardens of the Palace a pavilion had been erected large enough to entertain a thousand guests at dinner. Leading out of this pavilion was another and smaller pavilion, decorated with flowers and shrubs to resemble a tropical garden, in which the Khedive was to entertain his royal guests.

All Ismailia was beflagged. Triumphal arches had been erected in the streets in honor of the various royal visitors. A crowd of about forty thousand people jostled each other in the streets. Soup kitchens were maintained at the Khedive's charge to feed all those who had not been invited to more formal entertainments. There was, of course, a good deal of muddle, even for the invited guests. Fromentin tells us that many lost their luggage, missed their transport, failed to find their sleeping quarters, and were hard put to find any food. Some fell ill, many became exasperated. There were, as one may easily imagine, impromptu protest meetings hurriedly convened by famished, unshaven, and infuriated French savants. But to whom could one protest? Resolutions were passed, deciding on a boycott of the celebrations and an immediate return to France. But how? One searched vainly for one's traveling companions and suddenly found somebody one had known in Paris twenty years before and had not met since. But, before you had had a chance to greet him, he was swallowed up in a crowd of camels, donkeys, horse carriages, soldiers, and screaming women. The whole thing had a dreamlike, sometimes a nightmarish, quality.

On the morning of November 18th the Empress disembarked with her nieces and, accompanied by Lesseps, set out on horseback to the Jisr cutting, her suite following in two carriages fitted with enormous wheels to enable them to get through the sand. The cavalcade was escorted by a guard of Bedouin dressed in red and white and mounted on white camels. At Jisr the Empress dismounted and looked at the long stretch of the canal visible from the top of the cutting. A picnic luncheon was then served, after which the Empress asked to be allowed to ride on a camel. She made her ladies-in-waiting do likewise, and it was in this way that the party returned to Ismailia in time for a reception given for the Canal Company ladies at Lesseps' villa. After this no doubt rather boring entertainment, the Empress took a stroll in Lesseps' garden and picked some roses, before mounting her camel once more and setting off for the landing stage in the midst of what Fromentin calls "a scene of indescribable confusion."

In the afternoon there was horseracing. Soldiers lined the route from the landing stage to the plain outside the town where the races were to take place. Bands were playing at intervals along the route. The Empress Eugénie and the Emperor of Austria traveled in the leading carriage, followed by the Crown Prince of Prussia with the Princess of Holland, and by the Viceroy, driving his own phaeton and accompanied by his son, Prince Tewfiq. There was a tremendous crowd to watch the races, some on foot, some mounted on horses, donkeys, or camels. Fashionably dressed ladies stood on the seats of their carriages to try to get a view, as if they were at Longchamps. Fromentin was not impressed by the standard of horsemanship, which he thought inferior to what he had seen in the Sahara. He thought that the Arabs from Sinai were the best horsemen of a poor lot.

After the racing the more distinguished guests were conducted round the Bedouin encampment, which had been decked up for the occasion with carpets, polished Damascus blades, flintlocks chased with silver, and burnished copper cooking utensils. The Bedouin chiefs themselves, wrapped in new sheepskin cloaks, with which they had no doubt been presented for the occasion, courteously did the honors, offering sherbet, coffee, and tobacco pipes, and entertaining their guests with dancers, jugglers, singers, sword-swallowers, and contortionists.

On one of the houseboats, Ismail Sadiq Pasha, Ismail's Minister of Finance, who some years later was to be secretly murdered by his master,[5] gave a very recherché little party at which some of the lesser-known attractions of Oriental dancing were displayed for the benefit of a select little group of invited guests, most of whom took the precaution of going there incognito.

After nightfall there were more fireworks, and the ships on the lake were illuminated with electric bulbs. In the encampments, sheep were being roasted whole in huge improvised kitchens for the entertainment of thousands of the Khedive's humbler guests. The more exalted ones were to eat at the Khedive's Palace. In the confusion they had to make their way to the Palace as best they could—some in carriages, some on horseback, some on donkeys, some on foot, and some not at all. Fortunately, it was a fine night. The carriage reserved for M. de Buest, the Austrian Chancellor, did not turn up. His Excellency did his best to proceed on foot but, having got stuck in the sand, was pleased to be able to commandeer a small black donkey, on which he completed his journey through the illuminated town to the gates of the Palace.

In the Palace all was scented and luxuriant confusion. The salons, vast as they were, were not large enough to accommodate the four or five thousand guests who were assembled. In compliment to the Empress they had been decorated in the atrocious style which we now call Second Empire—long mirrors, colored glass windows, marble-topped tables, gilded woods, and huge crystal chandeliers and lusters. Many of the Oriental guests were, according to their custom, seated cross-legged on the costly carpets and divans. Others, overcome by the fatigues of the day, or by the Khedive's excessive and indiscriminate hospitality, were stretched out fast asleep. There was an immense variety of colored uniforms and gold braid. There were decorations of every grade of importance and splendor. M. de Buest, who wore two diamond crosses which had survived the donkey ride, clutched at them nervously, fearing they might be stolen. There was no room to move, but it was desirable to occupy a post of vantage for the Sovereigns' entry. Ladies stood on divans; bull-necked, jack-booted Prussian officers, with a characteristic disregard for other people's property, climbed onto marble-topped tables which buckled beneath their weight.

At last the Sovereigns appeared. The Empress Eugénie, on the arm of the Emperor of Austria, was dressed in cerise-colored satin covered with diamonds; on her head was a magnificent coronet. The Emperor and the Crown Prince of Prussia were in civilian costume. The crowd somehow managed to sort itself out into a double line through which the Sovereigns passed. An orchestra played dance music, but there was no room to move, let alone dance. At midnight there was yet another fireworks display. Supper was not due until one o'clock, but long before that the famished guests could wait no longer, and the buffet tables were taken by assault. In the Sovereigns' dining room, matters proceeded more decorously, and a twenty-four-course dinner was somehow consumed. An Egyptian Minister complained to one of the European Ministers of the Khedive's reckless extravagance. "We are eating up the Pyramids stone by stone," he grumbled. "Never mind, Your Excellency," replied his European companion, "you can borrow money from us and then you can buy from us the cement to replace them."

On November 19th *l'Aigle* weighed anchor from Lake Timsah at 1230 hours and steamed southward through the Serapeum cutting toward the Bitter Lakes, arriving at the south end of the Bitter Lakes at 1630 hours. She was joined before nightfall by fifteen other vessels which were making the whole journey through the canal, including the British Admiralty yacht *Psyche* and the gunboats *Rapid* and *Newport*. The fleet anchored for the night in the Bitter Lakes: "There was something solemn and imposing about this group of vessels, surrounded by desert, anchored on an artificial lake created by the genius of one man." The evening was occupied by ceremonial exchanges of visits, accompanied by the usual salvos of artillery and the inevitable fireworks display.

The less distinguished of the foreign guests found some difficulty in completing the journey to Suez. Steamers had in theory been reserved for them. "At half-past eight in the morning," relates Fromentin, "six or eight of us went to the landing stage with our luggage. There was a boat there getting up steam. There was also a vast crowd of travelers waiting to board it. We spoke to some of them. 'It's impossible to travel by this thing. There are no lifeboats.' 'What are you going to do then?' 'I'm going straight back to France. I've had enough of this.'" An illustrious crowd of French savants milled indecisively to and fro. The more timorous stayed behind or went to fight their way onto the Cairo train. The bolder spirits went on board the steamer, which brought them safely to Suez, where there was no accommodation reserved for them. After some difficulty most of them managed to get a shakedown aboard one or other of the numerous ships in the harbor.

Suez, like Port Said and Ismailia, was *en fête*. The ships in the harbor, which included two P. & O. liners, a British troopship, and a Turkish frigate, were dressed overall. At half-past eleven on the morning of November 20th, *l'Aigle,* still at the head of the procession, steamed out of the canal, having taken four hours on the trip from the Bitter Lakes. The great journey was over. In *l'Aigle*'s logbook the following entry was made: *"Mouillé sur le rade de Suez (mer Rouge) le 20 novembre à onze heures et demie du matin,"* and signed by the Empress Eugénie and her entourage, by Ferdinand de Lesseps, and by the captain and officers of the imperial yacht.

It was a day of triumph for Ferdinand de Lesseps, one which he celebrated, at the age of sixty-four, by his marriage, *en secondes noces* (his first wife had died in 1853), to a young French girl from Mauritius, Hélène de Bragard. The ceremony took place at a little chapel near the bank of the canal at Ismailia.

Congratulations poured in on Lesseps from all over the world. One of the most effusive letters was from the British Foreign Minister, the Earl of Clarendon, who wrote:

The intelligence which has reached England within the last few days of the successful opening of the Suez Canal has been received with great and universal satisfaction, and in doing myself the honour of congratulating you, as well as the French Government and people who have taken such a deep and consistent interest in your labours, I am sure that I represent accurately the feelings of my countrymen. Notwithstanding the obstacles of every kind against which you have had to contend, and which were the necessary result both of physical circumstances and of a local state of society to which such undertakings were unknown and where the removal of difficulties depended on your own genius and resource, a brilliant success has finally rewarded your indomitable perseverance. It is a matter of real pleasure to me to be the organ of conveying to you the congratulations of Her Majesty's Government on the establishment of a new channel of communication between the East and West, and on the advantages, political and commercial, which may confidently be expected as a result of your labours.[6]

It was, perhaps, too much to expect that the noble lord should have acknowledged that the principal obstacles with which Lesseps had had to contend were those deliberately placed in his path by Her Majesty's Government, of which Clarendon himself, at most of the material times, had been the Secretary of State for Foreign Affairs.

Lesseps may have valued more highly a laconic tribute from the Royal Navy, telegraphed to the Admiralty from Suez by Admiral Milne immediately after the transit of the canal by the Admiralty yacht *Psyche* and its two escorting gunboats: "Empress, *Psyche, Rapid, Newport* arrived. Canal is a great success. Milne."[7]

The making of the Suez Canal was very much the personal achievement of one great man. The fact that he was well served by many of his collaborators is yet another testimony to his genius, since he had, to a remarkable degree, the quality of inspiring other people, both high and low, with something of his own enthusiasm, energy, and dedication to the job in hand. Colquhoun, the British consul general in Egypt, wrote of him: "Not the least merit of this active and persevering man is the power he has of selecting and attaching to himself a staff of men of first-rate ability. He is however the moving spirit of the whole and I doubt, if he were removed, whether the staff, composed of the most heterogenous elements, men of all countries and of all parties . . . could hold together."[8]

When one considers Lesseps' great and varied contribution to the success of his project—his vision, his imagination, his diplomacy, his perseverance, his indomitable optimism, and, it must be added, his financial chicanery, one is inclined to give pride of place to his quite exceptional quality as a manager and overseer of men on the job, a quality which is particularly singled out for admiration by all British observers of the construction works. He shewed unfailing good humor and resource in handling difficult and delicate situations with a recalcitrant labor force, with thieving Bedouin tribesmen, with temperamental French engineers driven to the edge of despair by the physical discomforts imposed by the climate and by the mental frustrations inseparable from the supervision of a major engineering work in the middle of an Eastern desert. He was always cheerful. He knew instinctively when to be tough and when to be sympathetic. He never interfered unnecessarily, but he was always on the spot when he was really wanted.

This account has devoted most attention to Lesseps' activities in Cairo, in Constantinople, and in Paris, during the early years of negotiation before large-scale construction had started. It has had comparatively little to say of his activities between 1866 and 1869, when the construction work was at its height and when Lesseps spent months at a time touring the isthmus, organizing, encouraging, reprimanding, arbitrating, cajoling, driving the work ahead under the impulse of his indefatigable energy, his incomparable charm, and his matchless resource. He was a man for whom his subordinates worked as they would have worked for nobody else.

Perhaps the man to whom Lesseps owed most during the actual work of construction was the contractor Lavalley, who devised most of the dredging machines, who displayed an inexhaustible inventiveness in overcoming the various physical difficulties which cropped up from time to time, and who shared Lesseps' determination to let nothing stand in the way of getting the canal finished by the appointed time. Lesseps was particularly good with his European contractors, always giving them public credit where credit was due for good work, and never seriously quarreling with those who, like Hardon and Ayton, had to be paid off and replaced.

All in all, Lesseps the boss, in his shirtsleeves, on the job in the isthmus, is a much more attractive figure than Lesseps the diplomat, in Paris and Constantinople, playing a delicate game of blackmail and intrigue with emperors and empresses, with ambassadors and viziers, with financiers and industrialists, or than Lesseps the concessionaire, in Cairo and Alexandria, cajoling Said and threatening Ismail and bleeding the Egyptian Treasury white with the assistance of the more complaisant French consuls general, like Tastu, and of that unattractive figure Ruyssenaers, the Dutch consul general, who had his fingers in so many pies, who had his shady contacts at so many levels in the Palace and in Egyptian Government offices, and who seems to have been the moving spirit behind most of Lesseps' plans for extracting money from the Egyptian people.

Lesseps' judgment was not always infallible. He sometimes made mistakes which nearly wrecked the whole project, as when he wrote his threatening letter to Mohammed Said in June, 1859, and when he refused to come to Paris to negotiate with Nubar in the autumn of 1863. Generally, his handling of the canal finances seems to have been clumsy. The original subscription was mismanaged. His attempts to get Mohammed Said to take up the unsubscribed shares were unsuccessful. He seems only belatedly to have realized the financial advantages of a deal with Ismail over the questions of forced labor and lands. In these matters he seems to have been rescued from the results of his precipitancy either by Ruyssenaers in Egypt or by the Conseil d'Administration in Paris. For much of the time he was having to fight, not merely for the canal itself, but for his own position in the Canal Company. At various times, powerful combinations were organized to oust him from supreme control. Ismail, Morny, Nubar, Oppenheim, many of the more important shareholders and even, perhaps, some members of the Conseil d'Administration, all, at one time or another, lent their support to these combinations. These people variously disliked Lesseps' dictatorial methods, his financial unscrupulousness, his habit of putting out misleading information, his dangerous tendency to commit the Imperial Government to imprudent courses, his total indifference to the interests of the Egyptian economy, his bland disregard for the niceties of diplomatic protocol, his shameless exploitation of his relationship with the Empress.

But in those days, as in these, great enterprises, if they were to be successful, had to be conducted without giving too much attention to the canons either of good taste or of orthodox finance, without paying too much regard either to democratic habits of consultation or to diplomatic considerations of protocol, and without attaching very much importance either to truthfulness or to the interests and feelings of other people. In comparison with, for example, Hudson, the great English railway magnate, Lesseps was almost a model of financial and personal probity.

Financially, it was almost impossible to reconcile the needs of a great enterprise with the requirements of orthodox finance. There were too many Company promoters chasing too little capital. Shareholders were not the meek and dim beings with whom boards of companies are accustomed to dealing today. They demanded quick and lavish returns for their money. It was almost always necessary alternately to divert their exigencies by feeding them with false information and to calm them by distributing money which had been irregularly raised from some other source. Raising money from shareholders, and particularly from French shareholders, was very much like riding a tiger. Annual general meetings partook less of the character of quasi-religious ceremonies and more of the character of feeding time for the carnivores at the zoo than is usually the case today. Lesseps, with all his charm and with all his exploitation of that bourgeois chauvinism which was such an unattractive feature of the Second Empire, was particularly good at shareholders' meetings. But he could not possibly have managed his shareholders without a good deal of hard lying and without the continual subventions which he managed to extract from the Egyptian Government.

It is unreasonable to judge Lesseps, as it was unreasonable to judge Hudson, by the standards of top-hatted respectability which are rightly expected today from promoters of public-utility companies. The world of company promotion and high finance was very much a jungle where the ferocity of a tiger, the hide of a rhinoceros, the impudence of a monkey, and the cunning of a serpent had to be combined with the underground habits of a mole, the adaptability of a chameleon, and the acquisitiveness of a jackdaw.

After the successful transit of the canal, the Sovereigns and their representatives dispersed. On the afternoon of November 20th the Khedive, the Emperor, the Crown Prince of Prussia, and the British, Russian, and Austrian ambassadors left Suez for Cairo by special train. The Prince and Princess of Holland left the next day. The Empress stayed on at Suez for another day, during which she visited Moses' Well in Sinai and was taken to see the house at Suez which had once been occupied by Bonaparte and which was preserved as a monument to the great conqueror by a Muslim admirer of his genius. On November 22nd *l'Aigle* returned through the canal to Port Said where the Empress stopped to unveil a monument to Thomas Waghorn, the English pioneer of the overland route, who thus received, through the influence of Lesseps, a posthumous tribute which his own compatriots had never thought of paying him.

On November 24th the Empress took leave of Lesseps and of her Egyptian hosts and began the return journey westward, toward Marseille, Paris, Sedan, and Chislehurst.

The opening of the Suez Canal gave a particularly brilliant start to the Cairo winter season. The Opera House, on the edge of the Ezbekieh Gardens, had just been completed, and had been opened by the Khedive on November 1st.

When the curtain rose the audience were regaled by a cantata composed in honor of the Khedive by Prince Poniatovsky. In the middle of the stage was a huge bust of Ismail Pasha. Behind this bust were the eight singers executing the cantata, dressed respectively to represent Justice, Clemency, Renown, Melody, History, Agriculture, Industry and Commerce. There was a burst of loyal applause at the conclusion of the cantata, after which the opera *Rigoletto* was performed.

The Superintendent of Theaters had been able to engage an Italian opera company for Cairo's first opera season. They included in their repertory the finest productions of Verdi, Rossini, and Donizetti—*The Barber of Seville, Traviata, Il Trovatore, Semiramis, Lucrecia Borgia*—fifteen operas and ballets in all, of which the costumes and décor had been especially made in Paris by Mme. Zina Merante. The *première danseuse* of the Paris Opéra House and M. Mazillier were in charge of the corps de ballet, which consisted of about forty young girls, between fifteen and eighteen years of age, chosen principally for their beauty. Some attempt had been made to teach them to dance as well. Most of the girls had brought their mothers with them. The most elaborate precautions had been taken to guard their virtue. At Alexandria they were taken direct from the ship to the train without stopping in the town. Once arrived in Cairo, they were lodged behind barred doors in the Ezbekieh Police Station.

On November 3rd there was a slight accident. *Rigoletto* was again being performed. Toward the end of the first act, when nearly all the company was on the stage, the explosion of a gas lamp set fire to the scenery. The artistes rushed to the front of the stage and jumped into the orchestra; the spectators dashed for the exits. The Khedive, who was present, appeared in front of his box calling on the audience to remain calm. The fire was almost immediately put out; there was very little damage apart from the bruises sustained by the artistes, who could not, however, be persuaded to continue the performance.

Another theater, where vaudeville, comedy, and light opera were played, opened at the beginning of October. On this occasion, in the presence of the Khedive and Prince Tewfiq, three one-act pieces—*Le Feu au Couvent, La Rose de Saint-Fleur,* and *Une Fille Terrible*—were played. The company which had been engaged had a large repertoire of French plays from the Comédie-Française, but what the Cairo audiences really preferred was vaudeville, which, unlike the comedies, always drew a full house. The light-opera company played *The Duchess of Gerolstein* and *Orpheus in Hades* and ten other pieces by Offenbach. The leading singer was Mlle. Marguerite Joly, whose voice was not remarkable and whose principal attraction was a fine bust from which her dress always seemed to be on the point of slipping.

There was yet a third theater, the Cirque, which opened on October 15th and which continued throughout the season, giving a variety of productions ranging from pantomime to historical tableaus.

The Khedive's return to Cairo with the remaining royalties on November 21st was the signal for another round of entertainments. The Emperor Francis Joseph, now that Eugénie had departed, was the principal guest and was lodged at the Gezira Palace. The Crown Prince of Prussia, sulkily adorned with the laurels of Sadowa, departed for Upper Egypt. On November 21st a reception was given for the Emperor at the Kasr-el-Nil Palace. The whole city was decorated in his honor. Fromentin, wandering through the Khan-el-Khalil, the Bazaar Quarter, noted: "All the houses were beflagged and covered in lights; an enormous crowd; music everywhere, and the crowds beating out the time with hand-clapping and foot-stampings; all the women dressed in white. Carriages full of ladies of the harem; sounds of girls singing from curtained balconies. . . . The Khan-el-Khalil is fantastic; masses of carpets; everything displayed in the open; incredible richness; dazzling color. At midnight Cairo is gay and alive, much more so than at midday when most of the shops are closed for the siesta."

On November 22nd there was horseracing at Abbasieh, on the northeast outskirts of Cairo. On November 23rd there was an excursion to the

Pyramids and Sakkara. The royal party left Cairo in the morning by steamer for Memphis, a few miles upstream, where luncheon was to have been served. "But," reports the unfortunate M. de Buest, whose misfortunes at Ismailia will be remembered, "this luncheon, instead of preceding us, followed us, and was therefore not at Memphis when we arrived. The Emperor, who was in a hurry and is not very particular about his food anyway, decided to leave straight away across the desert to Sakkara and back by way of the Pyramids. The rest of us, with our more greedy habits, were reduced to a very low diet, for all we were able to get was a few hard-boiled eggs." At the end of this tiresome day the poor Chancellor was compelled to attend a *pas seul* called "The Dance of the Bee," which was two hours late in starting and for which the musicians failed to appear at all, so that the dancer had to do her piece without any other accompaniment except that provided by the exasperated De Buest, who was singing Arab songs to himself and beating time with his fists on his top hat. The party did not get to bed until three o'clock and had to be up in time to catch the train for Alexandria at six.

On December 2nd another reception was given by the Khedive at the Kasr-el-Nil Palace in honor of Ferdinand de Lesseps and his new bride, who had just returned from their honeymoon. On December 12th a dance was given in honor of the Crown Prince of Prussia, who had returned from Upper Egypt after the departure of the Austrian Emperor. On December 16th the Prince and Princess of Holland were similarly entertained.

In the 1860's no extravaganza would have been really complete without a balloon ascent. Accordingly, on December 13th, Messieurs Godard and Poilay, two eminent Parisian balloonists, "took off" from the Ezbekieh Gardens in a balloon appropriately named *Sphinx,* in the presence of a shouting and milling crowd of enthusiastic Cairenes. The prevailing north wind blew the balloon southward in the direction of the Faium. Toward nightfall, when the balloonists were over the desert near the Pyramids of Dashur, about twenty miles south of Cairo, they decided to come down. It is not recorded whether there was any transport organized to bring them and the balloon back to Cairo. It seems unlikely. And so we close this account of the inauguration ceremonies of the canal, leaving the two Parisian balloonists, no doubt wearing the knickerbockers and peaked caps in which balloonists, and indeed any other sportsmen of the day, were wont to attire themselves, trudging mournfully across a cold and windy desert toward the distant lights and uncertain welcome of some village in the Nile Valley.

NOTES

1. Journal, V, 307.
2. Stanton–Stanley 11.11.68. FO 78/2118.
3. Elliot–Clarendon 13.6.69. FO 78/2118.
4. Most of the quotations in this chapter, as well as most of the facts about the opening ceremonies, are taken variously from the following accounts of these ceremonies, and will
receive no specific acknowledgment: (*a*) *Règne du Khédive Ismaïl* by G. Douin, Vol. II,
Chap. XVI, pp. 431–475; (*b*) Lesseps' Journal, V, 318–351; (*c*) *Ferdinand de Lesseps,* by
G. Edgar-Bonnet, Vol. I, Chap. XII, pp. 477–501. The quotations from Fromentin's *Voyage
en Orient* are taken from M. Edgar-Bonnet's biography of Lesseps.
5. Ismail Sadiq's mother had been Ismail's nurse, and the two children had been brought up
together. From 1867 until his disappearance in 1876, the Mufattish, as he was called, was
in charge of the Egyptian Treasury, and on him fell the onus both of squeezing the last piastre
of taxation out of the Egyptian fellahin and of trying to satisfy the ever-increasing exigencies
of the European bondholders. When Messrs. Goschen and Joubert came to Egypt in 1876,
on behalf of the British and French bondholders, to negotiate a scheme for the settlement
of Egypt's debts, they found that the Mufattish was inexorably opposed to the measures of
control on which they insisted. In the midst of the negotiations, Ismail had the Mufattish
arrested. He subsequently disappeared, and it is almost certain that he was murdered on
Ismail's orders as a means both of diverting the odium of past oppressions from himself
onto the Mufattish and of appeasing the demands of Messrs. Goschen and Joubert, who were
insisting that the Mufattish must be removed. An interesting account of his disappearance
and murder is told in *Egypt Under Ismail,* by J. Carlile McCoan, pp. 191–204.
6. Clarendon–Lesseps 27.11.69. FO 78/2118.
7. Admiral Milne to Board of Admiralty 20.11.69. FO 78/2118.
8. Colquhoun–Russell 6.4.65. FO 78/1896.

CHAPTER *fourteen*

Britain Takes Over ⁊

᳹ THE Rake's Progress of Egyptian Government extravagance led, in 1875, to the selling of that Government's holding in the Suez Canal Company to the British Government and, subsequently, to bankruptcy, to Anglo-French financial control and, finally, to the British occupation of Egypt in 1882. This Rake's Progress can be said to have begun in 1858, when Mohammed Said started to raise money by issuing bills on the Egyptian Treasury bearing interest at anything from 12 percent to 18 percent in order to pay for his extravagances.

Said loved to live like a great man. Lacking his father's great natural gifts, he was neither a good judge of men nor a good administrator. He did not crush the people under exorbitant taxes and *corvées,* and he did not steal land from the people for his own personal enrichment. But he did impoverish the State by reckless expenditure on his caprices and fantasies, and by ministering to the greed of speculators and favorites. Often he really wanted to put the finances into some sort of order, but he was incapable of following any regular plan. His only notion of economy was underpaying his officials.[1]

By the end of 1859 Treasury bills to the value of 40 million francs, representing nearly one-half of Egypt's total annual revenue, had already been issued. These Treasury bills had mostly been subscribed by foreign banks in Egypt who found the interest rates offered more profitable than the 6 or 7 percent they could have obtained from the financing of commercial transactions. But, before long, these banks and their European principals began to feel some concern about the security of these bills and began to think in terms of enabling the Viceroy to raise a loan in Europe, which would be secured on some specific part of the Egyptian revenue, and which could be used, in part, to redeem the Treasury bills. In 1860 the first of what was to be a long series of such loans was negotiated, with the assistance of the French Government, with the French banking house of Charles Lafitte et Cie. and the Comptoir d'Escompte, for 18 million francs on the security of the customs receipts at Alexandria and on condition that no further Treasury bills were issued during the period of repayment of the loan.

It was obvious that this system of foreign loans, involving as they did some measure of foreign supervision over Egypt's revenue and expenditure would, if persisted in, tend to place Egypt's affairs progressively more and more under the control of the European bondholders. The assistance of the French Government over the first loan is probably explained by this consideration. The French consul general, soon after its negotiation, wrote: "If the Viceroy wants a further loan, would it not be better for him to obtain it from France rather than from any other country? When one is authorized, as a result of arrangements made in the interests of our capitalists, to exercise some measure of control over the finance of the state, one is well on the way to controlling the whole of the affairs of the state."[2]

In this way the Powers were led to compete with one another in pandering to the extravagance of successive Viceroys, and it was in this way that their consuls general, who were fully alive to the effect of these loans on the Egyptian economy,[3] and who at first opposed the giving of any encouragement to this extravagance, soon found themselves, first competing in the role of moneylenders to the Viceroy on behalf of the various international bankers who enjoyed the backing of their respective governments, and then, on behalf of these same bankers, bringing diplomatic pressure to bear on the Egyptian Government in order to obtain indemnities in compensation for some real or pretended infringement of the conditions of the loan which they had previously succeeded in selling.[4]

The proceeds of the first loan were spent by Mohammed Said almost entirely either in paying off claims for various indemnities or in gifts to various of his relatives,[5] and it was not long before he wanted another one. After a somewhat unsavory process of bargaining conducted on behalf of the Comptoir d'Escompte by the French, and on behalf of Oppenheim & Co. by the British and Prussian consuls general, a second loan of 60 million francs at 11 percent interest was negotiated with the house of Oppenheim in March, 1862. When Mohammed Said died in January, 1863, the Egyptian Government debt amounted to 367 million francs, partly in bonds secured on various parts of the Egyptian revenue, partly in unsecured floating debt.

This Rake's Progress was continued, and accelerated, under Ismail, who was even more extravagant than Mohammed Said. There were the expensive commitments which he entered into with the Canal Company. There were the large bribes paid in Constantinople for the purpose of extracting successive installments of independence from the Porte. There were the expenses of military campaigns in Africa. There were undoubtedly a number of useful public works by which Ismail increased Egypt's productivity and, in consequence, her taxable capacity. But there was also reckless extravagance in speculation, in gifts to hangers-on, in luxurious entertainments.

Speculation in Egypt during the sixties was encouraged by the cotton boom arising from the American Civil War which prevented the export of cotton from the southern states to the European markets, and which consequently created a rapidly increasing demand for Egyptian cotton. Lured by high cotton prices, and by the blandishments of various European bankers and their representatives, the Egyptian Government was persuaded virtually to act as guarantors to three large companies—the Egyptian Trading Company, the Egyptian Agricultural Company, and the Azizieh Shipping Company—formed to exploit the cotton boom. When the boom broke after the end of the Civil War, the Egyptian Government inevitably found itself paying out large sums in indemnities to the European directors of these companies and to their Egyptian "straw men" under the blackmailing threats of the European consuls, who were able to forget their rivalries and make common cause in the now fashionable sport of spoiling the Egyptians. As the French consul general remarked, "Whenever the British and French act together they can always bring to Egyptian Government to heel."[6]

Levantine hangers-on acting, or reputed to be acting, as spies or agents on behalf either of the Sublime Porte or of some European Power, abounded at Ismail's Court. The most famous of them were Seffer, a Polish adventurer; Lavison, a French exquisite; and Bravay, an army contractor. Ismail, partly seduced by their charm, partly afraid of their influence with their supposed principals, allowed such men to plunder him almost at will and to inveigle him into innumerable schemes which had as their sole object the spoliation of the Egyptian Treasury. The insensate extravagance of the entertainments attending the formal opening of the Suez Canal has already been described. It was the biggest, although by no means the only, example of this sort of extravagance.

Since the death of Mohamed Ali, the Egyptian Viceroys have loved to live in a sort of perpetual fairyland of parties and celebrations. This taste for ostentation attracts them towards the more superficial aspects of Western civilisation whenever the slightest opportunity is afforded. Whether it be an anniversary, or a return from a journey, or the arrival of a distinguished visitor, there are balls, horseraces, operas, banquets, illuminations, all contrasting vividly with the state of abject poverty in which most of the people live.[7]

"I cannot describe to you the misery here now. Every day some new tax. Now every beast, camel, cow, sheep, donkey, horse, is made to pay. The fellahin can no longer eat bread; they are living on barley-meal mixed with water, and raw green-stuff, vetches etc. . . . The taxation makes life almost impossible. . . . The prisons are full of headmen whose villages cannot pay their taxes . . . whole villages are deserted and thousands have run away into the desert."[8]

Ismail raised his first loan, for £5 million sterling, issued at 92 percent and carrying 7 percent interest, in 1864. By 1875 Egypt's foreign indebtedness amounted to some £68 million sterling, her internal loan indebtedness to about £14½ million sterling and her floating debt to about £16 million sterling. The annual interest payable on foreign loans amounted to about £5 million sterling, which was more than Egypt's total annual revenue at the beginning of Ismail's reign. Although this revenue had considerably increased during Ismail's tenure, as a result both of merciless taxation and of increased productivity, most of the proceeds of each new loan had to be devoted to the service of previous loans.

The Sublime Porte, during Aali Pasha's grand vizierate, had done its best to prevent this continual recourse to loans, which endangered the payment of the annual tribute, which mortgaged the future of what was, after all, Ottoman territory, and which was gradually transferring into European hands what little remained of Ottoman influence over Egypt. But corruption at Constantinople, and the influence which the great European banking houses were able to exercise on the European governments (including the Ottoman Government, which itself was heavily in debt to them), rendered all such efforts ineffective.

Every desperate device, except any attempt at good management and financial economy—taxation collected in advance, enfranchisement of estates from future payments of land tax against ready cash payments—was resorted to in an attempt to stave off the inevitable end. One of these devices was an attempt to market, on the most favorable possible terms, the Egyptian Government's ordinary shares in the Suez Canal Company which, at par, were worth some 88 million francs. But the shares were at a discount during the first few years of the canal's operations;[9] moreover, the value of the Egyptian Government shares had been diminished by the fact that interest and dividends had been mortgaged until 1894, and voting rights in respect of the shares forfeited for the same period in order to raise the 30 million francs payable to the Canal Company under the terms of the 1869 convention.

The defeat of France in the Franco-Prussian War had an adverse effect on the Canal Company's international influence, in that the French Republican Government was less able to help the Canal Company than the Imperial Government had been, because the French defeat had, for the time being, tilted the balance of influence in Near Eastern affairs away from France and toward Britain. This lessened ability was, however, partly compensated by an open and unwavering, if not always successful, support for the Canal Company given by the French Republican Government. Charles de Rémusat, the French Foreign Minister, stated in the Chamber of Deputies that "we must by all means prevent this truly French enterprise from passing into other hands."[10] Sir Henry Elliot, in Constantinople, complained that the French Government allowed Lesseps to "assume the position of a supplemental Ambassador at the Porte,"[11] and Lord Lyons wrote from Paris: "It was therefore most discouraging to find that in all our dealings with the French Government we invariably encounter M. de Lesseps, and in all our dealing with M. de Lesseps, we are immediately encountered by the French Government."[12]

This French official support was almost certainly forthcoming, not for any strategic reasons, but in defense of the financial interests of the French shareholders, and it seems probable that the French defeat had finally set to rest those residual British fears about the possibility of France occupying Egypt as a means of threatening the British possessions in India. But this specific fear was replaced by a more generalized apprehension. It was axiomatic in British strategic, political, and commercial thought that England's worldwide trading and imperial interests had been built on the foundation, and could be maintained only by the continuance, of that British command of the high seas which was exercised by the Royal Navy and which, since the days of the Napoleonic Wars, had not been seriously disputed. The effect of the completion of the Suez Canal had been to divert the route of a substantial proportion of England's overseas communications away from the high seas, where Britannia ruled the waves, and into a narrow passage over which control was not automatically conferred by the existence of naval supremacy. Down the years, the root of British apprehensions about the canal had been precisely this appreciation that the effect of the canal would be to diminish the value of sea power, to tilt the balance away from the blue waters, where Britain was supreme, to a continental strategy where Britain was at a disadvantage.

All through the nineteenth century in England, where governmental economy was at least as much of an article of faith as commercial expansion, and where indeed governmental economy, and consequent low taxation, was regarded as an essential condition of commercial expansion, there had been a very genuine British reluctance to extend responsibilities landward and a consequent determined resistance to any developments—like the Suez Canal—which seemed to involve the extension of landward responsibilities as a condition of safeguarding British interests. The British policy of trying to maintain the integrity of the Ottoman Empire and, specifically, of trying to maintain the reality of Ottoman control over Egypt was mainly dictated by a desire to avoid the expense and trouble of new landward responsibilities by "neutralizing" those areas which, in default of "neutralization," would, according to current British strategic and commercial concepts, have to be occupied by Britain as the only means of safeguarding vital British interests. It is a measure of British reluctance to extend their landward responsibilities that, even after it had become apparent that there was no further possibility of effective Ottoman control over Egypt, successive British governments sought an effective alternative form of "neutralization" in some sort of international control of Egypt. Such international control, if it were to be effective from the British point of view, demanded an effective British share in the exercise of that control, since neutrals could not be trusted to maintain neutrality.

In her endeavors to maintain the reality of Ottoman control over Egypt, Britain had been fighting a losing battle. The development of Egypt's natural resources by Mohammed Ali and his successors, proceeding contemporaneously with a steady decline in the rest of the Ottoman economy, made it inevitable that the subordination imposed by the terms of the 1841 Hatti Sharif would be progressively eroded, both by evasion and by amendment, to a point where it no longer had any effective existence. The endless negotiations in Constantinople during the sixties and early seventies, when successive Ottoman governments, backed by successive British ambassadors, tried to maintain some sort of effective control over Ismail's activities, had been in the nature of a series of rear-guard actions in which the tide of battle, temporarily swinging one way or the other as a result of bribes paid, follies committed, or obstinacy displayed by one side or the other, was moving inexorably toward Egyptian independence. Similarly, in her endeavors to prevent the construction of the Suez Canal, Britain had been fighting a losing battle. Given the nineteenth century climate of technical achievement and commercial expansion, it was inevitable that the canal should be built, either by Lesseps or by another.

It is only of symbolical significance that the death of Lord Palmerston, in 1865, approximately coincided with an almost imperceptible shift in British policy—the almost instinctive movement of the helm by an experienced mariner who feels the wind blowing too directly onto his cheek, by which Britain, instead of continuing to oppose the onset of Egyptian independence and the completion of the canal by Lesseps, began to think in terms of accommodating herself both to the one and to the other.

As regards the canal, the reason for this shift was the realization, imposed, as it appears, on the British Government by Sir Henry Bulwer, that, in spite of some remaining financial and physical difficulties, and in spite of a certain amount of wishful thinking, Lesseps had already given sufficient proof of his ability to overcome difficulties as to make the canal, to all intents and purposes, a *fait accompli*. As regards Egyptian independence, the Ottoman link had already been all but severed, not merely, or even mainly, by the existence of the canal, or by Ismail's ambitions, or by the material development of Egypt in comparison with the rest of the Ottoman dominions, but principally as a result of the increasing European loan investments in Egypt, which meant that the ultimate control of Egypt's affairs was irrevocably passing away from the Ottoman Empire and into the hands of Egypt's European creditors. The levers for controlling Egypt were in future to be manipulated, not in the ministerial offices of the Sublime Porte, but in the parlors of the great European banking houses.

The traffic figures for 1870, the first full year of the canal's operations, underlined the extent of British interest in the canal. In that year 489 ships, totaling 437,000 registered tons, passed through the canal, of which British shipping contributed 324 ships with a total tonnage of 291,000.[13] That is to say, something like two-thirds of the Canal Company's revenue was being contributed by British shipping.

In the 1856 Concession it had been laid down that tolls to be charged on ships transiting the canal should not exceed "*10 francs par tonneau de capacité des navires et par tête de passager.*" In the Company's navigation rules, published on August 17, 1869, it was laid down that, in calculating these tolls, the Company should accept the tonnage shown on ships' papers. Subsequently, on February 1, 1870, this ruling was amended by the Company to provide that measurements should be taken in accordance with the net tonnage according to the Moorsom system, which was the generally, although not universally, recognized method of tonnage calculation.[14] During the first two years of the canal's operations, revenue was found to be insufficient to meet expenses, which included not only the running costs of the canal but also the payment of 5 percent interest on the ordinary shares and provision for the amortization of these shares. (The half-yearly interest coupons were not paid for the years 1871, 1872, 1873, and for the first half of 1874; the shareholders were eventually paid from the proceeds of an issue of bonds with shares valued at 85 francs each—being the value of the seven outstanding half-yearly interest coupons less 2.5 francs tax—bearing interest at 5 percent and repayable after forty years.)[15]

In March, 1872, the Company announced that, in future, tolls would be collected on the basis of gross instead of net tonnage, calculated on a scale which added about 30 percent to the rate of tolls previously being charged.[16] This ruling immediately brought protests from shipowners all over the world, and also raised the question of jurisdiction. In the 1866 convention it had been provided that disputes between the Company and third parties should be adjudicated *"par les tribunaux locaux suivant les formes consacrés par les lois et usages du pays et les traités."* According to the Company, this meant that disputes in which the Company was defendant should be tried before the French consular courts in Egypt, since the *usage* which had grown up in Egypt (although it had no basis in any of the "capitulations" treaties) was that such disputes should be tried under the jurisdiction of the defendant party.

The British Government's reaction to the increase in tolls was not, at first, robust. The Board of Trade, in a sentence which deserves to be more widely known, stated in a Minute that "Under the circumstances it becomes necessary for Her Majesty's Government at once to take steps to place themselves in a position for forming an opinion on the subject."[17] The Foreign Office wrote to the British ambassador in Constantinople that "Her Majesty's Government considers that the construction put by the Company on the words *'tonneau de capacité des navires'* is a fair one, i.e., gross tonnage after deduction for engine and coal bunker space. With respect to jurisdiction, the Suez Canal Company is an Egyptian Company and, as such, disputes in connection with the Company must, in Egypt, be submitted to that Tribunal which has jurisdiction over the defendant."[18]

A month later the British Government, moved no doubt by agitation from British shipowners, completely reversed themselves. In a dispatch to Sir Henry Elliot dated August 31st, Lord Granville, the Foreign Secretary, stated that "Her Majesty's Government cannot admit the right of the Company to place its own construction on the terms of the Concession and . . . cannot admit the assumption and process by which the Company appears to have arrived at the meaning they place on the words *'tonneau de capacité'* and . . . are of opinion that the Egyptian Government should be supported in maintaining that the Company is, for the purposes of jurisdiction, Egyptian and not French."[19] The question of jurisdiction was still further complicated by the fact that the Messageries Maritimes, the French shipping line, had taken its case against the Company into a French court, which had ordered the Company to revert to the original system of tonnage calculation.[20]

In face of the protests from governments and shipowners, including French shipowners, Lesseps adopted the truculent attitude of a monopolist. In a letter to Sir Daniel Lange, the Company's representative in the United Kingdom, he wrote: "As far as we are concerned, we can only reply to those who are not satisfied with our terms . . . that they can either avail themselves of the Egyptian Railway or, if they prefer doing so, go round the Cape of Good Hope as before. . . . Those who do not pay the dues [namely, the increased dues] in advance will not be permitted to pass their ships through the canal."[21] This truculence was, in part, due to the fact that, through the influence of Barthélemy St. Hilaire, who was at one time closely associated with Lesseps in the canal scheme, Lesseps had secured the support of Adolphe Thiers, the President of the Third Republic, whose secretary St. Hilaire was.[22] Lesseps naturally made the most of Thiers's name in Constantinople, and it required considerable pressure from the British Ambassador to prevent the Porte from giving its sanction to the new rates.[23]

In January, 1873, the Porte, under pressure from the British Government, agreed to call an international conference at Constantinople to determine the basis on which tonnage dues might properly be charged. As a result of Lesseps' delaying tactics, which were supported by the French Government, the conference did not meet until the autumn of that year. During the period of delay, a commission set up by the Ottoman Government found that the Canal Company was not, by the terms of the 1866 firman authorizing the canal, justified in unilaterally raising the tolls. But, in spite of pressure from the British Government, the Ottoman Government took no steps to prevent the Company from charging the new rates. The report of the International Conference, which Colonel Stokes, the British representative, had taken the predominant share in drafting, was issued toward the end of 1873. It recommended a reversion to the Moorsom system of net tonnage as a basis for calculating tolls, but in consideration of the Company's financial difficulties it recommended that they be allowed to impose a temporary surcharge over and above the maximum rate of ten francs per ton of capacity. The maximum rate of surcharge was to be four francs per ton, diminishing with increases of traffic and disappearing altogether when traffic attained a minimum of 2,600,000 net tons per annum.[24] These recommendations were arrived at as the result of a long course of bargaining with the French Government representative who, opposed by all the other international representatives at the conference, fought an obstinate battle on behalf of the Company's shareholders. They were adopted by the Sublime Porte, which informed Ismail that they must be put into effect by the Canal Company within three months.

Lesseps at first refused to accept the Porte's decision, and behaved with an arrogance which was, by this time, becoming habitual with him. He threatened to close the canal; he threatened the Porte with demands for indemnities; he expressed the intention of continuing to apply the new rates. But the French Government (the French representative had, on his Government's instructions, associated himself with the conference's recommendations) was not prepared to back him to this extent. The Porte, with the British Government pushing them from behind, instructed Ismail to occupy the isthmus by force if the Company had not complied at the end of the three-month period of grace. It was not until Egyptian troops were already on their way to the isthmus that Lesseps, at last, gave way.

In fact, he had been making a fuss about nothing, since the rates recommended by the conference and accepted by the Porte were only slightly less than the rates the Company had attempted to impose. But the point had been established that rates were not to be varied unilaterally by the Canal Company without international consultation, and Lesseps' monopolistic arrogance had received a decisive check.

The diplomatic tussle which took place before Lesseps' capitulation is illustrative of the increased power of Britain and the decreased power of France, both in Constantinople and in Cairo. The Porte's reluctance to issue unequivocal instructions to Ismail was overcome by the fact that, first Austria, then Germany, then Russia, followed Britain in insisting that the Canal Company's counterproposals and requests for delay in implementing the conference's recommendations should be rejected. The same governments joined Britain[25] in assuaging the Khedive's fears lest he be forced to pay further indemnities to the company if he acted according to the Porte's instructions. France was left isolated and, eventually, the Duc Decazes, the French Foreign Minister, publicly[26] advised Lesseps and the Conseil d'Administration at the end of the three-month delay period that they could expect no further help from the French Government if they persisted in their recalcitrance.

By their intervention the British Government had shown both their determination to ensure that the Canal Company should be subject to some sort of international control in external matters, and their appreciation that this control should not prevent the Canal Company from operating at a reasonable profit. They had been able to express their determination by the conventional route, through the Sublime Porte, because, in this matter, there was something like a united front of the Powers against France. But the matter of the tonnage dues did not really affect the broader question of the necessity, from the British point of view, of securing some more direct influence on the administration both of the Canal and of Egypt.

The Egyptian Government's ordinary shareholding in the Canal Company had for long been a matter of interest both to the British Government and to the European bankers. As we have seen, Lesseps himself had for some time been anxious to get these shares into the control of the Canal Company's administration. In 1867 he had proposed to Ismail that he should surrender his shares to the Company in exchange for the Company's abandonment of *"tout ce qu'elle possède dans l'Isthme a l'exception du Canal proprement dit."* The principal motive for this proposal had almost certainly been a fear that such a large block of shares might get into potentially hostile hands, since there was always a danger that the Khedive might be driven, by his increasing financial embarrassments, to dispose of them. The decreased attraction of the shares brought about by the forfeiture of the interest coupons and the deprivation of voting rights was no doubt also inspired by the same motive. But the Company was in no financial position itself to make an offer of purchase, and it could only watch the position anxiously.

The possibility of the British Government, or of some British interest, acquiring the Egyptian Government shareholding had long been in the air. At the end of 1870 Stanton, the British consul general, writing to the Foreign Office about the Canal Company's financial difficulties, had quoted Ismail as saying that "the only way to ensure the Canal being made really serviceable for general navigation is for an English Company to obtain possession of it." Stanton went on to express the view that "a great opportunity may shortly occur of consolidating British influence in the country and of securing our communications with India by obtaining possession of the Suez Canal, a possession which would in my opinion be attended by most important political advantages for Her Majesty's Government."[27] Stanton's suggestion was circulated to various government departments for their opinions. The India Office replied favorably, but the Board of Trade replied that "there are considerable objections to encouraging the transfer of the Canal to an English Company." They did not, however, state what these objections were.

Four months later Sir Daniel Lange, the Canal Company's representative in the United Kingdom, wrote to Granville suggesting the acquisition of the canal by Britain and saying that he was trying to bring Lesseps round to the same view. At that time Lesseps was in England trying (unsuccessfully) to raise a loan of £600,000 in order to provide for interest payments to the shareholders.[28] In spite of a discouraging reply from Granville,[29] Lange wrote later that Lesseps was prepared to ask shareholders to agree to a proposal by which the whole of the ordinary shares would be offered for sale at a price of 12 million francs provided that the buyer assumed all obligations toward the Canal Company's creditors, involving payments of 10 million francs per annum over a period of fifty years.[30] Granville replied that the British Government regarded the proposal as "premature."[31] In December, Lange returned to the charge, proposing to Granville a scheme by which Turkey might purchase the shares, acting as a "straw man" for the British Government. He added, "I discovered on my last visit to Paris that M. de Lesseps had lost a considerable portion of his former sway over the Share and Bond Holders who, at the last Meeting, to his surprise, would scarcely listen to him and refused to adopt his financial report."[32] But Granville was still uninterested.

The shareholders had some reason for dissatisfaction. Their 1871 half-yearly-interest coupons had not been paid, and were not to be paid for another three years. During 1871 the 500-franc ordinary shares touched their lowest point at 163 francs. During 1872 they fluctuated between a high point of 490 francs and a low point of 185 francs. In 1873 the Company, in order to raise money to provide for the unpaid interest coupons, offered for sale 200,000 bonds at 100 francs each, bearing 8 percent interest and repayable after thirty years at 125 francs. Notwithstanding the favorable terms, only 120,000 bonds were subscribed.[33] Toward the end of 1873, however, steadily increasing traffic had enabled the Company to turn the corner. In 1874, assisted by the settlement of the tonnage dues dispute, and the authorization for a temporary surcharge, a second and larger bond issue, for 35 million francs, bearing only 5 percent interest and repayable at par after forty years, was fully subscribed, enabling all the arrears of interest to be paid off. In 1875 the market value of the ordinary shares, for the first time, went to a premium. With the specter of bankruptcy receding, the Egyptian Government's shareholding once more became a matter of general interest.

While the position of the Canal Company was improving, that of the Egyptian Government was deteriorating. Toward the end of 1875 a crisis seemed to be approaching. It was necessary for the Egyptian Government to find between three and four million pounds sterling to meet foreign-debt interest coupons falling due on December 1st, and there was no money in the Egyptian Treasury. The sources of borrowing had almost been exhausted. Revenues from the customs, the railways, and the Crown estates were already pledged for the service of existing loans. Land taxes had either been collected in advance or had been remitted in consideration of internal loans raised a few years previously, the proceeds of which had already been spent. Interest payments on the government's holding of canal shares had, as we have seen, been hypothecated until 1894. But the shares themselves, shorn of their interest coupons (and of their voting rights) still remained unmortgaged and thus represented a possible form of security for yet another loan. Now that the value of the shares on the European market had risen to something above par, they had become an acceptable form of property, either for outright sale or for security against a loan.

There were two French banking houses who were both, for different reasons, interested in the shares.[34] The Crédit Foncier had discounted unsecured Egyptian Treasury Bills, to the amount of 170 million francs, representing part of the Egyptian floating debt, and were thus anxious to convert the floating debt into a long-term loan adequately secured as regards both principal and interest. To this end, they were negotiating with the Egyptian Government, through the Anglo-Egyptian Bank in Cairo, for the funding of the floating debt, which amounted to a total of some £16 million sterling, using the Egyptian Government's holding of Canal Company shares as part of the security for the operation. The French Government, which was concerned at Crédit Foncier's large holding of unsecured Egyptian Treasury bills, knew about and supported these negotiations.

Meanwhile Ismail had been approached by André Dervieu, an Alexandrian banker and partner in the firm of Dervieu et Cie., who were the correspondents in Egypt of the Société Générale. At the beginning of November, 1875, André Dervieu obtained from the Khedive an option, expiring on November 16th, for the outright purchase of the Egyptian Government's shareholdings for 92 million francs, with 8 percent interest paid by the Egyptian Government for the nineteen remaining years during which the shares did not rank for interest or dividend. M. André's brother Edouard Dervieu, who lived in Paris, and who had previously been a well-known banker in Egypt and closely concerned with Ismail's financial affairs,[35] immediately set about trying to raise the money within the period of the option. The Dervieu brothers and the Société Génèrale were operating, if not on behalf of, at all events with the backing of, Ferdinand de Lesseps and his associates, who were not interested in Egypt's creditors and who were anxious to ensure that Egypt's financial straits did not result in the Egyptian Government's shareholding passing out of the Viceroy's and into foreign or cosmopolitan hands. But they soon ran into difficulties over raising the 92 million francs required, as a result of the Crédit Foncier's proposal for funding the floating debt which involved the necessity, for the time being, of the Egyptian Government holding onto its canal shares in order to provide security for the funding operation.

M. Edouard went to see the Baron de Soubeyran, the Subgovernor of the

Crédit Foncier, who told him about the funding operation and warned him that the Crédit Foncier would do everything possible to prevent him from raising the money for the purchase of the shares. After having ascertained that the Crédit Foncier's attitude was supported by Léon Say, the French Finance Minister, M. Edouard went to see M. Barrot, the Khedive's agent in Paris, and succeeded in obtaining an extension of the option until November 19th in order to give him a few more days in which to try to raise the money. Edouard Dervieu and Lesseps then went to the Duc Decazes, the Foreign Minister, and tried to impress on him the desirability of having the shares purchased outright by a French interest.

Here they met with a further objection. While Léon Say had been concerned for the solvency of the Crédit Foncier, with its mass of unsecured Egyptian paper, and anxious that the funding operation should go through, Decazes was concerned at the possible effect on the British Government of the purchase of the shares by a French Bank. On November 18th, in an attempt to meet the objections both of Léon Say and of Decazes, the Dervieu brothers amended their previous offer for the outright purchase of the shares and replaced it by an offer which, subject to acceptance before November 26th by the Société Génèrale, provided that the Egyptian Government would receive a loan of 85 million francs at 18 percent interest, repayable in three months, against the security of the Egyptian Government's holding both of the Canal Company ordinary shares, and of the preference shares entitling the Egyptian Government to 15 percent of the net profits. Since it was almost certain that the Egyptian Government would not be able to repay the loan at the end of the three months, it was clear that this new proposal was simply a device to try to get over the objections expressed by both Léon Say and Decazes to the outright purchase of the shares. In fact Lesseps, who was closely concerned in these negotiations, appears to have admitted as much to Decazes[36] who, writing to Gavard, the French chargé d'affaires in London, on November 19th, instructed him to find out what the British Government's attitude would be to the purchase of the Egyptian Government's holding by a French concern, without mentioning the possibility of a loan. As might have been expected, and as Decazes undoubtedly did expect, Lord Derby's reply to Gavard's inquiry was to the effect that the British Government would strongly object to any such transaction. In a dispatch to Decazes on November 20th, Gavard wrote:

The Principal Secretary of State told me that the Khedive was trying to mortgage his Shares in the Suez Canal Company with the Anglo-Egyptian Bank. [We shall see later how Lord Derby had got this not wholly accurate piece of information.] I then asked him if the question had not also been raised of selling their Shares to the Société Générale. "I do not conceal from you," he said, "that I should see serious inconvenience in such a course. You know what my opinion is respecting the French Company. It has run all the risks of the enterprise; all honour is due to it and I would not dispute any of its claims to universal recognition. . . . But since we use the Canal more than all the other nations put together . . . I should be very glad to see the time come when it would be possible to buy out the Shareholders and replace the Company by a Syndicate or Administration in which all the Maritime Powers would be represented. In any case we will do our utmost not to let an undertaking on which so many of our interests depend be monopolised by foreigners. The guarantee resulting from the control of the Porte is now no longer sufficient. If we lost that offered by the participation of the Khedive we should be absolutely at the mercy of M. de Lesseps. . . . The French Shareholders already possess 110 millions out of the 200 million [francs] which the capital of the Shares represents. It is enough." After some words on the subject of the Suez Canal Company I reverted to the mortgage loan of which Lord Derby had spoken to me. He answered that he did not wish the Khedive to mortgage his Shares but that, after all, mortgaging them was not alienating them and they could always be recovered. In conclusion he insisted on the bad effect which would be produced under present circumstances by the sale of the Shares to a French Company and stressed his desire to avoid reawakening old rivalries which an action of this sort would be sure to provoke.[37]

Lord Derby was not being altogether frank with the French chargé d'affaires. For, by this time, the British Government was already actively interested in purchasing the Egyptian Government's shareholdings themselves. On November 15th Lord Derby had sent the following telegram to Major-General Stanton, the British consul general in Egypt: "I am informed that a combination of French capitalists is offering to buy from the Khedive his interest in the Suez Canal and that his difficulties are such that it is thought probable he may consent. Please state if there is any truth in this report."[38]

It is not absolutely certain how much the British Government knew and from where it had obtained its information. The most generally accepted story is that Frederick Greenwood, the editor of the *Pall Mall Gazette,* had been told about the Dervieu option by Henry Oppenheim, the banker, during a dinner conversation on November 14th and had, with Oppenheim's permission, given the information to Lord Derby next morning. It appears that Oppenheim, who was interested in several of the secured loans which had already been granted to Ismail, was also interested in the Crédit Foncier's and the Anglo-Egyptian Bank's negotiations for the funding of the Egyptian floating debt.[39] He was therefore interested in defeating the proposal, expressed in the Dervieu option, for the outright purchase of the shares by the Société Générale, since such an outright purchase would have nullified the Crédit Foncier's proposals for the funding of the floating debt. He must have known about the Dervieu option from Soubeyran, who had spoken to Dervieu, and his use of Greenwood to convey the information to the British Government must have been inspired by the belief that the British Government would also be interested in defeating the Dervieu plan. He probably did not calculate that the British Government's reaction would be to make an offer for the shares themselves.

There was in fact no reason to suppose that such would be the British Government's reaction. As we have seen, Lange's soundings on the subject had been coldly received by the previous government. The only public indication of the attitude of Disraeli's government was a reply made by Lord Derby in the House of Lords on June 5, 1874, to a question asking whether it would not be advisable for the British Government to purchase the shares. On that occasion he had replied that "if a proposition for the transfer of the Canal to an International Commission were to come before us, framed in such a manner that all Governments would participate in the advantages of the Canal on equal terms, I do not say that that might not be a fair proposal to entertain."[40] It appears that Lord Derby and Sir Stafford Northcote, the Chancellor of the Exchequer, were both personally opposed to the purchase of the shares by the British Government[41] and that the policy adopted by the British Government as a result of the information received about the Dervieu option was forced upon the Cabinet by the Prime Minister, Disraeli, who may not have been correctly informed about the strength of the French opposition, both from the Crédit Foncier and from the French Government, to the Dervieu plan and who may, in consequence, have overestimated the very slender prospect of the Dervieu brothers' ability to raise the money for the purchase.

Stanton, in reply to Derby's cable of November 15th, cabled on November 16th, "I am informed that the report referred to in Your Lordship's telegram of yesterday is true and, as the Viceroy's difficulties are most pressing, there is great reason to believe he will be forced to accept the offer made unless other means can be found to procure funds necessary to meet obligations falling due within the next three months." In an immediately following cable, Stanton added: "With reference to my telegram of this afternoon I have ascertained that the Société Génèrale has offered to purchase the Viceroy of Egypt's Shares for ninety million francs. . . . Another offer is made through the Anglo-Egyptian Bank to advance eighty million francs on the security of the Viceroy of Egypt's Shares and repayment in nineteen years. At my request negotiations are suspended till Thursday evening to allow me to communicate with Your Lordship."[42]

Neither at this point nor subsequently was Stanton very well informed about what was happening. He was approximately correct about the Société Génèrale's offer to purchase and he was on the right track in reporting that the Anglo-Egyptian Bank was interested, not in the purchase of the shares, but in their use as security for a loan. (It does not, however, appear that the Crédit Foncier ever got to the stage of making a formal offer of a loan against the security of the shares. At this stage they were simply interested in trying to ensure that the Khedive did not dispose of his shares to a third party.) But Stanton did not realize that the proposals advanced by the Crédit Foncier through the Anglo-Egyptian Bank had already virtually put the Dervieu plan out of court and that there was, owing to the French Government's support of the Crédit Foncier, no immediate possibility of the purchase of the shares either by the Société Génèrale or by any other French interest. There can be no doubt that Nubar Pasha, the Foreign Minister, and Sharif Pasha, the Garde des Sceaux, who, although at odds with each other, were both anxious to have the shares sold at the best possible price, each, privately and separately, made it their business to give Stanton the erroneous impression that the shares might well be sold at any moment to the French unless the British Government stepped in with a good offer without delay.[43] The British Government, as we shall see, rose to the bait.

On November 17th, after the receipt of Stanton's two cables of November 16th, there was a Cabinet meeting in London, after which the following cable was sent to Stanton: "It is of great importance that the interest of the Viceroy of Egypt in the Suez Canal should not fall into the hands of a foreign Company. Press for suspension of negotiations and intimate that Her Majesty's Government are disposed to purchase if satisfactory terms can be arranged."[44]

Commenting on this Cabinet meeting to the Queen on November 18th, Disraeli wrote: "It is vital to Your Majesty's authority and power at this critical moment that the Canal should belong to England, and I was so decided and absolute with Lord Derby on this head that he ultimately adopted my views and brought the matter before the Cabinet yesterday. The Cabinet was unanimous in their decision that the interest of the Khedive should if possible be obtained and we telegraphed accordingly."[45]

A cable from Stanton dispatched on November 17th crossed the cable to Stanton telling him of the British Government's willingness to purchase the shares: "I find it is absolutely necessary for the Viceroy of Egypt to procure from three to four millions sterling before 30th. inst. in order to meet December engagements and to clear the situation until March when His Highness hopes to be able to make arrangements for conversion of the floating debt. His Highness assures me that he will not sell his interest in the Suez Canal Company at present, but he will be forced to accept the offer of an advance on the mortgage of his Shares. This offer, I now understand, is to advance eighty million francs against Treasury Bonds repayable at short date (not nineteen years as stated in my telegram yesterday) on the security of the Canal Shares which will be forfeited in the event of non-fulfillment of the engagement."[46] It appears that Stanton had got mixed up between the Anglo-Egyptian Bank negotiation for the funding of the floating debt and the second Dervieu option then being negotiated between Ismail and André Dervieu.

On receipt of Derby's cable on the evening of November 17th, Stanton immediately conveyed its contents to the Khedive and, at midnight of November 17/18, sent the following cable to Lord Derby: "I have acquainted the Viceroy of Egypt with the purport of Your Lordship's telegram of this afternoon. His Highness expressed his acknowledgment and renewed the assurance that he has at present no intention of selling his Shares and further indicates, should he change his views on this subject, to immediately inform Her Majesty's Government and give them the option of purchase. His Highness added that he would be obliged to accept the offer of an advance from the Anglo-Egyptian Bank to effect a conversion of his floating debt on reasonable terms."[47]

After receiving this cable, the British Government, not surprisingly, was anxious to know whether there was any possibility that the mortgage of the shares to the Anglo-Egyptian Bank, which was known by the British Government to be acting on behalf of the Crédit Foncier,[48] might lead to the forfeiture of the shares to a French interest. They therefore sent the following cable to Stanton: "Her Majesty's Government have received with satisfaction the assurance that the Khedive does not at present contemplate selling his Shares and that if he should do so hereafter he will give Her Majesty's Government the option of purchase. As however it appears that a transaction is in progress for the mortgage of the Shares to the Anglo-Egyptian Bank, Her Majesty's Government would be glad to learn details and more especially to know that there is nothing in the arrangements which would preclude the Khedive from redeeming his Shares."[49] Stanton appears to have replied to this on November 18th with a cable of which there is no trace in the British archives for, on November 19th, the Foreign Office returned to the same point in a cable to Stanton which reads: "Your telegram of November 18 scarcely sufficient. The members of the Bank ought to be known at Cairo. We could not ask without creating suspicion. We have heard that the Bank is only a cover for the Crédit Foncier and that your communications with the Egyptian Government were at once known to the French Government. Nubar Pasha should be more frank with you. If he is not careful he will greatly injure Egyptian credit in this country."[50]

On November 21st Stanton cabled: "I am assured by Nubar Pasha that the arrangement with the Anglo-Egyptian Bank is not concluded in consequence of their excessive demands. A fresh offer has been made by the Société Génèrale to advance Fcs.85 million for three months, they undertaking to present before 5 January a project for the conversion of the floating debt including the amount advanced by them and to have until that date preference in proposals of equal terms. If after three months the money is not repaid they become possessors of the Viceroy's Canal Shares. . . . The Viceroy is unwell and cannot transact business but Ministers are prepared to accept on receiving proof that the proposal is genuine . . . reasonable proposal from English capitalists might save situation should offer of Société Génèrale not prove serious. . . ."[51]

Derby replied on November 23rd: "Her Majesty's Government are anxious that the Khedive should obtain such assistance as he requires on reasonable terms and they believe that if details can be arranged satisfactorily this can be done. They would if requested send a confidential agent. Make every endeavour to suspend the conclusion of any arrangement to sell or pledge the Khedive's Shares."[52]

It is clear that Nubar and Sharif were, between them, engaged in the process of what is vulgarly known as "bringing the man up to scratch." On November 23rd at 1930 hours Stanton cabled: "Sharif Pasha has just called stating that he was charged by the Viceroy to inform me that the offer for an advance on mortgage of his Canal Shares has been withdrawn and offers for purchase alone are now being made. Fcs.100 million are offered through M. de Lesseps who has telegraphed to His Highness offering to undertake the placing of the Shares in Paris and London without commission or profit. His Highness will sell the Shares to Her Majesty's Government for that amount. M. de Lesseps' offer is supposed to be made on behalf of the French Government. An answer is requested by Thursday next, 25th. inst."[53] In an immediately following cable Stanton stated, "I should add that the Egyptian Government will pay interest at 5 percent for the amount paid for the Canal Shares until the coupons are free."[54]

There is no evidence, apart from Sharif's statement to Stanton, that any such offer had been made to the Egyptian Government by Lesseps or by anybody else. By November 23rd it was already clear that, owing to the French Government's attitude, the money would not be available in France to enable the second Dervieu option, which was due to expire on November

26th, to be taken up, and the Egyptian Government probably knew this. Therefore, since the Crédit Foncier and the Anglo-Egyptian Bank were primarily interested in funding the floating debt, the only immediate prospect of raising money on the shares in order to meet the December interest coupons of the secured debt was to induce the British Government to purchase before the end of November. The alleged Lesseps offer of 100 million francs seems to have been a complete invention by Sharif Pasha with the object of stampeding the British Government into purchasing the shares themselves for that sum, which was 8 million francs more than had been offered in the first Dervieu option and 15 million francs more than had been offered in the second Dervieu option for 85 million francs, which also included the reversion of the Egyptian Government's 15 percent share of the net profits.

One reason for the large difference between the first Dervieu proposal, which was made at the beginning of November, and the second, in the middle of December, was in the price movement of the Canal shares during the intervening period. In a note dated November 19th to Lord Derby by Colonel Stokes, the British representative at the Constantinople Conference on tonnage dues, who had returned to Royal Engineers' duty at Chatham but who was still retained by the Foreign Office on a part-time basis to advise them on Suez Canal affairs, he stated that, "The Share market has fluctuated considerably during the last three weeks, the Fcs.500 Shares have gone down from Fcs.730 on 21 October to Fcs.685 on 9 November."[55] In the same note Stokes expressed the view that "an offer of Fcs.3½ million (Fcs.87.5 million), without any stipulation for interest in lieu of the detached coupons" would be gladly accepted by the Khedive. The 100 million francs which the Egyptian Government had, in effect, quoted to the British Government, represented, on the assumed Egyptian Government holding of 177,642 shares, a price of 560 francs per share, which was considerably below the current market price. The Egyptian Government shares were, however, in a special category in that they did not rank for interest or dividend until 1894, and the sale was virtually a forced sale in view of the Egyptian Government's urgent need for money.

On November 17th, after the Cabinet had decided that they would, in principle, be prepared to purchase the Egyptian Government's shareholding, the question arose as to ways and means. Parliament was not sitting and, even if it had been, the need for secrecy would have made it impossible for the government to have asked the House of Commons for the money. The sum involved was, in those days, far too large to enable it to be "smuggled" through any of the existing Estimates. Buckle, Disraeli's biographer, tells us that the Prime Minister instructed Corry, his private secretary, to wait outside the Cabinet room on November 17th and, when Disraeli gave him the signal, to go immediately to Baron Rothschild and tell him that the Prime Minister wanted four million pounds sterling "to-morrow." According to this story, Corry carried the message to Rothschild who "picked up a muscatel grape, ate it, threw out the skin, and said deliberately, 'What is your security?' 'The British Government,' replied Corry. 'You shall have it.'"[56] It seems probable that the affair was, in reality, arranged in a rather less picturesque way, although it does not seem to have been arranged through the Chancellor of the Exchequer, Sir Stafford Northcote, who disapproved of the whole transaction.[57] At all events, the contract between Rothschilds and the Treasury was signed in time for the British Government to make their bid for the shares on November 24th. The terms of the contract were as follows: "Messrs. Rothschild will charge commission of 2½% upon a sum of up to Four Million Pounds Sterling which they undertake to provide and they will receive the 5% interest which the Khedive undertakes to pay until the date of repayment by Her Majesty's Government."[58]

Armed with the Rothschild promise of a loan of four million sterling, the Foreign Office sent the following cable to Stanton on November 24th:

The Khedive's offer is accepted. Her Majesty's Government agree to purchase the 177,642 Shares from the Khedive for four million pounds sterling and to recommend to Parliament to sanction the contract. In the meantime Messrs. N. de Rothschild & Son will be the agents of Her Majesty's Government in London to carry out the transaction. They will be prepared to hold One Million Sterling on 1 December at the disposal of the Egyptian Government upon the Shares being handed to you on behalf of Her Majesty's Government. The remaining Three Millions will be provided in December and January as may be arranged between the Egyptian Government and Rothschilds. Her Majesty's Government assumes that the 5% interest on the sum which is to be paid to Her Majesty's Government until the coupons are liberated will be a charge on the revenues of the Egyptian Government.[59]

Later in the afternoon of the same day, the Foreign Office, anxious not to risk spoiling the ship for a ha'porth of tar, sent another cable to Stanton: "Confidential. With regard to the security of the 5%, you will mention it as instructed and press the point if you see a chance of success but do not let the bargain go off upon it."[60] On receipt of the first cable, Stanton, as he subsequently related in a mailed dispatch, "lost no time in proceeding to the Palace to inform His Highness of the acceptance of his offer to dispose of the Canal Shares to Her Majesty's Government. I was unable at that hour[61] to see the Khedive as His Highness' medical advisers would not allow him to be disturbed, but I informed the Minister of Finance,[62] whom I saw in the presence of Nubar Pasha and of the Khedive's Garde des Sceaux, of the nature of the communication I had to make and shortly afterwards received the assurance that the terms were agreed to. Being however anxious to prevent any misunderstanding on the subject, and also to prevent the possibility of any successful intrigue interfering with the arrangement, I told the Minister I would draw up an agreement for signature. . . ."[63]

After signing the agreement, Stanton cabled the good news. "Agreement for the sale of the Canal Shares is signed. The Shares are to be deposited with me to-morrow morning. The number being only 176,602. I have stipulated that the value of the 1040 Shares short . . . will be deducted from the sum to be paid by Her Majesty's Government."[64] And, on the following day, he cabled, "Seven large cases containing Suez Canal Shares have this day been deposited in HBM's Consulate here. They have been corded and sealed with the seals of the Finance Minister, HM's Agent and that of the Consular Court pending verification of the numbers."[65]

In due course, after the shares had been checked and counted (temporary clerks being engaged at the British Consulate for the purpose),[66] and after Stanton had complained of the amount of room the seven large cases were taking up in the consulate, they were taken to Alexandria by special train and shipped to England by the troopship *Malabar,* which made a special call at Alexandria in order to take them on board. They arrived safely at Portsmouth on December 31, 1875.

The news of the purchase, announced in *The Times* on November 26th, was greeted in England with general, but not universal, satisfaction. The Chancellor of the Exchequer, in a private letter to Disraeli on the day of the announcement, wrote: "Our policy, or our proceedings, with regard to the Canal, has not been such as to gain us much credit for magnaminity. We opposed it in its origin; we refused to help Lesseps in his difficulties; we have used it when it has succeeded; we have fought the battle of our ship-owners very stiffly; and now we avail ourselves of our influence with Egypt to get a quiet slice of what promises to be a good thing. . . . I don't like it."[67] The Opposition in the House of Commons, when the transaction was debated in February, 1876, was critical, although the criticism was concentrated more on the amount of the commission paid to the Rothschilds than on the principle of the purchase itself. But generally, the reaction in England was favorable. *The Times* probably expressed the view of most educated people in its leading article on November 27th:

The possible results of this national investment are so large and indefinite that it would be vain to speculate upon them, and yet they present themselves persistently to the imagination. It is plain that we acquire an interest in Egypt and its administration which will compel the constant attention of the Queen's Government. We have purchased nearly half the Shares of the Suez Canal. We are the largest proprietors, and it need not be said that the others will look to us for the management of the property, the maintenance of satisfactory relations with the local Government and with the other Powers of the world. To this country will belong the decision on every question, whether scientific, financial or political; administration and negotiation will be in our hands, and as we have the power, so we shall have the responsibility before the world. . . . We have now an abiding stake in the security and welfare of Egypt.

Abroad, the reaction was varied. "France was grieved and bruised. The war, the defeat, and also the alarms which always follow great misfortunes, had heightened her sensibility."[68] The French Government feared that the transaction would lead to a progressive increase of British interference in Egyptian affairs. The Duc Decazes was violently criticised in the French press for his subservient attitude toward Britain.[69] Both the Austrian and Italian governments expressed their pleasure.[70] Bismarck, always pleased at any development which tended to set France and England at odds, congratulated the British Government.[71] The Sublime Porte was "not . . . without apprehension that the step taken by the Viceroy without consultation with the Porte may be seen with displeasure by the Sultan by whose Firman the construction of the Canal by a private Company was authorised."[72] In reply to this expression of Ottoman fears the British Government assured the Porte that "Her Majesty's Government have no intention of derogating from the sovereignty of the Sultan and that the purchase of the Suez Canal Shares was a necessary measure to prevent them from falling into the possession of parties who might have made use of them in a manner prejudicial both to the Porte and to England."[73]

The Khedive's reaction was to try to persuade the British Government to purchase his 15 percent share of the net profits of the Canal Company by representing to Stanton that the French had offered between thirty and forty million francs for this.[74] On this occasion the British Government did not rise to the bait. Lesseps himself accepted the situation with a good grace. In a letter to Lord Lyons dated November 24th,[75] he wrote: "The English nation now accepts that share in the Canal which has been loyally reserved to her from the outset; and if this action is to have any effect, that effect, in my opinion, can only be the abandonment by the British Government of the long-standing attitude of hostility towards the interests of the original Shareholders of the Maritime Canal, whose perseverance has been at once so active and so well-directed. I therefore look upon the close community of interest about to be established between French and British capital, for the purely industrial and necessarily peaceful working of the Universal Maritime Canal, as a most fortunate occurrence."

What was the real significance of the purchase? The immediate reason was undoubtedly the fear that the shares would be bought by a French interest and probably (on the basis of the information supplied by Stanton in his telegram of November 23rd) by a French interest dominated by Lesseps. That this fear was chimerical does not detract from its genuineness. There is no reason to doubt the British Government's statement, made in the dispatch to Sir Henry Elliot which has been quoted, that the purchase of the shares was made in the genuine belief that it was a "necessary measure to prevent them from falling into the possession of parties who might have made use of them in a manner prejudicial . . . to England." There is no reason to suppose that the British Government was actuated either by the macchiavellian intentions attributed to them by French public opinion and, to some extent, by the French Government, or that they shared the somewhat grandiose visions expressed in *The Times* leading article of November 27th.

Even Disraeli who, in a letter to Lady Bradford, expressed himself in terms of ridiculous hyperbole about the whole transaction, does not seem really to have regarded it as any more than what modern capitalists are accustomed to calling a "defensive investment." "After a fortnight of the most increasing labour and anxiety, I—for between ourselves and ourselves only, I may be egotistical in this matter—I have purchased for England the Khedive of Egypt's interest in the Suez Canal. We have had all the gamblers, capitalists, financiers of the world organized and platooned in bands of plunderers, arrayed against us, and secret emissaries in every corner, and have baffled them all, and have never been suspected."[76] Disraeli's plunderers and secret emissaries were indeed "men in buckram." But some exaggeration may be allowed to a man boasting of his exploits in a letter to a lady friend.

The British Government's purchase of the Khedive's Canal Company shares was simply an incident in that increasing manifestation of British interest in Egypt which began with the British acquisition of India in the Seven Years' War, which was stimulated by the construction of the Suez Canal, and which culminated in the British occupation of Egypt in 1882. It was dictated by the principle, first expressed by Dundas in 1798, and repeated in various forms by British statesmen throughout the nineteenth century and the first half of the twentieth century, that "the possession of Egypt by any independent Power would be a fatal circumstance to the interests of this country."

It is possible that the Victorian obsession with property caused British public opinion to exaggerate the importance of the shares transaction as a factor in conferring control of the canal upon England and in preventing that control from falling into other hands. In the light of British sea power, and in terms of British nineteenth century strategy, British strategic control of the canal could be secured either by the effective neutralization of Egypt or by a British military occupation of Egypt. Occupation was resorted to, and maintained, when the alternative policy of neutralization, which had been pursued since the expulsion of the French from Egypt at the beginning of the century, was regarded as being no longer effective. The financial ownership of the canal was quite irrelevant to the concept of strategic control.

A predominant share in the financial ownership was, however, relevant, both to the question of commercial policy and to the interests of British merchant shipping which contributed more than half of the total revenues of the Canal Company. In the light of experience over the tonnage and other disputes during the first five years of the canal's operations, it was clear that the newly acquired British shareholding could be a useful weapon with which to counteract the authoritarian tendencies of Ferdinand de Lesseps and the Anglophobe proclivities of many of the Canal Company's officials in the day-to-day commercial operation of the canal.

We have already seen that, by a decision of the 1871 general meeting, the holders of the Khedive's shares had been deprived of all voting rights until 1894 as a result of the interest coupons having been detached up to that date. Apart from this, the Statutes of the Company provided that no one shareholder, whatever the number of shares he might possess, was entitled to more than ten votes. The purchase of the shares had not therefore conferred on the British Government any statutory right to any control at all over the operations of the Canal Company (a circumstance which the government omitted to explain to Parliament when seeking retroactive approval of the transaction). Colonel Stokes expressed the view that the decision of the 1871 general meeting was illegal and that the Khedive's shares retained their full voting rights despite the alienation of the coupons, and recommended that the British Government should allocate their Shares to 706 trustees, each possessing the minimum number of shares entitling him to ten votes, and send these trustees to general meetings with the power of casting 7,060 votes on behalf of the British Government.[77] This ingenious suggestion was not adopted, and Colonel Stokes was directed to negotiate with Lesseps on behalf of the British Government for the regulation of the British Government's share in the management of the Company.

By the terms of the Stokes-Lesseps Agreement, arrived at on February 3, 1876,[78] it was provided that the voting rights should be restored to the shares, giving the British Government ten votes, and that three British directors, nominated by the British Government, should join the Board (Conseil d'Administration) of the Company. (This agreement was ratified at a general meeting held in July, 1876, at which the total number of directors was reduced from 32 to 24, thus giving the British Government one-eighth of the total membership of the Board.) In a subsequent agreement, arrived at between Stokes and Lesseps on February 21, 1876,[79] the Canal Company agreed: (*a*) to spend a minimum of one million francs a year for the next thirty years on capital improvements to the canal and (*b*) to vary the decisions of the 1873 Constantinople Conference on tonnage dues by making progressive annual reductions, between 1877 and 1884, in the surcharge authorized by the conference, with a view to reverting to the basic rate of 10 francs per ton net from the beginning of 1884, irrespective of the amount of tonnage carried by the canal. This agreement was also, in due course, ratified by a general meeting of shareholders. A subsequent agreement arrived at in 1884 between the Canal Company and a conference of British shipowners, and accepted by the British Government, provided: (*a*) for the nomination of three official and seven unofficial British directors, including a British vice-president and British member each on the Executive and Finance committees, out of a Board increased once more to 32 members,[80] and (*b*) for a sliding-scale reduction of tonnage dues below 10 francs per ton net to operate *pari passu* with increases of tonnage.[81]

As we have seen, the idea of digging a maritime canal through the Isthmus of Suez had, since the seventeenth century, been inextricably bound up with French and, to a lesser extent, with Austrian ambitions to restore to the ports of the Mediterranean that commercial supremacy in the Eastern trade which had been transferred to the Atlantic ports as a result of the discovery and exploitation of the Cape route. For France the idea had also been bound up with an imperial dream, nourished by memories of the Crusades, in which France was to be the means of restoring European and Christian civilization to the lands of the eastern Mediterranean, which would become linked to each other and to western Europe by the waters of a French Mare Nostrum, and which, by means of the Suez Canal, would serve as a cultural and commercial link between western Europe and the teeming populations of Asia.

The attainment of this ambition and the realization of this dream were never consistently pursued by the makers of French policy, either before or after the Revolution. But the ambition was kept alive by the merchants of Marseille, and the dream was always a potent, unpredictable, and disturbing element in the pattern of French intellectual, cultural, and political thought.

After the Seven Years' War, practical ambitions were sharpened and crusading dreams secularized by a growing popular hostility toward England which found expression in a desire to find compensation in the eastern Mediterranean for the French colonies in the East and West Indies which had been lost to England and, by so doing, to pose a threat and to set a limit to the expansion of the British Empire in the East.

Bonaparte's Egyptian expedition was an attempt to fulfill the ambition and to realize the dream. This attempt failed. The failure was symbolized, dramatically if not altogether accurately, by Bonaparte's defeat before the walls of Acre by Anglo-Turkish forces commanded respectively by Sir Sidney Smith and Jezzar Pasha. But the expedition had one important result. The work of the French savants who accompanied the expedition laid that foundation of French cultural and technical expertise on Egypt which was to be translated into political terms as a result of subsequent French involvement in the social reforms and political ambitions of Mohammed Ali. This expertise and this involvement concentrated practical French interest on the Suez Canal and paved the way toward Lesseps' triumphant achievement. But, at the same time, they aroused British suspicions and excited British opposition. These suspicions and this opposition were manifested in the events of 1840 which represented a major diplomatic defeat for France in the eastern Mediterranean, and in the British attitude toward the Lesseps project. The French official attitude toward the Lesseps project was determined on the one hand by a desire to support an enterprise which was both meritorious in itself and which was in perfect accord with traditional and legitimate French ambitions and aspirations, and on the other hand by an appreciation of the relative material strengths of Great Britain and France, by the Second Empire policy of alliance with Britain, and by a consequent desire to avoid any serious affront to British susceptibilities.

We have seen how Lesseps triumphed over the political obstacles. But this triumph did not change basic political and strategic realities. These realities dictated that the price the French would have to pay for the achievement of the canal would be the handing over to England of the strategic control of the canal. This, in effect, meant an ultimate French acquiescence in the British occupation of Egypt.

The opening of the Suez Canal did not, in itself, invalidate that policy of neutralizing Egypt which had been pursued by Britain since the beginning of the century and which, from the British point of view, was the preferable alternative to a British occupation of Egypt. It was the combination of three things—the growing weakness of the Ottoman Empire, the growing and predatory interest in Egypt being shown by her international creditors, and the opening of the Suez Canal—which, in British eyes, invalidated the neutralization policy and brought a genuinely reluctant Liberal Government to the alternative of military occupation.

On the surface, the existence of the Suez Canal was the least important of these three factors in determining the course of events in Egypt between 1875 and 1882. But, under the surface, the existence of the Suez Canal was probably a more important factor than the interests of British bondholders in determining the increasing British involvement in Egyptian affairs from 1876 onward. And, when the exigencies of the bondholders' representatives had led to an armed revolt against the authority of the Khedive, fears for the security of the canal rather than fears for the security of the bondholders' money were probably the decisive factors behind the British occupation. The fact that the British Government was the largest shareholder in the Canal Company was irrelevant. What counted, in 1882 as in 1956, was not the security of British dividends, but the security of British communications. Whether or not British fears for the continued security of their communications, either in 1882 or in 1956, were chimerical, is another matter.

This book is an account of the consummation of a French physical achievement and the frustration of a French political dream. It is fitting to conclude it with a brief description of the events which extruded the French from any future share in the political destinies of Egypt and which laid the foundations of that British Empire in the Middle East whose end was signalized, seventy-five years later, by a piece of political violence and poetic justice, when the Ruler of Egypt took possession of the canal over which European statesmen had wrangled and for which Egyptian peasants had paid.

Within a few days of the purchase of the shares, the Khedive, who was beginning to display the hectic optimism of a gambler nearing the end of his tether, and who hoped to use the increased British involvement in Egyptian affairs to his own advantage by playing off France against Great Britain and vice versa, asked the British Government to send a financial expert to Egypt to examine and make recommendations about the state of Egypt's finances. The British Government accepted this invitation and sent Mr. Stephen Cave, MP. This acceptance, coming on top of the purchase of the canal shares, was ill received in France, where it was regarded as one more stage in a concerted British plan to assume control of Egypt. The French Government was still interested in the Credit Foncier's plan to fund the floating debt and, as a reinforcement for the Anglo-Egyptian Bank, sent Outrey, who had previously been French consul general in Egypt and who enjoyed Ismail's confidence, to Cairo in order to help counteract the supposed intrigues of Cave and his mission.

The Cave Report,[82] which was published on April 3, 1876, while castigating Ismail's extravagance, gave him full credit for the economic expansion which had taken place and for the public works which had been undertaken during his reign; it also made it clear that Egypt's financial plight was mainly due to the extortionate terms on which Egypt's foreign loans had been contracted, as regards both commission and interest. The report particularly instanced the ruinous Oppenheim loan of 1873, which was for a nominal value of £32 million sterling but of which the Egyptian Treasury received only £11 million sterling in cash. The report recommended that arrangements should be negotiated with the secured creditors to accept a lower rate of interest and a longer period of repayment in order to reduce what the report recognized to be an insupportable and unjustifiable burden upon Egypt's revenues.

On April 6th, three days after the publication of the Cave Report, the Egyptian Government announced that, pending a new and comprehensive arrangement for the settlement of the Egyptian debt which was being negotiated, payment of the April and May coupons would be delayed for three months. This technical act of bankruptcy marked the beginning of an Anglo-French rapprochement over Egypt which was soon to take the form of an Anglo-French condominium over Egypt and which, had it not been for the quite unjustifiable tenderness shown by both Governments toward the interests of the bondholders, and the failure of these Governments to recognize and make allowances for the resentments aroused in Egypt by the impact of the foreign controls imposed on Egypt in the interests of the bondholders, might well have formed a viable third alternative to neutralization or to British occupation. As it was, the representatives of the British and French governments, acting with varying degrees of willingness as bailiffs for an anonymous horde of foreign bondholders, provoked resentments which could be dealt with only by the application of armed force. When it came to the crunch, the French Government, for domestic political reasons, was unwilling to apply the armed force. So the British applied it by themselves, and occupied Egypt, thereby convincing the French that this was the final stage in a carefully conceived and long-matured plan.

At the beginning of May the Khedive, as a result of his negotiations with Outrey and the Crédit Foncier, issued two decrees, the first of which created the Caisse de la Dette, a body to be manned by one French, one British, one Italian, one Austrian, and one German member, for the management of the foreign debt, and the second of which provided for the consolidation of the whole of the secured and floating debt at a sum of £91 million sterling bearing interest at 7 percent, and committing Egypt to an annual payment of about £6½ million sterling per annum, or about two-thirds of Egypt's total annual revenue, in interest and sinking-fund payments. The British Government, seeing that this was a French-inspired scheme, motivated principally by the Crédit Foncier's desire to obtain some security for its mass of unsecured Egyptian paper, refused to recognize this settlement, and refused to nominate a British member to the Caisse de la Dette, on the ground that the settlement was unduly favorable to the holders of the floating debt. Eventually, an Anglo-French Mission (the Goschen-Joubert Mission) was sent to Egypt, which negotiated a new settlement, less favorable to the owners of the floating debt, and which, backed by the authority of the two Governments, caused Ismail to accept a very large measure of Anglo-French control over the revenue-producing departments of his Government. (It was during the visit of the Goschen-Joubert Mission to Cairo that Ismail Sadiq, the Mufattish, who was Ismail's Finance Minister, and who was regarded by the bondholders' representatives as being obstructive to their interests, was arrested by Ismail and subsequently murdered.)

It is unnecessary, in this account, to follow in detail the history of what became known as the Dual Control which, at one time, extended to the appointment of British and French Ministers at the Ministries of Finance and Public Works, respectively. The Anglo-French aim was to establish an effective control over both income and expenditure and to establish a proper differentiation (which had never yet been established) between the Khedive's privy purse and the state budget. Ismail's aim was to avoid the reality of any control over either his own personal expenditure or that of the state, and to use the Dual Control as a convenient means by which payment of his debts might be evaded, scaled down, or delayed. Ismail's natural astuteness, and the authority which he wielded in the country, enabled him, time and again, to evade most of the promises and commitments which the Dual Control was able to extort from him. Finally, in 1879, the British and French, in their undignified capacity of debt collectors, joining forces for once in the corridors of power at Constantinople, prevailed upon a not over-reluctant Sultan to issue his firman for the deposition of Ismail and, in accordance with the terms of the 1867 firman, for the succession of his eldest son Tewfiq who, as titular Prime Minister under the Dual Control, had already given proof both of his opposition to his father and of his subservience to Anglo-French interests.

After Ismail's deposition, opposition to the Dual Control came, not from the Palace, but from the growing resentment both of the Egyptian Army and the Egyptian notables. When Ismail was on the throne, his had been the only effective Egyptian voice to be raised. When Ismail turned, they all turned. But when Ismail went, most of the authority of the throne went too. The mere appearance of Ismail was sufficient to quell an incipient mutiny. A frown from Ismail was enough to send a Minister into exile, as Nubar had gone, for a short spell, in 1876. In the same year, a word from Ismail to an army sergeant was all that was necessary to procure the murder of another Minister, Ismail Sadiq, because it suited the Khedive, for the time being, to conciliate the Goschen-Joubert Mission. Under Tewfiq, all that was changed. This was due, not so much to Tewfiq's character as to the circumstances of his accession. He was known to be the nominee, the creature, of the foreigners. And all the resentment which had been gathering against Ismail—for his despotic ways, for his oppressive taxation, for his having mortgaged the country to, and for having wasted the substance of his country upon, foreigners—but which had not been visited upon Ismail because of the prestige he enjoyed and because of the fear he evoked, now gathered round the head of his luckless son and successor, who had inherited Ismail's liabilities without any of his personal assets.

The Dual Control found themselves identified with a despotism which, when it had been exercised by Ismail, they had done their best to discredit, and by a xenophobia which, by the manner as well as by the matter of their inevitably unpopular proceedings, they had done a great deal to arouse. They now found themselves obliged to support the new Khedive's authority against an incipient mutiny in the army, and against a demand for constitutional government from the Chamber of Notables, which had been convened in an attempt to appease the mounting popular discontent.

The crisis came at the beginning of 1882, when the Chamber of Notables, angered at the refusal of the Dual Control to allow them to debate the Budget, joined forces with the army. On February 3rd the Prime Minister, Sharif Pasha, who had been trying to hold the balance even between the army, the Chamber of Notables, and the Dual Control, resigned and was replaced by Mahmud Sami, a nominee of the army, who appointed Ahmed Arabi, the leader of the army movement of revolt, as Minister of War. From that moment onward, until the British occupation in August, Arabi, with the army behind him, was the real master of the country.

The situation had completely escaped from the control of that French-speaking, Turkish-Albanian-Circassian aristocracy which had previously dominated affairs in Egypt and which could be dealt with by diplomacy, flattery, bribery, threats, and cajolery, and had got into the hands of native-born Egyptians who regarded Albanian princes and Turkish courtiers with the same xenophobic dislike that they extended to Jewish bankers and Anglo-French officials.

For the previous six years there had been an unusual community in the

Egyptian policies pursued by France and Britain. This community had originally been resorted to in order to try to put a stop to Ismail's attempted exploitation of the endemic divergencies between them. It had been continued as a result of the partnership imposed on the two countries by the day-to-day working of the Dual Control. In the early days, when Disraeli was Prime Minister in England, it had been England which had taken the lead in insisting on the imposition of effective measures of control, with France faintly protesting but resolutely pursuing. Later, with Léon Gambetta as Prime Minister and Foreign Minister in France, and with a Liberal government in power in England, it was the French Government which took the lead and the British Government which, dubiously but obediently, followed. When the crisis came, Gambetta had just fallen from power, and Charles de Saulce de Freycinet was the French Premier and Foreign Minister. Granville, the British Foreign Minister, was still moving forward with the impetus Gambetta had applied to him, at a time when the new French Government was beginning to have doubts about Gambetta's forward policy in Egypt.

There were four matters which the British and French governments were at one in wishing to provide for: the maintenance of the authority of the Khedive; the protection of the European population in Egypt; the security of the Suez Canal; and the interests of the European bondholders. The first three matters were all the legitimate concern and responsibility of Turkey, the Suzerain Power. The predominance given over the past six years by the British and French governments to the fourth of these matters—the interests of the bondholders—with which Turkey was not concerned, and which had been the basic cause of the trouble, had tended to diminish the importance attached to Ottoman suzerainty by these two governments, and they showed at this stage a reluctance to encourage Turkish intervention, with its corollary of probable future Turkish interference. On the one hand, if things blew over, Turkish intervention might prove unnecessary; on the other hand, if things did not blow over, it was the Ottoman habit to compound with, rather than to try and crush, successful rebellion. There was, in fact, reason to believe that Ottoman emissaries were already in touch with Arabi.

If the British and French governments were opposed to Turkish intervention, the other European Powers were opposed to Anglo-French intervention. The dispatch of British and French naval squadrons to Alexandria in the middle of May was viewed with suspicion not only in Constantinople but also in Vienna, Petersburg, Berlin, and Rome. And so, at the end of May, on British initiative, a Conference of the Powers was convened to meet in Constantinople.

Meanwhile, in Egypt, the appearance of the British and French squadrons off Alexandria had enabled the Khedive to dismiss the Sami Ministry and to reappoint Sharif Pasha as Prime Minister. This reassertion of the khedivial authority was, however, short-lived and, before long, Arabi Pasha was back in power, this time as Prime Minister and virtual ruler of Egypt.

At the beginning of June the Conference of Powers met in Constantinople. The Ottoman Government had given permission for the Conference to be held, but declined to participate in it. Instead, they sent a commissioner, Darwish Pasha, to Egypt, to see how the land lay. It had long been the Ottoman habit, in its dealing both with the Powers and with its own vassals, to "roll with the punch," and to accept, as far as possible in advance, events they were unable to resist. With the attitude of the Powers still uncertain, they were by no means disposed, without further information, to commit themselves to any future action with regard to Egypt. The conference opened impressively with a solemn declaration, subscribed to by the representatives of all the assembled Powers—Great Britain, France, Austria-Hungary, Russia, Germany, and Italy—that they sought in Egypt no territorial gains, no exclusive privileges, and no commercial advantages which were not equally available to any other nation. The conference then adjourned until June 23rd. While it was in recess, an antiforeign outbreak in Alexandria on June 11th resulted in the death of some fifty foreigners. As a result, a large part of the foreign colony in Alexandria sought refuge with the Anglo-French naval squadrons lying off Alexandria.

When the conference resumed its sittings, discussions centered on what measures, if any, were to be taken for assuring safety of transit through the Suez Canal, which, it was generally agreed, was a matter of legitimate concern to all the assembled Powers.

On July 11th there appeared the first sign of a rift in the united front which, up to that time, had existed between the British and French governments in their attitude toward the Egyptian crisis. Admiral Seymour, in command of the British squadron off Alexandria, noted that some of the coastal batteries west of Alexandria were being put in a state of readiness. After consultation with the British Government, and after a request to the Egyptian Government, which was ignored, to cease work on the batteries, the British admiral informed his French colleague that he proposed, on the next day, to open fire on the offending batteries. The French admiral, Conrad, on instructions from his government, weighed anchor and sailed from Alexandria in the direction of Port Said. On the day after the bombardment the Khedive, who was in Alexandria during the bombardment, and who appears to have given the order to reply to Admiral Seymour's fire, sought the protection of the British squadron. Thereafter, British military action against

Egypt was undertaken in the name of the Khedive with the object of restoring him to his throne. Immediately after the bombardment Arabi, apprehending a British landing and an advance on Cairo, withdrew with his troops from Alexandria and established himself along a defensive line near Kafr el Dawar, the gateway to the Delta. On the Khedive ordering him to return to Alexandria, he refused, and was declared by the Khedive to be in rebellion.

On July 20th a British military expedition, commanded by Sir Garnet Wolseley, sailed from England for Alexandria.

It was clear to the representatives of the Powers assembled at Constantinople that Britain was resolved on armed intervention in Egypt, either alone or in cooperation with the Powers. The near prospect of an invasion of Egypt immediately raised the question of the neutrality of the Suez Canal, for, in view of the difficult terrain and the presence of the bulk of Arabi's forces between Alexandria and Cairo, the most propitious route to Cairo for an invading army was through the canal to Ismailia and thence along the line of the Sweet Water Canal to Cairo.

The neutrality of the Suez Canal had been declared both in the 1856 Concession and in the 1866 firman, but these declarations had never been incorporated into any international convention. If the canal were not neutralized, there were, in view of the probability of an attempted invasion of Egypt, two principal dangers to be apprehended, either of which would jeopardize free passage through the canal. The first was that the Egyptian Army might cut off supplies of Nile water from the isthmus by blocking or diverting the Sweet Water Canal. The second was that they might sink vessels in the Maritime Canal in order to block the passage of an invading armada along the canal to Ismailia. These were real dangers which might, and which probably would, have been averted by an internationally subscribed guarantee of neutralization. On the other hand, such a guarantee would seriously have tied the hands of an invading army by committing them to a single difficult and well-defended approach route to Cairo. The British Government, which for this reason was opposed to neutralization, had, since before the bombardment of Alexandria, been trying to persuade the French Government to join with them in a regular patrol of the Maritime Canal with gunboats and in the occupation of strategic points. The French Government, although hard pressed by the Suez Canal Company which was, naturally enough, in favor of neutralization, was disposed to agree, merely stipulating that any such Anglo-French action should be approved both by the other Powers and by the French Chamber of Deputies.

Both the other Powers and the Chamber of Deputies showed some reluctance. On July 29th, while the Constantinople Conference was still discussing the matter, the Freycinet Government was defeated in the Chamber on a motion asking for a credit of 9.5 million francs for measures for the protection of the Suez Canal. The government thereupon resigned. The Chamber, where the opposition to the government motion was led by Clemenceau, had, in effect, voted the French out of Egypt.

Meanwhile Admiral Seymour, on the instructions of the British Government, had obtained from the Khedive authority to "occupy all those points in the Isthmus of Suez which you consider necessary to ensure freedom of traffic through the Canal, and the protection of the population of the Isthmus, and to suppress any forces not recognizing my authority." On August 7th the British Government informed the Powers that, acting under the authority of the Khedive, British forces would take such measures as they considered necessary for the protection of the canal.

At this point Ferdinand de Lesseps, by this time an old man seventy-seven years of age, arrived in Egypt. Without any effective support from the French Government, he embarked, single-handed, on a forlorn campaign for the recognition of the neutrality of the canal, alleging (probably correctly) that he had already obtained from Arabi an assurance that this neutrality would be respected by the Egyptian forces. It was, of course, as much to Arabi's interest, as it was against the British interest, to have this neutrality recognized. "The old rogue is playing us tricks," commented Lord Granville,[83] and asked M. Duclerc, the French Foreign Minister, to intervene.

On the night of August 19/20 the British invading force under Sir Garnet Wolseley arrived at Port Said, occupied the Canal Company's installations, and entered the Canal, which was closed to navigation for the next five days. The Canal Company's officials, under orders from Lesseps, refused to provide pilots and refused any form of cooperation. On August 24th, after the British force had been landed at Ismailia, Wolseley returned the control of the canal to the Company and normal navigation was resumed. Largely as the result of Lesseps' defiant attitude, the disturbance to the normal working of the canal, and the derogation from the Canal Company's authority, had been reduced to a minimum. But the principle of neutralization, for which Lesseps had fought since the beginning of the enterprise, had been breached. And the canal had proved to be—literally as well as metaphorically—what Mohammed Ali had always feared it would be—a channel up which the English would sail and occupy Egypt.

Having landed at Ismailia, the British force advanced toward Cairo along the line of the Sweet Water Canal. On September 13th they met and defeated Arabi at Tel el Kebir, just on the verge between the desert and the

Delta. Twenty-four hours later the British occupied Cairo, where they were to remain for the next sixty-five years.

The last word must be with M. Jean Lemoinne, Senator and Member of l'Académie Française, who, in an article published in *la Revue Politique et Littéraire* on November 1, 1884, wrote:

Egypt was lost for France on the day when the man who has been called the Great Frenchman completed the Suez Canal. The British had always opposed this great enterprise. Lord Palmerston, the incarnation of British chauvinism, had attacked it by every means in his power. . . . The energy, the perseverance, the obstinacy, the unquenchable fire shewn by Lesseps triumphed over all obstacles. But, on the day the Suez Canal was opened, the British said to themselves: "We have got to have it" (*Il doit être à moi*).

And thus was completed the metamorphosis by which the act of consummation of the marriage between East and West (in the Saint-Simonian phrase) was converted into a British imperial lifeline, an object which, in course of time, became of almost sacramental significance to the British Conservative Party. After England had lost her last territorial possession on the mainland of Europe, Mary Tudor, the reigning English Queen, was said to have declared that, when she died, the word CALAIS would be found engraved on her heart. It may also be said that, when the last British Imperialist is lowered into his grave, the word SUEZ will be inscribed on his coffin.

NOTES

1. Sabry, *L'Empire Egyptien* . . . , p. 85.
2. Beauval–Thouvenel 18.5.61. CP 29.
3. E.g., Bruce–Clarendon 25.3.57. FO 78/1313.
4. E.g., Sabry, *op. cit.*, 95–96, in which he describes how Beauval obtained for the banks concerned an indemnity of 840,000 francs in consideration of an allegation that Mohammed Said had issued Treasury bills in contravention of the conditions of the 1860 loan. It appears that these "Treasury bills" were in fact salary claims on the Egyptian Government by unpaid officials which they had given in lieu of cash payments to various local tradesmen who, in turn, had attempted to cash them from the Egyptian Government.
5. Sabry, *op. cit.* p. 90.
6. Outrey–de Lhuys 28.6.66. CP 38.
7. McCoan, *Egypt Under Ismail*, pp. 81–82.
8. *Ibid.*, quoting Lady Duff Gordon, an English visitor to Egypt.
9. The average price of the ordinary shares for the first six years of the canal's operation were (par francs 500), according to J. Charles-Roux (*L'Isthme* . . . , II, 291):

1870	Fcs. 262.868
1871	208.135
1872	355.133
1873	434.935
1874	422.190
1875	674.052

10. Lyons–Granville 2.4.73. FO 78/2311.
11. Elliot–Granville 2.4.73. FO 78/2311.
12. Lyons–Granville 18.4.73. FO 78/2311.
13. FO 78/2256.
14. Hallberg, *The Suez Canal*, p. 223. The Moorsom formula for net tonnage was based on an estimate of available cargo space after deductions made for space occupied by crew, bunkers, and engines.
15. J. Charles-Roux, *op. cit.*, II, 289.
16. Hallberg, *op. cit.*, p. 224.
17. FO 78/2256.
18. Granville–Elliot 31.7.72. FO 78/2256.
19. *Ibid.*, 31.8.72. FO 78/2256.
20. This judgment was reversed on appeal. See Lyons–Granville 12.3.73. FO 78/2310.
21. Lange to Board of Admiralty 3.1.73. FO 78/2310.
22. See letter from St. Hilaire to Lesseps of 14.3.73 in M & D, Vol 15: "The President of the Republic is entirely favorable to the interpretation which you give to the expression '*tonne de capacité*' in the Concession." See also Elliot–Granville 16.3.73. FO 78/2310. With a strange prescience Lesseps had cultivated the acquaintance of Thiers, then in opposition, during the years 1855–1857. See Lesseps' letter to Hippolyte la Fosse in Journal, I, 155.
23. "The Turks are very afraid of Lesseps and his French backing" (private letter from Sir H. Elliot to Lord Tenterden, Under Secretary of State for Foreign Affairs, 19.3.73, FO 78/2310). In fact the extent of French backing seems to have been appreciable. Elliot complained that British dispatches from Lord Lyons in Paris which had been shown in confidence to the French Foreign Minister had been immediately transcribed and sent to Lesseps, who spent most of 1873 in Constantinople trying to extract from the Porte permission to apply the new rates.
24. Hallberg, *op. cit.*, p. 226.
25. The steady pressure exercised on the Porte and on the Khedive by the British Government was not affected by the change of Administration which took place in February, 1874, when Disraeli replaced Gladstone as Prime Minister and Lord Derby replaced Lord Granville as Foreign Secretary.
26. Publicly in the sense that Decazes's instructions to the Marquis de Vogüé, French ambassador at Constantinople, were "leaked" to the Paris press (Paget–Derby 17.4.74. FO 78/2320).
27. Stanton–Granville 30.12.70. FO 78/2256.
28. Lange–Granville 3.4.71. FO 78/2256.
29. Granville–Lange 4.5.71. FO 78/2256.
30. Lange–Granville 2.6.71. FO 78/2256.
31. Granville–Lange undated FO 78/2256.
32. Lange–Granville 29.12.71. FO 78/2256.
33. J. Charles-Roux, op. cit., II, 298.
34. For a detailed account, from the French point of view, of the the transactions leading to the purchase of the Canal shares by the British Government, see *L'Invasion Anglais en Egypte: L'Achat des Actions de Suez,* by Charles Lesage (Paris, 1906).
35. For an interesting account of Edouard Dervieu's financial career in Egypt during the sixties, see *Bankers and Pashas,* by D. S. Landes (Heinemann, 1958).
36. Hallberg, *op. cit.*, p. 238.
37. Quoted by Fitzgerald, *The Great Canal at Suez,* II, 280–282.
38. Derby–Stanton 15.11.75. FO 78/2432.
39. See Sabry, *op. cit.*, pp. 160–161.
40. Parl. Debates, Lords, 3rd. Series, Vol. 219, p. 1036.
41. Hallberg, *op. cit.*, pp. 241–242.
42. Stanton–Derby 16.11.75. FO 78/2432.
43. In this connection see Stanton's mailed dispatch to Lord Derby 18.11.75. FO 78/2432.
44. Derby–Stanton 17.11.75. FO 78/2432. This cable was sent off at 1500 hours and was drafted in Derby's own handwriting with a note by him that it carried into effect a Cabinet decision.

45. *The Life of Benjamin Disraeli, Earl of Beaconsfield*, by G. E. Buckle, V, 443.
46. Stanton–Derby 17.11.75. FO 78/2432.
47. *Ibid.*, November 17/18, 1875, FO 78/2432.
48. See correspondence below.
49. Derby–Stanton 18.11.75. FO 78/2432.
50. *Ibid.* 19.11.75 FO 78/2432.
51. Stanton–Derby 21.11.75. FO 78/2432.
52. Derby–Stanton 23.11.75. FO 78/2432.
53. Stanton–Derby 23.11.75. FO 78/2432.
54. *Ibid.* 24.11.75. FO 78–2432.
55. *Ibid.* 19.11.75. FO 78/2432.
56. Buckle, *op. cit.*, V. 446–447.
57. See *The Life, Letters and Diaries of Sir Stafford Northcote, First Earl of Iddesleigh*, by Andrew Lang, II, 85.
58. FO 78/2432.
59. Derby–Stanton 24.11.75. FO 78/2432.
60. *Ibid.*
61. It was early in the morning.
62. Ismail Sadiq. See Chapter Thirteen, Note 5.
63. Stanton–Derby 27.11.75. FO 78/2432.
64. *Ibid.* 25.11.75. FO 78/2432.
65. *Ibid.* 26.11.75. FO 78/2432.
66. Correspondence dealing with arrangements for paying these temporary clerks appears to have consumed more paper than was consumed by the correspondence dealing with the purchase of the shares.
67. Lang, *op. cit.*, II, 85–86.
68. Lesage, *op. cit.*, p. 144.
69. Hallberg, *op. cit.*, p. 252.
70. *Ibid.*, p. 253.
71. *Ibid.*, p. 252.
72. Elliot–Derby 30.11.75. FO 78/2432.
73. Derby–Elliot 4.12.75. FO 78/2432.
74. Mailed dispatch by Stanton to Lord Derby 27.11.75. FO 78/2432. The 15 percent share of the net profits was sold to the Crédit Foncier in 1880 for 22 million francs (Wilson, *The Suez Canal*, p. 109).
75. Parl. Papers, Egypt No. 1 (1876), Lyons–Derby 30.11.75., enclosing translation of letter from Lesseps. If the date of Lesseps letter—November 24th,—is correctly transcribed, he must have had exceptionally sure and rapid means of information about what was happening.
76. Buckle, *op. cit.*, V, 449–450.
77. Stokes–Derby 31.12.75. FO 78/2540.
78. Parl. Papers, Egypt No. 9 (1876).
79. J. Charles–Roux, *op. cit.*, II, 32–33.
80. The first British vice-president was Stokes, by then Lieutenant General Sir John Stokes.
81. J. Charles–Roux, *op. cit.*, II, 120–137. This sliding-scale provision was denounced in 1900 without any protest from the British Government. See Wilson, *op. cit.*, p. 112.
82. Parl. Papers, Egypt No. 7 (1876).
83. *Life of Lord Granville* (Fitzmaurice), II, 272.

BIBLIOGRAPHY

BIBLIOGRAPHY

This "selected bibliography" consists of a list of those documents, books, and so on, actually consulted during the course of writing this work. It makes no pretense of being a complete bibliography on the subject.

PRIMARY SOURCES

(i) LESSEP, FERDINAND DE. *Lettres, Journal et Documents pour Servir à l'Histoire du Canal de Suez;* five vols. Didier et Cie., Paris, 1875-1881.

(ii) ARCHIVES FRANÇAISES. "Egypte, Correspondence Politique" (CP), Vols. 18-47.

"Egypte, Mémoires et Documents," Vols. 13-15.

(iii) FOREIGN OFFICE RECORDS (prefix "FO"). 97/411, 97/408, 78/1156, 78/1340, 78/1421, 78/1489, 78/1556, 78/1715, 78/1795, 78/1796, 78/1849, 78/1850, 78/1895, 78/1896, 78/1897, 78/1898, 78/2014, 78/2118, 78/2257, 78/2265, 78/2310-2319, 78/2368-2373, 78/2405, 78/2430-2432, 78/2498, 78/2500, 78/2503, 78/2504, 78/2540, 78/2632, 78/2634, 78/2854, 78/2862.

(iv) PUBLISHED ENGLISH STATE PAPERS. Parl. Papers. Egypt Nos. 1, 2, 4, 5, 7, and 9 (1876), and Egypt No. 3 (1881) and Egypt Nos. 1, 5, and 17 (1882).

SECONDARY SOURCES

D'ALLEMAGE, H. R. *Prosper Enfantin,* Paris, 1930.

ASHLEY, HON. EVELYN. *Life of Viscount Palmerston,* 2 vols. Bentley, 1876.

BALDWIN, GEORGE. *Political Recollections Relative to Egypt.* London, 1801.

BEATTY, CHARLES. *Ferdinand de Lesseps.* London, Eyre & Spottiswoode, 1956.

DE BELLEFONDS, LINANT. *Mémoires sur les Principaux Travaux d' Utilité Publique Exécutés en Egypte.* Paris, 1872-73.

BOULENGER, MARCEL. *Le Duc de Morny,* Paris, Hachette, 1925.

BUCKLE, G. E. *The Life of Benjamin Disraeli, Earl of Beaconsfield,* Vol. V, Murray, 1920.

CHARLES-ROUX, F. *Les Origines de l'Expédition d'Egypte,* Paris, Plon, 1910.

———. *L'Angleterre, L'Isthme de Suez et L'Egypte.*

———. *au XVIIIme. Siècle.* Paris, Plon, 1922.

———. *Bonaparte, Gouverneur d'Egypte.* Paris, Plon, 1935.

CHARLES-ROUX, J. *L'Isthme et le Canal de Suez,* 2 vols. Paris, Hachette, 1901.

COURAU, ROBERT. *Ferdinand de Lesseps.* Grasset, Paris, 1931.

CRABITES, PIERRE. *The Spoliation of Suez,* London, Routledge, 1940.

DOUIN, GEORGES. *Règne du Khédive Ismaïl.* 4 vols. Société Royale de Géographie d'Egypte, 1933.

EDGAR-BONNET, GEORGES. *Ferdinand de Lesseps,* 2 vols. Paris, Plon, Vol. I, 1951; Vol. II, 1959.

D'ELBEE, JEAN. *UnConquistader de Génie.* Editions Littéraires de France, 1943.

FITZGERALD, PERCY. *The Great Canal at Suez,* 2 vols. London, Tinsley Bros., 1876.

DES GARETS, COMTESSE. *Auprès de l'Impératrice Eugénie.* Paris, Calmann-Lévy, 1928.

HALLBERG, CHARLES, W. *The Suez Canal,* New York, Columbia University Press, 1931.

HEROLD, J. CHRISTOPHER. *Bonaparte in Egypt.* London, Hamish Hamilton, 1963.

HOSKINS, H. L. *British Routes to India.* London, Longmans, Green, 1928.

LANDES, DAVID S. *Bankers and Pashas.* London, Heinemann, 1958.

LANE POOLE, S. *The Life of Stratford Canning,* 2 vols. London, Longmanss, Green, 1888.

LANG, ANDREW. *Life, Letters and Diaries of Sir Stafford Northcote, First Earl of Iddesleigh,* 2 vols., Longmans, Green, 1890.

LESAGE, CHARLES. *L'Invasion Anglaise en Egypte; L'Achat des Actions de Suez.* Paris, 1906.

DE LESSEPS, F. *The Isthmus of Suez Question.* London. Longmans, Green, 1855.

McCOAN, J. CARLILE. *Egypt Under Ismail.* London, Chapman & Hall, 1889.

MALCOLM-SMITH, E. F. *The Life of Stratford Canning.* London, Benn, 1933.

SABRY, M. *L'Empire Egyptien sous Mohammed Ali et le Question d'Orient* (1811–1849). Paris, Paul Guenther, 1930.

———. *L'Empire Egyptien sous Ismaïl et L'Ingérence Anglo-Française* (1863–1879). Paris, Paul Guenther, 1933.

SENCOURT, R. *The Life of the Empress Eugénie.* London, Benn, 1931.

SMIT, G. BARNETT. *The Life and Enterprises of F. de Lesseps.* London, W. H. Allen & Co., 1893.

VOISIN BEY. *Le Canal de Suez. Historique, Administratif et Actes Constitutifs, 1854–1902,* 7 vols. Paris, 1902–1907.

WILSON, SIR ARNOLD. *The Suez Canal,* London, Oxford University Press, 1933.

INDEX

INDEX